Me~
Musical
Life across
Borders

BANDA

Mexican Musical Life across Borders

Helena Simonett

WESLEYAN UNIVERSITY PRESS

Middletown, Connecticut

Published by Wesleyan University Press, Middletown, CT 06549
© 2001 by Helena Simonett

ISBN 0-8195-6429-X cloth
ISBN 0-8195-6430-3 paper

Printed in the United States of America

Designed by Richard Hendel
Set in Quadraat, Smokler, and Matrix types by
B. Williams and Associates

5 4 3 2 1

CiP data appear at the back of the book

A los banderos, parranderos
y otros aficionados de la tambora

Contents

Illustrations

MAPS AND FIGURES

Acknowledgments

This book has become a reality because of the help and encouragement of many people. I am indebted to them for sharing their time, experience, stories, knowledge—and above all, their love for banda music.

Fortunately, musicians in Los Angeles have kept a valuable Mexican custom: to esteem hospitality and to share time. I usually would approach them at their worksite, the nightclub. They generously shared their time between sets, discussing, explaining, and helping me to make contacts with other persons who they considered could be beneficial for my research. I would like to express my gratitude to all of them. A very special thank-you goes to Felipe Hernández, Armando "El Serrucho" Bastidas García, and Bernabé Martínez in Los Angeles. In Sinaloa, it was somewhat easier to find the musicians. Their sincerity and assistance have made it possible to realize this study. I owe my deepest gratitude to Isidoro "Chilolo" Ramírez Sánchez, Ramón López Alvarado, Teodoro Ramírez Pereda, Guadalupe "El Sirola" Castro Ibarra, José Luis "El Indio" Ramírez Sánchez, Germán Lizárraga, Luis Ramírez Vizcara ("El Gigante"), Mariano López Sánchez, Francisco "Chico" Herrera, and José Ángel "Ferrusquilla" Espinoza. This book is dedicated to all the musicians, from whom I have learned about the social and cultural power of Sinaloan banda music and its significance to their lives—and ours. ¡Muchísimas gracias!

In retrospect, it was much easier to conduct fieldwork in Sinaloa than in California. The Los Angeles metropolis is a tough place to do fieldwork because of its size and its hectic life style. To gain access to people in the music industry or promoters of singers and bandas was very often difficult, if not impossible—they were either at meetings or out, or simply would not return my phone calls. I wish to thank those who responded to my inquiries: Jesús "El Peladillo" García and Juan Carlos Hidalgo (KLAX), Fidel Fausto and Rosy González (KBUE), Félix Castillo (Furia musical), Fernando A. González (Discos Musart), Jenny Rivera (Cintas Acuario), José Ferrera (El Lido), and Abel Orozco (El Parral). A special thank-you goes to Marisela Vallejo and Adán "El Compita" Sánchez. I am particularly grateful to Victoria Soto, Irma Reyes, Christina Castellanos, Elydia Reza, Lotty Nava, Veronica Zamora, and Marina Sánchez for their readiness to speak about their dance experience; to Benjamín Hernández for teaching me the quebradita; and to Bonifacio Pérez for inviting me to dance events to which I would never have had access otherwise.

Heartfelt thanks go to Arturo Santamaría Gómez and Manuel Gómez Rubio, who both generously allowed me to consult their large book collections. I am grateful for their interest in my work and for their comments and suggestions. Manuel "Chino" Flores Gastélum and Miguel Valadés Lejarza have both helped me to understand the major elements of banda's history. I have also benefited from conversations with Enrique Peña Bátiz, Hernando Hernández, Elisa Pérez, Rubén Rubio Valdez, Antonio Coronado, Luis Astorga, and Sam Quiñones. I would like to express my appreciation to the staff of the Archivo Municipal in Mazatlán and the Hemeroteca in Culiacán, and to Héctor Carlos Leal Camacho from the Centro Regional de Documentación Histórica y Científica. Many thanks go to Roger Savage, Tim Rice, Colin Quigley, and Steve Loza, my academic advisors from the University of California, Los Angeles, where I submitted my dissertation on banda music; to George Lipsitz for his continuous interest in my discoveries and my writings; to my friends and colleagues for cheering me up; and to my teacher Wolfgang Laade, who initiated me into ethnomusicology many years ago in Switzerland.

I would also like to acknowledge the help of Carlos M. Haro, Daniel García Blanco, Manuel Contreras, and Maricela Contreras Herrera (Fonorama), María de Jesús "Chuyita" Lizárraga, and all my friends in Mazatlán. A special thankyou goes to Mireya García and José Solórzano for helping me with the transcription of the songs, to Olivia Nickel for verifying the English translations of the song lyrics, and to Barbara Norton for her superb editing. I would also like to express thanks to those who read parts of the manuscript in its different stages, especially Manuel Gómez Rubio for his insightful comments on part II; Jane Sugerman for reading chapter 1; and Richard Haefer for his helpful remarks regarding the mariachi chapter. For their hospitality and generosity I am indebted to my friends Arturo Santamaría and Sandra López, Bob Reyno, Héctor and Natalia Fattorini, Ellen Sinatra, and Giuseppina Colicci. Last but not least, I wish to thank my family and my husband, Gieri Simonett, for his continuous support and encouragement, for his unconditional love, and for sharing my passion for Mexican music. This book is also dedicated to him and to Oriana and Lara who are already kicking up their heels to the sound of the tambora.

Introduction

Ya llegó la banda, vamos a bailar
ya llegó la banda, la vida hay que gozar.
Salvador Sandoval, Banda América

It was in September 1992, just one week after my arrival in Los Angeles, California, that I first heard banda music. My husband and I drove the twenty miles from our new home in the San Fernando Valley to downtown Los Angeles to join the Mexican Independence Day celebration. It was the first time we had visited El Pueblo, the historical center of Los Angeles; "El Pueblo" and "Los Angeles" are both short forms of "El Pueblo de Nuestra Señora La Reina de los Angeles de Porciúncula" and refer to the city's Spanish-Mexican origin. As I learned later, it was a group of Mexican pioneers from the northwestern states of Sonora and Sinaloa who laid the pueblo's foundation in 1781.[1] Mexican culture has provided the core of the city with much of its charm. Olvera Street, *La Placita*, and the surrounding area were crammed with festive people. Mariachis dressed up in traditional *charro* and sombrero were playing in the iron bandstand at the center of the Plaza. The celebration was in full swing: Mexican tunes mingled with the smell of barbecued chicken and caramel. If this was Los Angeles, I knew I was already falling in love with this city! Through the layers of different noises I picked up a familiar sound. From down the street, sounds of an oompah-oompah bass line reached my ear. Curious about its origin, we approached the throng gathering in front of a band on a small stage and forming pockets around some young dancers. There were too many people to see much more than the dancers' hats. Some of the spectators seemed baffled, others amused. The band, which I later learned was a *tecno-banda* [technoband or technobanda], consisted of seven musicians playing trumpets, trombones, keyboard, electric guitar, and percussion. I could neither see nor hear a lot, but I expected that this would not be the last time I would attend such events, since I had applied for the graduate program in ethnomusicology at the University of California, Los Angeles. The celebration, sonorous and colorful, its atmosphere saturated with angelic scents, had awakened my appetite, both physical and spiritual. The first I immediately appeased with a couple of juicy *tacos de pollo*. To satisfy the latter I would have the years to come.

But there was a long journey from this first encounter with a technobanda to the discovery of the sounds of the *banda sinaloense* [Sinaloan band], the *banda de viento* [wind band], the *banda-orquesta* [orchestra band], and the *banda del pueblo* [village band]—all of which are synonyms or variations of the *tambora*, a regional ensemble of Mexico's northwest coast named after its characteristic double-headed bass drum. For me, as for many young Mexicans and Mexican Americans in the United States, technobanda and the dance craze it triggered was a detour to learning about the existence of and eventually appreciating the *música de tambora*, the regional music of Sinaloa.

Whereas the band's characteristic bass line immediately reminded me of the town band in Switzerland in which my father used to play the horn, the festive people of Mexican provenance around me seemed to recognize the music as inherently Mexican. Banda had struck different strings: while I was curious about banda's affinity with Central European band music and thus wanted to learn more about the music's history, young Mexicans and Mexican Americans in the United States began to appropriate the new sound that emerged just at a time when conservative forces and the California governor were about to launch a new political attack to silence the voices of a growing minority. Banda music was their cultural answer.

Crossing Borders

The power of technobanda was enormous. It had a tremendous social and cultural impact on hundreds of thousands of young people during the early 1990s. But not just north of the border: its contagious rhythms spread, and everywhere Mexican youths started dancing the *quebradita*. This new dance style was the backbone of the banda movement. Nightclubs mushroomed. The demand for live music grew rapidly, and a vast number of musicians began to tune into banda. Moreover, banda music swiftly conquered Los Angeles's airwaves. In 1992, for the first time in its history, the city's top radio station was a Spanish-language one. Along with the music and the dance came a specific dress code, the *vaquero* or cowboy style. Many of the new compositions addressed both the quebradita dance and the clothes: *vaqueros, botas y sombrero* [jeans, boots, and hat]. The fondness most of the quebradita participants north of the border felt for technobanda became a strong identity statement. They began to wear an array of accessories that pointed to their Mexican heritage. Their message was: being Mexican is something to be proud of. It was a feeling that many of them had never experienced before. Technobanda events offered them the opportunity to be *orgulloso*, to foster self-esteem and self-respect—yet the sense of self these young people were reclaiming was that of something more than an individual, isolated self: rather, it was a sense of the self as part of a community.

Banda music was catching on, and its rapidly growing success motivated young musicians to start their own bands. One of them was Banda América, a group of eight male and three female musicians aged eighteen to twenty-five. Banda América's song "Ya llegó la banda" [The Banda Has Arrived] was more than self-promotion:[2]

Ya llegó la banda,	The banda has already arrived,
vamos a bailar	let's go to dance
ya llegó la banda,	the banda has already arrived,
la vida hay que gozar.	life has to be enjoyed.
Everybody, get together,	
have a good time. . . .	

The song, with its bilingual refrain, also signified Banda América's particular way of transcending multiple borders. In December 1994 I visited Fiesta Studio in downtown Los Angeles, where the band was in the midst of recording its second compact disc. At that time the members had been playing together for a year and a half, and they were moving in a new direction, incorporating non-Mexican rhythms such as reggae. But their statements were not only musical: they had chosen a name and a logo that represented themselves. The colors of the logo "Banda América"—red, white, and blue—and in particular the star-shaped dot on the letter "i" in "América" indicate the musicians' identification with the United States. Yet "America" is a word that exists in both the Spanish and the English languages, and it implies that the band is bilingual as well as bimusical. Further, "America" is also the name of the large continent of which Mexico is part. Knowingly or not, Banda América sent a strong message: music does not know any borders, especially not political borders. To find out more about where this contagious music was coming from and where it was going to, I had to cross borders many times myself.

Doing Fieldwork

The last stanza of a popular corrido resounded in my ears when I headed for Mexico in the summer of 1994 to conduct preliminary research for my dissertation. The corrido talks about brave outlaws, "men who kill for little reason," and violence related to drug trafficking. The *corridista* [balladeer] reminds the listener that "when you go south, don't forget that in each of these states there are very dangerous people." I had heard Banda Machos's interpretation of "Escuadras del sur" [Squads of the South] many times on the radio before, but I had never really thought much about its content until I was ready to leave. Traveling alone in Mexico did not concern me; I had already spent several months in the capital and in the southern states. But I had never been in Mexico's northwest, and I did not really know what to expect. The words of the corrido and the well-intended advice of some of my friends left their imprint. Sinaloa—was it really the "Wild West" they described? Were its people different from the friendly, hospitable Mexicans I had known so far?

The purpose of my travels, which took me from Mexico City to Guadalajara, to Zacatecas and Durango, and to Mazatlán, was twofold: first, I wanted to get some impression of the areas most of Southern California's more recent immigrants were originating from. And second, I wanted to collect as much information as possible on the subject matter.[3] The conspicuous lack of material on Sinaloa's music forced me to question why this was the case. Mexican ethnomusicology in general still tends to focus on indigenous musical practice. Except for mariachi music, the musical expressions of the mestizo population, which would include rural and urban popular music, seem to be of little interest to scholars. Apparently, *banda sinaloense* has never been seen as significant.[4]

This academic neglect reflected general attitudes toward banda music, so it was not surprising that Sinaloans usually would first react to my interest with amazement. Later, however, it became obvious that they were flattered that a foreigner would like their music. Although the scarcity of written sources was disappointing, the trip helped me to establish personal relationships with different individuals and served as a basis for subsequent fieldwork. These contacts also helped me to approach banda musicians in Los Angeles.

The results of my research rely mainly upon data collected through firsthand observation such as observing musical performances and participating by dancing; listening to radio stations, cassettes, and compact discs; and interviewing musicians, singers, composers, dancers, radio programming directors, disc jockeys, record producers, nightclub managers, security guards, waitresses, aficionados, and intellectuals (including some individuals who dislike banda music or do not approve of the dancing). Moreover, I skimmed over tons of old newspapers hoarded up in Mazatlán's Archivo Municipal and browsed the microfilms of the Hemeroteca in Culiacán. After completing my dissertation in 1997 I continued my research on historical data in various libraries in the United States as well as in Mexico City and Europe. I also went back several times to Sinaloa, most importantly to participate in the centennial celebration of Mazatlán's carnival, and to Los Angeles, to learn about the new musical trends and the changing life in the city's Mexican nightclubs.

Since I am fluent in Spanish, people were sometimes confused about my ethnic background. Although I am a *güera*, a person with light skin and brown hair, people found it hard to believe that I was actually Swiss, residing temporarily in California in order to study Mexican music. Inside Los Angeles's nightclubs, where the lights were dimmed and the music was loud, I could pass for a Mexicana or a Chicana. Dancers and waitresses almost always addressed me in Spanish. In many situations it was definitely an advantage to be European instead of a U.S. citizen. The tour of the well-known Banda El Recodo to Europe in 1995 had built a bridge to that continent, and my assurance that they were warmly welcomed over there and that I myself loved banda music helped my credibility enormously. Moreover, I felt strong emotional bonds between some recent immigrants and myself, although our experiences differed greatly. Curiously, they thought that my situation was worse than theirs, since I was so far away from family and homeland and entirely cut off from my culture. Their compassion helped me a great deal to endure my occasional emotional lows and my nostalgia.

Doing fieldwork in Los Angeles, however, was not always fun, and people did not always meet me with friendly openness. California's current sociopolitical situation affected my work in a way that made me aware of how sensitive ethnomusicological research can be. For example, in January 1996, U.S. Immigration and Naturalization Service raids led to the arrests of clients at a county-run mobile clinic offering disease-control services in the City of Industry, Los Angeles. INS agents detained suspected undocumented immigrants in two apparel factories on the Eastside and hit a commercial parking lot in Industry where day laborers used to gather. The INS calls such immigration raids "surveys."[5] These raids raised the awareness of many Mexicans as well as Mexican Americans. At that time I was interested in obtaining information for a survey I was conducting on banda and quebradita. I had designed a questionnaire for participants in banda events and intended to distribute copies in front of various nightclubs. The purpose was to get feedback from a large group of people that was not accessible in any other manner but that I felt was crucial for my research. However, under the circumstances, it was not advisable to use words such as "research" [*investigación*] or "questionnaire" [*cuestionario*] in Spanish—any person asking too many questions, even if anonymity was assured, was suspicious or potentially dangerous. Although I was able to interview a dozen dancers who responded to the questionnaire and provided me with their phone numbers, the overall result was not what I had hoped. Eventually, after some more attempts in the summer of 1996, I gave up this project.

Yet local politics is not confined to the local any longer: California's affairs touch Mexicans south of the border as well. Nowadays, news travels fast and reaches even Mexico's countryside via satellite. Some of it may generate unexpected and uncomfortable situations for the ethnographer. On Holy Saturday 1996 I joined Banda Los Chilolos on a trip to a small town along the dusty highway that connects Mazatlán and Culiacán, where they were contracted to play for a fiesta. Late at night, I went to the restaurant across the street to warm myself up. I chatted with the innkeepers while having a cup of coffee. Some of the guests were still eating, and the television was on, pouring pictures from the outside world into the house. Nobody seemed to notice until video cameras captured the sight of Riverside County sheriff's deputies bashing immigrants at the end of a wild chase. Suddenly the room got quiet—all eyes were glued to the screen in disbelief. The Mexican television station broadcast the scene of the immigrants being struck with batons over and over again. Anger grew. The beating seemed so forceful, so unnecessary. I felt miserable and embarrassed. My discomfort increased when I suddenly became aware of how people positioned me: I was from el otro lado, the other side, and I sensed that they expected me to tell them that what we had just seen was not true or, at least, not the usual way Mexican immigrants were treated in the United States. But it was true. At that moment I was glad I had mentioned why and with whom I had come to visit the town and that I was Swiss. After a while the others at the inn started discussing the pros and cons of immigration, referring to the many things that had happened either to themselves or to some acquaintances. In the course of time, their anger—initially directed at the sheriff's deputies—shifted toward the immigrants: "It is in Mexico where they belong. Why do they have to go north, anyway?" For me, it was not only a lesson in how power relationships work, but also an intense experience of how other people perceive me.

Because banda is a man's world, there were many advantages to being a female researcher. However, the fact that I was married but not accompanied by my husband occasionally caused slight confusion. Mexican men would not have allowed their spouses to go alone to the places where I usually met the musicians. Nor does Mexican culture allow a decent woman to enter bars or certain types of nightclubs without a male protector. Some cantinas in Mexico are for men strictly. A sign next to the door discourages women to enter. It usually reads either "Prohibida la entrada a menores de edad, uniformados y a mujeres" or "Prohibida la entrada a menores de edad, armados y a damas" [Entry is prohibited for minors, men in uniform/armed men, and women / ladies]. However, since I was not Mexican, these principles did not strictly apply to me. Usually men felt responsible for my well-being and they would offer me protection, though I was not always sure why I had to be protected and against whom or what.

The main site for my fieldwork in Los Angeles was the nightclub. Thus,

1. The author in front of a cantina in Mazatlán, 1997. The inscription reads: "Entry prohibited to minors, women and men in uniform." Photo by Gieri Simonett.

much of my research took place late at night and in rather unsafe neighborhoods. It was not easy to find the sites where banda music was actually performed, since newspapers such as *La opinión* advertised only the huge banda concerts at Pico Rivera Sports Arena. After I became a regular listener to the ranchero-format Spanish-language radio stations that announced upcoming events in and around Los Angeles, I grew more familiar with the nightclub scene. To do research in nightclubs is indeed fun and pleasurable, as some of my colleagues enviously remarked—but not always. Most of the burgeoning Mexican part of Los Angeles is a sagging area. The signs of urban neglect and decay are everywhere: fenced stores and houses, graffiti-covered and boarded-up buildings, empty lots strewn with litter, and plenty of car dealerships, fast-food restaurants, and gas stations. Even the most gleaming and alluring neon signs cannot obscure the poverty and shabbiness of these neighborhoods. I remember that I often lost my enthusiasm and curiosity when I finally arrived at the parking lot of a nightclub after having driven twenty miles or so to get there. More than once, I reconsidered my initial impulse and decided to drive home again, scolding myself as a coward.

I would not have wanted to miss any of my experiences, since they were constitutive for my understanding of cultural practice as meaningful action. Moreover, it became clear to me that my own situation was unique, and I realized how deeply my interpretations were affected by interactions with other people and their traditions. Likewise immersed in a larger context, these people had their own unique experiences. It was my hope to bring these different voices, worldviews, life experiences, value systems, and beliefs together—not to level them out but to establish a dialogue that illuminates how music and dance can be meaningful and significant in many different, maybe even contradictory, ways. Since any discourse is multivocal, it is open to several readings. My interpretation is to be understood as only one of several possible openings into a world of meanings. Like any ethnomusicologist at the beginning of the twenty-first century, I am aware that ethnographic practice and writing inevitably participates in the politics of representation. I hope I was able not only to hear different voices when doing fieldwork, but also to represent them in this book.

Writings on Banda Music

Banda is a product of *mestizaje* [culture blending], but unlike mariachi, which was close to the center, where culture and notions about culture were being forged, it has never been considered a musical form worthy of scholarly attention, neither in Mexico nor in the United States or elsewhere. None of the standard histories of Mexican music includes *banda sinaloense*. Neither the renowned Mexican musicologist Vicente T. Mendoza, in his extensive work, nor Juan S. Garrido ([1974] 1981) mentions the musical traditions of the northwestern states. Rubén M. Campos included a brief chapter titled "Las bandas de música populares y las grandes bandas militares" in a book published in 1928, though with an emphasis on Mexico's highly-ranked military bands.[6] While at that time the military bands were already integrated in Mexico's national institutions, *bandas populares* [popular bands] were still in the process of becoming standardized. Regional characteristics and the lineup of the popular bands, now also referred to as *bandas regionales* [regional bands], were about to consolidate.

Although historically related, *bandas populares* are not a direct offshoot of the military bands. In the mid-1800s, civilian brass bands were being introduced into every European colony overseas, where they took root and flourished in their new environment. *Bandas populares* were a ubiquitous feature of Mexico's musical life in the later nineteenth century and thrived in both urban and rural areas. The many *kioskos* [bandstands or rotundas] and their prominent and central place in the villages, towns, and cities continue to testify to the bands' pivotal role in community life. During the Mexican Revolution in the 1910s, many local musicians joined the military bands. When the revolution ended, they returned to their villages, bringing with them a new musical repertory. The military, on the other hand, was strongly involved in Mexican civic life after the revolution and in the shaping of Mexican nationalism. Efforts were made by the new government to reintroduce civilian bands, so-called *bandas municipales*. Nowadays, most towns still have a municipal band whose duty is to play at public festivities. The repertory typically includes popular, military, and classical pieces. *Bandas populares* or *bandas de viento* [wind bands] still play an important role throughout Mexico, particularly among indigenous groups such as the Zapotecs, Maya, Mixtec, and Nahua.[7]

Having grown up within a pattern of local culture, popular bands have always been identified with particular localities. Their names suggest that they were seen as essentially civic organizations associated with the public and community life of their own village, town, or city. Thus, bands are usually named after the place of origin.[8] Some of them add the name of the bandleader or call the whole band after individuals or their nicknames.[9]

In different regions, bands have acquired vernacular names pointing to their most notable characteristics: the *tambora* [bass drum] in Sinaloa or the *tamborazo* [drumbeat] or *alborota güeyes* ["scandalous sonority"] in Zacatecas. Since bands have never been severed from the broader popular social life that sustains them, local names often reflect how the bourgeois stratum of society perceived them. Bands' reputed low-class status is reflected in names such as *terribles hueseras* [a terrible bunch of bones], *perrada* [a pack of dogs], or *chile frito* [fried chili] and *frijol' con hueso* [beans with bones], both of the latter typical dishes of the poor.

Not surprisingly, then, the bands' role in Mexico's musical life has so far not been given proper credit. Scholars have invariably ignored their history and cultural significance. If mentioned at all, bands tend to be discussed in vague and indiscriminate terms regarding regional developments of distinct popular band types. Not only has the musical expression of a large segment of the society been rendered marginal, musical life in Mexico's peripheries in general has been overlooked. Even in more recent works on Mexican popular music, the northwestern states are either ignored or subsumed within the vast north.[10]

The first book on Sinaloa's regional music was published in 1980 by Manuel Flores Gastélum, a cornet player and music teacher from Culiacán. Based on interviews with local musicians as well as on his own lifelong experience as a player in a brass band, Flores's work contains a wealth of information and of names. Unfortunately, a lack of precise dates, the inconsistent use of terminology, and assumptions about readers' prior knowledge make this book very difficult to read. Flores began his music career at the Internado del Estado in Culiacán in 1933, where he eventually became the director of the Banda de Música. The idea of documenting the history of Sinaloa's popular music occurred to him when he still was a student at that institution: he had to witness the deliberate incineration of musical material, a measure taken by the then director to clean up "all the old stuff" stored in the archive. Flores believed that the archive contained material—instruments, methods, manuscripts, and printed music—that went back to the French Intervention in the 1860s and that would have been of great value in documenting Sinaloa's musical history. Because of the scarcity of written historical material, Flores resorted to oral history, interviewing such musicians as Conrado Solís, Aristeo Castro, Jesús Escobar, Pedro Alvarez, and Rafael Lomelín. He endeavored to retrieve facts concerning the origin of the regional bands, the repertory, the composers, and "anything that could be of interest to the next generations," as he told me when I visited him in 1996 in Culiacán, just one year before he died. I am very grateful to him for sharing his knowledge as well as his collection of historical photographs, some of which are included in this book.

The scarcity of written information about Sinaloa's musical tradition became strikingly apparent when technobanda exploded onto the scene in Los Angeles.[11] The music-and-dance phenomenon made headlines in the national news media in 1993. While major newspapers reported on the dance craze and the awakening and growing self-respect of the Hispanic population, business-oriented magazines reported on the breakthrough of the Spanish-language radio station KLAX-FM and its subsequent leading position in the Los Angeles radio market. During technobanda's formative years, a few academic writers began to pay attention to the new style and its sociocultural impact: in 1994 *Selected Reports in Ethnomusicology* published a twelve-page review by Carlos Haro and Steven Loza of the musical heritage of banda and its evolution into its contemporary popular form. The cultural studies specialist George Lipsitz (1999) took technobanda as a means to observe demographic changes in southern California. Aside from my dissertation (1997), I have published a series of articles on both technobanda and *banda sinaloense* (Simonett 1996–97, 1999, and 2001a).

Theoretical Background

Like my ethnographic understanding, my academic background has been shaped by a number of individuals and texts, and in different settings. During my studies of musicology at the University of Zurich in the 1980s I was exposed to hermeneutics and reception theory, including reception aesthetics and reception history, and through the study of literature I became familiar with French structuralism. While continuing graduate school at UCLA I became aware of the many valuable ethnomusicological works applying ideas from American structuralism, deconstruction, and poststructuralism. The many years I spent in academia on both sides of the Atlantic have, I believe, made me "bitheoretical" and have helped shape both my fieldwork and this book. It is thus necessary to elucidate some of my main concerns and perspectives regarding culture, history, tradition, agency, and popular music.

CULTURE AS DISCURSIVE PRACTICE

The definition of culture has been modified and reformulated many times since the term was introduced into the English language by Edward B. Tylor over a century ago, and it continues to be redefined as the fields of anthropology and ethnomusicology develop. The notion of culture I find most intriguing is derived from leading philosophers of hermeneutics.[12] The significance of Ricoeur's philosophical reflections for my own approach to studying banda music and its cultural context both south and north of the border became more and more apparent as I read and reread his many essays on language and meaning, on text and action, on interpretation and subjectivity, on explanation and understanding, and above all, on time and narrative. Ricoeur's thoughts have helped me to clarify many ethnographic obstacles, notably questions of how to grasp and interpret lived experience. Texts, as Ricoeur has repeatedly pointed out, are not confined to written texts but also include acts of discourse. Acts of discourse, in turn, bring language into the dimension of action. Particularly engaging is his notion of "text as meaningful action."[13] If we understand music as meaningful action, it allows for the possibility of extending the interpretive practices of text to music.

Culture is formed through and informs discursive practices. It consists of intersecting, overlapping discourses that embrace "a plurality of voices orchestrated by common themes, idioms, meanings, resonant with the participation of others in the past and here and now," as the anthropologist Janice Boddy (1989: 7) has summarized so perceptively. It is thus necessary to engage in a dialogue with other people, to make them tell "their story." The German philosopher Wilhelm Schapp ([1953] 1985: 94) wrote half a century ago that "the story stands for the person," or, in other words, it is only through the stories that we can gain access to others. Each story stands in a lively relation to the other stories. Hence, the story of each individual is entangled in the stories of numerous others. But the (hi)story can become known only through the process of narrating. Telling, following, and understanding stories is the continuation of these untold stories.

Each individual and each community has its narrative identity. Without the recourse to narration, there would be neither personal nor communal identity. "Individual and community are constituted in their identity by taking up narratives that become for them their actual history" (Ricoeur 1988: 247). Moreover, the stories we tell and retell are significant because they are our experience of history. Inasmuch as time is more than just a bridge for the recovery of the historical, these stories not only tell the past, they also shape the present and embrace the future. The act of telling a story converts natural time (clock time) into a specific "human" time. This is one reason, I suppose, that scholars interested in other cultures continue to practice ethnography despite their questioning of anthropological knowledge, the validity of authority, and the legitimacy of representation (see Clifford and Marcus 1986).

THE NARRATIVITY OF HISTORY

In most European languages—English is the exception—no linguistic distinction is made between "story" and "history." The Spanish word *historia*, the French *histoire*, and the German *Geschichte* retain "the rich ambiguity of designating both the course of recounted events and the narrative that we construct. For they belong together" (Ricoeur 1981: 294). Indeed, the discourse of history, or historiography, is an accumulation of stories about past events. More precisely, it is the sum of particular narrative practices and, hence, particular views of those who dominated the course of history. Human beings have used power not only to master or dominate but also to be remembered and recollected in narrative discourse, to be memorable. These existential and historical implications of narrativity are very far-reaching, because they determine what is to be "preserved" and rendered "permanent" in a society's sense of its own past, of its own identity.

Authority over history is bound up with restrictive narrative practices. In nineteenth-century Sinaloa, for instance, narrative practices were shaped and regulated by the newspaper reporters, who, being part of the educated class themselves, shared the canonical view of their upper-class readers (see Voss 1982). Their agency, power, and narrative perspective direct and impinge on our attempts to write about popular culture of the past. Established by particular sociohistorical conditions, notably in conjunction with the formation of the Mexican nation-state, and through a complex historical process, a distinctive discourse emerged as dominant and legitimate. This official discourse not only silenced the lower classes, it never gave them the chance to raise their voices in the first place.

"Peripheral" narrative undoubtedly existed, but it was not preserved in writing. Nevertheless, those who were most deprived in terms of economic and cultural capital did express themselves in the diverse settings of everyday life—in their music for instance. Although banda music had been left out by those who wrote history, it was always remembered by the people. Paradoxically, the written documents lost their power as they sank into oblivion, whereas the elusive musical sound gained power as it was interpreted and reinterpreted during the centuries since. The history that was kept silent by the official discourse has been and continues to be narrated by the music itself. If we wish to understand banda's historical dimension, we have to listen to the music. Banda's true historical meaning lies in the music, with those who make and live it and with those who listen and dance to it.

TRADITION

Although there seems little consensus among scholars of what tradition precisely means, it is a concept that has not lost its validity for those whose object of study is "tradition" and "traditional music."[14] Scholars continue to use the term, shifting and bending its meaning for their own theoretical and methodological purposes. For my own attempts to unravel and formulate a concept that works for banda music, which is simultaneously traditional and modern, ancestral and contemporary, inherited and appropriated, it seemed helpful to again resort to hermeneutical philosophy for inspiration.

Hans-Georg Gadamer, for example, reminds us that tradition is far from a static entity or simply a permanent precondition. Rather, he stresses the etymology of the term, the root sense of *traditio* as continually passing on or handing down. Tradition entails a constant process of readjustment of constrained and bound improvisation and adaptation. "The fact is that in tradition there is always an element of freedom and of history itself. Even the most genuine and pure tradition does not persist because of the inertia of what once existed. It needs to be affirmed, embraced, cultivated" (1994:281). Gadamer's insight that we are always situated within a tradition or traditions, that we are always affected by the past, was taken up and further developed by Ricoeur: "The temporal distance separating us from the past is not a dead interval but a transmission that is generative of meaning. Before being an inert deposit, tradition is an operation that can only make sense dialectically through the exchange between the interpreted past and the interpreting present. . . . The notion of tradition, taken in the sense of traditions, signifies that we are never in a position of being absolute innovators, but rather are always first of all in the situation of being heirs" (1988: 221).

Moreover, the reality of our cultural way of life is distinguished by both the preservation of a heritage or tradition and the possibilities it holds out. The dialectic between innovation and sedimentation, the process by which innovation settles into tradition, is crucial for an understanding of creative processes with regard to the power of cultural imagination to create cultural identity.[15] As Ricoeur has argued, "[W]e understand ourselves only by the long detour of the signs of humanity deposited in cultural works. [The cultural work] is the very *medium* within which we can understand ourselves" (1981: 143). Thus, the key to understanding how people see and distinguish themselves lies in their cultural practices. Music making, for instance, communicates powerful messages about what society has been and could become. Or, as Barry McDonald has put it, tradition is "a human potential which involves personal relationship, shared practices, and a commitment to the continuation—out of the past and into the future—of both the practices and the particular emotional/spiritual relationship that sustains them" (1996: 119).

INDIVIDUAL PERFORMERS, ACTIVE AUDIENCES

I have also been inspired by other scholars who have analyzed music in its social and cultural context employing practice theory as outlined by Pierre Bourdieu (1977) and who focus on individuals as "agents."[16] As a result of scholars' critiques of their own concepts of culture, culture is no longer viewed as a cohesive totality—a shared world of ideas that includes the intellectual, moral, and aesthetic standards prevalent in a community and the meanings of communicative actions. Practice theory is an individual-centered approach that focuses on the role of the individual and of individual strategies and practices, and suggests that the study of classes of individuals helps to avoid cultural generalizations. As early as 1973, Clifford Geertz acknowledged that symbolic systems are "historically constructed, socially maintained, and individually applied" (1973: 346; see also Rice 1987). The individual is not perceived as a "free agent" but rather as an "individual caught in culture," bound by forces of society, history, economics, gender, and so forth. Thus, studies that focus on the individual experience call upon both the effects of history and the social world as necessary to its interpretation.

Practice theory has been widely used in recent ethnomusicological works focusing on musical practice, in particular on musical experience at the site of its making and reception. The performer is understood as a "social actor" and human activity as the performance of specific learned roles and rules of interaction. The performance event itself is the "text"—in the extended sense of text as meaningful action, which includes music making and dancing. A theory that focuses explicitly on the event is intriguing because it encompasses both performer and audience in a mutually participatory act of textualization.

In the 1960s, some scholars in the field of literary criticism began to stress the importance of the audience for the analysis of literary texts. Their emphasis shifted from the written text itself to the reader, now understood as an active participant in the production of meaning. Reader-response criticism, as this novel development was called in the United States, provides a framework for understanding the interaction between text and reader and endeavors to reveal the ways in which the reader's faculties are both acted upon and activated.[17]

New trends in continental literary theory in the 1960s were inspired by Gadamer's landmark contribution to philosophical hermeneutics, *Wahrheit und Methode* [Truth and Method]. In Germany, the shift of attention to the reader became known as reception theory and reception aesthetics. In the ensuing decades, reception theory became a widely accepted interdisciplinary theory. Although the works of its main exponents, Wolfgang Iser (1978) and Hans Robert Jauss (1982), have been translated into English, reception theory never became widely known in the United States.

The new awareness of the audience as a reading community inseparable from the notion of text led both Iser and Jauss to concretize the dialectic relationship between text, reader, and their interaction. Both reintroduced the concept of aesthetic experience, of pleasure and enjoyment, into literary theory. Iser's theory of aesthetic response holds that the reader's aesthetic response to the text brings into play his or her imaginative and perceptive faculties.

Jauss's hermeneutical approach to audience-oriented criticism draws from Gadamer and seeks to situate a text within its historical "horizon," that is, the context of cultural meanings within which it was produced, but then explores the shifting relations between and the changing horizons of its historical readers. Hence, Jauss is concerned with the ways in which the experience of the text by its reader or audience mediates between the past and present. He draws upon Gadamer's notion that all interpretation of a past work consists in a dialogue between past and present and that all interpretation and meaning is situational, shaped and constrained by the historical contingencies of a particular culture. Moreover, the meaning of a text escapes the intentions of its author: as a text passes from one cultural or historical context to another, new meanings may be drawn from it—meanings that were never intended or anticipated by its author or contemporary audience. Jauss also insists that the reception of art is not simply a passive consumption; rather, it is an aesthetic activity that depends on assent and rejection. The theoretical questions posed by Iser and Jauss have encouraged me to formulate my own questions regarding the role of the audience. My analysis of technobanda as a music-and-dance phenomenon, in particular, shows the importance of an active, participating audience in shaping popular culture. I have tried to go beyond merely explaining my view of the participants' role in this process and recover their agency by including the voices of those who listen and dance to the music.[18]

PEOPLE'S MUSIC

The music of "common people" has been a subject of investigation since the emergence of the discipline called comparative musicology, the forerunner of ethnomusicology, at the end of the nineteenth century. This interest became institutionalized in 1948 with the foundation of the first scholarly organization of the field, the International Folk Music Council (IFMC). The category "folk music" was seen as distinctive from other kinds of music and was defined as "the product of a musical tradition that has been evolved through the process of oral transmission." Continuity, variation, and selection were listed as determining factors that shape folk tradition. Moreover, folk music "has been evolved from rudimentary beginnings by a community uninfluenced by popular and art music."[19] Although in 1969 the IFMC was renamed the International Council for Traditional Music (ICTM), its conventional notion of musical categories did not really change. Tradition was still viewed as passed on from generation to generation as a time-honored body of knowledge and values. The historical dimension of folk music, in particular the question of authenticity—that is, the old, unchanged music untouched by the modern world—was fundamental to most scholars of the older generations.[20] Questions of origin and evolution were of particular interest to the early comparative musicologists. Questions concerning the historical dimension of orally transmitted music continue to be important, one reason being that the belief in the antiquity of folk music is still widespread, especially in the nonscholarly world.

After 1950, the study of recent and current change under conditions of acculturation and influence from Western culture became the main focus of ethnomusicological research. Some scholars called for an integration of popular music and dance into the study of music. However, this did not happen until the hegemony of folk music was challenged, that is, until popular music was actually admitted into the domain of ethnomusicological study.[21] Paradoxically, it was folk music that began to draw ethnomusicologists to urban ground—a shift that was kindled by large-scale migration of the people who were regarded as the tradition bearers into the cities. Analogously, for a long time folklorists shied away from confronting issues such as urbanity, modernity, and technology. It was not until the 1970s that American scholars began to discuss folklore in the urban experience seriously.[22] Most earlier folklore studies suffer intensely from romantic naiveté and the idealization of traditional life. In more recent research that focuses on folk expressions in modern society, folklorists have come to the conclusion that both conservative and innovative forces operate on the traditional cultures that rural immigrants bring with them. They acknowledge that the new contexts for social life generate new traditions of their own that are genuinely urban. Folk music in the city does acquire divergent meanings that are subject to continuous transformations. Thus, folk music is no longer viewed as a symbol of the stability and continuity of rural traditions. On the contrary, scholars recognize that tradition is in a constant stage of disarray and people strive to restore and maintain it in new rituals, displays, and diverse forms of entertainment—constructed and if necessary invented (Hobsbawm 1983).

At first glance, the term "popular music" seems less ambiguous than "folk music." It is usually understood as emerging from urban centers and being disseminated through sheet music, radio, television, and commercial recordings. It is readily comprehensible to (and perhaps also performable by) a large proportion of the populace, it is used primarily for entertainment, and its appreciation presupposes little or no knowledge of musical theory or techniques. The music so defined, thus, comprises pieces of modest length with a prominent melodic line (often vocal) and a simple restricted harmonic accompaniment (Lamb 1980: 87). However, the repertory of popular music, from its very beginnings in the nineteenth century on, cannot always be sharply distinguished from those of folk music traditions and art music because they overlap substantially. In fact, popular music genres in Mexico such as the *son*, the *corrido*, and the *canción ranchera* were often urban renditions of folk genres, whereas the most popular "folk songs" were influenced by nineteenth-century European salon music.

Although there have been some attempts in academia to adjust the terminology to actual musical practices, it seems that the conceptualization of city/popular (mass-mediated) music and countryside/folk music continues to be firmly established in the public's mind. There is an additional problem in the Spanish language, since the term *música popular* actually means "music of the people," encompassing what ethnomusicologists call "folk" and "traditional" as well as "popular urban" music. In the 1930s, Mexican scholars began to use terms such as *música folklórica*, *folklore musical*, or simply *folklore* to distinguish this type of music from *música popular* understood as commercial music.[23] Nonscholars, on the other hand, refer to commercial popular music as *música pop* or *música comercial* and continue to perceive *música popular* as "the people's music." Musicians who play the people's music are called *músicos del pueblo*. The word *pueblo* denotes the place (village) as well as the people (villagers). This duality of meaning is no linguistic coincidence, for "in the Hispanic view, the place where the people dwell is the people, and the people are the place" (Sage 1990: 5). Depending on who is using the term, "popular" may also carry a strong connotation of low class and backwardness.

Notably, when I talked with banda musicians about "traditional" Sinaloan music, they used neither the word *tradicional* nor *auténtica* to refer to this type of music. Instead, they would say *la música vieja* [the old music], *canciones antañas* [songs from long ago], or similar expressions that indicate a passage of time but are free of value judgments. They refer to their own music as *música regional* or *música popular*—popular in the sense of "liked by the people"—which indicates banda's strong regional roots and localized identity.

The term "technobanda" has been created to distinguish the modernized banda which includes electric instruments from the "traditional" acoustic banda. Although technobanda is undoubtedly recognized as a popular music form—popular in the sense of commercialized and urban—it does elicit feelings that are related to a traditional rural life style. Moreover, young people of Mexican heritage claim that they like technobanda because it is their parents' and grandparents' music. How can a popular, commercialized, mass-mediated music style be traditional at the same time? Do the terms "popular" and "traditional" really contradict each other or has this opposition been created artificially by scholars' attempts to categorize musical expressions in either/or?

During the last two decades the body of academic studies on popular music has grown rapidly and is evidence that this neglected topic has developed into a respected field of scholarly inquiry. While earlier works have treated music as a reflection of the pattern of social organization, more recent studies recognize that musical discourse and social context do inform each other. In his seminal essay on the aesthetics of popular music, Simon Frith (1987) has suggested asking how popular music constructs "the people" rather than what it reveals about them. He proposed looking at popular music in terms of how it articulates meaning, how it organizes our collective sense of time and memory, and how it contributes to the social construction of individual identities. Furthermore, he pointed to popular music's particular power to create intense emotional experiences—experiences, however, that always contain social meaning and that are placed within a social context. With the awareness that popular music is always intimately entangled with feelings of identity and notions of community, I consider technobanda as both a site of social significance and a site of cultural contestation.

Referring to the emerging popularity of Dominican *bachata* music in the 1980s, Deborah Pacini Hernández has noted that "changes in the social status and mass dissemination of genres rooted in the musical practices of the poor . . . always reflect transformations in the larger social context, although they are usually launched by individuals who are able to successfully translate these class-bound musics to broader mass audiences by providing them with a veneer of social respectability" (1995: 2). Like bachata, the new techno version of banda was able to transcend the social context in which it originated. And like tango's detour to Paris in the early twentieth century, or calypso's recognition as Trinidad's unique musical form by British and American audiences in the 1960s, banda music had to travel abroad and conquer a less prejudiced audience before it could return to Mexico City and become a "reputable" Mexican music. Although technobanda had already conquered new terrain in Mexico, especially in Jalisco, its relocation into a different social context accelerated the process of its popularization. Particular social conditions in the United States helped banda not only to overcome its marginality and "low-class" stigma but also to become a commercially successful popular music genre much faster and to a much larger extent.

Framework

Book-length studies of particular musical genres typically begin with the music's origin and follow its development in chronological order. I decided to deviate from such an approach by first exploring the technobanda movement and then tracing the music back to its roots. This is admittedly somewhat unorthodox, but I think it underlines one of the central points of a culture concept I firmly believe in, and which I have outlined above: the power of a tradition lies in its contemporary practice, the dialectical exchange between the interpreted past and the interpreting present, which enables our cultural imagination to create a cultural identity. Rather than being a new genre, technobanda reached deep into local tradition for inspiration, but its success was rooted in its capability to transcend spatial, temporal, and social boundaries. Moreover, with my decision to begin the book with technobanda, I follow the path of my own discovery leading from technobanda to the Sinaloan banda tradition. Hence, my own experience is reflected in the succession of the chapters. The narrative mirrors my personal travels, both literally and metaphorically, and my learning process as an ethnographer. The structure of the book is thus a result of the logic of question and answer as I ventured to learn about banda music. It is also an invitation, especially to those who witnessed and/or participated in the technobanda movement, to explore the music's roots, its social history, and its cultural power.

The body of the book consists of three parts, each of them divided into three chapters that address different but related issues: "The Technobanda Craze in Los Angeles: Popular Music and the Politics of Identity"; "A Social History of Banda Music: From Rural/Local/Traditional to Urban/Transregional/Commercial"; and "The Transnational Dimension of Banda Music: Narco Subculture and Contemporary Influences."

Part I explores the "banda movement" that swept southern California in the early 1990s and attempts to explain why and how this musical style emerged and became popular among a vast audience within very short time. For decades, Mexican newcomers who settled in the traditional Mexican barrios of Los Angeles and, more recently, in the industrial heartland of the city remained invisible (and inaudible) to the main population's political, social, and cultural concerns. When politicians and the news media began to blame California's economic recession—triggered by cutbacks in the aerospace and defense industries in the 1980s—on the growing number of immigrants, technobanda exploded in popularity and became a unifying symbol of pride in one's own culture and traditions.

Recent studies have shown that popular music may provide a system for publicly presenting and negotiating identity and for constructing alternative sources of power and meaning, particularly under conditions of pervasive demographic, political, and social change (Waterman 1990; Erlmann 1996). This first part, thus, describes and analyzes technobanda as a transnational music-and-dance phenomenon that allowed its participants to raise their own voice, to make their presence visible and audible, and, at the same time, to create a livable place for themselves in an environment that has not welcomed them and that grew increasingly more hostile to anyone of Mexican or Latino descent. It emphasizes the role of music promotion, radio stations, and nightclubs in the making of popular culture as well as in the formation of a powerful cultural self-understanding, community consciousness, and solidarity.

Part II sketches banda's social history from its beginnings in Sinaloa in the mid-1800s and follows its development through the twentieth century. While I had to resort to historical documents to reconstruct banda's early history, my account of its unfolding in the twentieth century is based on historical memories that are being handed down from generation to generation and on personal stories and individual experiences of a number of banda musicians. Responding to both the customs that retain handed-down practices and the technological and commercial innovations, these musicians are simultaneously tradition bearers and agents who continually create and recreate what has been passed on to them.

Banda's early history as laid out in this part is based on what has survived of nineteenth-century popular culture: written texts such as newspaper commentaries in which the urban upper classes voiced their worries about the behavior and morals of the subaltern classes, as well as travel reports describing local customs filtered through the eyes of foreign observers. These accounts help to recover aspects of everyday life that have been left out of the historical record, but they have to be interpreted with caution. For, as a North American traveler warned a fellow countryman who visited Mazatlán around 1900, "social customs here are as foreign from our own as lemonade from tequila." Moreover, because language and social life are inextricably linked, written texts always bear the traces of the social structure that they both express and help to reproduce.

With industrialization and the development of capitalism during Porfirio Díaz's regime (1877–1911), a different configuration of class distinctions arose, and classes began to identify themselves through particular cultural practices. In Mexico, the struggle to define and dominate the cultural domain coincided with the formation of the modern nation-state after the revolution of 1910. Yet, the state's increasing influence on popular culture did not affect banda's development to the same extent as it did mariachi's, for instance. While mariachi eventually became accepted as national Mexican music, banda was denigrated as provincial and low class. Crucial points in this discussion are the influence of center and periphery, and the domination of the elite in the crystallization of the culture concept.

Part III emphasizes interrelations and linkages between local settings and larger regional and transnational structures and processes. It addresses banda's transnational dimension and assesses contemporary influences, notably the economic power of Sinaloan drug traffickers to influence and coerce musicians and their repertory. Here I argue that the celebration of the revolutionary hero of the modern Mexican nation-state in the emerging mass media helped shape the image of the brave man—an image, however, that under the commercial imperative quickly deteriorated but still continued to inform the collective mentality of a society, mainly by means of motion pictures and popular music. Likewise, the images and stereotypes of the Sinaloan man have been created and perpetuated by banda music. To a certain degree, banda itself is responsible for some of the less favorable popular images, for, in its tightly male world, banda has continually cherished the self-aggrandizing bravado of the macho: the bullies and boosters in the songs, as well as in reality, are, of course, always accompanied by a banda.

Banda is fully transnational. It is part of today's increasingly globalized world characterized by the circulation of people, money, goods, information, and meanings. Even though Sinaloan musicians have traveled across the border and maybe even settled in metropolitan Los Angeles, they remain oriented to the places from which they have come, and they maintain close social relationships with people back home. But moving to a new place and working in a new environment mean engaging with people here and now. In order to survive economically, musicians are forced to respond to local needs. Thus, when technobanda emerged in Los Angeles's burgeoning Mexican neighborhoods, banda musicians saw themselves pushed to once again innovate their tradition.

As banda's and technobanda's rootedness in local identity suggests, regionalism is of central importance to the music's past as well as its present. Understandings of locality and community, however, are discursively and historically constructed. This book is an attempt to deepen the understanding of particular places and people by focusing on a music that, in the course of its long passage, has encountered many challenges and crossed many borders.

Terminology and Translation

It is common in the literature concerning "ethnic" groups in the United States that the authors legitimate their choice of "label." Labels do change over time, reflecting changes in how groups of people see themselves in relation to the larger society. Although in the 1990s the word "Mexican" was often used in a derogatory way in California's political arena, some young U.S. citizens of Mexican heritage began to refer to themselves as Mexican or *Mexicano/a*. In fact, many of those who responded to my quebradita questionnaire were second- or even third-generation U.S. citizens and admittedly more fluent in English than in Spanish, but chose Mexican or Mexicano as their ethnic belonging. Thus, in this book *Mexicano* is used as a general term to refer to the population of Mexican origin residing in the United States, regardless of nativity or generational status. *Mexican* is used when referring to those born in Mexico, while *Mexican American* and *Chicano* are used to refer to the American-born population. Sometimes *Latino* is employed instead of *Mexicano* in order to include other Latin Americans.

Translations begin in the field with our ethnographic work and our "cultural translation" of others' stories, experiences, and expressions. Foreign languages further complicate this process and involve an additional translation. Although I am fluent in both English and Spanish, I faced innumerable problems, particularly when translating song lyrics. I could not avoid an immediate and irreparable loss in sonority, rhythm, rhyme, and sometimes even reason. However, it is my hope that in general the Spanish texts, on their migration into the English language, have not lost too much of their fluidity and vitality. I translated all interviews conducted in Spanish more or less literally. While short quotes are embedded in the text, longer narratives are visually set apart. Quotes from written sources are directly translated without giving the original version.

PART I

**The
Technobanda
Craze in
Los Angeles**
*Popular Music
and the Politics
of Identity*

A New Sound in "Nuevo L.A."

Entre espinas de nopales
crecieron mis padres y ahí nací yo
y entre la tierra mi padre soñaba
con darme una vida mejor.
Ya no vivo entre tanta pobreza
vivo como mi padre soñó
no ambiciono tampoco riqueza
la sangre de indio que traigo es mejor.
   José Arturo Rodríguez González, Banda Machos

Cultural expressions of marginalized communities usually go unnoticed in the national news media unless they relate to or affect American culture at large. Banda was the music of an "invisible minority" of recent Mexican immigrants and blue-collar workers until the extraordinary and persistent popularity of a new "Mexican" radio station began to threaten the hegemony of the English-language radio industry in Los Angeles.

According to Arbitron, a nationwide company that assesses the number of listeners per radio station, KLAX, a hitherto unknown Spanish-language FM station, became number 1 in the city of Los Angeles in the fall of 1992.[1] This sensational breakthrough in the nation's biggest radio market stunned the broadcast industry and generated a flood of articles in business-oriented magazines and national newspapers. Although an earlier published report had indicated a strong upward trend, "Los Angeles broadcasters were still shocked when the fall Arbitron ratings were released and Spanish outlet KLAX, which programs Mexican 'ranchers' music, was at the top of the heap."[2] How could a Spanish-language radio station that aired "rural" Mexican music surpass twenty commercially significant stations and become number 1?

The first reaction of some radio people was to question the accuracy of the Arbitron ratings. The rock station KLSX-FM, which dropped from fourth to ninth place during the same period, complained that Arbitron may have incorrectly credited some of their listeners to the new station because of the similarity of the stations' call letters. The skepticism was fueled by Howard Stern, whose New York–based morning talk show is aired by KLSX, and an independent auditor was hired to investigate.[3] Yet the 1993 winter Arbitron ratings affirmed KLAX's leading position, and *Billboard* acknowledged, "[T]he station proved that feat was no fluke by rising nearly two full share points (5.3–7.2)."[4] "The hottest sound in L.A. is banda," proclaimed the *Los Angeles Times* boldly. "The Mexican music with German roots has caught on big with young Latinos and the format has propelled KLAX-FM to No. 1."[5] The fact that there were no instantly effective marketing strategies to regain control over the city's airwaves seemed to distress Los Angeles broadcasters and radio program consultants. Apparently, KLAX had found a format that appealed to a large audience that wanted to listen actively. The new radio station continued to keep its top-rated position, ruling the airwaves in "the pop music capital of the world" for almost three years.[6]

Just Another Fad?

When "la bomba explotó" [the bomb exploded], as the KLAX deejay Jesús García ("El Peladillo") described the station's sudden success, it pulled banda music out of the barrio and brought it into the limelight. The vibrant new sound that had emerged in "Nuevo L.A.," as the city's burgeoning Mexican neighborhoods were called, began to reverberate. By 1993 banda music had become impossible to ignore.

The print media was first to "discover" (techno)banda. The new music-and-dance craze made headlines in such major newspapers as the *Los Angeles Times*, the *New York Times*, the *Wall Street Journal*, and the *Washington Post*. Los Angeles's Spanish-language newspaper, *La opinión*, printed several articles on banda and quebradita in 1993. Many posed the question, Is banda's current success just a passing fad, a trend that comes and goes, or a sign of cultural reawakening? Is it a simple dance craze or a "cultural revolution"? At that time, nobody really knew what exactly banda music was, nor where it had come from.

Despite the scarcity of dependable references, journalists, apparently unconcerned about disseminating pseudoknowledge and assumptions, managed to write eloquently about technobanda's roots. All the articles quoted here share a certain geographical vagueness and historical inexactitude, if not inaccuracy, made up for by articulate descriptions. Eric Boehlert summarized for *Billboard* magazine: "Historically, Mexican villagers in the Pacific coastal state of Sinaloa would gather in the town square after church and listen to banda (or tambora, as it's also called). Devoid of vocals, the music, with its signature tuba and row of festive horns, often sounded strangely German, as if the musicians had been practicing in Frankfurt beer halls. The music's 'oom-pa-pa' streak did in fact come from Germans: German farmers who settled in regions of Mexico during the nineteenth century. The music remained essentially traditional and ceremonial until the last decade, when vocals were added, tubas replaced by bass guitars, and saxophones added into the mix."[7] Banda music indeed "often sounds strangely German," but Boehlert's explanation does not work: the bulk of German farmers who migrated to Mexico during the late nineteenth century settled in the Texas-Mexico border area, not along the Pacific coast. The *New York Times* writer Margy Rochlin argued likewise: though giving credit to Sinaloa as the place of banda's origin, she traced the "oom-pah-pah ruckus" to the German and Austrian immigrants of the border area as well. As if banda's "signature tuba and row of festive horns" were not enough, Rochlin generously added saxophones and euphoniums, instruments that do not belong to the lineup of traditional bandas (the tuba may occasionally be replaced with a euphonium, but only one bass instrument is used); technobandas, on the other hand, were stripped of their wind instruments, consisting of electric bass guitar and synthesizer only:

The evolution of the regional music called banda began decades ago in the northwestern Mexican state of Sinaloa. Unlike mariachi bands, which usually feature guitars, violins and trumpets, or the accordion-driven norteño music made fashionable by Los Lobos, banda groups use up to fifteen musicians playing trombones, trumpets, saxophones, clarinets, euphoniums, bass drums, cymbals and tuba. No guitars and, originally, no vocalists, a tradition dropped by a majority of today's banda groups. Technobanda, a more recent innovation, substitutes an electric bass guitar for the tuba and depends on a synthesizer instead of wind instruments. Depending on the arrangements, banda groups can perform heart-wrenching, emotional ballads or use the blend of the blaring horns and crashing cymbals to give the feel of a wild marching band; other tunes rely on the honking tuba to create an oom-pah-pah ruckus, an influence that can be traced back to the wave of German and Austrian immigration to the United States-Mexico border in the late nineteenth century.[8]

While both Boehlert and Rochlin neglected to explain how some "German farmers" and Austrian immigrants settling in the U.S.-Mexico border area, across the rugged Sierra Madre mountain chains and at a distance of six hundred miles from the Pacific Coast, had managed to influence the regional music of Sinaloa, the *Wall Street Journal* located banda directly in the "norteña territory" of south Texas, whence it had allegedly spread to the west in recent years. Moreover, the fact that many bandas had long been popular, urban, and even highly commercialized ensembles that played a variety of dance rhythms escaped the writer's attention: "In some ways banda music is hardly new. It originated in the 1800s, when German polkas from South Texas European settlements caught on with the local ranchero musicians. Not until a saucy repertoire of dances evolved a few years ago, though, did banda spread to nightclubs and airwaves—first across the West, then to Hispanics in other U.S. cities."[9]

Rather than acknowledging the regional influence of the Sinaloan banda on technobanda, the authors of the *New Republic* linked the "new generation of banda music" to Mexican municipal brass bands and their predecessor, the military band of the French-Austrian imperialists who seized parts of Mexico in the 1860s. These authors, too, missed the presence and activities (entertaining, recording, and touring) of popular, professional, and commercial bandas throughout the twentieth century:

Banda music—the fruit of Mexico's popular town orchestras appropriating the instruments of the Emperor Maximilian's military bands—has taken over L.A. A fixture of small-town Mexican life since the mid-nineteenth century, banda bands, with their tubas, trumpets, snare drums, still escort religious processions and perform free on Saturday afternoons in plazas throughout Mexico. It probably would have stayed that way had it not been for a radio station on Sunset Boulevard, just off the Hollywood freeway. On August 1, 1992, KLAX 97.9 was reformatted to showcase a new generation of banda music—technobanda—which added vocals and synthesizers and replaced the traditional guttural coughs of the tuba with the electric bass.[10]

Scarce historical data was even more critical for the producers of the documentary *La Banda: Dance of a New L.A.*,[11] for their medium requires visual documentation. None of the historic material used in this otherwise well-made film displays a Sinaloan banda. The producers inserted three black-and-white still photographs showing a group of Mexican bandsmen, as well as clips from a (silent) movie with a group of two fiddlers, a harpist, and a marimba player, and a man (maybe a street entertainer) dancing, or rather jumping about, with no musician present. While the bands in the photographs included a saxophonist and thus could not have represented a Sinaloan banda, the ensemble in the movie most likely stemmed from Mexico's east coast, the Yucatán peninsula. What is remarkable, however, is that journalists and film producers alike showed an interest in stressing technobanda's roots. They sensed that the historical dimension of this new music style was crucial not only to its current popularity among Los Angeles's Latino youth but also to its endurance in the world of popular musics, with its fast pace of change. All of the filmers' young interviewees in the documentary affirmed the importance of the music's roots and tradition, and everybody agreed that "banda is here to stay."

Yet technobanda's deep roots in traditional regional Mexican music also prevented it from being noticed and/or appropriated by other, non(-Latino)-Mexican, audiences. In the spring of 1993, one month before Banda Machos's first nationwide tour of the United States, *Billboard* wrote: "They may go unrecognized at most American record stores, but the eleven members of Banda Machos, who hail from Villa Corona in Jalisco, Mexico, make up one of the most popular Latin music acts today and are helping to change the face of contemporary Mexican music on both sides of the border with their widely popular banda songs" (Boehlert 1993). Banda Machos's two albums, *Casimira* and *Sangre de indio*, were already sales hits in 1992, and they remained among the top twenty on Billboard's Top Latin Albums/Regional Mexican chart. *Billboard* declared 1993 as "the banda year."[12]

Technobanda's Birth and First Years

Before the creation of commercial technobanda, various local musical groups equipped with electric guitars and synthesizers were already experimenting with Sinaloa's traditional repertory. In some sense, these bands were technobanda's predecessors, yet the innovative experiments of these musicians reached only a small audience.

For a new product to break through commercially, it is not enough to carefully orchestrate its promotion and dissemination. It is the predisposition of the targeted audience that decides whether or not a product will be successful. Technobanda apparently found the right place, the right time, and the right circumstances: a ready and enthusiastic young audience for whom this new, catchy, and danceable rhythm became a style of life and a strong force of cultural identity.

The first technobanda recordings were made by Fonorama, a studio in Guadalajara, Jalisco, in the mid-1980s. At that time, Mexico's commercially most successful music was produced by *grupos*, ensembles with synthesized instruments and vocalists playing a repertory of easy-listening Mexican and international pop ballads—groups such as Los Bukis, Los Temerarios, Liberación, and Los Fugitivos. In the search for a new style of popular music, Manuel Contreras, the general manager of Fonorama, was experimenting with different combinations of existing ensembles: banda, mariachi, norteño, Tex-Mex, and grupo. Of all the hybrids, Contreras liked the grupo version of a Sinaloan banda best. He replaced the traditional tuba and horns with electric bass and keyboard synthesizer, added a vocalist, and recorded a selection of *música tropical* (Caribbean music, in particular cumbia and salsa) with norteño flavor.[13] And so technobanda was born. After recording Banda Kora in this new style, Contreras further modified the ensemble's lineup and made recordings with the nine-man band Vaquero's Musical, consisting of electric guitar and bass, electronic keyboard, percussion, saxophone, three trumpets, and voice.[14] "Well, [Vaquero's Musical] recorded and we promoted it for some two or three years. The radio stations [in Guadalajara] didn't accept it right away. They refused because people here didn't like banda music. Here in Guadalajara they are very conservative when it comes to music. . . . They didn't like banda at all. So I kept promoting [the new style] from '85, '86, '87 to '88. Nobody wanted to play it until one day, we were given the opportunity to put it on a radio morning program. The audience liked it very much. And from then on, it flew off and it gave way! It gave way. Other grupos which came for recording sessions copied the style right away" (interview, 1994, Guadalajara). People from all residential districts in Guadalajara called the radio station requesting that they repeat these new songs. One reason technobanda gained popularity, Contreras assumed, was its "general style" and versatility, which appealed to very diverse audiences. He took great satisfaction in having initiated a "musical revolution" that generated so many opportunities for musicians and other people who live from the music business. Yet, he modestly admitted, "To tell you the truth, it was [the new style] I was looking for. But I never imagined that! I never imagined it would go that far! I don't want to presume that I ever thought in such large dimensions. I thought in nothing more than two states—Sinaloa and Nayarit. I didn't even think in Jalisco! But it went, and went, and went. And look at where it went! [This music] is indeed very strong. . . . Now it even enters El Salvador. These are things that one cannot expect. One only initiates them" (interview, 1994, Guadalajara).

Indeed, popular culture is not predictable. As John Fiske has noted, "The people discriminate among the products of the culture industries, choosing some and rejecting others in a process that often takes the industry by surprise, for it is driven by the social conditions of the people at least as much as by the characteristics of the text" (1989: 129). The power of popular music is based on its relevance to the immediate social situation of the people who feel attracted to it. Once it loses this immediacy, it has to give way to another, more suitable music style.

Acknowledging music as a mediating element within the urban experience, Contreras believed that in the late 1980s the noisy city of Guadalajara was ready for "a loud and strong music like banda." Youth cultural expressions, in particular, are "shaped in and through the relations established with music and with the living environment of the city" (Riaño-Alcalá 1991: 87). Loud and strong music has always had a contagious effect on young people, for it gives them a sense of empowerment. But even Contreras was completely taken by surprise by technobanda's success.

The tongue twister "El ranchero chido" [The Conceited Rancher] by Jaime

García, recorded by Vaquero's Musical, was in several ways pioneering: it was the first technobanda hit, and it set the subsequent standard for technobanda songs. Like "El ranchero chido," most of the new compositions are in a fast tempo. The lyrics—and thus the vocalist—stand in the center. Lyrics often refer to banda events, the quebradita dance, dance steps, dancers, and clothes. They employ wit and irony and even dare to ridicule sacrosanct symbols, such as men's mustaches. There is a preference for creative use of language and double entendre, generally sexual. Of course, some of the new technobanda compositions are romantic and in a slow tempo. Like the Mexican *ranchera* and *balada* [ballad], these songs drip with emotions and sentimentalities. Apart from novelties, a great number of technobanda songs rely on contrafacta (setting new words to existing tunes) of traditional rancheras and corridos from the banda and norteña repertories.

Although Vaquero's Musical is generally recognized as the pioneer technobanda, other bands also claimed to have "invented" the new musical style. The dispute was carried out in the fan magazine *Furia musical*, which further encouraged the contention by printing biased headlines.[15] Banda El Mexicano, a four-man band from Mazatlán that created *el ritmo de caballito* [the rhythm of the little horse] in 1988, accused other bands of having copied its rhythm: "We invented the style and we want the people to know that. We are the pioneers who converted banda into a dance. The quebradita dance didn't exist before. Some bandas renamed [our rhythm] to put us aside. They are against us because they don't want us to succeed. That's why it occurred to them to baptize our rhythm 'quebradita,' even if its real name is 'caballito,' the name used by El Mexicano. At the beginning some called [the rhythm] 'de brinquito' [the dance of the little leap] or 'de ranita' [the dance of the little frog], but we gave it the name caballito."[16]

Banda El Mexicano promoted the caballito dance in its songs "Pa' que lo bailes" [So That You Dance It] and "No bailes de caballito" [Don't Dance Caballito]. In another song, "Nena, vamos a bailar" [Baby, Let's Dance], the singer states that quebradita and caballito are the same.[17] Promoting itself as "The Creators of the Caballito Dance" (see Mazatlán's Yellow Pages), the band began using a little horse as its trademark. In an interview with the fan magazine *Furia musical*, Banda El Mexicano said that bands that substitute only two or three acoustic instruments with electric ones have not earned the name "technobanda." In return, some of these bands, which have up to thirteen musicians, accused El Mexicano of distorting the original sound and, because of its reduced size, referred to it disparagingly as "a quarter banda."

Soon after Vaquero's Musical succeeded in Jalisco, new technobandas sprang up. Many musicians who used to play mariachi, *música tropical*, or *rocanrol* [rock

2. Poster featuring Banda Machos, published in the fan magazine *Furia musical* (January 1997). Photo by Luis Sánchez. © Furia Musical/Editorial Televisa. Used by permission.

'n' roll] switched to banda. According to Manuel Contreras, about 80 percent of all performing musicians became *banderos* [banda musicians]. The demand for live music was high: "Every business in these neighborhoods here hires bandas. Here, if there is no banda, there is no dance either. It's incredible—and that in a state where banda is disliked!"

Among the most commercially successful new groups were Banda Machos and Banda Maguey (both from Villa Corona, Jalisco, formed in 1990 and 1991, respectively), Banda Móvil and Banda R-15 (both from Nayarit, the latter formed in 1991). Raúl Ortega, the lead singer of Banda Machos, described their music as a fusion of modern technology and traditional music: "We have profited from the merit of the traditional bandas. But because we are pushed to modernize [the sound], we use technology. So we replaced the tuba, the tumba [*sic*], the tambora, the saxophones [*sic*] and the cymbals with the keyboard, the drum set, and the electric bass. We have both a good light and a good sound system which we'll soon boost."[18]

Indeed, the use of a sound system was a significant break with the traditional practice of playing banda. To put it somewhat simplistically, technobanda was born when the bands began to use amplifiers. This innovation also allowed the new bands to integrate a vocalist whose voice could be amplified to be heard above the loud wind and percussion instruments.

Technobanda's Cradle

Born in Guadalajara, commercial technobanda migrated northward together with its earliest fans. It first conquered Los Angeles and the Southwest, then Chicago and, to a lesser degree, Texas. After its success in the United States, technobanda flowed back to Mexico and was eventually embraced by Mexico City. Among the audience in the United States were many Guatemalan and Salvadoran fans who helped to disseminate technobanda in their home countries.

The steady flow of immigrants from Mexico and Central America has long been changing the face of California. The Los Angeles metropolitan area, more than any other place in the United States, is a magnet for immigrants, notably from Mexico. Latinos, in particular Mexican Americans, are gradually becoming a demographic majority. As of 1990, Latinos (including newcomers and American-born Latinos) made up 40 percent of the Los Angeles area's thirteen million inhabitants; over three million Angelenos speak Spanish at home. From the historical Mexican barrios—East Los Angeles, Boyle Heights, and Pico Union—Mexican newcomers have spread into the San Gabriel Valley in the east, San Fernando in the north, and San Pedro in the south. Newcomers have also spilled into the traditionally African American South Central, Watts, Compton, and Inglewood areas. Many recent immigrants have settled in the five cities that in earlier decades comprised the industrial heartland of the county: Huntington Park, South Gate, Bell Gardens, Cudahy, and Maywood (Acuña 1996: 3; see also Waldinger and Bozorgmehr 1996; Clark 1996; and Ortiz 1996). As many as 80 to 90 percent of the population of this mega-barrio, also known as "Nuevo L.A.," are Latinos. Half of them are not U.S. citizens, and half do not speak English and thus are quite segregated from the mainstream. Most recent immigrants, undocumented ones in particular, are not able to participate in American society in any way. Yet, through their music these invisible and muted people have contributed to Los Angeles's urban culture, and they have been able to carve out their own cultural space.

It was in these neighborhoods that technobanda first gained a foothold. Local radio stations promoted the new style and, soon people's demand for places to dance to the new rhythm was propelling Nuevo L.A.'s night life. Latino clubs began to feature technobandas, and numerous new nightclubs emerged. José Ferrera, the manager of one of the first large nightclubs to put bandas on their stage, recalled:

El Lido opened in 1988. But back then we didn't feature banda and norteño, we featured cumbia. No one with headgear would enter here; they were pulled out at the door. If someone came with a hat on, he had to hand it in. If someone with a hat comes now and

1. Greater Los Angeles.

you tell him to hand it in at the entrance, it is as if you'd tell him: "Enter nude!" . . . I remember that before on Saturdays here, there was not a single person with a hat. Within six months, everybody here had a hat. Those who didn't wear one had to go elsewhere because nobody wanted to dance with them. If you wanted to dance at El Lido, you put on your hat and your boots. If not, the girls wouldn't dance [with you]. That was a very ponderous fashion. (Interview, 1996, South Gate)

When asked how he would explain this sudden change in fashion and taste in general, El Lido's manager, himself a native of Spain, responded:

Where do I live? [I'm] entirely surrounded by Mexicans, and what they like is banda and norteña. Here isn't Hollywood or Los Angeles where they have salsa nightclubs and where they don't let 'em enter with hats. I'm in South Gate and 95 percent of the people here are Mexican. . . . Mexicans of this area are very different from the Mexicans in East L.A. They don't seem to be from the same country! The latter have been here 100, 200, 300 years. They speak English, they don't speak Spanish anymore. . . . The Mexicans who arrive in this area—South Gate, Bell, Bell Gardens—are a different type of Mexican, very different from the one who lives in East L.A. Many of them don't speak English. And they arrive with their music. It's here where banda and norteña started to catch on. The Mexicans from East L.A. didn't like [banda]—well, they like it now because they began to identify themselves [with the music]—they were ashamed to speak Spanish. On the contrary, the Mexicans who come to live here in this area are very proud to speak Spanish, they don't feel embarrassed. . . . The very, very, very center of Mexican music is this area here. Of course, there are other Latin dance halls, but it is this area, South Gate, where everything is emerging, where [Mexican music] is very strong. If it hits here, it will spread all over Los Angeles; later it will spread all over California, and from there all over the United States. But the first place where it has to succeed is here. . . . Música tejana [Texas-Mexican music], for example, doesn't work here. I tried to put on tejana, but the people felt offended. Unbelievable! To upset people here at El Lido, you have to put on either very bad music or music they don't like at all. [Tejano] left the dance floor empty. Whereas when a drum strikes like this—wam!—people start to dance. Once we had a problem with the sound system—I still don't know what happened. At nine o'clock the place was jam-packed and we didn't have sound. It took me half an hour to find the problem. It was a tremendous noise, a bad contact that could have been caused by any wire. The band that was here had wind instruments. When they began to play the tambora and the trumpet, the people got up and danced; they didn't care, they just danced and danced until I resolved the problem—and the beautiful night continued. (Interview, 1996, South Gate)

In the early 1990s the demand for live dance music grew rapidly, and the number of bands multiplied. In the space of just a year, technobanda had given rise to dozens of groups. Los Angeles's night life in the barrios began to flourish anew. Stores selling accessories for banda dancers soon lined Pacific Boulevard in Huntington Park. Among Mexicans, Huntington Park and la Pacific are better known than Hollywood or Rodeo Drive. It is the place where new fashions materialize. At last, the culture industry had discovered technobanda.

From Local to Transregional/Transnational

Once a local music has been spread by the broadcasting and recording industries to other regions and across the borders of nation-states, it becomes a transregional or transnational music.[19] Whether audiences will choose one music style over another does not depend on its availability and visibility alone, but on the consumers' aesthetic sensitivities. Despite the efforts of multinational recording corporations to plan and control the music market, products and consumer desire cannot be entirely gauged beforehand.

"Know[ing] what the people want," remarked Scotty Dupree in the magazine Mediaweek, "may seem a simple and obvious idea, but it's one that the radio program consultants tend to miss." KLAX-FM "may not only have filled a void in the Los Angeles radio market, but it could prove one of those wondersome happenstances in radio that comes about when a station finds an audience that listens actively. It went from nowhere to No. 1, in one book, with a format it calls 'rancheras'."[20] The program directors who started to broadcast (techno)banda music in the Los Angeles area sensed banda's potential, yet they could not foresee that this new musical style would catch the imagination of such a huge audience and trigger a cultural revolution. Indeed, nobody could envision that a radio station featuring "Mexican hillbilly music," as technobanda was labeled by the American media, would break all records in terms of ratings and make radio history in Los Angeles.

Before KLAX adopted the banda format, different local Spanish-language AM stations had already been serving their audiences with the sound of their choice. Radio KALI 1430 AM, called Radio "Kaliente" ["hot radio"], was one of the first local radio stations to put banda music on the air. The deejay Enrique "El Cora" Galindo, one of the main advocates for banda and quebradita, later joined KLAX. Fidel Fausto also began to experiment with banda music on a local radio station in Oxnard, KOXR 910 AM.[21] In August 1991 he created a program called A toda banda. Against the advice of his colleagues, Fausto put banda music on the air, and the program was a success. When asked why he anticipated a positive audience response, Fausto said that he already had a feeling that banda might become a strong force after Antonio Aguilar's two radio hits in 1984 and 1985, "Lamberto Quintero" and "Triste recuerdo" [Sad Memories].[22] The popular Mexican ranchera singer and actor had recorded both songs with Banda La Costeña, one of Sinaloa's most venerable bandas. According to Fausto,

[p]eople recognized the song by the singer, not by the banda. Only people from Sinaloa—and maybe from Zacatecas and Durango—were acquainted with banda. . . . When I joined KLAX in 1992, I remember that Alfredo Rodríguez, the general manager, asked me: "How are we going to program this FM?" I said: "First, regional Mexican music, and second, 60 or 70 percent banda." And he said: "Are you crazy?"—"No, I'm not crazy. I know that banda is going to come strong." And he: "Do you have enough banda?" —"Not enough. But if we play a lot of banda, we are going to force the record companies to record more banda." At the beginning we played Banda El Recodo, Banda La Costeña, Banda Sinaloense Ahome, Los Mochis, and a lot of other bandas from Sinaloa: Banda Culiacán, Banda Los Tierra Blanca. But then more and more groups came on the market, not bandas but technobandas. (Interview, 1996, Hollywood)

KLAX 97.9 FM

In August 1992 KSKQ-FM , with its blend of romantic international hits, became KLAX-FM, with a format based on banda and ranchera music. Within a short time, and despite the station's limited promotion budget, an enormous number of people were tuning their radios to 97.9 FM . Without competing directly against the dominant Spanish-language station KLVE-FM, with its easy-listening, international pop baladas, KLAX managed to attract a Spanish-speaking audience. With regional Mexican music and its "street-smart on-air style," KLAX, "La Equis" ["The X"] for short, succeeded in reaching a huge but neglected audience: recent immigrants, Mexicans from rural areas or small towns, and blue-collar Mexicanos.

KLAX belongs to the Spanish Broadcasting System (SBS), which is headed by Raúl Alarcón Jr. With seven radio stations in Los Angeles, New York, Miami, and Key Largo, SBS is the nation's largest Hispanic-owned media company.[23] Deep financial debts troubled the company in the early 1990s and made restructuring necessary. The new format at KLAX was a key step in the successful restructuring. In an interview with *Billboard*, Alarcón gave full credit for the turnaround to KLAX's general manager, Alfredo Rodríguez, who was lured away from KWKW-AM, a popular local station that featured Mexican regional music.[24]

KLAX's success story offered the *Mediaweek* writer Scotty Dupree an opportunity to criticize a common lack of creativity among most radio programmers. "The rub here is that programming consultants are not tuned into popular culture—they can't be, given the national nature of their business. Popular culture is inherently local. That's why the KLAX story is significant" (1993).

3. The modest building of Los Angeles's most successful radio station of the 1990s, KLAX-FM. Photo by Helena Simonett.

Successfully programming without knowing the musical preferences of the audiences is indeed impossible. The people who risked putting banda on the air were intimately familiar with the predispositions of their targeted audiences. Alfredo Rodríguez told *La opinión* that "In order to know how to present a type of radio that pleases the majority, it was necessary to go out on the street."[25] Instead of relying on data from industry research firms, he went to visit restaurants, bars, nightclubs, and other public places to find out what kind of music people really liked. "We didn't plan to do it with banda only. The original idea was to create an FM station with a unique sound and an AM station with oldies. Because we wanted to develop *una identidad propia* [an identity of our own] for the FM, we looked around to see what music was not covered by other FM radio stations. We began to play all types of Mexican music including the four or five bandas that existed at that time. We created more interest. New bandas were formed and, suddenly, there was a musical explosion—a musical explosion that turned into a social movement" (interview by Carlos M. Haro with Alfredo Rodríguez, 1994, Hollywood).[26]

KLAX's success drew national attention to the Latin market in Los Angeles and raised Spanish-language broadcasters' hopes that mainstream advertisers and agencies would begin to recognize the potential of Hispanic stations. In fact, the increase in audience enabled KLAX to quadruple its morning ad rates from $120 to $500 per sixty-second spot (which was, however, still only half

4. Members of El Club del Sheriff de Chocolate visiting with deejay Juan Carlos Hidalgo at KLAX in 1994. Photo by Helena Simonett.

what English-language stations might charge).²⁷ According to *Hispanic Business*, SBS's "flagship radio station" helped to push its 1993 revenues to $42 million, an increase of 45 percent over the 1992 revenues. In fiscal year 1994, KLAX represented nearly half of SBS's total revenues.²⁸

Because the supply of technobanda recordings was still limited in 1992, KLAX "adopted" a promising young band from Jalisco called Banda Machos and turned it into "La Reina de las Bandas" [The Queen of the Bandas] using a clever programming strategy. As Rodríguez emphasized, beyond the format— the type of music that distinguishes the radio station—the station has to have *una filosofía propia* [a philosophy of its own]. KLAX's principle was to communicate positive values, to foster political and social awareness, and to integrate its listeners into the program. The station's commitment to the community was carried by its deejays, in particular its morning team, "Juan Carlos y El Peladillo."

Both Juan Carlos Hidalgo and Jesús García were teenagers when they left Mexico in the mid-1980s and crossed the border illegally. Both endured the adversities of life as undocumented immigrants picking fruit in Californian fields. Hidalgo eventually enrolled in a Spanish-language communication school in Oxnard in 1987 and then began to work at KTRO, a local radio station. During the same period, García worked at a Thrifty drugstore while attending broadcasting school at night. The two aspiring young men met at a Halloween party organized by the students of the school. García had come to the party dressed as the legendary Mexican comedian Mario Moreno, alias Cantinflas, a raggedy scoundrel with a sharp tongue. In 1989 Hidalgo introduced García to KTRO. Next the team worked at KELF in Oxnard and later at KOFY in San Francisco, where Hidalgo became program director. In 1992 Rodríguez lured them to Los Angeles, where they started to work as morning deejays. Immediately the team became popular as "Juan Carlos y El Peladillo." "Peladillo" was more than just a copy of the legendary Cantinflas—he was García's alter ego. The main reason for his success, García believed, was not the perfection with which he played his role, but the love for Cantinflas he shared with his audience. He felt grateful that listeners accepted him not only as an entertainer, but as one of them: "I want to entertain and to give joy and pride. But I'm like everybody else. I'm a human being with the same affections as all human beings out there. What I like most is a *tostada* with beans. We [the deejays] are humble people. . . . We went through the same stuff that our listeners did. That's why people identify with us. That's why they believe us" (interview by Carlos M. Haro with Jesús García "[El Peladillo"], 1994, Hollywood). Hidalgo, too, insisted that they were not "the hilarious deejays" that were celebrated by their fans and the press. The audience simply liked them because they shared their feelings, and because they talked about their own experiences as undocumented arrivals in the United States. "People trust us," Hidalgo said, "because they know the pain and the suffering." The audience's trust enabled the deejays to be more than simple entertainers:

The microphone gives us a lot of power. It gives us the opportunity to educate our people through the music we put on the air. But we also see ourselves as [political] leaders when we criticize [California's Governor] Wilson, or when we encourage the people to become politically involved by convincing them that they don't betray their fatherland when they become [U.S.] citizens. We, the deejays, have the responsibility to act as role models. . . . Hopefully, some youths will leave the gangs and give up their bad habits. We would like to see that even the young people here learn to speak Spanish, that they know their traditions. We would like them to recognize that each of us who came to this country is equally valuable. (Interview with Juan Carlos Hidalgo, 1994, Hollywood)

Music was seen as a strategic tool for transmitting tradition and heritage to a younger generation. The station's foremost goals were to instill cultural pride, to further validate Mexican customs, and to create a strong sense of community. One of KLAX's actions "to instill cultural pride" was to encourage the cre-

5. KLAX deejay Jesús García, "El Peladillo," doing community work in a Los Angeles Latino neighborhood, 1995. Photo by Helena Simonett.

ation of dance clubs. It was one of the deejays' most important promotional functions to sponsor these clubs. Hundreds of them registered with KLAX, asking the popular deejays to act as their *padrinos* [godfathers]. Registered clubs were entitled to promote their events on air. KLAX's activities outside the studio were a mixture of public service and self-promotion. For instance, after the 1994 earthquake, the team organized food and goods for the communities that were hardest hit; they ran a project for young people to paint houses; and they were present with music and giveaways at community events, high school festivities, and anti-drug campaigns.

KLAX offered its listeners face-to-face encounters with the deejays. Its studio on Sunset Boulevard in Hollywood was open to anyone who wished to meet the staff personally. Many took the opportunity, as could be heard over the airwaves when the deejays encouraged the visitors to make use of the microphone themselves. The power of the radio station was based on its successful mediation of an apparently immediate experience of a "knowable community" rooted in place, tradition, and locality. KLAX's choice of an exclusively ranchera format made apparent its determination to nurture the distinctiveness and the integrity of regional Mexican cultures against the threatening forces of Americanization, in particular forces of deterritorialization and homogenization.

Despite the genuine intentions of KLAX's deejays "to further our valid customs, to value the audience and not to offend it, be it with words or music," their street-smart style was not appreciated by all listeners. The criticism kindled a controversy which was carried out in letters sent to *La opinión's tribuna del público* and to *Teleguía*. Opinions about KLAX printed between January and April 1993 ranged from "La 'X' es la mejor" [The "X" is the best] to "La 'X' es un mugrero" [The "X" is a greaser]. The latter statement, made by a reader from Los Angeles, offended many KLAX fans. It was not only an attack on the radio station and its personnel but also an insult to everybody who identified with the station. A reader from Long Beach responded that KLAX's ratings should be proof enough that a huge majority loved the station exactly the way it was. "I even dare to say that this person [calling La 'X' a greaser] is not [a real] Mexican," read his counterattack. Another reader, who apparently disliked the deejays' on-air style, argued that the deejays seemed to compete with each other to determine who was the more ridiculous one: "I rarely listen to the radio station because I find it embarrassing to listen to the type of radio that reigns in this 'Big Ranch' which is called Los Angeles. The Angeleno radio is plagued by vulgar disc jockeys with a lack of communicational sensibility."

KBUE 105.5 FM

During the third year of KLAX's unparalleled domination of Los Angeles's airwaves, new competing Spanish-language radio stations began to have an impact on its ratings. In early 1995, Liberman Broadcasting Corporation bought a radio station in Los Angeles to establish KBUE 105.5 FM as a Spanish-language banda station.[29] Fidel Fausto left KLAX to become program director of KBUE, also called "KBuena" (pronounced *que buena* [how good]).

On March 1, 1995, I started a new FM [station] in Los Angeles, KBUE. At KLAX they were still playing almost 60 or 70 percent banda. Considering that banda had lasted for almost ten years in the market, I said, well, I have to find out which will be the next type of music to be strong enough to last for the next ten years. So I started on KBuena with more norteña music—60 percent norteña and 40 percent banda. Now [a year and a half later], norteña is in fact stronger than banda. I believe that in the next years norteña music will become even stronger and banda will come down. Natural [acoustic] bandas are now in favor. Technobandas are already dead. We still play Banda Machos, which was once number one, and Banda Maguey—but they are not strong anymore. (Interview, 1996, Hollywood)

With its slightly different format, KBUE tried to reach an audience other than KLAX. Whereas the latter focused more on teenagers, KBUE targeted adults, "people who have the potential to buy." According to a survey of 1995, KBUE listeners were between 18 and 44 years old, the majority of Mexican origin from small towns and ranchos. Although Fausto emphasized the differences between the two competing stations, KBUE's programming strategies and its on-air style were in fact very similar to those of KLAX. The success of both stations was based on the skills of their deejays in reaching their audiences.[30] Rosy González, KBUE deejay, saw herself in the role of a communicator rather than a commentator: "We are very informal, very casual. Other radio stations are more formal. We relate very well to our listeners, and they relate to us. We are talking *to* them, not *at* them. I hope I can make listeners feel like they're part of my family, my friends. We, the deejays, are the icing on the cake" (interview, 1996, Hollywood).

Both the general manager and the program director of a radio station may be regarded as cultural gatekeepers, for they determine the format of the station, outline its philosophy, and decide which recordings will be aired. Although both Rodríguez (KLAX) and Fausto (KBUE) have stressed that it is the audience that makes the radio station, their own power to determine what their audience will like is enormous. Asked about how a music is made popular, Fausto replied that the power to decide what will become popular lies entirely in the hands of the program director: "How much the people are going to like a new song depends on how many times I have played it. Seventy to seventy-five percent of the songs are forced upon the people by the station. If we play the song a lot, the people are going to like it. . . . If I play a song six or seven times a day, within one week, people are going to like it. That's why the company needs to select a person for the programming who places at least 80 percent hits."

Yet, the shaping of an audience's taste only works to a certain degree. Any successful program director must have a feeling of what the audience might like next. In Fausto's words: "I force something that I know *they* are going to like." But what are the criteria for playing a certain song? Fausto responded in an interview:

FF: Every day I receive a lot of new CDs. [*He points to the stacks of CDs that pile up all over his office.*] I have to listen to all these CDs in order to decide what we are going to play. When I have time, I check them one by one, song by song. I listen to all the ten or twelve songs and decide which one is the best.

HS: *How do you decide?*

FF: How? By feeling. By my heart.

HS: *So . . . it is your taste.*

FF: That's right!

HS: *If you like it, you think the audience will like it too?*

FF: Yes. Well, when I listen to the song, I don't listen "by myself." If you want to know which one is my type of music: I like Tchaikovsky, Beethoven, Mozart, Carrillo. I was at the Conservatorio Nacional de Música in Mexico. But if I would decide to play that type of music, they wouldn't listen to me. So when I listen to a tape or CD, I'm taking *their* position. (Interview, 1996, Hollywood)

Key individuals in marketing innovations and trends in popular culture do not necessarily share the audience's taste. For example, Manuel Contreras, who created the new banda style, prefers to listen to "a more refined instrumental music." He only listens to banda during a recording session or when he goes to an audition to hear how they play. "I don't listen to it to enjoy," he admitted, "My ears hurt when I hear a bad banda, and I get a terrible headache. If everybody bought as many cassettes as I do, there would be no business with banda." Both Contreras and Fausto seem to have sensed the needs of the listeners before the listeners did. Both were able to detect a gap in the music market and to fill it. The masses who buy into popular culture are rarely aware how much their tastes, desires, and needs are manipulated by the music and media industries.

The number of listeners is a determining factor in the radio business. The larger the audience, the more a station can charge for advertisements. Arbitrend provides radio stations with monthly feedback on where they stand in comparison with other stations. In addition, radio stations do random research themselves by using a method called "hook on the phone" (a few seconds of a song are played to see if people recognize it). Another way to evaluate public taste and to recognize tendencies is to do a survey. In November 1995, to decide whether KBUE was on the right track, Liberman Broadcasting Corporation hired a company to evaluate audience preferences. Fifteen hundred randomly selected persons who regularly listen to Spanish-language radio stations in Los Angeles and who agreed to test music for six to eight hours were invited to the Sports Arena and exposed to eight hundred hooks (bits of songs). Fausto, who prepared the hooks, included all the songs KBUE was playing (at that time around five hundred) and, in addition, songs other stations such as KLAX were playing and songs he thought should be played. Such surveys are necessary for the long-term planning of a station. Immediate feedback about which songs appeal to listeners is also obtained by the "pre-request on the air." Three times an hour, people can call KBUE to request a specific song. The deejay has to write the title in the space the program director leaves blank when he prepares the Broadcasting Data System (BDS), the station's logbook. A careful evaluation of the BDS reveals not only the listeners' preferences but also the programmer's skill in manipulating the audience.

One of the strategies to keep people listening is to "presell." This can be done by simply telling the audience what is coming up in the next hour or by enticing listeners with easy competitions where they can win cash prices, compact discs, or concert tickets. To be able to participate in the competition, listeners have to stay tuned—sometimes for hours. For several years, KLAX gave away "keys" to callers allowing them to participate in the monthly raffle of a car. Both stations also developed a code that callers had to give before they could request a song or send their greetings. To the deejay's question, "¿Cómo se escucha La 'X'?" [How does La "X" sound?], the caller had to answer, "¡De peluche!" [Plushy!]. KBUE's deejays asked, "¿Cómo está?" [How are you?], and callers replied: "¡Bien buena como la KBuena!" [Very good, just like KBuena!]. To give listeners codes and keys is a clever way not only to grant them access to the radio station, but also to foster the feeling of belonging to a community.

Furia musical

In September 1993 *Furia musical* [Musical Fury] was created in Mexico City to fill a gap in the market of fan magazines: *la onda grupera* [the grupo movement]. *Furia musical* contains plenty of colorful pictures to look at and little text to read: "You won't be simply a reader; you'll be a spectator who participates directly in our stories; you'll have the opportunity to learn about your favorite groups and travel with them, to win prizes, and to attend great concerts." The magazine entices its readers with gossip ("We'll explore the intimate life of the artists so that you can know them at heart") and lures them with photo montages ("A great magazine that will present your favorite groups in the most natural way").[31]

A biweekly fan magazine with its U.S. headquarters in Miami, *Furia musical* has a strong circulation in the United States: each issue sells between 300,000 and 750,000 copies. The target audience is between eighteen and thirty-four years old, Spanish-speaking or bilingual, of both sexes, and from a low socioeconomic sector with little education. *Furia musical* is, as the editors claim, for individuals with an interest in who's who in Mexican popular music. The center of attention is the stars—their careers, awards, romances, weddings, divorces, and accidents. The magazine is owned by Fonovisa, which for its part is owned by Televisa, the world's largest Spanish-language media company, with headquarters in Mexico City.[32]

After Fonorama's first technobanda recordings in the late 1980s, other Mexican labels also began to record the new groups. MCM (Metro Casa Musical, Monterrey), Disa (Monterrey), and Musivisa (Mexico City), companies that had already specialized in Mexico's "rural-rooted sounds" of norteña and ranchera, began to sign banda acts. Yet banda products from Mexico remained largely ignored in the United States. Without retail distribution, fans were forced to trade and copy tapes they had brought across the border from Mexico. In 1992 Fonovisa Records, which has a U.S. distribution agreement with Banda Machos's Mexican label, MCM, released the *Casimira* album.

After the unprecedented inroads of "rural-rooted sounds" into Mexico City, new labels were created, among them Raza by Warner Music Mexico in 1994. EMI Music Mexico showed interest in acquiring DLV, a company specializing in norteña music. BMG International (Bertelsmann, New York), Sony Discos (Miami), and Capitol Records' EMI-Latin (Los Angeles) signed norteña and banda acts. The Mexican label Discos Musart (distributed by Balboa Records, Los Angeles) competes with labels operating in Los Angeles such as Fonovisa (Van Nuys) and La Sierra Records (Panorama City). Fonovisa has U.S. distribution agreements with Mexican labels such as Musivisa, Disa, MCM, Fonorama, and LMC (Luna Music Corporation, Los Angeles). Since modern technology allows the producers to record and mix at different places, material is often sent back and forth between studios until the product is ready for distribution. Local artists and young vocalists in Los Angeles record with smaller labels such as Discos Linda (Pasadena) and Kimo's and Cintas Acuario (Long Beach), or create their own label, as did Chalino Sánchez (Rosalino Records).

Televisa has multiple interests in promoting grupos and bandas.[33] It owns Melody Records, which is affiliated with Musivisa, a label that signs grupos and bandas. Televisa also developed Río Nilo, a 540,000-square-foot multipurpose facility in Guadalajara, where music and dance shows routinely draw between seventy thousand and ninety thousand fans and where norteños, grupos, and bandas compete with each other. *Furia musical* promoted Río Nilo as the "perfect scenario" for "battles between grupos and bandas."[34] Univisión, Televisa's co-owned U.S. network, promoted Banda Machos in the United States after its triumphant beginning in Jalisco. Although Hispanic television contributed much to the popularization of banda music and bandas through the dissemination of their images, it had been rather slow in "discovering" and promoting banda. But once discovered, Televisa turned banda into a commodity for the masses, propagating it nationally and internationally.

Potential for Crossing Over?

The text of one of Banda Vallarta Show's songs, "Rock y banda," addresses the successful integration of a Mexican into American society and reflects this cultural approach musically by fusing banda and rock 'n' roll (the song, however, is still recognizably banda and not a *rock en español* hybrid). The song tells the story of a banda dancer who enters an American nightclub dressed in his Mexican outfit: boots and hat. When a girl invites him to dance rock 'n' roll, he feels ashamed for not knowing the steps. But finally they overcome the cultural barrier by learning from each other: dancing, they discover a new style, which eventually becomes a hit in the discotheque. According to the protagonist, he is not only accepted as who he is, but he is also actively contributing to American culture by creating a new dance style. Appearing at a time of rapid expansion of the banda movement and optimistic confidence in the music's potential for a successful blending with Anglo-American pop styles, we might interpret the dancer's story as a reflection of Banda Vallarta Show's own hope of crossing over to, or even of having a direct impact on, the Anglo mainstream.

Banda's success indeed made multinational recording corporations take notice and sales managers look into the possibility of marketing technobanda in the "Hispanic," "Latino Pop," or even "world beat" categories. However, a few years after the initial boom, only a small selection of technobanda albums were to be found in national outlets such as Tower Records or Blockbuster. Unlike tejano music, technobanda had not burst out of its Mexican American boundaries as culture industry executives had hoped when the new sound emerged in the early 1990s. Banda's rootedness in the particularities of its local culture apparently did not suit mass marketing. The barriers to a smooth crossover into common-denominator Latin pop seemed impossible to overcome. Even a singer like Ezequiel Peña, who was tremendously popular among Mexican audiences, hardly fit the image of an American pop star. Despite his good looks and highly promoted *ojos verdes* [green eyes], his outward style would never have appealed to mainstram expectations. Peña's group, Banda Vallarta Show, dressed in fancy costumes dotted with thousands of gleaming sequins, cowboy boots with appliqués, and black hats, looked as if they had sprung from the entertainment world of Las Vegas or Puerto Vallarta, a popular tourist destination on Mexico's Pacific coast. The group's name, Vallarta Show, reflected the international, modern flavor its music embodied. The Americanism "Show" pointed at the choreographic display Peña and his band put on at performances. The visual spectacle was indeed an essential ingredient in Peña's appeal. His shows in the United

States, held at huge arenas like Pico Rivera in Los Angeles, would regularly attract tens of thousands of spectators, most of whom were of Mexican origin. Yet, technobanda failed to capture non(-Latino)-Mexican audiences and their tastes. Or, to put it differently, technobanda successfully resisted being appropriated into the mainstream music industry, for some of the reasons discussed earlier.[35]

The Global-Local Nexus

Specialists in world economy and policy studies have repeatedly pointed out the threat global (Western) popular culture poses to local traditions.[36] Since globalizing processes bring about a certain homogenity, many still tend to believe that the culture industry and contemporary communication technology are turning the world into a "global village," a homogeneous, integrated, and interdependent place. On the other side are those who argue that Western hegemony is now being eroded from below by burgeoning local and regional cultures (see Garofalo 1993; Featherstone 1995). Thus, the "global village" is not a village, but an urban complex of global diversity, including all the ethnic neighborhoods contained within the city, as stated by Don Ihde (1993: 66). Moreover, globalism is always countered by localism, as John Fiske has argued in a recent paper on the hybrid vigor of popular culture in an increasingly diversified society such as the United States (1996: 46). What we will find is that locals continually bend global practices by appropriating specific elements in order to create their own cultural practices, which articulate their own historically and socially specific experiences. Thus, the interaction of global mass culture with local cultures produces hybrid musical forms that suggest not the elimination of cultural diversity, but rather opportunities for counterposing diverse alternatives.

Like other observers of Los Angeles's youth culture, the *La opinión* writer Henry Muñoz Villalta marveled at the phenomenon of young Latinos dancing to the beat of ranchera music: "While youths in Latin American countries ardently adhere to music from the U.S., young people of Aztec origin residing in California nostalgically prefer the music of their parents, the type that most fully identifies with their cultural roots."[37] Without considering the different social situatedness of these youths, he went to call their preference for rural Mexican music, including technobanda, "paradoxical." Yet the fondness for ranchera music among young Mexicanos in the United States was anything but paradoxical. With technobanda they had finally found their own voice—a vibrant, fresh, and modern voice which allowed them to acknowledge and live out their otherness. For these youths, technobanda confirmed a continuing attachment to values shared with parents and rooted in their "homeland," while simultaneously allowing for social attitudes, trends, and aspirations derived from Anglo youth culture. Thus, this music was relevant not only to their life style but also to their cultural needs.

Taste and aesthetic inclination are always socially informed, and emotional experience is the key to a music's aesthetic pleasure. "Sangre de indio" [Indian Blood], a rather sentimental ranchera composed by Josué (José Arturo Rodríguez González), was one of Banda Machos early hits and was played extensively on KLAX in 1992 and 1993.[38] The song lyrics reflect values that are generally esteemed in Mexican society (respect for parents, hard work, irrelevance of material gain) and convey pride in one's race and roots (Indio heritage, land):

Por las venas de mi padre	Through my father's veins
le corre la sangre también como a mi	runs the blood, as it does through mine
sangre del indio que calla	that of the Indio who remains silent
que llora, que ama, que sabe sufrir.	who cries, who loves, who knows how to suffer.
El indio aquel que mi madre amó	That Indio whom my mother loved
porque sabe que es un hombre fiel	because she knows he is a faithful man
gracias a Dios que es mi padre	thank God, he is my father
y que yo he heredado ser indio como él.	and that I have inherited being Indio as well.
Entre espinas de nopales	Among cactus thorns my parents grew up
crecieron mis padres y ahí nací yo	and there is where I was born
y entre la tierra mi padre soñaba	and on that land my father dreamed
con darme una vida mejor.	of giving me a better life.
Ya no vivo entre tanta pobreza	I don't live in such poverty anymore
vivo como mi padre soñó	I live like my father had dreamed
no ambiciono tampoco riqueza	I don't seek for wealth either
la sangre de indio que traigo es mejor.	the Indio blood I carry is more.
La piel de bronce que tengo	My bronze-colored skin
es herencia de mi padre	is my father's legacy
y este corazón que siento	and this heart that I feel
éste me lo dio mi madre	my mother gave it to me
los dos me dieron la vida	they both gave me life
los dos me dieron su sangre	they both gave me their blood
y gracias a Dios que me hicieron	and thank God they made me
un indio como mi padre.	an Indio like my father.
Mis hermanos también llevan	My brothers have the same
la sangre de indio como llevo yo	Indio blood as I do

sangre que pintó la tierra	blood that painted the land
la tierra que mi padre tanto labró.	the land my father worked so much.
Dejó mi padre la sierra	My father left the sierra
mi madre llorando trás él caminó	my mother followed his steps crying
dejaban todo por darme	they left everything to offer me
lo que ya más tarde la vida me dio.	what life, later, has given me.
Ya no vivo entre tanta pobreza [etc.]	I don't live in such poverty anymore [etc.]

As simple as this song may sound, it was able to vitalize the social imaginary of immigrants and estranged people and to set free strong emotions. Both song lyrics and music constitute a powerful way of belonging: Indio identity is firmly rooted in local attachments (la tierra) and in local traditions.

Rather than being a new genre in its own right, technobanda reaches deep into local tradition for inspiration. Yet, as a genre directed at the mass market, it depends on production and consumption systems and strategies developed by the popular music industry. On the one hand, technobanda emphasizes its roots in particular localities and thus reasserts its independence from and re-sistance against Anglo-American hegemony; on the other, it is subjected to mainstream popular culture. If we understand technobanda as a cultural prac-tice entangled in a dynamic global-local nexus rather than as part of a static binary of hegemony and resistance, we may come to the conclusion that tech-nobanda's appeal was grounded precisely in the tension between elements of nationalistic resistance (the reinterpretation of regional Mexican music) and conformity to the hegemonic power of the culture industry, with its MTV-inspired high-tech music. Participation in banda events allowed both Mexican immigrants and Mexican Americans to reclaim and renovate their own tradi-tion while enjoying the commercial seduction and standards of MTV and its re-lated industry. Within a short time, technobanda engendered a powerful cul-tural self-understanding among its mostly young listeners and provided them with an invigorating sense of belonging and a shared sense of purpose.

As has been pointed out in this chapter, the broadcast media played a crucial role in the formation of a collective self-consciousness and the creation of an "imagined community" centered around shared traditions and memories.[39] KLAX helped to construct an alternate public sphere, a form of community consciousness and solidarity that maintained identification with the "home-land" in order to facilitate the newcomers' life in the United States as "others." For longtime residents and Mexican Americans, on the other hand, the "imag-ined community" created by the radio station had the encouraging effect of (re)identification with their prior home. Among younger Mexicanos in particular, the vibrant technobanda scene was valued not only because it reinvented a traditional genre, but also because it made the Mexican presence in the United States visible and audible. The importance and power of the music in the struggle for identity and difference are discussed more fully in chapter 3.

The Quebradita Dance Craze

Vamos todos a bailar
este ritmo sin igual
a bailar la quebradita
con Vaquero's Musical.
    Toreko, Vaquero's Musical

"Move over, salsa. Forget lambada. The dance of the day is *la quebradita*, and the sound that drives it is *banda*"—so read the Entertainment Supplement of the *Los Angeles Times*. Another journalist at the same newspaper observed: "Hotter than a jalapeño, the dance fever has been gaining steam among Latino teen-agers—particularly those of Mexican descent—and now it seems to have burst onto the scene, dominating CD players at junior high and high school dances, *quinceañeras* [coming-of-age parties for girls] and parties from East Los Angeles to Lynwood, from Hollywood to Huntington Park. *¡Que cool!*"[1]

It is certainly not an easy task to introduce a new dance style to an uninitiated readership. Yet, to keep their readers informed about the newest cultural trends, newspaper writers had to grapple with the obstacles to describing the nonverbal practice of the quebradita. Obviously, the most fruitful way to write about a new dance style was to compare it with already familiar styles and to emphasize its difference: "*La quebradita*, a dance that combines country-Western with cumbia, salsa and occasionally flamenco. The dance gets its name, *la quebradita* ('the little break'), when one partner, usually the guy, swings his mate into a backward bend and, balancing her body in one arm, barely brushes her against the floor while rocking to the beat. For sure, this is not the Mexican hat dance. It's more like lambada meets limbo rock" (Quintanilla 1993). Or: "*La quebradita*, less overtly erotic than other recent Latin dance crazes, looks something like the Texas two-step combined with the fast and furious footwork of a Highland fling. The upper body remains fairly rigid as dancers kick their heels fore, aft and around in circles, occasionally dipping their partners backward into a *quebradita* (break)" (Easley 1993). Moreover, "acrobatic lifts and sombreros spinning like Hula-Hoops" are in vogue while "too much salsa-style wiggling" is despised. The *Wall Street Journal* reported that couples were "clicking their boots" on the floor "and blending sensuous Latin ballroom, country and western two-step and old-fashioned polka."[2] In an article on "MexAmerica's border culture" in *Newsweek*, quebradita was described as "a mix of lambada, jitterbug and hoedown, but more formal and dignified."[3] The *New York Times* writer Margy Rochlin described the "industrial-strength dancing" in more detail:

To the untrained eye, it might appear that there are a wide variety of ways to dance to banda. Essentially, there are only two—el zapateado and la quebradita. Reserved for the faster-paced numbers, the former dance has a hard-to-translate meaning involving heelwork and hard-to-describe look—it's something like the fusion of bandylegged clogging and the up-and-down arm movements of the Monkey, a 60's go-go dance. La quebradita which is performed during the slower tunes, has been said to incorporate the theatrical touch-dance choreography of the flamenco, the lambada, salsa dances, the Texas two-step and the tango. Mostly, it appears to be the Mexican equivalent of dirty dancing, with much synchronized writhing, dizzying twirls and naughty hip grinds. The trademark of la quebradita is its eponymous move, which literally translated means "the little break" and involves the male partner's swinging the female partner from side to side while simultaneously bending her so far backwards that her hair swabs the floor. It's an athletic feat that must be seen to be believed; improperly executed, la quebradita can be a humbling, if not bruising, experience.[4]

The "banda movement" that swept Southern California in the early 1990s was indeed carried by the music's danceability. Technobanda's accelerated tempo and powerful amplification enabled dancers literally to feel the music. Quebradita, the new dance style that had emerged and evolved as a way to dance to technobanda, was the backbone of the movement. This chapter focuses on banda as a music-and-dance phenomenon in general, and on the dance events in particular, where social imagery, identity, *communitas* (the collective aspect of dance rituals), and aesthetic meaning are produced in performance—sensorially, audibly, and visually—through music, kinetics, gesture, and dress.

The Quebradita Craze

Soon after the new banda style had conquered the airwaves, many grupos turned into technobandas, and vocalists who had never before considered recording with a banda released their new compact discs. Banda Toro, for example, a ten-man band from Zacatecas that put the hit "La noche que murió Chicago" [The Night Chicago Died] on the charts and whose vocalist used to sing mariachi, explained that it too wanted to be part of "the current new wave, the wave of the quebraditas and the banda music."[5] The dance fever spread and nightclubs prospered. The quebradita craze gained momentum. On the one hand, the demand for live music encouraged the formation of new techno-bandas, and on the other, the growing number of bands propelled the cities' nightlife on both sides of the border. Banda Arkángel R-15, a technobanda from Nayarit, advertised the new dance and itself musically in "La quebradita":[6]

Todos para bailar la quebradita	Everybody let's dance the quebradita
todos para gozar la quebradita	everybody let's enjoy the quebradita
pues es un baile nuevo, se baile ahorita	for it's a new dance, dance it now
Arkángel R-15 ahora te invita.	Arkángel R-15 invites you.
La quebradita está de moda	The quebradita is in fashion
la quebradita les va a gustar	you're going to like the quebradita
pues ese baile es una fiebre	because this dance is certainly a fever
solo con banda se ha de bailar.	which with banda can only be danced.

In another song, the band had raised the question, "¿De dónde viene este baile?" [Where Is This Dance From?]. There is no definitive answer, because it seems that the quebradita style emerged at several locations around the same time. South of the border, Maricela Contreras (of Guadalajara's Fonorama) remembered that people started dancing the quebradita on the steps of the Lienzo Charro Santa María Tequepexpan, Guadalajara's arena, when the first technobandas were contracted to play for the *jaripeos* [rodeo-like shows] in the late 1980s: "Quebradita was born here. The truth is that the movement was born in Guadalajara." Responding to the dispute over the authentic name of the new rhythm and dance style, Vaquero's Musical, the pioneering technobanda from Jalisco, affirmed its leading role through the song "A ritmo Vaquero's":[7]

(Y de nuevo con ustedes, los creadores	(And again with you, the creators
del estilo banda, Vaquero's Musical)	of the banda style, Vaquero's Musical)
Toda la gente pregunta	Everybody is asking:
¿de dónde es la quebradita?	Where is the quebradita from?
Se los voy a contestar:	I will answer you:
en mero Guadalajara	in Guadalajara itself
le llamaban "de brinquito"	they called it "de brinquito" [short-leaping]
con aquel "Ranchero chido"	with that "Ranchero chido"
de Vaquero's Musical. [etc.]	from Vaquero's Musical. [etc.]

Así es este baile de quebradita	That's how this quebradita dance is
de caballito, de perrito, de brinquito	of caballito, of perrito, of brinquito
[o] como le quieren llamar.	[or] whatever you like to call it.

North of the border, however, Radio KALI DJ Enrique "El Cora" Galindo, insisted that "the quebradita was born in Los Angeles. Juan Pedro González, owner of the dance club Jalpa in East Los Angeles, was the first to call it 'la quebradita'."[8] Banda Arkángel R-15 had its own answer ready in the song "¿De dónde es la quebradita?"[9]

La quebradita es un baile	Quebradita is a dance
que baila toda la gente	which is danced by all people
se oye bonito su ritmo	its rhythm sounds pretty
tiene sabor diferente	it has a different flavor
¿de dónde viene este baile?	Where does this dance come from?
aquí pregunta la gente	people here ask
¿de Sinaloa o Jalisco	From Sinaloa or Jalisco
Durango o Aguascalientes?	Durango or Aguascalientes?
Es de Durango, de Guanajuato	It's from Durango, from Guanajuato
de Zacatecas y de Jalisco	from Zacatecas and from Jalisco
es de Colima, de Michoacán	it's from Colima, from Michoacán
y de Sonora, de Sinaloa	and from Sonora, from Sinaloa
es de Chihuahua y de Guerrero	it's from Chihuahua and from Guerrero
de California y de Nuevo León	from California and from Nuevo León
¿de dónde es la quebradita?	Where is the quebradita from?
[coro] También es de Nayarit.	[chorus] It also is from Nayarit.

With this diplomatic response, Banda Arkángel R-15 not only bypassed the dispute over the quebradita's origin, but also contributed a substantial idea, namely: the quebradita comes alive where it is being danced.

The Dancing Style

The basic quebradita step is quite simple, based on a two-step pattern consisting of rocking back and forth between the left and the right foot in time with the bass and percussion beats. Dancers may combine the basic pattern with a variety of turns, spins, and breaks. Quebradita's characteristic gesture, as the dance's name suggests, is the "little break," the backward bend of the female dancer. If not properly executed, "la quebradita can be a humbling, if not bruising, experience," as one journalist has accurately noted. In its song "La quebradita," Banda Arkángel R-15 alerts the male dancer: "Lift her up, bend her

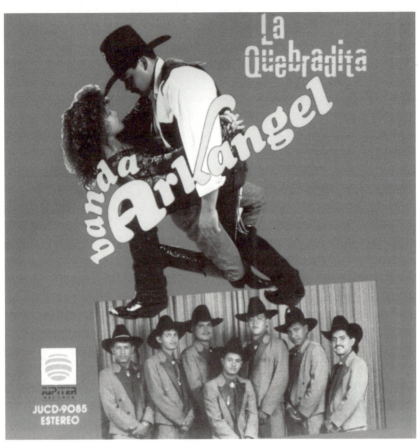

6. Banda Arkángel R–15 CD cover. © 1993 Luna Music Corporation.
Used by permission.

down, lift her up. Be careful when you dance it, when you lift her up by her waist, that you're not going to break her." In another song, the female dancer is being warned to not underestimate the momentum: "Hold on, Nicolasa, hold on and don't let go. Even if you're slight, this quebradita is very strong." Although it is the male dancer who, with a sudden but controlled movement, dips his partner backward, the gesture is performed by both dancers. If the woman does not sustain the momentum, she will "break" his back too. While fine-tuned cooperation between the dance partners is essential, it is the man, as in other couple dances, who leads and outlines the dance's choreography. In dance competitions—organized by many nightclubs at midnight to keep the party in full swing—the audience used to shout "¡Québrala!" to animate the dancer to "break her." Most often, however, dancers only indicated the quebradita gesture, especially on crowded dance floors without sufficient space for expansive movements. Hence, dance-fanatic couples often showed up early (before nine o'clock) to practice and to enjoy their dancing unhindered by other dancers. Later at night, they would dance at the margins of the dance floor—sometimes using ground not marked as part of the dance space—to execute the "little break."

For fast-paced pieces that were not danced as a pair, skilled dancers performed highly complex footwork, borrowing from traditional Mexican dance steps such as the *zapateado* [a heel-and-toe stepping dance] and from *ballet folklórico* [staged folklore dances].[10] In fact, the quebradita combines various dance styles from different regions of Mexico, in particular from the north and northwest, with simplified steps and gestures from folklórico dances and with steps from contemporary popular Latin dances. The dance scholar Benjamin Hernández, with whom I took some quebradita classes at East Los Angeles College in 1994 and who demonstrated and compared selected steps from the quebradita and folklórico repertory, told me that in the aftermath of the Chicano movement, the barrio youths went to ballet folklórico classes as part of their bilingual education. These classes not only gave them a distinct awareness of Mexican traditions, but also provided them with a cultural experience that they now, as adults, "reexperience" in quebradita events.

Both folklórico and quebradita steps integrate gestures that are related to the rural Mexican lifestyle. Because of its centrality in a rancher's life, the horse has become an important status symbol. Hence, many of the dance steps imitate its movements. The basic quebradita step is "trotting." One of the quebradita's remarkable leg gestures is called the "horsetail" (except for the quebradita, names of other dance gestures seem to have been invented on the spot). The horsetail is a combination of kick forward, twirl at the knee (with the knee as a fixed point), kick back, and twirl at the knee, and is performed without disrupting the dance rhythm. If the twirl with the lower leg is repeated in a fast tempo, it resembles a horsetail flicking away flies. According to Hernández, the horsetail is a variation of "the rooster," a gesture from the folklórico repertory of Jalisco. Another combination of leg gestures, the so-called getting on the horse, is a simplified version of "the little horse" in folklórico dance. Still another of quebradita's leg gestures, the "lasso," a loop performed with the lower leg in front of the body, corresponds to the folklórico gesture called the "bottle" (loop with the leg around a bottle on the floor) and the "atole" (arm gesture of stirring cornmeal mush). The quebradita gestures were usually done by men and occasionally by women, depending on the situation and the dancers involved.[11] Generally, male dancers had a larger and more playful repertory of dance movements than women; for instance, they would imitate riding on horseback or spin their hat on their fingertips. For men, the

¡A BAILAR La Quebradita!

"ZAPATEADOS", "QUEBRADITAS" Y LO MAS NUEVO... "EL PASO DEL VIEJITO"

7. "¡A bailar la quebradita!," instruction video of how to dance the quebradita. © 1993 Luna Music Corporation. Used by permission.

dance floor was very much a site of contention where they could demonstrate masculinity by executing sensational footwork and showing off their ability to move well.

If dance is cultural behavior that is partially determined by a people's values, attitudes, and beliefs, as suggested by the dance scholar Judith Hanna (1979), then it necessarily reveals both consensual and conflictual cultural processes. The reaction among Mexicans and Mexican Americans in the United States to the new dance style was not unanimously positive. The emerging controversy centered on arguments involving tradition, generation, gender, class, and nationality. The focus of the polemic was the *quebrar*, the bending backward, which was interpreted by some (mostly elderly) people as too sexually suggestive. Twists and acrobatics were denounced as "amoral pirouettes," vulgar and obscene gestures disfiguring "the tradition" and "betraying Mexico." In an angry letter to *Teleguía*, a reader from Bell Garden wrote:[12] "I am a Mexican from Guadalajara, and it makes me very sad to see these so-called 'Quebraditos' here [in Los Angeles] who try to show off with vulgar behavior. . . . They don't have any idea what it means to wear a hat and boots; that hat and boots are worn because of tradition and custom and not to ridicule and humiliate us in front of the other people who live in this country. . . . To all these 'Quebraditos': Show respect, morals and principles; hat and boots are our roots; wear them with dignity; it is a very fine heritage that our ancestors have left us. I hope this falseness will end very soon."

Yet young dancers who grew up in Los Angeles showed little appreciation for such criticism. Most just ignored the polemic provoked by the quebradita. Quite a few female teenagers, I was told, went dancing at nightclubs without the approval of their parents, telling them they were visiting with a girlfriend or some such excuse. I observed girls changing from their regular clothing into dressy skirts or provocative shorts in the ladies' restroom—hardly with parental consent. In Banda El Mexicano's song "No bailes de caballito" [Don't Dance Caballito], a mother's authority is being questioned:[13]

Cuando vas al baile	When you're going to the dance
¿qué te dice tu mamá?	what does your mom tell you?
¡No bailes de caballito	"Don't dance any caballito
que te voy a regañar!	or I will scold you!"
Cuando llegas al baile	When you arrive at the dance
¿qué te dice tu papacito?	what does your boyfriend say?
¡Vente, mamacita	"Come on, darling
a bailar de caballito!	let's dance some caballito!"
Te toma bien apretada	He hugs you very tight
te coge por la cintura [etc.]	he grabs you by your waist [etc.]

Parents may have worried for their offspring less because of the dancing and more because of the drug dealing, shootings, and so forth they feared were going on at the dance halls. Young nightclub-goers, on the other hand, tended to play down the inherent danger. As one female dancer told me: "The nightclub itself it a safe place. That's why [my parents] let me go out. It's safe. There is security everywhere. If you are under age, they don't let you drink. My parents would not let me go otherwise. . . . Both my parents went to the Lido. They checked it out. They know what it is like. They also went to this other place, El Jalpita, where my friend and I are going to dance." Asked about the quebradita polemic, in particular the dance's sexually suggestive gestures, my interviewees in Los Angeles freely shared their own experiences regarding dancing, pleasure, sexuality, and *costumbres* [customs, tradition].[14] Addressing the apparent suggestiveness of the dance style and the generational conflict, one young dancer said:

My parents don't like [techno]banda, but they didn't reject it either. Just when la *quebradita* came out, some of the moves, like when they would fly the girls around—[my parents] were totally shocked: "What are they doing there?" Like, when [the male dancers] were moving the girls back and forth: "Oh my God! They are having intercourse!" Or something. That's a question a lot of people ask that are older: "The guys, don't they get excited dancing so close to the girls?" It's a question that comes up a lot. To me, if you are into dancing, why should you be somewhere else? But also young people. . . . Some American friends I have, I took them to a nightclub one time, and they: "Oh my God! You're dancing for the first time with them and you're already hugging them." Totally shocked that guys just come up to you, they just hug and start dancing back and forth [the quebradita movement]. See, it has nothing to do with sex, it's just dancing. You can tell from the way a guy hugs you, if it's too tight. . . . This new hip movement, I like it, there's nothing wrong with it. Older people that see it for the first time may be shocked. My grandmother would probably pray for me or something.

Another dancer related:

Certain moves are sexually suggestive. My mother would interpret it like that. Older people would say: "Oh, look what she is letting him do?" But to me, it's not a sexual contact. I don't know how the guy may take it, but to me, it's nothing. And I'm sure all these people are just dancing. Sex doesn't even come to their mind at that time. . . . You're dancing—that's all. I can dance with anybody, I won't get offended if he holds me like this. That's the way they dance. Outside the dance floor, you can't be so close. I've always thought: Why can you hold someone and it's OK to hug someone while you're dancing, but outside the dance floor you can't hold someone like that? How come you can hold a stranger on the dance floor but not outside? From where I come from [the Mexican countryside], if you dance consecutive dances with someone, that means a lot. It's not like here where you're just dancing. It's the kind of society you're in. Here people don't get scandalized over little things. Most Hispanic people come from small towns, rarely from the city. If they are from the city, they're more open minded. Here you have more freedom. It all depends how you're raised and what values you have. For some it's decent, for others not. In my family, we had to go with my mom's values, even though we were in the United States. Even now, when I'm going to the nightclubs she gets upset, she says: "That's not right. You're a mother of two. You shouldn't be in these places." And I get a whole story. But I tell her: "We are in America. I'm old enough now to know what I'm doing."

The Dress Code

In the PBS documentary *La Banda: The Dance of a New L.A,* broadcast on 14 April 1994, the host, Rubén Martínez, invited the viewers to explore together the newest dance craze that had swept the city: "Maybe you've been wondering about all those Mexican-looking cowboys and cowgirls if you were strolling along the streets of L.A. lately. Well, I'm here to tell you: It's a cultural revolution, it's a social transformation, it's a political movement—well, at the very least, it's a dance craze. The music is called banda; the dance is called quebradita; the *vaqueros* and *vaqueras,* as the cowboys and cowgirls call themselves in Spanish have been dressing themselves up and are coming down to get in clubs like this, A Mi Hacienda in La Puente [in the eastern part of Los Angeles]. So, what's all the fuss about? I don't know, *raza* [folk]. Come on down, let's check it out."

Fashion is a very important ingredient of youth culture in general. Like other dance crazes, the quebradita came along with a characteristic style of dress: the vaquero attire. As any uniform does, the quebradita dress style helped to forge unity among the participants. Vaquero's Musical, the pioneering technobanda, seems to have been a trendsetter in matters of clothing. The nine cowboys appear on the cover of their first cassette dressed in a dark brown three-piece suit, white shirt, black tie, boots, and black Stetson. Soon, they dressed up in a flashier norteño-vaquero style: multicolored, fringed leather jackets, matching boots, and plenty of gold jewelry. Appliqué and embroidery turned plain cowboy boots into multicolored artworks. Banda Machos's dark outfit—including their trademark, a long black trenchcoat—became more colorful too. Banda Vallarta Show and its lead vocalist, Ezequiel Peña, displayed a unique style: garish costumes dotted with thousands of gleaming, glittering sequins. The musicians encouraged the *quebradores* [quebradita dancers]: "Take off your sneakers, put on your boots." Dance enthusiasts embraced the new fashion quickly. The basic outfit for a man included boots, *tejana* [Stetson hat], tight-fitting jeans, belt, and a nice shirt, and was affordable for anybody. However, it was easy to spend a fortune for more expensive clothes: a good hat may cost up to $1,500; boots go for $800 or more (especially snakeskin or ostrichskin boots); a belt of the same material is worth $600; the same is true for the *cinturón piteado*, a belt embroidered with maguey fibers; if it has a valuable buckle, its price has no upper limit. Fringed leather vests were optional. In some nightclubs, it seemed that good dance skills were directly related to the value of the quebradita outfit of the dancers. One friend of mine who did not consider himself a splendid quebrador refused to wear expensive clothes so as not to create unrealistic expectations in female dancers. The importance of appearance is affirmed in various technobanda songs. According to Banda Maguey, women "who like to dress up elegantly and who enjoy calling others' attention" should put a miniskirt, a leather vest, hat, and cowboy boots.[15] Banda Súper Zapo, on the other hand, mocks a light-skinned cumbia-dancing cowboy with his elephantlike boots with spurs and his well-arranged hat: "He is a modern cowboy because he's dancing the quebradita."[16]

A woman's wardrobe shows more variety. Her basic outfit corresponds to the man's, including the Stetson. However, she could also wear fringed shorts, knee-high boots, and a skintight top. Other *quebradoras* [female dancers] preferred to dance in short skirts and high heels. Banda Arkángel R-15's singer complained about his partner's cheap excuse for not dancing in "Báilame quebradito":[17]

La banda ya está tocando	The banda is already playing
y tocando quebradita	and playing quebradita
vamos a bailar, mi vida	let's go dance, my darling
no te quedes sentadita.	don't stay in your seat.
Yo no vine a este baile	I didn't come to this dance
a quedarme sentadito	to remain seated
si no baila usted conmigo	if you don't dance with me
yo voy a bailar solito.	I'm going to dance all alone.
Me dijo que sus zapatos	She told me that her shoes
le apretaban sus piecitos	were pinching her little feet
y tanto yo le dije	to which I replied:
y bailemos descalcitos.	Then let's dance in bare feet.

To have the right shoes for dancing the quebradita is one of the central themes in technobanda songs. Banda Zeta, for instance, sings about a quebrador who would not stop dancing even after he ruined his new shoes dancing through the night ("Zapatos de bailador"). While Banda Pequeño Musical praises a dancer's magic sneakers ("Tenis mágicos"), Banda El Mexicano urges the dancers to exchange their sneakers for boots ("Quítate los tenis"). Banda Z invokes a pair of old shoes in "Zapatos viejos," and Banda Vaquero's Musical tells of a mishap: chewing gum that got stuck on the toe of his shoe impeded the dancer from enjoying the night ("Chicle pegao").

Boots were more than a fashion statement. The shape of cowboy boots has an influence on the dancer's body posture as well as on the kind of steps he or she will or can perform. Boots force the dancer to bend the knees slightly; slant-cut heels facilitate the quebradita's trotting step. Hence, the upper body of the quebrador is not straight and upright, but slightly bent over, a posture that forces the female partner to bend backward at the waist. The quebradora could tire quickly in this position if she does not hold on to her partner firmly. On the other hand, the shift of the center of gravity out of the vertical plane of the body facilitates the execution of the turns by giving momentum to the movement. In addition, the brim of the hat (or hats) prevents dancers from changing this bent position, as well as from hopping and jumping too much.

Except for the *cuarta*, a small horsewhip, most of the characteristic quebradita accessories are just adornment. Fixed at the belt of the male dancer, the cuarta serves as a kind of handle for the quebradora to hold on to during the performance of the "little break." Also swinging off the belt is the *correa*, a leather strap engraved with the name of the Mexican home state of its wearer, or the *pañuelo*, a bandanna with embroidery in the colors of the Mexican flag. Such affirmation of nationalism is mentioned in "El jaripeo" by Julio C. Preciado, at that time the lead singer of Banda El Recodo. As described in this song, the jaripeo, a popular entertainment containing shows of horsemanship, bullfights, and banda music, takes place in Guadalajara's arena Santa María Tequepexpan:[18]

Me gusta vestir de moda	I like to dress in fashion
con mezclilla y con tejana	with jeans and with hat
con botas de los potrillos	with cowboy boots
con mi paño y con mi cuarta.	with my bandanna and my horsewhip.
Arriba mi Sinaloa	Sinaloa forever
arriba a Guadalajara	Guadalajara for ever
arriba los mexicanos	Mexicans forever
que bailamos con la banda.	let's dance with the banda!

Contrary to Banda El Recodo's statement, explicit demonstrations of regional and national identities in the form of cuartas and pañuelos were practiced only in the United States. Quebradores in Mexico did not exhibit such overt nationalism. When I went to the jaripeo in Guadalajara in the mid-1990s, I did not spot anybody with such accessories. Manuel Contreras, too, noticed that young people in Guadalajara usually dressed up in a plain cowboy style: "I think that this kind of dressing up in Texan clothes was started by [Mexicans living in the United States]. Here [in Guadalajara], they don't use these things that dangle [horsewhips and leather straps] and additional details. Here, they don't use so much adornment. Tejana [hat], vest, jeans, and boots, nothing else. However, I did observe a big change: many former *cholos* [gang members] now dress up as cowboys. Many of them walk around like that also during the week. They probably feel more virile in cowboy gear" (interview, 1994, Guadalajara).

The various accessories that were part of the vaquero outfit in the United States reflect how important the quebradita movement was for the self-esteem of the participating youths north of the border. It gave them a strong sense of unity and power. For many, it was the first time in their life they would, or could, admit their origin and show pride in their Mexican heritage. In a long article titled "The Dance of Nuevo L.A." published in the *Los Angeles Times Magazine*, Steve Loza is quoted as having said: "People are saying that we don't have to look like Prince or Madonna. We can wear our boots and hats. The *vaquero* style is important as a symbol. When a Mexican puts on that suit . . . you can walk into that club and be proud that you're a Mexican."[19]Symbols that express difference and social boundaries indeed help people in their construction of identity and place. Politics of identity will be addressed in more detail in the next chapter.

The Nightclubs

In 1990 most Latin dance halls in Nuevo L.A. featured *música tropical*. When banda music began to gain ground and the dancing public asked for the novel rhythm, local musicians had to face the new situation. *Tropical* musicians, of course, resented the inroads being made by the *banderos* [banda musicians], who not only usurped valuable performing opportunities but also changed the public's taste. In order to survive, many musicians acceded to the altered popular demand, whether they liked banda or not. José Ferrera, the manager of El Lido, one of the most prominent nightclubs in South Gate, observed the transformation of *salseros* [salsa musicians] into banderos as the new sound took over:

When banda got at the height of its power, many of those who before used to dance cumbia changed to banda. It started in '90, '91. Wherever they put a Sinaloan banda to play, the place filled up. It was a very ponderous fashion. The [cumbia] musicians were mad. . . . I talked with many professional musicians. They said: "They took away my work; they don't give me work at the dance salons where I always used to play because the banda snatched it. On top of it, I have to play a music I'm fed up with just to survive." It dashed a lot of musicians. In those times, many starved; either they moved away from Los Angeles or they played banda. Salsa bands transformed into Sinaloan bandas . . . I remember that some members [of the bandas] were people from South America who used to be *salseros*. "Hey you, aren't you a *salsero*?" "Yes, but I have to eat, boss, and what hits right now is banda. . . . " They didn't like to play banda music. They didn't live it. It was a disaster how they played banda. When they play *tropical*, one can feel it. First, a musician has to believe in himself. They didn't move, they didn't dance, just: bom-bom! Banda music is very simple but it has its things. You have to live it. You have to have it in your heart. Look, how the people dance—with pleasure! There was a time in '92, '93 when 70 percent of the musicians switched to banda. (Interview, 1996, South Gate)

El Lido was one of the first larger nightclubs to contract technobandas and Sinaloan bandas as well. The moment banda was put on stage, the nightclub's popularity exploded. Ferrera recalled:

This place opened at the right moment with banda. Banda arrived and made us strong and popular. In those times there were not many places with banda, so we put banda— and up we went! The quebradita started at a very little place here in Los Angeles, called "Jalpita." The problem is, it doesn't have parking. Everybody was talking about how [Jalpita] started to play quebradita, how well it was received, how much people liked it. But because it was so small, people came over here and asked: "Listen, why don't you play banda?" So did the [dance] promoters. One said: "I bring you a banda and I guarantee that I will make this place burst!" I: "But these people are too hot-blooded— lots of problems. You know how these banda people are." We worried about doing it. He organized the dance [and it was] full. Full! A tremendous bomb. And that was when I realized and said: "*Caray!* Banda comes very powerful." (Interview, 1996, South Gate)

The novel rhythm was electrifying and the quebradita fever spread rapidly. The attraction for many young people who had been used to "canned music" (disco) was that the music in these nightclubs was live: "If they didn't play live music in nightclubs, I probably would not go so often. It's not the same. I like the live bands. During the break, the deejays play records, but it's not the same." Another dance aficionado concurred: "What draws me to the nightclub is the energy of the music. I dance banda because it's so fast and there are live instruments: it's a complete band." The nightclub scene drew more and more young people of Mexican heritage, most of whom grew up in the United States. Participating in American popular culture, they used to listen to rock, rap, heavy metal, or deep house, and they would never have imagined that they would one day tune into Mexican music and engage in a vaquero dance fad. One eighteen-year-old woman told me: "Before it started with Banda Machos, I didn't like Spanish music. . . . I listened to English music, techno, et cetera. Then banda became popular and everybody started liking it. All these songs came out. . . . And when the clubs started, that's when I started too. And since then, that's all I listen to." Analyzing what made her eventually embrace Mexican music, another young banda aficionado related:

I grew up with it, but I didn't like Mexican music. I was one of those dumb girls—you go to a family party and you don't like Spanish music. It was not until I was turning eighteen when I started liking banda. When you come to the U.S. at an early age, you get kind of dumb. You develop a different taste. I used to be into heavy metal. I used to wear long black hair, boots, platforms. At eighteen I wasn't yet clubbing much on weekends, I would just go on Thursdays with my sisters. We are eight girls, eight sisters in the house. I used to go out with them since I was fifteen. I used to go to Leonardo's right there on Manchester and Vermont. [At that time] they played *tropical*, they had salsa. In the [intermission] it was very usual that they played English music like hip-hop. The reason why I started listening to banda music was that I was forced into it. Banda was coming on so strong that I found myself going to family reunions, *quinceañeras*, and everybody would look at me just very weird because I was dressed in that particular way I would go to the parties with English music. [Banda] was so in, that they were all playing the music and wearing the music: leather vests, *cuartas*. It got to a point where I wouldn't dance the whole night because nobody would take me up to dance. They must have thought that I wouldn't dance [banda]. So I kind of mellowed down on that kind of dress. But I still don't dress pants and boots.

Several technobanda songs address the apparent change in taste among youths. Banda Zeta, for example, wonders why two women sit in a banda nightclub where they obviously do not feel comfortable. After observing them, the singer concludes that "they are a little too refined, with attitudes from over there [the United States], I'd even say they seem to be conceited." In fact, when asked why they are about to leave, the girls reply in a snippy way: "Ash, to be frank, we just don't like this music. Ash, this ambience is gross." Whereupon the singer orders the banda musicians to stop "this music and these trumpets," because what the girls like is heavy metal.[20] Banda Arkángel R-15, on the other hand, tells about a pleasant encounter on the dance floor: while dancing quebradita, "a pretty *güera* with a slender waist, beautiful hips, and hair of golden color" teaches the song's protagonist that one does not necessarily have to know Spanish in order to like "this rhythm of trumpet and saxophone."[21]

Changing Styles

Popular dance styles are known for changing rapidly. The new dance style that allegedly had emerged in La Jalpa nightclub developed into a dance craze that was fueled by mostly young people, many of them second- or third-generation Mexican Americans. They danced the quebradita by adding their own steps. Since many of these youths had already been dancing to rap, they developed distinctive steps derived from hip-hop. The transformation of both the youths into vaqueros and the quebradita into *brinquito* was observable at nightclubs such as El Lido.

Because of an increasing number of violent, gang-related incidents in the 1980s and 1990s in and around youth dance clubs in South Gate and surrounding cities, authorities closed them one after another. Young people of these neighborhoods were left with no place to gather and to dance. Thus, the main reason youths went to banda nightclubs may not necessarily have been the type of music featured, but the prospect of meeting and dancing. José Ferrera recalled:

Well, when banda became very strong—Let's go to dance banda! Who cares about banda? What is important is to dance. If you really like to dance, the music is not important. So they had to come to places like this. They also formed [private] clubs. Not because of banda, but because they wanted to dance. Their music [rap] is in English: it heats up their blood. It talks about their stuff and they understand. On the contrary, banda is in Spanish and since they hardly understand, it doesn't matter what the music says. But they do understand the songs in English: they sing about what happens to a homeboy or what happens to a gang. That's why this music heats them up and when two gangs cross each other, well . . . for them, our doors were closed: "You don't have the age; you can't dress like this." . . . Many of them didn't even speak Spanish. But they didn't care: here was the ambience, here was the youth. (Interview, 1996, El Lido, South Gate)

Afraid of drive-by shootings, the El Lido security guards prevented youngsters in baggy clothes from gathering in front of the nightclub. The vaquero dress code was imposed on those who wanted to enter. At first embarrassed to dress up as cowboys, many youths had a feeling that banda was forced upon them. Yet, the nightclubs' appeal was too strong to resist; eventually they exchanged baseball caps and oversized clothes for cowboy hats and tight jeans. Transformed into "urban cowboys," but with a techno or hip-hop past, they became a driving force in the modification of the dancing style: "The way they dance it here is different from how it is danced in Guadalajara. Many people think that the real quebradita is how it is being danced here, and I agree because it was here where the dance got mixed, where the youths blended in their own steps. Elderly people don't like to dance the quebradita. They say that it ruins the banda music, that banda has to be danced differently. Well then, who gave quebradita its distinct touch? The *cholos* [gang members], the youths" (interview, 1996, El Lido, South Gate).

Over the years, the quebradita style evolved and *el caballito* ["the little horse"] began to dominate the nightclub scene, followed by *el brinquito* ["short-leaping"]. As its name suggests, brinquito is danced with a lot of jumping. While Banda Ritmo Rojo claimed in one of its songs that caballito, quebradita, and brinquito are the same, Banda La Costeña seemed to be closer to the pulse of the nightclubs and described the new dance style in "El brincaíto": "Look how savory this rhythm is, darling, the one that's called *brincaíto*, *caray* . . . It's important that you enjoy, that you never stop jumping. Don't discipline your feet, just let yourself be carried away."[22]

To dance "de brinquito," the cowboys had to take off their hat and boots. Instead, they dressed in comfortable dancing shoes and baggier pants. Accessories that boosted regional and national pride disappeared. Instead, dancers expressed their regional self-esteem in distinctive dancing styles. In Nuevo Los Angeles, people from Jalisco tended to gather at the Lido, while Sinaloans preferred the Farallón and Parral: on Saturdays, many of them would meet at the Potrero. A dancer from Jalisco, who won several prizes at El Lido's dance contests, summarized the different trends:

Quebradita is the first style, when banda started coming in with the technomusic. Quebradita means break. Before, they would get the girl on a very low level and that's why it was called "breaking." Caballito says it. They also have another name for it, brinquito: that is what we do. It's trotting, what horses do, they trot [*shows the trotting step*]. Right now, we're mixing quebradita with caballito. Specially at the contests in Lido's. Quebradita is acrobatic. Caballito doesn't have a lot of acrobatics. We did a step that's called "caballito," my dance partner and me. You probably saw it. He gets me, and he flips me over [his back]. We call it "caballito" because it [looks like] saddling the horse. We do mix a lot of tango and steps borrowed from everywhere. But when there is a *zapateado*, it always has to be done the same way. I would never change a step in *zapateado*. It's the imitation of the way animals dance. . . . A lot of people that wear the *avestruz* [ostrich-leather] boots love *bandas sinaloenses*. They hate technobandas, and they might also hate the way we dance. They say that's not the way it is supposed to be danced. You are supposed to dance it together and in a hugged style. I have talked to a lot of guys when I go out alone. They take me out to dance, and if a good song is played, say "La quebradora," I want to dance it separate. They say, "No, that's the way you're supposed to dance, only crazy people dance it separate." They find us who jump around too innovative, too modern; they think it's clownish. But both groups, the guys that are wearing the *botas de avestruz* and we who like to dance brinquito, we all love banda. A lot of us go to Banda El Recodo [concerts], but also the people who drive the fancy trucks will go. We both like the same music, but they disapprove of the way we dance. We think it's too boring they way they're dancing. It's peculiar. They do criticize us a lot. If you go to Farallón dancing the way we dance in Potrero, everybody will criticize you. We don't go there anymore.

Private Quebradita Clubs

The first quebradita club was organized in Huntington Park in 1990 when eighteen youths decided to start a fan club for Banda Vallarta Show. Calling themselves after one of the band's hits, "Te ves bien buena," the youths met regularly to dance quebradita. Within the next five years, hundreds of dance clubs emerged all over the city. The organization of young people into dance clubs was strongly supported by the radio station KLAX. The aim was to engage youths in a healthy leisure activity and, by doing so, keep them out of trouble. In early 1994 the *Los Angeles Times* ran an article on its front page in which a staff writer, Diane Seo, asserted that the dance craze provided an alternative to violence.[23] Police and school officials observed that many youths had given up gang banging or were less active because of their club involvement. As one eighteen-year-old member of the Casimira Club told the journalist, "I used to be a tagger and would write stuff all over the walls and on the MTA buses. I used to make fun of people who liked banda music. But then I went to one party, saw all the pretty girls, and then went out and bought myself the boots and the hat." A police officer expressed what many parents had hoped for: "By God, if we could get all the kids in Santa Ana in clubs, dancing like this, we could stop all the shootings on the street."

The quebradita club scene attracted both former and present gang members. With their new "uniform" emblazoned with the regions of their ancestors and the name of their club, the quebradores looked much like gang members and were sometimes mistaken as such. But instead of flashing signs to signal a progressing gang fight, hand gestures became indicators to which quebradita club the youngsters belonged. José Ferrera commented on the dance craze:

When banda started to catch the ear, look at them, the cholos, with their cars that have a sound system that makes them vibrate. What do you think came out of these sound systems? Rap? No, banda! And you start talking to them and they hardly stutter in Spanish. . . . And later the [private] clubs began to emerge: the Club of the Crying Indian, the Club of . . . this or that Indian. And look who's in those clubs, precisely these young people. The cholos baptized their clubs in Spanish, just because the banda was in vogue.

They replaced the name of their gang with that of a banda club. They transformed themselves. I think it happened because they didn't have any space. Since banda music offered them a space, the young people changed their taste. Throughout this area, the majority of the youths transformed themselves. That's how the music expanded even more. (Interview, 1996, South Gate)

Apparently, quebradita clubs carried out similar functions as gangs, but without the violence: they created a social space for young people, provided a stage for (healthy) competition, forged collective identities, and thus nurtured feelings of belonging. Moreover, dance clubs held the potential for social change. Hence, the significance of these clubs for young people who used to be engaged in violent and antisocial activities should not be underestimated.

A good number of the emerging quebradita clubs consisted of individuals of all ages who shared a passion for dancing to banda music. The aim of these clubs was to organize parties where their members could indulge in their favorite leisure activity: dancing the quebradita. Banda América, for example, encourages in one song: "To animate the fiesta, to invite couples to move the hips, there is nothing like dancing with banda. Cheer up, guys, don't restrain your desires to dance to the rhythm of this delightful banda."[24]

Often technobandas were hired to play for parties held in the backyards of private houses, in community halls, or in parking lots. Such events attracted singles, couples, and families alike. Children dressed up as little vaqueros imitated and practiced the steps that the grown-ups were dancing. Some of them even tried to mimic the gestures and pelvic movements of their favorite vocalists, whom they had watched on videos or television. Events such as these quebradita parties familiarized children and adolescents with the social world of their parents and with one of the community's most important leisure practices, dancing. Furthermore, fiestas attended by multiple generations provided a much deeper sense of community solidarity than gatherings of people of the same age.

Discourse about Dance and Body

Jane Cowan, who has explored the articulation of gender politics in northern Greece through body and dance, argues that "the way the body is conceived, used, and experienced necessarily reflects the practical and symbolic structure of the outside (natural, social, and political) environment."[25] Drawing from symbolic anthropology, which defines culture as a system of symbols, Cowan identifies the body as "a sign that can be read by other people." As a vehicle of meaning, the body plays an important role in the life of a society. Since social dance allows for intimate physical contact between men and women, dance events are the subject of ongoing vigorous contestation and negotiation. Depending on generation, gender, origin (rural versus urban), and individual conceptions of proper comportment, interpretations of the dancing bodies in quebradita events may greatly diverge.

Dancing is much more than just knowing the steps or analyzing the "motor act," as José Limón has done for his study on working-class Texas-Mexican polka dancing.[26] Rather, a dancer has "to feel the music," and the men have to be able to transmit this feeling to their dance partners. A female dancer I met at El Lido defined "a good male dancer": "The music has to be in his body. You can relax, lose yourself, close your eyes—just feel his body moving. If he isn't a good dancer, it's no pleasure because you have to concentrate too much. You can't relax because you have to figure out what he'll do next. You get all cramped, and you're glad when the band changes the rhythm so you may dance separately or say 'Thank you' and go have a seat. With a good dancer, you just hope the music doesn't stop and he doesn't get tired of you."

For a deeper understanding of what is going on between dancers and between the dancing bodies and the music, it is essential to acquire a lot of dancing experience. In other words, it is only by dancing that one can fully understand dance. Bodily experience helps not only to reach a deeper understanding of what it means to dance but also to understand the music differently—by feeling the music through the body. Moreover, dancing makes one realize that mind and body, reason and sense, reflection and experience do not oppose each other but rather intertwine.[27] Experience, for instance, is an ongoing integrative process based on both lived experience and reflection. Cognition and knowledge are not merely intellectual matters but involve the entire person, including the body.

As with many other dance styles, the role of the quebradita is to allow one to let off steam, to have fun, to work out, to feel one's body, and to show off one's ability to move well. Technobanda provokes a surge of physical energy that, as fans would say, "just pulls you out of your seat." The only remedy for such bodily desire is to dance until the physical demands on the body eventually result in exhaustion. Banda Súper Zapo thus sings:[28]

Vamos, negro, con la banda	Let's go, my dark one, with the banda
mira que quiero bailar	look, I want to dance
mi cuerpo desesperado	my desperate body
oye solo hablar de banda	only hears talk of the banda
me pongo a bailar, bailar	I begin to dance, dance
la sangre se me alborota	my blood is getting excited
me tengo que remediar.	I must dance for relief.

Negro, ya no puedo ma-ma-más	I can't any-any-more, my dark one
mira, como estoy cansao	look, how tired I am
la rodilla me ha aflojeao	my knee has gotten weak
de tanto bailar, bailar	from so much dancing, dancing
mejor me voy a sentar	I better have a seat
porque estoy desbaratao	because I am a mess
qué buena la banda va.	how good this banda is!

Dancing is first of all a physical activity. Inasmuch as it is practiced in public, it is also a social activity. Although quebradita dancers also may have had other agendas, one of the forces driving them to attend dance events was to enjoy the pleasure of sociability. Banda América affirms both the irresistibility of the rhythm and the dance event as a community experience: "Everybody get up, leave your seats. Let's go all together to dance with the banda. Banda for you, banda for me, banda for everybody who's here."[29]

One of music's effects is to intensify the experience of the presence. As the popular music specialist Simon Frith has put it: "One measure of good music is, precisely, its 'presence,' its ability to 'stop' time, to make us feel we are living within a moment, with no memory or anxiety about what has come before, what will come after. This is where the physical impact of music comes in—the use of the beat, pulse and rhythm to compel our immediate bodily involvement in an organization of time that the music itself controls. Hence the pleasures of dance and disco; clubs and parties provide a setting, a society, which seems to be defined only by the time-scale of the music (the beats per minute), which escapes the real time passing outside" (1987: 142). Technobanda's exuberant rhythm and the nightclub ambience had a contagious effect. One dance-crazy young woman told me, "This past week I wasn't able to go out. Now, I feel desperate. What draws me to the nightclub is the energy of the music." Another dancer said, "The rhythm and the volume are most important. If you dance, that's what you listen to. I hardly listen to the lyrics—sometimes I do, but most of the time it's just the rhythm. Makes you just get up and dance . . . Dancing is to forget about everyday life, to feel good, to clear the mind. And it is a good workout." Or: "Dancing is a way of living in the imaginary world of the music." In the many conversations I had with quebradita aficionados on the dance floor and outside the clubs, words such as "fun," "pleasure," "exuberance," and "energy" were most often mentioned to explain the music's electrifying appeal to dancers.

Gender Relations

Not only are social and cultural identities inscribed in dancing bodies, but gender ideas and gender relations are enacted on the dance floor. In this sense, public dance events contribute to the continuity of the established social system, encouraging both men and women to act according to their gender roles. The setting is largely determined: it approves of men's aggressive role in courtship and women's wait-and-see attitude. Cultural concepts of masculinity, however, are valued by both men and women. Conventions such as the formal invitation to a dance are viewed as positive values of manhood—the gallant *caballero*—and are much appreciated by women. Heightened by the rhythmic sound, the lyrics, the light show, and (in some cases) the alcohol, the display of machismo (in the sense of male bravado) seems to be socially tolerated by all participants.[30]

"I'm not here to challenge macho traditions. I'm here to enjoy dancing," replied a college-educated young woman when confronted with questions about the ambivalent role of social dancing in gender relations. On an abstract level, however, she concurred that dancing as a social action is informed by largely concealed structures of value that help to maintain and reproduce social power. Despite the conventions of the dancers' comportment ("Why is the guy leading and not the girl?"), the female dancers I interviewed did not feel patronized in any way. On the contrary, many thought that "for men dancing is a lot of pressure," while for themselves it provides much pleasure. Conventions that seem to support male domination are often interpreted inversely: men are not really in charge, even if it is they who decide with whom they want to dance. "She can say no. It's very embarrassing for a guy to invite a girl for a dance and she says no." Thus, decisions over dancing empower her rather than him. Moreover, some female dancers have developed strategies that allow them to feel and to be more active. For instance, if making eye-contact does not work, a girl may approach the dancer of her choice directly. Thus, although general conceptions of proper comportment are largely maintained on the dance floor, certain conventions are in flux. Dance events are, as Iain Chambers has argued for music, an important "counter-space" in our daily lives. The impetus of dance events "lies in a temporary suspension of the division between the 'private' and the 'public,' between the imagination and the routines, roles and social relations in which we regularly find ourselves locked" (1985: 209). Despite customary social patterns, the roles of both men and women involved in dance events are constantly being defined and redefined: "Imagination and 'reality' are brought together in a significant friction and exchange. And the major side of this encounter is the frequently repressed zone of the body. . . . It is the body that ultimately makes, receives and responds to music; and it is the body that connects sounds, dance, fashion and style to the subconscious anchorage of sexuality and eroticism" (1985: 210).

Dance is a vital feature of leisure culture, entertainment, and sexuality. For

8. Dancing quebradita at the Salón Pacífico in Mexico City, 1998.
Photos by Helena Simonett.

women and girls in particular, "dance has always offered a channel, albeit a limited one, for bodily self-expression and control; it has also been a source of pleasure and sensuality" (McRobbie 1984: 132–133). Dance-fanatic young women unanimously affirmed that "[i]f a woman goes to a nightclub, she usually wants to dance." Rather than seeing dancing as simply promising or providing sexual opportunity, men too have come to acknowledge it as an absorbing and pleasurable activity in its own right. Although "some guys just go to the nightclub to drink, to stand around, and to look at the dance," one quebradora said, "I think most of them just want to dance, to be close to somebody else, to be hugged—to feel good."

Dancing Bodies

Although in Mexican culture dancing is the social act par excellence, nightclub dancing, next to smoking, was one of the first acts of women liberating themselves from traditional social constraints (Dallal 1982). A young woman who dared to enter a nightclub made a step toward indecency that would detach her from a way of life that had been designated for her by a traditionally patriarchal society. As a result of "the narrow identification of woman with sexuality and the body in a society that has for centuries displayed profound suspicion toward both" (Bartky 1990: 73), dancing may still be viewed as indecent behavior by some people. By dancing in public, women deliberately display their bodies to the male gaze: "Look how they move their hips, these beautiful girls who dare to dance" (Banda Ritmo Rojo). Moreover, women who indulge in public dancing are believed to provoke aggressive male courting and ultimately to expose themselves to indignity and dishonor.

Some song lyrics give a detailed description not only of the dance and dress code, but also of the dancing bodies. Since the great majority of the composers and vocalists are men, song lyrics reflect a male perspective. The male gaze turns the female body into a sexual object: "Whatever clothes you wear, I undress you with my eyes." The parts of the female body most often noticed in new songs are the hips and the waist: "I love to dance with you . . . your waist, your back, your hips, your legs, and your pretty miniskirt"; "You are a girl with very fine hips, you look very well, you look like a Coca-Cola bottle." Banda Vallarta Show's lead singer went into raptures over a female dancer: "If one sees how she's dancing, how this woman moves, how she moves these hips, she drives me mad" ("Esa chica me vacila" [This Girl Shakes Me]). Banda Zeta devoted a whole song to the parts of the female body men like best ("Caderas lait" [Light Hips]). In "La mini mini," Banda Legendarios hold that women dress in miniskirts simply to provoke and to conquer men: "The cowboys like to look at girls in a miniskirt. They get very excited when they see the panty lines." It must be noted, however, that the sexuality seen on the cassette and CD covers of other Latino musics (in particular Caribbean musics) is not central to the images projected by technobanda covers.

On the other hand, there is no technobanda song, to my knowledge, that describes the body, or parts of the body, of male dancers explicitly. References to the outward appearance of men point out some characteristic such as the apparel or the mustache: "He was a Stetson-hat type, very much cowboy and with a big mustache." More often, however, men distinguish themselves by their virtues ("un hombre a toda ley" [a reputable man]) and actions ("hold on, Nicolasa, because I'll show you how to dance the quebradita. I know you'll like it"). Song lyrics also reflect men's concern about their masculinity. This concern is often expressed in a humorous way. Since the mustache denotes manliness, it is a preferred theme of new songs:[31]

Es el novio, un muchacho muy galante	"He's the fiancé, a very elegant young man
que las quiere y las sabe enamorar	who knows how to treat girls and make them fall in love"
muy atentas comentaban las vedetas	the girls commented very attentively
y algo más que yo no pude descifrar.	and something more I couldn't make out.
Entre risas y miradas maliciosas	Between wicked smiles and glances
las muchachas cuchicheaban sin cesar	the girls whispered ceaselessly
el bigote de Tomás era divino	that Tomás's mustache was divine
susurrando por lo bajo este cantar:	murmuring this song:

Como pica, pica, pica	How it pricks, pricks, pricks
como raspa, raspa, raspa	how it rasps, rasps, rasps
como pica el bigotito de Tomás	how Tomás's little mustache pricks
como pica, raspa y pica cuando besa	how it pricks, rasps and pricks when he kisses
el hermoso bigotito de Tomás.	Tomás's beautiful little mustache.

The majority of Banda Arkángel R-15 musicians live up to the Latino image of masculinity and wear a mustache. According to their song "El bigote" [The Mustache], which is full of ambiguous sexual allusions, the mustache makes a man more appealing to women. Yet, they let their question, "Why is it that women like the mustache, which has been in fashion for so long?" go unanswered. The mustache as a symbol of manliness is also evoked in situations where men do not comply with the dominant cultural ideal of manhood. "Bigote mojado" [Wet Mustache] by Vaquero's Musical is one example:[32]

Todas mis penas llevan tu nombre	All my pains carry your name
tu nombre escrito en mi corazón	your name is inscribed in my heart
se me he olvidado que soy un hombre	I forgot that I am a man
y el hombre llora con discreción.	and that a man cries in secrecy.
Estoy cansado de este tormento	I'm tired of the torment
cansado de andar así	of going around like this
con el bigote siempre mojado	with my mustache always wet
[de] llorar por ti.	from crying for you.

Interestingly, new compositions that address a man's pain and his desire to show his emotion by crying have become very popular—for example, "Cuando los hombres lloran" [When Men Cry], by Banda Móvil, and "Un indio quiere llorar" [An Indian Wants to Cry] and "Los machos también lloran" [Machos Also Cry; original title: "Los hombres también lloran"], by Banda Machos. The latter song asserts that weeping does not take away from a man's manliness: "And even if you cry, buddy, it doesn't take the *macho* away from you! . . . Cry, cry, cry, and even the most *macho* men have feelings and know to cry."

One of music's social functions is to give us a way of dealing with our public and private emotional lives. Love songs, for example, are important "because people need them to give shape and voice to emotions that otherwise cannot be expressed without embarrassment or incoherence" (Frith 1987: 141). Technobanda's romantic songs, such as Banda Machos's hit "Mi luna, mi estrella" [My Moon, My Star], or Banda Maguey's "Si tú no estás" [If You Are Not Here], touch intimate feelings and deal directly with the private, emotional sphere. Romantic songs with particular messages—confessing love, expressing admiration, admitting yearning—indeed, were often requested at KLAX, to be dedicated to specific named or unnamed individuals of the opposite sex. On the dance floor, songs in slower tempos allow couples to dance closely. Those who have memorized the lyrics are given a welcome opportunity to share their feelings for their partner by singing along. Thus, the pleasure one feels when listening and dancing to music is associated with the direct emotional intensity of one's musical experience.

The bulk of the new technobanda compositions, however, do not invite romantic daydreaming. Rather, the lyrics are witty, droll, and diverting and often refer to the quebradita dance and the vaquero attire. The songs are in a fast tempo and call for an energetic dance style. Thus, the pleasure these songs produce is linked to cultural enjoyment and identity, as well as to the cultural enjoyment of identity. It is, as Frith has put it, "a pleasure of identification" with the music, with the performers of that music, and with the other people who like it" (1987: 140). Beyond this rather innocent "pleasure of identification," however, technobanda provided the means by which its listeners, practitioners, and participants constructed, asserted, and mobilized their ethnic particularity at a time when "their community" came under attack. Thus, the "banda movement" cannot be understood properly outside the wider power relations in which it was embedded and that also nourished its growth.

Technobanda and the Politics of Identity

Me gusta la banda, me gustan los grupos
me gusta lo contry, me gusta el norteño
también el mariachi de corazón
yo soy muy latino y a mucha honra lo digo yo.
    Ismael Gallegos, Banda El Chante

In the 1980s, California's deteriorating economic condition, caused by cutbacks in the aerospace and defense industries, had a polarizing effect on its society. Many residents began to blame the economic recession on the growing number of undocumented immigrants who were pouring into the state. The news media readily assisted in creating an atmosphere of crisis linking joblessness with illegal immigration and illegal immigration with crime. White middle-class residents in Southern California felt specially threatened by the "flood" of Latino immigrants. As they saw Los Angeles become transformed into the "capital of the Third World,"[1] overrun by brown-skinned people, they easily bought into the campaign against illegal immigration waged by Republican Governor Pete Wilson and other politicians. This aggressive campaign against "illegal aliens" turned into full-blown anti-immigrant hysteria. Racial tensions increased. In 1995 a majority of California's voters supported Proposition 187, the so-called Save-Our-State initiative, which sought to deny public education and nonemergency health care to undocumented immigrants and their children. Anti-immigrant feelings were affected by a perception that immigration was out of control and that most Latinos were in the United States illegally.[2] Hence, not only did recent immigrants feel unwelcome in California, but also longtime Latino residents and Mexican Americans of several generations were faced with growing resentments, open hostility, and thinly disguised racism.[3]

Immigrants, on the other hand, felt that they were being unfairly blamed for

California's economic adversities. The Spanish-language radio station KLAX-FM, oriented to the needs and interests of immigrants, began to oppose Governor Wilson's xenophobic rhetoric. "He's using immigration like a political campaign for publicity," declared the KLAX deejay Juan Carlos Hidalgo. "How can the governor talk about these people when they provide the food on his table? They are humble, but they pay taxes like everyone else."[4] In an effort to mobilize the station's listeners to register to vote, the morning deejay team launched "the Juan Carlos and El Peladillo Show, the program Governor Pee Pee Wilson hates most."[5] Although residents of Mexican ancestry constitute the area's largest single ethnic bloc (40 percent of Los Angeles County's thirteen million inhabitants are of Mexican origin), their electoral power lags far behind their numbers (Ortiz 1996: 247). This is attributed to the delayed pending naturalization of a large portion of the Mexican-born population and the disproportionately young average age of the U.S.-born generation. While a small minority still decides the fate of a large nonvoting majority, the impact of immigration on the community has been sudden and substantial: Los Angeles is experiencing a radical transformation of its ethnic composition. The banda movement is but one of many signs. In 1994, the *Los Angeles Times Magazine* published an essay by Rubén Martínez, who asked provocatively: "Anti-immigration fervor is at a fever pitch, but the real issue is this: When will the old (Anglo) L.A. join the new (Latino) L.A., and learn to dance the quebradita?" In a similar vein, Chicano scholars and commentators cherished the newfound Latino pride, interpreting the quebradita phenomenon as a "backlash against the anti-immigrant rhetoric."[6]

It is certainly no coincidence that technobanda popped up in Los Angeles at the same time politicians began to blame undocumented immigrants from Mexico and Central America for California's economic crisis. Technobanda had a profound impact on the development and expression of the cultural self-image of hundreds of thousands of young foreign- and American-born Latinos during a period of heightened awareness among California residents of large-scale immigration from Mexico and Central America. Since much of contemporary politics is organized around identity, this chapter examines (techno) banda and the quebradita as a site for negotiating identity among Mexicanos in the United States.

Wave of Ethnic Pride

In neighborhoods where Mexicans constitute demographic majorities, many do not regard themselves as members of an alienated and marginalized minority. Los Angeles's proximity to Mexico enables Mexican newcomers, as well as long-term residents, to maintain strong ties to their homeland. Rather than immigrants in the traditional sense, most of these people are transmigrants who remain attached to and empowered by a "home" culture and tradition.[7] Frequent travel back home and maintenance of multiple relations across the border enable them to cling to their accustomed ways of life. Because of their sheer demographic mass and limited contact with other Angelenos, Mexicanos have not only retained a strong sense of cultural identity, they also fashion their new place so as to feel at home.

Although the sense of being a "people" with historical roots was not new to Mexican Americans, Chicano scholars celebrated Latinos' newfound confidence, claiming that now, on the verge of the twenty-first century, "L.A.'s culture comes full circle": "Twenty years ago, sociological literature considered ethnic identification a deviant behavior. . . . Today Latinos have begun to value their own norms and ways of life. It is only the strength of our identity and our multirooted culture that can make the disaffected among us, particularly the youth, feel like they belong to the larger society. In fact, we are becoming the mainstream."[8] Summarizing the ambience at a Los Angeles nightclub when the quebradita craze was in full swing, Rubén Martínez asserted: "To say that there is Latino pride in La Puente tonight would be an understatement. It's more like a cultural revolution. We're Mexican, speak Spanish, dance quebradita and are damn proud of it."[9] But why so much pride? he asked. Why now? And why would American-born Mexicans proclaim themselves Mexicanos "on this side of the border"? The quebradita wave, Martínez argued, fueled a latent feeling that they too had a right to succeed in this country, where most of them were born. The dimensions of the movement let them recognize that others too felt the need to belong. Indeed, like other youths of foreign descent, Mexicanos are often more hurt and troubled by their exclusion from mainstream society than are their parents. Faced with discrimination and a more and more openly expressed racism, children and young adults have tried more fiercely to assert their ethnic particularity and to search for a musical voice to state unequivocally who and what they are.[10]

Banda music was something new for a generation of Mexicanos who had grown up listening to mainstream rock and rap music. By the mid-1990s, a large number of young Latinos had engaged technobanda as a space for cultural affirmation. Instead of American popular music, the latest banda hits now poured out of open car windows: this was their political statement. Technobanda was "their own" voice—and, a heavily amplified voice at that, not one to be ignored. A young banda aficionado told me:

Have you noticed that the more that things turn against the immigrants and the more laws they make against the immigrants, the more they are coming out? They are dressing more expressive[ly], they like to turn up their car radios more. They're proud of who they are, they are not intimidated any longer. The banda movement helped young people to address the issue of being Mexican. To tell who they are or to fight against injustice and discrimination. Definitely . . . I have friends that were ashamed of their roots, they didn't want to admit that they are Mexican. And now I see my cousins' friends, they're going to dance banda: "Yes, I'm Mexican!" Young people are aware of a lot of things—at a younger age.

Identity formation was encouraged by the mass media. KLAX-FM, which had developed a youth market among the teenage children of immigrants, also reached a young American-born audience. Committed to strengthening cultural bonds and to adhering to Mexican traditions and customs, the KLAX deejay Jesús García announced: "The banda movement opened my eyes. It is a great thing for the children. It will open their eyes too. Even when they don't dance quebradita any longer, they will continue to care about their roots. That's the most important thing—the traditions and the customs—and we encourage to keep them alive" (interview, 1995, Hollywood). Recalling her own experiences, the KBUE deejay Rosy González argued that the popularity of banda music was more than just a momentary inclination:

The reason why it became so strong among the youth is that for a long time young Mexican Americans didn't know much about their roots. I grew up here and I remember going to school and if you were listening to Mexican music, they'd say you are a nerd. Everybody was lying to themselves because they'd go home and what they would listen to at home was Mexican music. But among friends it was not cool to listen to Spanish music. Now, all the youths are enjoying the music, finding out more about their roots, about who they are really. They are proud of their music, of who they are, and I think that's great. At the same time it's a kind of a rebellion against politics here in the United States. (Interview, 1996, Hollywood)

Graciela Beltrán, a young Mexican American ranchera singer who started to record with banda when "the movement" was in full swing, asserted that she had never been a victim of the contradictions that affect many children of Mexican immigrants. She never had to hide her cultural preference: "At this moment, I feel most at ease with the folkloric wave. [Singing Mexican music genres] has allowed me to learn about and to love my cultural roots even more. I have found a way of expression that will be mine for the rest of my life."[11] The "banda movement" north of the U.S.-Mexico border will indeed be more than a simple footnote in the history of banda music.

Place Making: Theoretical Considerations

Since the 1960s, theories and methods of cultural studies have undergone profound changes. Stimulated by a changing world, scholars began to thoroughly rethink the predicament of culture. In his seminal work *Culture and Truth*, Renato Rosaldo called for new approaches in social analysis: "Modes of composition have changed because the discipline's research agenda has shifted from the search for structures to theories of practice that explore the interplay of both structure *and* agency. . . . Rather than stressing timeless universals and the sameness of human nature, this perspective emphasizes human diversity, historical change, and political struggle" (1993: xvii–xviii). While most traditional anthropological studies tended to favor representations of contained people, places, and identities, many recent studies concentrate on highly diverse social groups in multicultural settings. Thus, questions of conflict, change, inequality, disruption, and difference have moved to center stage. In Rosaldo's view, cultural anthropologists have reshaped their discipline in part because of what they have learned from conflicts about multicultural social realities.

Indeed, since the civil rights movement, more and more people living in the United States have affirmed and continue to affirm their right to a separate identity within the framework of a pluralistic society. The rise of ethnic self-affirmation under the banner of "one's own culture," "the right to remain different," "one's own tradition," and "being an independent people" is related to a broader political context that rewards such self-affirmation in one way or another. On the academic level, an earlier generation of sociologists, the so-called melting pot theorists, was followed by scholars such as Nathan Glazer and Daniel P. Moynihan (1963), Fredrik Barth (1969), Michael Novak (1972), and Werner Sollors (1986), who celebrated the triumph of ethnicity over assimilation. Rather than assuming upward mobility and inevitable assimilation (theoretical models that suited European immigrant experience), these analysts began to pay more attention to the subjective side of ethnic belonging and to cultural manipulation in interactive settings. Yet, the discourse continues to be dynamic as new voices arise—voices of minority intellectuals with different experiences of social reality and different understandings of America's past and present. By exploring cultural images of oneself and others, these scholars have begun to challenge prevalent ideas and conceptualizations of both the culture(s) and the society we live in.[12]

Of course, the definition of culture has been modified constantly since the term was introduced into the English language, and it continues to be redefined as the field of anthropology develops. Among the many contemporary notions of culture, the understanding of culture as the way of life of a people, or "culture as praxis," is of particular relevance to this study, as it is to any study of music, music making, or music reception. If culture is constituted by people's practical activities, self-representation and self-identity are crucial components. Identity, on the other hand, is linked to a sense of place, to networks (a wider set of social and spatial relations), and to memory.

Peter W. Preston proposes that we "think of identity as a shifting balance between what is remembered and what is currently demanded. Identity is thus always shifting; it is never fixed" (1997: 49–50). To stress the transformative aspect of identity, Stuart Hall (1990) has called identity a "meeting point," a point of temporary identification that constitutes and re-forms the individual so as to enable that individual to act. A close look at the micro level of the individual and the individual experience indeed helps us to rethink the outdated notion of identity as given, coherent, and stable. Rather than being an inherent quality of a person, identity arises in interaction with others, with institutions, and with practices (Sarup 1996:14).[13] Hence, in inquiring into identity, we have to focus on the performative aspect of identity, the process of identity construction through identification and affiliation, the sense of belonging, and the meanings of home, place, roots, and tradition. Subject to the continuous play of history, culture and power, identity emerges as a continually contested domain. Questions of identity, as Gupta and Ferguson recently pointed out, "demonstrate with special clarity the intertwining of place and power in the conceptualization of 'culture'." Moreover, "[b]y stressing that place making always involves a construction, rather than merely a discovery, of difference, the authors . . . emphasize that identity neither 'grows out' of rooted communities nor is it a thing that can be possessed or owned by individual or collective social actors. It is, instead, a mobile, often unstable relation of difference" (1997: 13–14).

Analogous to the notion of identity as fluid and dynamic, ethnicity is not a given but "something reinvented and reinterpreted in each generation by each individual" (Fischer 1986: 195).[14] Identifying oneself in ethnic terms meets the basic human need to express social belonging. Moreover, some sense of identity is based on the feelings of belonging to a tradition. Thus, people who have experienced the pain of social rejection or exclusion from mainstream society may resort to an even stronger identification with their ethnic community.[15]

In modern, industrialized societies, visible distinctions between socioeconomic levels are not immediately apparent, making it difficult for one to identify oneself as a member of a particular group. On the other hand, individuals are much more flexible in choosing or reinventing their ethnic identification.[16] "The struggle for a sense of ethnic identity is a (re)invention and discovery of a vision, both ethical and future-oriented," Michael M. J. Fischer has claimed.

"Whereas the search for coherence is grounded in a connection to the past, the meaning abstracted from that past . . . is an ethic workable for the future. Such vision can take a number of forms: they can be both culturally specific . . . and dialectically formed as critiques of hegemonic ideologies (e.g., as alternatives to the melting pot rhetoric of assimilation to the bland, neutral style of the conformist 1950s)" (1986: 196).

Much has been written in the last two decades about "the sense of place."[17] The initial focus of inquiry into "the sense of rootedness in place" has shifted in recent years to "the sense of displacement" and to place as a site of power struggles. Yet, "displacement is not less the source of powerful attachments than are experiences of profound rootedness" (Feld and Basso 1996: 11). As Clifford Geertz has so keenly noted: "For all the uprooting, the homelessness, the migrations, forced and voluntary, the dislocations of traditional relationships, the struggles over homelands, borders, rights of recognition, for all the destructions of familiar landscapes and the manufacturings of new ones, and for all the loss of local stabilities and local originalities, the sense of place, and of the specificities of place, seems, however tense and darkened, barely diminished in the modern world" (1996: 261). Thus, the consciousness and worldview of a collective people continue to be rooted in place, tradition, and locality. For people, whether dislocated or not, memory is not a simple nostalgic longing for or an illusion of home, but "a basis for ideas of continuity; a store of experience and knowledge to inform future activity; a sphere of reflective self-understanding; [and] a fluid sphere liable to alteration in the light of new events or merely via the passage of time" (Preston 1997: 52–53). Since music "evokes and organizes collective memories and present experiences of place with an intensity, power and simplicity unmatched by any other social activity" (Stokes 1994: 3), it provides the means by which we can look more closely into how notions of belonging, identity, and experience are linked to the relations of place and space—how place is constructed. Music is thus a privileged site from which to examine the politics of identity.

Music not only informs our sense of place, as various popular music specialists have pointed out; "music both creates and articulates the very idea of community" and helps people "to make sense of their social world and their place in it" (Frith 1992: 177). Although these statements are somewhat general, those who write about music usually assume a certain sense of community. Yet, like subcultures and ethnic groups, communities are not stable units of contained people, defined or self-defined. Perceptions of such groups are not only discursively and historically constituted, but boundaries and contents are constantly being negotiated and allegiances shift. Since people tend to identify with more than one musical genre, music as an "identity marker" is a good example of the volatility and the multiplicity of such allegiances.

Shifting Parameters, Shifting Musical Landscape

Studies of Mexican and Chicano culture in the United States reflect the tendencies of the debate over assimilation and resistance. Although some scholars continue to emphasize the conflicts minority groups face within the host culture, the focus on inner tension and ambivalence felt by minority Americans who are torn between solidarity with their traditional culture and conformity with the American mainstream has shifted.[18] Scholars of the borderland now emphasize that historically, Mexican immigration has been characterized by continuity rather than alienation, marginality, and social disorganization.[19] Rather than bemoaning the borderland as a world of confusion, they cherish it as a place of opportunity and innovation, where border people deal with the predicament of being caught between two nations and two cultures in the most imaginative ways. "Mexican Americans most closely resemble a transborder population, people whose living space transcends an international boundary. In many ways they are an in-between population, caught between competing ways of life and contrasting worldviews. But long ago they came to terms with their minority status in the United States and their ambivalent relationship with Mexico. Their adjustment to a dual way of life has been eased by direct and substantial participation in the shaping of the transboundary system in which they function, and on the whole they have managed to cope well enough with the challenges posed by cultural marginality" (Martínez 1994: 116). Border people are believed to perceive the national boundary in a positive way "as a bridge to greater human contact" and "as a unifier of different styles of life" rather than as a barrier or divider (Martínez 1994: 305). Challenged by living in between two cultures, such people often develop highly creative energies and rich cultural visions.

Appropriation and syncretic cross-fertilization are particularly apparent in music, as Steven Loza (1993) has demonstrated in his in-depth study of the postwar Mexican and Chicano musical life of Los Angeles. Loza suggests a theoretical framework called "networks of marginality" as an alternative to Manuel Peña's dialectic analysis of intercultural conflict.[20] In contrast to Texas-Mexican musicians who developed particular regional musical styles such as *conjunto* and *orquesta*, Chicano musicians in Los Angeles have adapted musical styles representative of the American mainstream: the rhythm and blues and rock bands of the 1960s and 1970s from East Los Angeles "assimilated, changed, and perhaps introduced a variety of musical styles that originated in both Mexico and the United States."[21] Like the East Los Angeles band Los Lobos, which has gained international popularity with its cover of "La Bamba," most Eastside bands have experimented with elements from their Mexican musical heritage in one way or another, Loza affirms. Their innovative use of "a transcultural Mexican musical framework of style and form" has made the Los Angeles Chicano musical landscape a vital and heterogeneous one.

More recently, George Lipsitz (1994) has analyzed the two "post-punk-neo-feminist-anti-racist-Chicana-bilingual-folk-rock-country-jazz-*ranchera* ensembles" Las Tres and Goddess 13. Like other Chicano and Chicana musicians, both bands draw from multiple musical sources. The two bands "offer a postmodernism grounded in concrete historical and social experiences," Lipsitz concludes. "Yet they also understand the powers of imagination and performance that are capable of creating ways of thinking and living on the terrain of culture that have not yet emerged as political forces and institutions" (1994: 146). In the "maelstrom of constant change, apparently under no-one's control and without direction [where] both the past and the future have collapsed into the present, and our lives are organized without any appeal to the place of the present within a historical continuum,"[22] these young Chicana bands have found a unique way to express their historical and social experiences. Their music represents "a dynamic culture of conjuncture and intersectionality" (Lipsitz 1994: 140).

In an earlier article Lipsitz expressed the opinion that "failure to assimilate into dominant cultures can bring exclusion from vital economic and political resources" (1990: 149). This may still be true for many immigrants to the United States. Yet, during the last decade major shifts have occurred in Los Angeles's society and culture. Many recent immigrants who are seeking a "home" in metropolitan Los Angeles are confronted with displacement, disruption, and loss of local stabilities. In particular, those who have moved from an impoverished region to the relatively wealthy metropolis of Los Angeles experience the "postmodern condition" (Sánchez 1993: 9). While in earlier years assimilation was the main goal of U.S. immigration policy, multiculturalism is now in the fore.[23] Ethnic groups are claiming the right to keep their own identity, to be different. Meanwhile, cultural institutions and the mass media have become aware of these ethnic groups as well. Thus, the recent trend toward celebrating ethnic diversity has led not only to a new awareness of multicultural Los Angeles, but also to an economic and political exploitation of the current circumstances. While in the 1970s many Eastside bands struggled to expand their networks beyond the barrio boundaries, nowadays major record labels have an eye on ethnically isolated musical cultures because such local musics may be "a potential addition to the pool of musical resources available to broader audiences" (Slobin 1993: 18).

Because of the prevailing multicultural climate, and, maybe more importantly, because of the sheer number of Mexican newcomers, Mexican and Mexican American musicians no longer need to assimilate to the "superculture" (the American mainstream). The Los Angeles Mexican and Chicano musical landscape is not only heterogeneous but shifting as well. Neither concepts of intercultural conflict nor networks of marginality seem useful any longer as theoretical frameworks. Accelerating processes of globalization ("mass mediaization" and transmigration) challenge us to rethink our culture concepts. What is needed when looking at contemporary musical landscapes is a mode of thinking that is open to these broader processes, one that includes at once the microworld and the global cultural flow, and that accounts for the complex interplay between local and overarching music systems.[24] The (techno)banda phenomenon is probably the most striking example of the power and efficacy of a transregional subcultural sound. While Los Angeles's spawning ground and local dynamics have been seminal in the unfolding of this music, a transnational culture industry involving big recording and entertainment companies north and south of the border catapulted technobanda out of the barrios. Yet, as pointed out in chapter 1, it seems that, in general, banda musicians consciously address Mexican (Spanish-speaking) audiences and do not aspire to penetrate the mainstream market. Banda Machos and other bands have become successful without giving up their Mexican identity. In fact, they are successful *because* of their Mexicanness. Thus, for musicians in Mexican Los Angeles, economic success is no longer dictated by the dominant Anglo-capitalist culture.

Boundary Construction

Like other migrants who move from a developing to a highly industrialized country, newcomers from rural Mexico who arrive in metropolitan Los Angeles are confronted with displacement, disruption, threat, ambiguity, instability, and discontinuity, as well as with a political climate that silences their voices. Sometimes it is difficult for Mexican newcomers to even find empathy from Mexican Americans, for "[t]he interplay between Mexican nationals and Chicanos at times brings to the surface the antipathy that exists between these two groups, a hostility rooted in economic differences and questions of identity" (Martínez 1994: 168–169).[25] The recent growth of the Latino presence in metropolitan Los Angeles not only frightens Anglo Californians—many Latinos too are fearful about the city's rapid transformation.

At school, immigrant children often face mockery and exclusion by their U.S.-born Latino classmates. A Mexican American eighth grader was quoted in the *Los Angeles Times* of having said: "The thing is we see ourselves as different even though we have the same culture. We're American and they're not."[26]

Hence, he and his friends called Mexican immigrants names such as "beaner," "Wehac" (a derogatory term for a Mexican immigrant of Indian descent) and, more recently, "quebradita people." An eleven-year-old immigrant student in return suspected that U.S.-born Latino classmates "might be envious of us because we are so proud of our culture."

Tensions in daily life between individuals and groups of individuals are inevitable. On the other hand, struggles and negotiations help to forge new allegiances. Festivals in particular disclose music's important role in the celebration of communities. For instance, while Latino (and pan-Latino) consciousness in the United States still remains mainly at the level of rhetorical unity, salsa music has become a strong symbol of *latinismo* (Sommers 1991). Similarly, the wide acceptance of technobanda among Mexicans, Central Americans, and Mexican Americans in Southern California reveals that music is able to establish relationships and engender narratives that have not previously been imagined or even valued. As Robert Walser has pointed out, "[Music's] potential to create new meanings for listeners is particularly great in mass media cultures, where music is mobile, sometimes the only means of contact among different ways of life. Thus, musical analysis of popular music can help us to make sense of the seemingly fragmented modern world; it can help us to understand the thoughts and desires of many whose only politics are cultural politics" (1993: 34). Walser's statement resonates strongly when one thinks of California's immigrant politics in the 1990s. Public controversies over multiculturalism and "English-only" reflect a deep uneasiness among many residents about contemporary conditions of life. Recent California gubernatorial election campaigns have not only shown how deep the division actually is between the opposed concepts of the melting pot (uniculturalism) and multiculturalism, but have also proved Rosaldo right: "These days questions of culture seem to touch a nerve because they quite quickly become anguished questions of identity" (1993: xxi).

Subcultural Affiliation and Identification

The cultural backlash generated by the prevailing anti-immigrant climate of the early 1990s reinforced the Latino communities in the Southwest. As young people of Mexican descent became more sensitive to racial discrimination and exploitation, they began to take an increased interest in their own and their parents' and grandparents' heritage and traditions. Musical replenishment from south of the border encouraged Mexicanos to reaffirm and bolster their ethnic consciousness and to express their cultural loyalty. People's choices of which particular subculture to affiliate with and belong to are not random, as Slobin (1993) has argued. Songs, sounds, and styles are important features in any subculture because they embody certain values and attitudes the group members share. Slobin criticizes the tendency in earlier cultural studies to analyze cultural expressions using a single parameter. British scholars in particular tried to map class onto the music of subcultures (see Hebdige 1979). They tended to see youth culture as a spin-off of a necessary "parent class," and style features such as clothing and music as emblems of identity with the parent class (Slobin 1993: 43). Banda aficionados or "quebradita people" easily fit the concept of a subculture, and an examination of the dance movements show strong affinities with Slobin's considerations.

While some quebradita participants told me that "the cowboy outfit is more like a fashion statement," others insisted on its symbolic value: "I wear a *tejana* [Stetson hat] because I'm proud of who I am." Indeed, the Stetson hat, the most conspicuous emblem of the "banda movement," mirrors the music's working-class origins and could entice one to analyze banda music as class confined, just as Keil and Keil (1992) and Peña (1985) analyzed the polka and Texas-Mexican *conjunto*, respectively, as working-class phenomena. But in spite of the fact that banda music was mainly nurtured by Mexican low-wage laborers and blue-collar immigrants in Southern California, technobanda was not solely a working-class phenomenon. Musical identities do not necessarily correspond with how people are placed in this world socially. The same music may be meaningful to a range of people who do not share class, nationality, age, or even language. Moreover, a music's connotation to backwardness or upward mobility may be perceived quite differently. For those aspiring to a higher social status, affiliation with "low-class" music is not desirable, while for individuals who have accommodated to their status in society, such music loses its threatening connotation. Representative of many young banda fans, one told me: "I'm more into [Mexican music] than my parents are right now. I'm listening to K BU E, while my mom is listening to oldies in English." Another related: "I had to defend the music and explain [to] my colleagues and friends that banda is beautiful. I also thought before that banda was low-class music. The music has that stigma." A Mexican-born interviewee analyzed the status of banda, pointing out the music's different reception: "Banda music has been around forever. I grew up with banda music. At that time, not very many people liked it. At least in Mexico, only the poor listen to that type of music. The rich do not listen to [banda]. They have Spanish pop-rock music, romantic music such as ballads. You go to a club, and it's divided: the rich and the poor. Even in TV shows and Spanish soap operas, when they make fun of the poor, the poor characters listen to banda. And you have the rich characters that listen to another, more sophisticated type of music. Here in California, it cuts through the classes. Here it doesn't matter."

In the United States, (techno)banda was able to leave its marginalized confines and to become the cultural expression of a very diverse people, thus transcending class boundaries. Rather than simply a class marker, music in contemporary America may be "at once an everyday activity, an industrial commodity, a flag of resistance, a personal world, and a deeply symbolic, emotional grounding for people in every class and cranny the superculture offers" (Slobin 1993: 77).

For many individuals who felt their ambiguous social position as Chicanos or Mexican Americans in the United States, participation in banda events was an alternative musical activity that also affirmed their political standing. As one college-educated young woman asserted:

I like the music, but it is also political. To me, a lot of it has to do with my parents' history. It is knowing my history. I like a lot of the lyrics, especially the old songs—the older lyrics talking about growing up in a small town. Banda Machos's "Sangre de indio" talks about moving away from the hometown, about being an Indian. They're talking of being proud of who you are. I know how it is to live in a small town because of my parents. I feel proud of listening to this kind of music. It reinforces what I was taught to believe. My parents always said: "You have to be proud of who you are." That's why my parents always took us back twice a year. When we were little, they would take us [for] the whole summer. [The music] brings back those memories for me, when I was little. I like hearing [the songs]. It's a statement about my parents' history and it validates the history, what they have been through. It also shows, in a political sense, "Yeah, we're also here and we are proud of being here. We're strong people."

Emotional Grounding

Music embodies imagined worlds. Yet, the banda movement has shown that imagination is not simple daydreaming or idle escapism, but rather an empowering force. Because music offers strong images of characteristic identities, it is a source of identity and pride. Richard Middleton has noted that "popular music has always been concerned, not so much with reflecting social reality, as with offering ways in which people could enjoy and valorize identities they yearned for or believed themselves to possess" (1990: 249). In particular, new compositions addressing the dance style and clothing encouraged banda fans to identify with the new style by participating actively in the dance events, dressed up as vaqueros. One of the dancers remembered the first years of the dance craze: "Technobanda was very strong. They dressed the music that was playing. Yes, they listened to it, they dressed it, and they drove it. Have you seen the trucks with the hats? That was very in, the trucks with the hats, with the ropes on the mirror."

Music and lyrics of many songs comprise features of a concept called lo *ranchero*. According to Peña,

> To understand the significance of the concept we must first be aware that it is a component of a larger ideology of romantic nationalism that is rooted in Mexican thought on both sides of the border. This ideology has been nurtured for a very long time . . . , but its most recent manifestations can be traced to the Mexican Revolution of 1910 and the intense nationalism it spawned. . . . Romantic nationalism in Mexico has exerted a unifying influence by appealing to the glory of the nation's "unique" heritage. As components of this nationalism, the concept of lo *ranchero* and the symbols that cluster around it—of which *música ranchera* is one—have contributed to the ideology by ennobling the existence of hacienda and rural life in general, portraying this existence as idyllic. (1985: 10–11)

Technobanda's innovation of adding a vocalist enabled the band to expand the traditional instrumental banda repertory and reinterpret songs from the vast pool of Mexico's lyric genres, notably the ranchera, a melodic and highly emotional song type that developed during the post-1910 revolution period. Although usually associated with mariachi, rancheras are performed by all regional Mexican music ensembles. Rancheras' affective intensity lies in both the sound, including the typical *gritos* [emotional yells], and in the song lyrics. As "momentary recreations of a simpler and romanticized folk heritage," they evoke feelings of nostalgia and patriotism, and therefore of Mexicanness (Peña 1985: 11).

The ranchera style is particularly suited for romantic songs about love, loss, and suffering. Most often, the subject of the pain and the nostalgic desire of such songs is a woman. Similar sentiments may also be caused by the separation from the beloved *tierra*, the place and, in a broader sense, the nation where one was born. The departure, forced or voluntary, from the purity of the rural homeland and the longing to return "home" are the theme of many rancheras, both old and new. A typical example is the traditional "Canción mixteca" [Mixteca Song], which nurtures nostalgic longings for the ancestral homeland: "How far away am I from the land where I was born! What immense nostalgia invades my thoughts! . . . I'd like to cry, I'd like to die of anguish."[27] In a similar vein, one of Banda Machos's hit songs, "Los machos también lloran" [Machos Also Cry; original title: "Los hombres también lloran"], regrets the loss ("I left the land where I was born . . . I left my father to work alone, I left him crying, alone and sad") and expresses the hope of returning:[28]

Yo le pido a mi Dios que me escuche	I beg my God to hear me
y que pronto se acabe mi pena	to soon end my suffering
pues yo quiero volver a mi tierra	I wish to return to my land

junto mis amigos,
    mis padres queridos
y vivir en paz.

to be with my friends
    and my beloved parents
and to live in peace.

The affective power of locality is also conveyed by "Mi tierra" [My Land], a song composed by Severiano Peña and interpreted by Banda El Chante, a young Sinaloan-style banda from Jalisco:[29]

(¡Un saludo para toda la gente del Chante
    y para todo Jalisco!)

(Greetings to all people from El Chante
    and for all Jalisco!)

Qué lindo es mi pueblo, qué linda es
    mi tierra
qué alegres charreadas se ven por allá
se ven esos charros jugarse la vida
con el alma henchida de tanta emoción.

How pretty my town is, how pretty
    my land is
what joyful rodeos they have
those horsemen who risk their life
with their heart filled up by so much
    emotion.

Tienen sus tabernas allá en los corrales
y brotan manantiales del vino mezcal

On their farms they have taverns
where mezcal wine gushes forth in
    abundance

se cruzan las copas y brindan con ellas

they cross the glasses and they toast
    with them

y tiran botellas a medio corral.

tossing the bottles in the midst of the corral.

Aaay, mi tierra, mi tierra natal
yo nunca te olvido porque eres mi nido
porque eres mi hogar.
Aaay, mi Chante, mi tierra natal
donde sus mujeres nos dan sus quereres
y no hay falsedad.

Aaay, my land, my native land
I will never forget you, for you are my nest
you are my home.
Aaay, my Chante, my native land
where your women give us their love
and where there is no falsity.

Se ven sus potreros plantear de espigales
y brotan maizales que es una emoción
se cruzan carretas y trocas completas
¡qué grandes cosechas nos da esa región!

To see the pastures planted with grain
and the thriving cornfields is such a joy
carts and loaded trucks pass each other
what a great harvest this region bestows on
    us!

Yo nunca te olvido, mi Chante querido
porque eres la cuna que el cielo me dio
y aquí me despido cantando el corrido
que con esta banda sus notas brotó.
Aaay, mi tierra [etc.]

I'll never forget you, my beloved Chante
because you are the cradle the sky gave to me
singing this song I say goodbye
accompanied by the sound of this banda.
Aaay, my land [etc.]

Like the peaceful rural homeland evoked in the Banda Machos ranchera, the village of El Chante is represented as a sanctified place, an imagined locus of purity, goodness, sharing, and neighborliness. Identifying itself with "its" village, Banda El Chante encourages the construction of both locality and community and consciously places itself in a tradition. For, as their names suggest, traditional bandas have always identified with particular localities, enjoying a special association with the public and community life of their own village or town.

Identity construction always involves notions of difference and social boundary; as one song says, "I am Mexican even though I am living among Americans." Since much of contemporary politics is organized around identity, asserting one's difference may lead to constructing a national or ethnic identity by emphasizing one's superiority: "Our culture is the best." Such bold nationalistic statements as those exhibited in "Yo nací pa' cantar" [I Was Born to Sing] are an exception, but nevertheless very popular among a large audience. Interpreted by Banda El Chante, this ranchera was played extensively on Californian airwaves in 1996. Again, the song's verbal patriotic assertions are invigorated by the ranchera character of the music:[30]

Me gusta la banda, me gustan los grupos	I like banda, I like *grupos*
me gusta lo contry, me gusta el norteño	I like country, I like norteño
también el mariachi de corazón	I also like the mariachi of my heart
yo soy muy latino y a mucha honra lo	I am very Latino and I say it with a
digo yo. . . .	lot of pride. . . .
Aaay, yo nací pa' cantar	Aaay, I was born to sing
le canto a mi tierra, mi raza querida	I sing for my land, my beloved *raza* [people]
digan lo que digan, nuestra cultura es	say what they say, our culture is the best . . .
la mejor . . .	
y nuestra gente es la mejor.	and our people are the best.
Aaay, me gusta la banda.	Aaay, I like banda.

The reassertion of nationalist discourses, as Grossberg has pointed out, is "based less on the idenitification of the nation and the state than on the assumed identity between the nation and ethnicity" (1996: 170).

In the diaspora, community, once understood as being rooted in particular localities, moves to the level of the nation and beyond. The shift from an explicit affirmation of regionalism to a cultural expression of (trans)nationalism was particularly noticeable at dance events in Nuevo Los Angeles. As one participant observed: "It was very powerful when that article came out in the L.A. *Times* [*Magazine*, by Rubén Martínez, 1993]. I remember I was reading it at school. Three years later, it's still the same big crowd. In terms of clothes, it is different. . . . All these accessories are gone, but they still react to the *saludos* [salutes to Mexican states]. It's not so territorial anymore. Just Mexico. Maybe there is an unconscious influence because there are so many things going on against Mexicans [in the United States] recently—they became the scapegoat for political reasons. It becomes secondary from what state you're from."

The fervent adherence to Mexican regionalism and nationalism may be attributed to feelings of uprootedness and dislocation among Mexican immigrants. Yet, kindled by an anti-immigrant rhetoric that does not distinguish undocumented immigrants from legal ones or from long-term residents and citizens of color, there has also been a noticeable resurgence of regionalist and nationalist feeling among Chicanos. Their participation in banda events may have been an attempt to redefine Los Angeles's cultural space so that they could feel at home in a city and society that favor a policy of rejection and estrangement. Because music is capable of creating a spontaneous collective identity, it serves well as an affirmation of ethnic and/or national difference.

Contemporary and Traditional

Technobanda allowed Mexicano youths to experience an attachment to values shared with grandparents and parents and rooted in their "homeland." On the other hand, it also allowed them to share social conventions, fashions, and aspirations derived from American youth culture. Like other recent popular musics of large migrant populations, technobanda's syncretic fusion of traditional elements and contemporary features is an expression of its listeners' and participants' own senses of identity. As pointed out by Peter Manuel (1995), cultural expressions of migrant communities often show an inclination toward postmodern aesthetics, while simultaneously retaining ties to premodern ancestral traditions. The coexistence of post- and premodern cultural attitudes in lower-class urban subcultures, though, is not a "postmodern pastiche" in the sense of a calculated play with elements from disparate discourses and subjectivities as employed by postmodern artists. "Rather, subcultures are often born into struggles against poverty and discrimination, in which the reconstitution of a sense of personal or collective subjectivity is not a casual pursuit, but rather an urgent task crucial to psychic survival. . . . [T]he migrant's search for a sense of identity, like that of modernizing societies in general, is not necessarily a post-modern process, but one which synthesizes traditional and contemporary subjectivities in an often profoundly emotional manner" (1995: 229, 235).

California's sociopolitical circumstances have contributed much to the power and force of banda music. In its modern garb, technobanda appealed to hundreds of thousands of young people. As a "traditional Mexican" music, it was a source of pride in one's own culture and race. Moreover, technobanda generated a taste for acoustic banda music and thus helped to release the concealed possibilities of the traditional Sinaloan banda. Banda's modernized version and the dance craze it triggered was a detour on the road to learning about and eventually appreciating Sinaloan banda music. As the KBUE deejay Rosy González emphasized, many young people found their roots, their "home," in banda music: "*Banda de viento* is a feeling that people have of back home. When I hear *banda sinaloense* I get the chills. That's why banda music, the original *banda de viento*, will always be around." Similarly, one young college-educated banda fan told me about her own experience: "When I was in high school, I wasn't very much into Spanish. I would come back to my parents' country, Mexico, Jalisco, twice a year. I never stopped because that's my roots. I have a lot of family there. Both my grandmothers are there. My father's family is there. My mom's family is also there. What helps is that they're both from the same small town, El Chante. Now, I like the tambora more than technobanda. It's the real stuff." Another banda fan summarized the tendency among young listeners in the United States to go back to their roots, "to seek out the real thing": "Technobanda and quebradita are not so hot anymore. Now, the real *banda sinaloense* is strong. They are very versatile—they play anything from quebradita to *tropical* to norteña. I think when the studios started to make these techno-mixes, that's what killed technobanda. It was the wrong direction. People wanted to go back to their roots, to hear the real music, played by real musicians—not by synthesizers and computers."

Most of the fervent banda fans in the United States, however, did not know anything about the social world of traditional, noncommercial banda music in its region of origin, nor about banda's association with Sinaloa's lower classes. They had hardly ever been exposed to the prejudices nurtured by many Mexicans (especially those from Mexico City), who associate banda music with disreputable social behavior, rural backwardness, and vulgarity. For most young people in the United States, technobanda and its catchy and danceable rhythms were something new, something that had no dark past yet was inherently Mexican. They would have been surprised to hear about how many of the banderos made, and continue to make, a bare living: in the *cantinas* [bars or brothels] and playing for *parrandas* [drinking sprees]. The glamorous world of technobanda, with its sophisticated lightshows and high-tech sound systems, does not in fact resemble the crude and often violent environment of the traditional banda, where a musician's life is frequently at risk, where in an instant a trifle could become a life-threatening affair, where musicians might be killed just because they do not comply with a patron's request. Banda's history is full of such stories;

they are told and retold among musicians and have occasionally made head-lines in local newspapers.

Music often serves as a "key to our remembrance of things past" (Frith 1987: 142), an observation that is especially true for the "banda movement" that swept the southwest in the early 1990s. Triggered by California's particular so-ciopolitical conditions, which increasingly polarized its population, young people of Mexican decent began to take more interest in their Mexican heri-tage, in their (assumed) traditions. They considered technobanda an intrinsi-cally traditional music—and as such, it helped them to build a consciousness of the past and to forge a vision of the future. Thus, traditional music does not simply belong to the past; rather, it overcomes temporal distance by virtue of its own meaningful presence. The sedimentation of cultural values holds the promise of the continuity of meaning and relevance of a way of life for its peo-ple as a distinctive group. Hence, to understand technobanda's power, we ought to consider technobanda a "popular traditional music"—a traditional music in modern garb whose success is rooted in its capability to transcend spatial, temporal, and social boundaries.

This ability, however, has always been banda's strength. Introduced by Eu-ropean merchants and settlers during the second half of the nineteenth cen-tury, bands constituted the primary entertainment of Mexico's elite and work-ing class as well. Appropriated by the lower strata of society, band music continued to be popular, surviving modern developments in the entertainment industry. Throughout the twentieth century, bandas flourished in cantinas and dance halls as well. Acceding to popular demand, they developed a repertory that embraced every musical trend: from polka and waltz to fox-trot, cha-cha-cha, mambo, cumbia, and, eventually, quebradita. The following chapters ex-plore banda's social and cultural history in more detail.

PART 2

A Social History of Banda Music
From Rural/Local/Traditional to Urban/Transregional/Commercial

The Sociohistorical Roots
of Banda Music

Los papaquis son aquí
y no serán más adelante
porque dicen que aquí vive
la mujer del Comandante.
    Popular verse

In our experience of time, the past does not exist as something remote, isolated from the present. The temporal distance that separates us from
the past, in Ricoeur's notion of traditionality, is not a dead interval but a generative transmission of meaning. He urges us to reopen the past, to reveal the
past as a "living tradition," so as to reanimate its still-unaccomplished potentialities (1988: 221; see also Kearney 1991: 55–73). It was with this notion of
past in mind that I dug for the roots of banda music in archives, in libraries,
and in people's memories.

The roots of banda music reach deep into the nineteenth century. Yet, inquiring into the musical life of any nineteenth-century populace is a strenuous endeavor. This is even more true if one ventures to explore the music of people living in the provinces, far from the center, where culture and notions about
culture were being forged. Musicologists have very often avoided examining or
ignored the musical life of such regions, either because of the scarcity of historical documents or because of the (assumed) irrelevance of regional expression
to culture at large. Thus, little is known about music making in the vast territories of northwestern Mexico. This region was geographically isolated, effectively
cut off from all but the Pacific coast by the Sierra Madre Occidental, a chain of
high and rugged mountains. Although the restrictions that had earlier prohibited foreigners from exploring the country were abolished after Mexico's independence from the Spanish empire in 1821, only a few visitors traveled through

2. Mexico.

Mexico's northwest. Foreigners usually arrived in Veracruz and made their way through Puebla to Mexico City, where most of them would reside. Guadalajara in the west, Guanajuato in the north, Oaxaca in the south, and the Yucatán peninsula in the southeast were their favorite travel destinations. In the mid-1800s, a European traveler noticed that "of all the states composing the Republic of Mexico, none are less known than Sinaloa, Durango, and Chihuahua. Partly from fear of savage Indians, partly from want of pecuniary means, they have been avoided by most travelers" (Seemann 1853: 159).

Mexico's northwest remained unexplored terra incognita until inventive merchants from the Old World recognized their chance for exploiting its dormant fortunes. Business, however, was carried on using the ocean highway; the overland routes were both unsafe and uncertain. Thus, Sinaloa's ties with the rest of Mexico continued to be weak throughout the century.

Contemporary comments on music in Sinaloa before the mid-nineteenth century are scarce, and those that exist are invariably nondescriptive and brief. References to "plebeian" traditions of music making are virtually nonexistent. One of the few available notes was written by Juan M. Riesgo, the first constitutional governor of Sinaloa, who reported in the 1820s: "The music is very underdeveloped despite the people's love for it. Only in Rosario [a mining town] is it somewhat advanced; of course, we refer to music on principle, because a violin can be found anywhere, even on the most miserable ranch. Some master the harp, the guitar and the jaranita [small guitar], instruments suitable for the Criollos [Mexicans of Spanish descent]. Although not having the elegance of European [instruments], for us they have a captivating charm" (Riesgo and Valdés 1828: 42).[1] Certainly music was played even in the remotest and most isolated regions. Mexicans' love for music and dance in general was often noticed and commented on by foreign visitors. For instance, Carl Christian Sartorius, a German emigrant who settled in Mexico in 1824, observed: "In town and in the country every one is fond of music; the Creole and the Mestizo have much talent; all the world plays and sings, and yet musical education is quite in the background. . . . Music is nowhere taught in schools. The young learn to strum on the piano, harp or guitar, without knowing a note, and even whole bands of performers on stringed and wind instruments only play by ear" (1961: 125).

It was not until the second half of the nineteenth century that references to the musical life of urban communities began to appear more frequently. Mazatlán's newspapers would regularly announce the Spanish zarzuela troupes that visited the city theater and the open-air concerts performed by the military band, which belonged to the garrison of Mazatlán. With the port's increasing importance in Asian and European trade, the number of foreign visitors to

Mexico's Pacific coast grew. Some of the sailors, adventurers, scientists, merchants, and diplomats wrote detailed descriptions of their journeys addressed to their countrymen at home.

These firsthand accounts are, of course, subjective and reflect not only the author's worldview but also his ability to appreciate a different world. Individuals without the necessary endurance to travel under uncomfortable conditions and without a certain openness and tolerance experienced Mexico as appalling, as did the Englishman who exclaimed: "If Humboldt, when he paid a visit to the city of Mexico, had examined it with the eyes of a humane philosopher, and had represented it in its unadorned colors, how much disappointment would have been spared to travelers and to Europe!" (Hardy [1829] 1871: 9). Most visitors, however, were enchanted by the land, its people, and their manners and customs. This fascination is reflected in their rich, descriptive, and often book-length travel reports, which were meant to be not detached chronicles, but personal narrations of adventures in a strange but picturesque land. Although filtered through the eyes of foreign observers, these accounts are a valuable source for the reconstruction of popular culture in nineteenth- and early-twentieth-century Sinaloa.

Sinaloa in the Nineteenth Century

Until the eighteenth century, only a small number of colonists had settled in northwestern New Spain (Jones 1979). After the subjugation and pacification of hostile Indian tribes and the Jesuits' expulsion in 1767, immigration to the frontier area was encouraged. New towns emerged as a growing number of Spanish newcomers to Sonora and Sinaloa settled in mining and agricultural districts and around presidial garrisons. The late development of a permanent Hispanic society in the northwest had two important consequences. First, it never became a stronghold of the Catholic church; and second, small urban centers were formed that were dominated by powerful, often interrelated families (Voss 1982: 32).[2] Geographically on the edge of the viceroyalty, the northwest experienced Mexico's struggle for independence, with its ideas of a common national identity, less strongly than any other region of the country. However, as Spanish dominance came to an end in 1821, the northwest began to expand its commerce, in particular with merchants from Europe and the United States.

The growing foreign and coastal trades were channeled through the ports of Mazatlán and Guaymas. European and North American merchants began establishing themselves in the two ports, marrying the daughters of prominent families of the interior's urban centers. Although the mining towns inland continued to be prosperous commercial and cultural centers, the maritime towns were growing steadily in size and importance. The economic and political power of the mining centers shifted gradually to the ports, where foreign capitalists competed with each other to gain control over the new territories.

In the early nineteenth century, Mazatlán was only a small fishing village; its military function was limited to the observation and protection of the coast. The place was of no particular importance until commercial vessels from Europe steered for its natural harbor in the 1820s. These foreign traders soon recognized Mazatlán's potential for mercantile interchange with Sinaloa's vast hinterland and established themselves in the port. It was this commerce that accelerated Mazatlán's urban development. A member of a British expedition that passed through Mazatlán several times remarked in 1846 that "[S]ome of us had seen Mazatlán in 1832 . . . but Mazatlán itself was no longer a rural village, but a commercial town, full of busy merchants and bustling traders; the apathy of the indolent Creole was supplanted by the activity of the English, the German, the French, and the American" (Seemann 1853: 122). In the mid-1850s a Prussian traveler described Mazatlán as "a pretty little town": "It is only some fifteen years ago that the increasing trade with the interior—the provinces of Sinaloa and Durango—made of a cluster of thatched huts a well-built little town. During the height of the Californian gold fever, Mazatlán made still more rapid advances, through the increase of trade in provisions with San Francisco and the number of passengers, Mexican and American, arriving and departing" (Tempsky 1858: 9). Lieutenant Wise, on board of one of the American frigates that blockaded Mazatlán during the Mexican-American War (1847–48), observed: "In the year 1830, Mazatlán was a miserable Indian fishing village; but owing to its advantageous position in affording a better harbor, and fresh water, than existed for large vessels north of Acapulco—its facilities for communication with the rich mining districts of Zacatecas, Durango and Culiacán, besides the market opened in the populous provinces bordering upon the Pacific, it soon increased in magnitude to a fine thriving little city of ten thousand inhabitants, and became the most important commercial point on the continent north of the equator" (1849: 143). By the 1850s, Mazatlán was "a modern little city [with] many handsome shops, cafés and *sociedads* [sic]" (Wise 1849: 148), social clubs where monte and other games of chance were played. Along its cobblestone streets were spacious, flat-roofed, one-story houses built of bricks that belonged to the wealthier citizens. Well-stocked commercial houses and shops lined the Calle Principal, which connected the Old Harbor and the custom house.[3]

Unlike the bulk of European immigrants to other parts of the American continent, newcomers to Sinaloa belonged to "the better class of their respective nationalities, numbering among them wealthy and accomplished merchants, and other learned men [with] a knowledge of mining, engineering, mechanics and other arts, industries and sciences" (Weidner 1882: 15–16). By mid-century Mazatlán had a church, a theater where the "beautiful people" and elite gathered to listen to Spanish plays of love and tragedy, two principal hotels kept by Frenchmen, and about five hundred shops and stores.[4] Most of the one hundred or so foreigners in the city were engaged in commercial business, and they allegedly owned most of the real estate in the city. Hamilton's guide for the "settler, miner and the advance guard of American civilization" commended Mazatlán as "a commanding commercial city of rapidly growing importance" that "has but few equals for its surrounding advantages, and invites to her municipal confines an intelligent class of immigrants, who will develop her latent energies and resources" (Hamilton 1883: 110–111).

Despite these eulogies on the natural beauty and wealth of Mexico's northwest, Sinaloa's economy toward the end of the nineteenth century did not prosper, nor did its people. Agriculture was at best stagnant, restricted to producing for the local market, and industry consisted of a few factories. The local governments were impoverished, and political power remained in the hands of a few prominent families. Within Sinaloa, "the overwhelming majority of municipalities had been, and remained still, small district market centers, quiescent and parochial, at best only minimally affected by the larger entrepreneurial currents" (Voss 1982: 193).

During the second half of the nineteenth century, there was a considerable gap between the two large urban centers, Culiacán and Mazatlán, and the numerous small district towns. Yet, the majority of Sinaloa's population lived in the countryside. Only one out of seven Sinaloans was living in a town of 2,500 or more inhabitants. The few roads that existed were rudimentary and impassable during the rainy season. Even the main road running the length of the state was of rather poor quality (Wheat 1857:55; Hamilton 1883: 106–7). Nineteenth-century travelers often complained about the bad roadways, infested with sheep ticks and, worse, with numerous outlaws—roaming bandits, brigands, and hostile Indians who made travel extremely dangerous, especially in remote regions. The poor and unsafe transportation system unfavorably affected not only business and economy but also any cultural interaction between urban and rural Sinaloa.

Sinaloa's Divided Society

Mexico's independence from Spain did not improve the social position of the subaltern classes. The local bourgeoisie, who had inherited the rules of colonial society and culture, was little concerned with the idea of a Mexican nation in which all Mexicans would be equal and caste distinctions abolished. The existing social inequalities were not questioned by the well-to-do.

Although culture does not derive simply from class, in early nineteenth-century Western societies and, by extension, in their colonies, "culture" was understood as cultivation, refinement, and edification, and thus inseparable from relationships of wealth and power. The term "culture" implied opposites such as nonliteracy, crudeness, and vulgarity. Consequently, society could be divided into those who had culture, the *gente decente,* and those who did not, the *pelados* [literally, "the shorn ones," a kind of urban peasant noted for his coarse, uneducated, and vulgar language and behavior].

In his report on the province of Sinaloa, Riesgo blamed the colonial government for its indifference toward the common people. According to the author, it was the lack of education that had retained the populace in a state of "barbarism" (Riesgo and Valdés 1828: 40). In the isolated periphery of the young nation, however, the local notables too suffered from the lack of refinement civilization had granted the upper-class citizens of the center. Entertainment was largely based on individual motivation. The lack of regulated recreation and cultural institutions such as theaters was made up for by ingenuity.[5]

Since entertainment in the province was scarce, people of all social strata took advantage of the many holidays included in the Catholic calendar. Church festivities were a great opportunity for diversions of all kinds. Foreign travelers, in particular the Protestant Anglo-Saxons, often commented on the bizarre religious rituals and practices they had observed—rituals that were "Indian, rather than civilized or intellectual . . . tasteless and barbaric" (Mayer 1844: 152).[6] Foreign mine owners were annoyed by the native laborers, for whom every church holiday was a pretext for taking three days off work. Visitors also noted the closeness of upper and lower classes that seemed unavoidable in Mexico: "And so, over the whole church, the floor was a checker-board of ladies and léperos—of misery and pride!"(Mayer 1844: 152).[7]

It was not until the end of the century, though, that native notables in the urban centers of the province began to notice this uncomfortable closeness in public places, especially at church, where they attended mass together with members of the lower classes. Thus, most comments on ecclesiastical matters published in Mazatlán's newspapers in the late nineteenth century contain a critique of the decay of Catholic morals. Although the encroachment on the sacred by the secular may be interpreted as a sign of the church's awareness of people's needs, Sinaloa's conservative churchgoing notables did not approve of this tendency. Some felt compelled to criticize changes in ecclesiastical traditions, especially when these practices, in their view, became a playground for the common people. Accompanied by various diversions such as bullfights, horse races, games of chance, music, and dance, celebrations of church holidays would usually "end with one or more injured persons."[8]

Military Bands and Urban Musical Entertainment

After Mazatlán became a garrison town in 1844, life was affected by the presence of the military. Military bands played for a wide range of functions, some of which were not strictly associated with the military unit. It is not known when the military bands began to give open-air concerts for Mazatlán's citizens, but it is likely that this custom already existed when an American naval unit seized the town in 1847 and let its own bands play for the Mexican audience. According to Lieutenant Wise, the American occupation of the port was rather amiable: "The townspeople began to look less gloomily upon their invaders . . . and the women . . . sought the main plaza in the afternoons, arrayed in tastefully flowing robes, and graceful *ribosas* [sic], whilst their surprisingly diminutive feet beat time to the music from our bands" (1849: 168).

Although not authorized by the Naval Academy until 1852, bands were common on ships before then (Hazen and Hazen 1987: 24).[9] Lieutenant Wise's frigate, the *Independence*, must have been one of those that were unofficially equipped with a band. Indeed, several officers of the Pacific Squadron (1846–48) wrote about music bands on board ship in their journals. Lieutenant Henry Bulls Watson, for example, noted that despite the extensive preparations for a ball on board of the sloop *Cyane*, none of the officers from the other ships showed up, and that four of the six "ladies" who attended the dance became seasick. Shortly after this unsuccessful social gathering, some American and English officers planned to give a public ball on shore. But because of a disagreement, the commodore of the frigate *Savannah* refused to send his band (Watson 1990: 80, 90).[10] Marius Duvall, ship's surgeon on the *Portsmouth*, recalled a calm night in the port of Mazatlán: "The night is moonlit, and I have just been listening to the music from the band on board the [frigate] Congress" (Duvall 1957: 59).

According to accounts by foreign marine officers, record-book keepers and sea travelers, it was common for bands employed on board also to play on shore if there was an opportunity. A member of a British expedition reported on its stay in the port of Guaymas, Sonora, in 1849: "We were very gay during our stay. The inhabitants behaved in a cordial manner, and our young people—in fact, old and young—fully entered into their dancing propensities. Tertullias [sic], balls, and *petit soupers* were the order of the day. We gave a grand ball on shore in the Punta de Arena, where a spacious tent and supper-room was fitted up, dancing kept up from nine o'clock in the evening until three or four in the morning" (Seemann 1853: 157).

When the French-Austrian army occupied the city (1864–66), the Mazatlecos were again exposed to foreign band music. During their stay, General de

Castagny's military band allegedly gave public concerts in the town square and played at village festivities.[11] Bands on board foreign ships that stayed in Mazatlán's waters continued to give concerts in the main square during peacetime (El correo de la tarde, 14 April 1899).

Although Mexican regiments had included music bands since the 1810s, and Jaime Nunó, the composer of the national anthem, was appointed inspector of the regiments' bands in 1854, the first official military bands were not established until after Mexico's triumph over the French-Austrian imperialists in 1867.[12] Presumably inspired by the bands of Maximilan's imperial guard and the French army, each battalion eventually got its own band. The military recruited its bandsmen nationwide from a large pool of excellent civilian musicians. Soon Mexico counted several outstanding military bands that could compete with the best in world (Campos 1928: 200, 202).[13]

The bands' outdoor concerts were intended to entertain the urban elite. Yet every citizen had unfettered access to the music. Military bands usually played a mixed repertory of marches and classical selections and hence offered many listeners their first experience of "serious" instrumental music. Later in the century, Mazatlán's weekly newspapers informed their readers regularly about the concerts of the infantry bands that played for the public in Plaza Machado and at the Old Port. The program included fantasies from Verdi's Il Trovatore, Bizet's Carmen, and Wagner's Lohengrin, polkas, mazurkas, pasodobles, and Mexican salon music (see, for example, El occidental, 18 April 1874; El correo de la tarde, 29 April 1895). A Colombian visitor to the port in the 1890s noticed that there were two infantry regiments in Mazatlán, each with its own band (Jaramillo 1899: 79). Apart from the serenatas [open-air concerts], they also played at the bullfights and for civic functions such as opening-day celebrations of public facilities.[14]

Toward the end of the century, the repertory became more eclectic, including arrangements of popular art music as well as national and patriotic melodies. The first public concert with canciones del campesino [peasant songs] was given in 1885 in Culiacán's main square, the Jardín Rosales (see González Dávila 1959: 655; Ibarra 1960: 319). The songs were harmonized and arranged for band by Angel Viderique, the director of the Banda de Música del Estado. By that time, however, civilian bands had already spread and were deeply ingrained in village tradition.

With the expansion of capitalism in the late nineteenth century, the class differences in Sinaloa's cities came to resemble those of modern urban society elsewhere in Mexico. Whereas the privileged minority could afford to enjoy music in privacy, most lower-class people had access to music in public places only—the square, the church, the theater, and the street. Although music performances in these public places were given primarily to entertain the notables, everybody was allowed to attend.

Apart from serenatas, which the military band played twice a week on the main square, music could be heard publicly on many other occasions. In the colonial mining and small market towns, where the parish church occupied a central position both visually and ideologically, sacred music was rooted in Spanish Catholic practice. In the newer maritime population centers, the influence of the church was not very strong. The architectural aspect of these centers was not determined by the traditional powers, but by trade and commerce. This is particularly true of Mazatlán, where a church was not built until 1842.[15] Lieutenant Wise noted a few years later: "There was but one church in Mazatlán, for the people are not piously inclined, and one Padre was all we ever saw" (1849: 148). A similar observation was made by an American traveler: "There was but one church in Mazatlán, and this is not very large; though sufficiently so to hold the church-going citizens. But few of the gentlemen attend church, and scarcely any of the foreigners" (Wheat 1857: 33).

The construction of the cathedral began in 1856 and was completed in 1899. Evidently, sacred music was far less important in the life of Mazatlán's citizens than secular music.[16] The iron bandstand on the square in front of the cathedral, donated by the German merchant house Melchers, was inaugurated in 1890.[17] According to Mazatlán's chronicler Miguel Valadés Lejarza, German merchants had a genuine interest in promoting music making since they sold, among other imported manufactured goods and industrial products, a variety of musical instruments (personal communication, Mazatlán, 1994, 1996, 1998).

Eustaquio Buelna reported on a scandal that occurred in Mazatlán in 1852 when entrepreneurs used an inventive strategy to avoid paying taxes. The merchants allegedly hired musicians to attract a crowd; then, they threw coins at the rabble, who started to shout, "Long live the merchants, death to the government!" The chief of police was summoned but had to retreat when pelted with stones (Buelna 1924: 36).[18] Although the kind of music is not further defined, one remark points to the possibility that it was the military band. In any case, one can imagine that brass instruments would have been the most efficient in attracting a crowd large enough to intimidate the police.

A detailed description of the life of foreigners in Mazatlán can be found in the memories of Adolph Riensch, a young German clerk who lived in the port from 1841 to 1844. Of special interest are his remarks about music making among the immigrants and the popular German customs they had carried to their faraway new home, such as *Fastelobend* (carnival), *Kirmes* (kermis), and *Liedertafel* (medley singing).[19] Although Riensch was an ambitious young entrepreneur, he was also inclined to enjoy life. Soon after his arrival in Mazatlán, he

9. Bandstand in front of the cathedral of Mazatlán, donated by the German merchant house Melchers in 1890. Photo by Helena Simonett.

got together with other German bachelors to indulge in music making: "[Jacob] Prisi grabbed his cello, [Roberto] Meyer played the piano and sang, and I joined in with my tenor voice. . . . We usually had many listeners, because in those times a very sociable ambience reigned in Mazatlán; business flourished, and at night everybody wanted to enjoy life. There was little difference between chief and clerk. We ate and drank together, we went for a ride and amused ourselves" (1960: 67–68). Some of the Germans kept an improvised bowling alley in a nearby cave, which they sometimes would convert into a "dance hall" by decorating the walls with mirrors, flowers, and pretty fabrics. After dancing all night long, the participants would return together in the early morning hours following the band.[20] In front of each home, the musicians would give a serenade for the departing person. These nightly processions must have been quite charming—at least for the participating youths.

Among foreign visitors and sailors, the port of Mazatlán was known for its amusements and recreations. A well-traveled visitor who arrived in the port in 1846 just when a ravaging cholera epidemic had paralyzed the town's whole social life exclaimed with much regret: "After a voyage of such long duration we met, instead of the much-needed amusement and recreation, death and mourning" (Seemann 1853: 149). The toll of the epidemic was high, but life was soon back to normal, as another traveler noted: "At night . . . when the whole population is out to enjoy the pleasant air, the men in their white shirts and the women in their bewitching rebosas; when some native band is playing, just far enough distant to drown the discordance; when the paper lanterns of the fruit-venders gleam at every corner, and the aristocratic señoritas smoke their cigars in the balconies above—Mazatlán is decidedly the gayest and liveliest little city on the continent" (Taylor 1850: 246–247).

Foreign visitors, some of whom belonged to the middle class of their respective nations, were not only more likely to come into personal contact with the lower orders of Mexican society than were members of the native literate class, but were also more eager to learn about them. In the larger cities in particular, "higher classes as they are called, withhold of themselves as much as possible from plebeian habits" (Sartorius 1961: 162). While the native upper class tried not to rub elbows with the *pelados*, visitors such as Lieutenant Wise would accept an invitation to a popular *fandango* held on the marshland outside Mazatlán that was also frequented by *léperos*, that is, day laborers, idlers, pickpockets, and cutthroats: "A large marquée had been erected in the middle of the open space, and around were smaller affairs, with numerous booths, sparkling with lights, music and merriment. It was not a very select affair, and I took the precaution to loosen my sword in its sheath. Presently we entered into the spirit of the frolic, and were soon hand in hand with leperos and their sweethearts—sipping from every cup—whirling away in waltzes—dancing to the quick *jarabie* [*jarabe*, a dance form], and making ourselves particularly ridiculous" (1849: 192). In June 1848, shortly before the Americans lifted their blockade of the port, Wise witnessed what he termed "the gamblers' fiesta." Actually, it was the popular Fiesta de Olas Altas, which was held annually in May until prohibited by decree in 1870:

Towards nightfall the population assembled on the Olas Altas, and the scene became very gay and animated—the monté tables were thronged—dollars and ounces of gold chinking incessantly—loto [lotto] banks playing for prizes of dulces or licores—Indians with figured boards and dice, making more noise than their *confrères* in the trade, betting coppers or fried fish. The cars and horses were filled with delighted paisanos, who were enjoying the pleasures of city life. At the fandangos, too! were girls in their gayest dresses, dancing to the enlivening music of harps and guitars, bursting forth at intervals with some shrill chaunt [chant] or ballad, to relieve their nimble feet, perhaps, from exertions attending the *jarabie* and *jota* [two dance forms]. It is altogether an attractive spot; and when one is tired of the monté, bowling at Smithers', or dancing at the fandangos, there is the sparkling surf at your feet, where the energies may be revived. (1849: 307–308)

Street music was a familiar aspect of the urban center. The American scientist Josiah Gregg wrote in his diary about his observations in Mazatlán in 1849:

My attention was attracted about midday (as it had also been on several previous occasions) by a band of music parading the streets, accompanied by several horsemen, fantastically dressed, in ridiculous representations of Indian costumes—and ahead of the cavalcade, a still more ridiculous "clown," who exerted his lungs in making speeches to a rabble of boys and vagabonds, who crowded the wake. This is the usual style, as well in the interior towns of the republic generally, as here, of publishing a circus or bullfight (or in fact, any other public representation), to come off in the evening. This is the *convite*. Sometimes we see a party with but a guitar and violin, and a couple of songstresses parading the streets. This is the *convite* to one of those disorderly fandangoes which infest some parts of the town, especially on Sunday evenings; for this is the day here, as well as everywhere else in the republic, for all sorts of public amusements. (1944: 336)

It was also customary for a band to parade through the streets during the daytime to publicize the theater program. An American visitor observed with amazement that "the poorer class are great lovers of the theater, and will live upon nothing, and go with bare feet for weeks, in order to save the treasured *dos reales* which shall give them the entrance to their favorite amusement" (Edwards 1883: 23). Yet another traveler noted: "I saw an interesting picture one evening, in front of the theater. A large band was stationed near the door, where they performed waltzes and polkas in excellent style—an idea no doubt derived from 'Scudder's Balcony' of the gambling-hells of San Francisco. It had the effect, at least, to draw a dense crowd of the lower orders to the place, and increase the business of the traders in fruits and drinks. A military band, of trumpets alone, marched up and down the principal street, blowing long blasts of piercing sound that affected one like the shock of an electro-galvanic battery" (Taylor 1850: 247).

Invited by wealthy citizens, foreign artist troupes had been visiting the port since the 1840s.[21] When in 1868 the Teatro del Recreo featured Verdi's opera *La traviata*, the local weekly newspaper *El Pacífico* noted enthusiastically: "Finally, Mazatlán's society has enjoyed for the first time the satisfaction of having hosted an opera company . . . The first composition put on stage was the most beautiful work of the famous Verdi, called the 'Traviata or La Dame aux Ca-mélias.' The plot of the work is exceedingly immoral, but its music is good" (*El Pacífico*, 26 December 1868).

In 1875, after ten years of construction, a new, bigger, and more luxurious theater was finally completed, the Teatro Rubio.[22] It was the pride of Mazatlán's elite; the newspaper published its program regularly and occasionally also printed theater critiques. In Culiacán, the construction of a sumptuous theater began in 1890 under the patronage of the entrepreneur Manuel Clouthier. The opening of the Teatro Apolo in 1894 was a grandiose show. Since many upper-class members of Culiacán were sensitive about their shortcomings in the arts, the new theater became a symbol of culture and modernity. The lower classes, too, benefited from the theater, as they did from the developing culture industry in general.

Mazatlán's garrison band played not only in public, but also for private cele-brations such as weddings, baptisms, saints' days, birthdays, banquets, and the so-called *kermesse*, a type of social gathering that was very much in fashion in the late nineteenth century among "la culta sociedad de Mazatlán," the city's cultivated residents, that is, the entrepreneurs, medical doctors, lawyers, and newspaper reporters.[23] Both the military bands and *orquestas* [orchestras]— small ensembles of three to four professional musicians playing soft-sounding instruments such as violin, violoncello, guitar, jarana, and flute—were con-tracted to play for such occasions.[24]

Around the turn of the century, the larger towns and the urban centers boasted of some prominent orchestras, among them Los Hermanos Mora (di-rected by Eligio Mora), the Orquesta Navarro (Enrique Navarro ["El Gordo"]), the Terceto Lizardi (Pedro Lizardi), the Cuarteto de Trujillo, the Orquesta de Cirilo Rivas, the Orquesta Francisco Torres in Mazatlán, and the orchestras of Braulino Pineda in Rosario, Abundio García in Cosalá, and Severiano M. Moreno in Escuinapa. The orchestras' domain was not confined, however, to tertulias and other private events. Despite their small instrumentation, they be-gan to take over some of the duties that before had been the responsibility of the military band. In Mazatlán, they not only gave open-air concerts in the city's squares, but were also contracted to play during the intermission at the Teatro Rubio or during lunch time at the Hotel Central, which had opened in 1888. Soon, the orchestras were being hired for all kinds of festivities and developed a popular dance music favored by the elite and the working people alike.[25] Interestingly, their program did not vary much from that of the military band. The repertories of both ensembles included marches, mazurkas, schottisches, polkas, pasodobles, waltzes, fantasias, and overtures by famous opera composers, and danzas composed by bandmasters.[26]

Orchestras were also often employed for a "walking serenade" called *andar de gallo*. This type of serenade was a popular mode of musical expression in the romantic nineteenth century. Performed outdoors and at night, these ad hoc concerts were usually arranged by bachelors in honor of an adored young lady. An American visitor to the port in 1875 remembered his sleepless nights, tormented by thousands of fleas and swarms of mosquitoes and kept awake by crowing cocks, barking dogs, "and worse than all, occasionally a man with a hurdy-gurdy," who was hired "to grind out his miserable tunes the whole night." And "sometimes a full band would come to serenade some fair *señorita* on her festal day, and rattle away till the dawn of morning. On these occasions it is usual to invite the musicians into the house, and keep the merrymaking there, but [if] the revelers have made too free before their approach, as is often the case, this custom is dispensed with, and, in revenge, they proceed to greater libations, and bang and toot away until the blush of day sends them to their homes" (Edwards 1883: 15). In the late 1890s, Mazatlán's local newspapers began to report such concerts more frequently.[27] Although probably most romantic when played by stringed instruments, *los gallos* were offered not only by vocalists, guitarists, and orchestras, but also by cylinder (hurdy-gurdy) players and most likely by village bands too. Rather than being pleased by these complimentary concerts, several fellow citizens must have perceived them as nightly disturbance like this critic who exclaimed: "What a horror, a cylinder player was also serenading. One's liberty to molest others seems to be unrestricted" (El correo de la tarde, 29 November 1897). The authorities eventually felt compelled to protect the night's rest of the citizens and thus took some measures against the serenading musicians. Prospective wandering musicians first had to obtain permission from the prefect. Those who did not apply and pay for the license risked being punished. Moreover, the duration of music making at a single location was limited to two hours. The authorities of Culiacán were less tolerant: a police edict restricted nightly playing to one hour (Mefistófeles, 23 July 1904).

The advent of modernity brought about social, economic, and cultural changes in Mexico's periphery toward the end of the nineteenth century. When the growing laboring class, the peasantry, and the urban poor began to assert their rights to share goods and services the privileged minority had previously monopolized, they could no longer be ignored. In its endeavor to integrate the subaltern groups into society, Sinaloa's ruling class was first of all concerned with keeping control over the masses. One mode of social control was the legal and bureaucratic regulation of the population. Since gaming, drinking, and spontaneous partying did not harmonize well with the modernistic ideas of the Porfirian elite who had elected themselves as society's moral guardians, local authorities in both cities began to issue regulations and decrees that prohibited indecency and excess of any kind. Among the victims of order and progress were the *pelados*, gamblers, drunkards, prostitutes, idlers, drifters, beggars, handicapped, and insane.

In Culiacán, newly issued decrees also prohibited the *mareaches*, popular dances held on the city's outskirts on Sundays, and affected other popular festivities as well. Because the subject of these regulations usually was the "ordinary people" and their entertainment, we can learn about certain widespread customs among the subaltern classes by indirect means. For instance, although the performance of the national anthem other than at official events was prohibited in the 1880s, local musicians continued to play the tune at popular festivities and in bars. Individuals who did not comply with the law were punished.[28]

Urbanization and Modernization

Until the third quarter of the nineteenth century, the notables and the lower social orders in the provincial cities tended to share the same pastimes: serenatas, walks in the square, horse races, bullfights, cockfights, patriotic and church celebrations, theater and circus performances, carnival, public dances, and gaming. With growing urbanization and advancing modernization, however, the separation of leisure activities along class lines increased. In Sinaloa, the liberalism of the Porfirian government favored principally the interests of Mazatlán's capitalists. As a consequence of the concentration of industrial production, the city began to attract a large number of laborers. Although economic development brought about steady improvements and a more refined culture, these benefited the ruling minority only. The working class suffered under terrible labor and housing conditions. While the affluent classes could enjoy all the modern amenities of the residential zone such as electricity, potable water, toilets, paved streets, theaters, hotels, and so forth, the lower classes dwelled in their barrios, lacking the most basic services (Beraud 1996: 82). This discrepancy did not escape even the cursory glances of foreign visitors to the port, one of whom noted in a somewhat romantic spirit: "Back of [the] homelike homes, in little tilted alleys, are the *chosas* of the poor—boatmen, laborers, porters, fishers—rude apologies to a complacent sky, with careless cane and rushes, and naked babes and laughter, and all the trade-marks of the tropics, where to be poor is not to want" (Lummis 1898: 155).

In the last decade of the nineteenth century the speed of technological modernization increased. The city was beginning to pulsate with modern life: bicycles enhanced the mobility of the citizens, and steam locomotives replaced the leisurely *arañas* [carriages pulled by mules or horses]. Large parts of the Mexican Republic were already connected by rail, the ultimate symbol of modernity, when Sinaloa's isolation was finally terminated by the construction of the Ferrocarril Sud-Pacífico. Culiacán was linked with the Nogales-Guaymas route in 1895 and with Mazatlán in 1906.

Coexisting capitalist and precapitalist economic formations furthered the unequal distribution of commodities and marked the division between the elite and the masses in the cities. Modernization was carried out at the expense of the peasantry and the urban poor, who became even more marginalized. Yet, from the point of view of the ruling class, it was precisely these *pelados* that impeded improvement and progress. According to the authoritarian liberal ideas prevalent during President Porfirio Díaz's time, it was necessary to domesticate this ungovernable population through economic modernization and education so that the illiterate masses would adapt themselves to civilization.

The Mexican Reform and the subsequent constitution of 1857 had proposed a new framework for Mexican society in which the working classes were considered a part of the nation-state. This recognition of the native population as a fundamental part of the nation called for its integration. Thus, Mexico's "modern elite" saw itself confronted with the difficult task of both keeping its dominance and putting an end to the isolation of the subaltern groups. Moreover, after the reform war "many commoners for the first time began to think of themselves as Mexicans. The people of the peripheral states, such as Sonora and Sinaloa, also began to consider themselves a part of the national context. Urban notables had to come to feel it strongly" (Voss 1982: 204).

The newspapers of Sinaloa's two major cities, Mazatlán and Culiacán, from the third quarter of the nineteenth century and the beginning of the twentieth century sketch a vivid picture of urban life, both its advantages and its adversities.[29] Addressed to a circle of literate people, the journalists reported and commented upon affairs they thought were of concern to their readership. Most of their commentaries were heavily biased in favor of politically powerful individuals. This social elite referred to itself as *los notables, las familias, la sociedad, la crème* or *high life*. Illiterate people and their activities were only documented when the literate upper class took an interest in them. But the elites' interest stemmed not from sympathetic curiosity but from disgust, as the newspaper editorials indicate. Most often comments were confined to criticizing the crude and vulgar behavior of the populace, its unpolished manners, its superstitious beliefs, its backwardness and immorality—in short, its otherness. "Ordinary people" were described in terms of everything the members of the upper class were not, or thought they were not. But the elite not only condemned the habits and customs of the lower classes, they also began to suppress any element of popular culture that disturbed the civilized image of the dominant society. Popular festivities came under attack.

Popular Festivities: Sites of Contest

Much of nineteenth-century popular culture took the form of festivals (Burke 1978: 65). The festival was a place where the cultural traditions of the two main social classes met: "the great tradition" of the educated elite, (the *gente de razón* or *gente decente* [rational, decent people], as the Mexican upper class referred to itself), and the "little tradition" of the unlettered communities (the *gente sin razón* [irrational people]).[30] As early as 1858, Sartorius recognized that "[i]f we desire to obtain a glance at the different elements of which the people are composed, we mix with the varying crowd in the market-place, or in the bustle of a popular festival, when all are found united" (1961: 48).

As mentioned earlier, in the second half of the nineteenth century the social elite, in particular the urban notables, began to withdraw itself more and more from the "little tradition," which was characteristically transmitted by informal means and in public places—in the street and the *plazuela*, at the market, at church, and in the cantina. Since the reform, holidays and festivals had "undergone a certain change with the substitution of republican ideas and the decline of religious influence" (Bancroft 1888: 621). National holidays were staged on two separate levels: one for the representatives of the state, the other for the masses. The basic structure of the program was the following: "The national holidays . . . are opened with artillery salvos and ringing of bells, followed by high mass, attended by the authorities and government officials. Then follows a formal audience at the palace, in front of which the people gather to listen to national speeches and music . . . . Then follow performances by athletes and actors, and general merry-making, with illuminations" (Bancroft 1888: 621).

National celebrations in the province had a similar structure. They were, as Bancroft, the historian, had noted, "somewhat numerous." In addition to the established festivities, the notables organized a number of festivals for the purpose of entertaining themselves.[31] Such festivals publicly demonstrated the power of the elite as well as its vision of social hierarchy, and they reinforced the cohesion of the institutionalized system in front of the masses.

Earlier in the century, the popular masses had celebrated Christmas rather boisterously, with masked balls and carnivalesque street revelry.[32] Instead of prohibiting the revelry, the authorities domesticated the festivities by imposing an official holiday: Christmas was given a civic meaning.[33] The new character of the celebration was supposed to help foster a feeling of national unity among the populace. A number of other national holidays were created for the same reason: the masses had to be reminded over and over again that they too were part of the Mexican nation-state. The elite seemed to recognize that the integration of the lower classes into society was best done on a cultural level.[34]

On the other hand, some members of the ruling elite were reluctant to welcome the lower classes into society. Everyday reality was marked by intolerance and prejudice rather than by idealistic political visions. Although members of the upper class tried not to mingle with the *pelados*, they could not avoid contact completely, especially at festivals. It was not surprising, then, that public celebrations such as the Fiestas de Mayo (the defeat of the French-Austrian imperialists on 5 May 1862) and Independence Day (16 September) gave rise to numerous complaints among the notables. For Mazatlán's columnists, the populace and its expressions—its music and its dances—were at best repugnant. But since popular dances were an already established and therefore inevitable element of national celebrations, the *gente decente* urged the authorities to at least remove these "expressive"—that is, impulsive, uncontrolled, and excessive—dances out of the sight of their cultivated eyes (El Pacífico, 21 September 1890).

Not only the eye but also the sensitive ear of the refined citizen seemed to be disturbed by the sound of the street musicians that arrived from their villages to celebrate Independence Day in the city. The musicians and their music as well were perceived as a plague: "The sound of the murgas [street musicians] that presented us with their notes during the 15th and the 16th [of September] reverberates. . . . After the official celebration was over, the bands that had come from nearby villages continued to roam the city followed by a numerous populace" (El correo de la tarde, 21 September 1891).[35] With little understanding of the historical and political situation of the lower orders within the nation-state, one newspaper columnist complained about their indifferent attitude toward the fatherland: "The populace is not even able to distinguish these memorable days from the others of the calendar" (El Pacífico, 8 September 1889). The writer thus requested readers to fight the common people's unpatriotic attitude by celebrating the national holiday with dignity and with edifying music, that is, to the notes of the garrison band. Although participating in the same celebrations, the attitudes and sentiments of the two classes were considered different: whereas the *gente de razón* recognized the deeper meaning of a patriotic celebration, the common people were believed to be simply dazzled by the spectacle. Because of the lack of a common denominator between the ruling class and the popular classes, however, it is no surprise that the disregarded people did not understand the meaning of Independence Day as a celebration of a united Mexico.

The notions of ordinary people held by the educated class, as reflected in such comments, show how deeply the notables saw themselves removed from the subaltern classes. Unfortunately, there are no documents concerning how the common people themselves perceived the given class distinction, the resultant discrimination, and the persistent tutelage. But undoubtedly, nineteenth-century rural and urban subaltern classes were a more powerful force than official history ever admitted, especially in the cultural domain. There were constant negotiations on a cultural level between the different social groups. Although the dominant group had some advantages on its side, the subaltern classes were actively involved in the bargaining. An example of such negotiation is the popular Fiesta de Olas Altas, gaming days celebrated in the month of May, which were supplanted by the *fiestas zaragozanas* (Fiestas de Mayo) and eventually prohibited by decree in 1870. In 1901, the people asked for permission to re-establish roulette, lottery, and other games during the month of May.[36] The leading citizens were outraged. Dr. Martiniano Carvajal, a self-appointed guardian of civic virtue and morality and mouthpiece of Mazatlán's *gente decente*, read the petition with indignation.[37]

The dominating class did not always get its way. More often, a compromise with the subalterns had to be negotiated, as in the case of the popular carnival celebrations. When the working classes and their cultural expressions eventually could no longer be ignored, the newspapers began to report more often on cultural affairs of the city's common people and of the neighboring villages.[38] These accounts often sound as if their authors just had noticed popular cultural expressions for the first time; as if they could not believe that such "crude" expressions could have an entertaining effect on any human being at all. El *correo de la tarde* reported about village musicians visiting the port:

The musicians from Siqueros: These modest sons of the arts got such a good hiding last Saturday that we doubt they will entertain the ears of the Mazatlecos again with the odd noise of their giant "fagot," their tremendous tambora and other instruments. The said musicians arrived here in the retinue of the Governor. The populace crowded around the musicians and accompanied them on their parade through the streets. Worn-out after continuous blowing, the unfortunate musicians wanted to retire, but the populace requested more music and thronged in front of Mr. Tomás Sarabia's inn, where the musicians had taken refuge from the mob that began to throw stones against doors and windows. The Chief of Police intervened and dealt some blows to the crowd, and the mob broke up but not without having injured one individual who was staying at the inn. Allegedly, three of the musicians were beaten up badly and their tambora, their deafening tambora, was broken during the quarrel. (El correo de la tarde, 7 February 1894)

A few years later, the refined ears of the civilized urbanites seemed to have become somewhat used to the noisy sound of the village bands. Their invigorating and enlivening effect on civic festivities was acknowledged in a favorable way:

Noisy were the festivities last Saturday which celebrated General Díaz's taking over of the presidency of the Republic. Early in the morning, the music bands roamed the streets of the city playing merry pieces and contributing to boost the public rejoycing. At night, the banda from Siqueros played the best selection of its repertoire in the Plazuela del Rastro which was beautifully adorned. (El correo de la tarde, 3 December 1900)

News from Rosario: Today the popular banda Quelite arrived in town [Rosario], making more noise than the two slaughter houses together. Amongst rockets and yells, one could hear the mellifluous notes of "las playas" and the "papaqui." The musicians wore splendid and lavish disguises. Next Thursday, they will give a grand concert in Hidalgo square as a present to [Mazatlán's] society. (El correo de la tarde, 23 May 1901)

According to the frequently published comments on popular entertainment, the working class was especially fond of band music:

The suppliers contracted the Banda del Quelite directed by Mr. Terríquez. (El correo de la tarde, 5 March 1899)

There was a strictly private fiesta at the Market where many families met to dance to the tunes of the Banda del Quelite. (El correo de la tarde, 10 April 1899)

The management of the Fundición de Sinaloa [foundry] contracted the banda Quelite to play during working hours in front of the factory. (El correo de la tarde, 12 April 1899)

New bands were formed as response to an increasing demand for musical entertainment in the city as well as in the surrounding villages: "The banda del Venadillo, which was recently founded in the village Venadillo under the direction of Mr. Valente Vélez, who had been a senior musician of the band of the 17th battalion, gave a very pleasing debut yesterday in the port. If Tiburcio's musicians don't make an effort, the peasants will soon leave them in the dust" (El correo de la tarde, 11 February 1901). The commentator referred to the Banda Rosales, organized by Tiburcio Navarro, a brother of the orchestra leader and composer Enrique Navarro. The band consisted of young craftsmen and gave its debut in November 1900. Interestingly, it was emphasized that the musicians wore special uniforms (*El correo de la tarde*, 28 November 1900).

Comments on popular music bands appeared with more frequency, especially in the months of September (Independence Day) and February (carnival). Mazatlán's boisterous carnival celebrations had become an irresistible attraction for the popular masses, urban and rural alike. Since noise had been an ingrained part of carnivalesque revelry, it was only natural that the bands of the surrounding villages would participate in the urban feast.

Masked Balls and Carnival Celebrations

Carnival was brought to the Americas by the Spanish and Portuguese colonizers.[39] Later the English, the French, and the Dutch colonized the smaller Caribbean islands and introduced their ways of celebrating the pre-Lenten season.[40]

The Spanish and Portuguese carnival celebrations lacked the finesse of the French and Italian masked parades, although in Cádiz, for example, the bourgeoisie and aristocracy borrowed traits from the Italian carnival of the sixteenth and seventeenth centuries, in particular the patrician practices of Genoa and Venice (Mintz 1997: xvi). Thus, in early eighteenth-century Spain, carnival developed on two distinct planes: as a fête of splendor, fancy decorum, balls, and operas held at the theater and in the private homes of the upper classes, and as a rowdy and disorderly party celebrated by the lower classes on the streets. Despite the prosecution of misconduct such as obscene dancing, sexually offensive displays, and mockery of religious, military, and political authorities, popular revelry continued to be quite tumultuous. Passersby were affronted and humiliated by various forms of mischief: standing on the balconies, revelers tossed buckets of water, threw flour bombs, or swung sacks of sand to knock off the hats of men strolling on the streets below. Since the crews of ships traveling between the Spanish ports and the New World came from the lower classes, these raucous carnival practices were imported to all the colonies.

As in other Latin American countries, popular carnival revelry in Mexico was primarily confined to the port cities on the east coast: Veracruz, Tampico, and Mérida. The center of the country was less directly affected by customs of the lower-class Europeans. However, street revelries were so exuberant in the capital in the 1830s that church authorities felt compelled to issue an edict prohibiting masquerades. They even threatened to excommunicate the disobedient. Although the police backed the church, they could not halt the people's masked revelry during Lent (see Widenmann and Hauff 1837: 305–307). By the early 1840s, the upper class apparently had withdrawn from the public festivities and left the theaters to the middle class.[41]

The development of pre-Lenten festivities in nineteenth-century Mazatlán parallels that of other Latin American and Caribbean celebrations. It seems that carnival celebrations in Mazatlán originated in the late eighteenth century among the black and mulatto soldiers stationed in the Presidio de Mazatlán (Olea 1985).[42] At that time, Mazatlán consisted of only a few huts. By 1804 Mazatlán had grown into a village of two thousand inhabitants, of whom one-third were white and two-thirds black or mulatto. Thus, it is conceivable, as Rafael Valdéz Aguilar (1993: 13) has argued, that blacks and mulattoes had a significant impact on the regional music, songs, dances, and carnivalesque festivities.

In 1823 the unloading of a shipment of foreign merchandise was not allowed because the government had prohibited high seas commerce during the carnival season. The following year, one could hear a verse related to this event. It became popular when it was used by the squadron stationed in the port to request payment of their salary in 1827 (Olea 1985):

Los papaquis son aquí	The *papaquis* are here
y no serán más adelante	and they won't be on ahead
porque dicen que aquí vive	because it is said that here lives
la mujer del Comandante.	the wife of the commander.

As in other port cities of the continent, sailors and foreign settlers played a crucial role in the formation of local customs. According to Riensch (1960: 77), one of the entertainments of the young German entrepreneurs in the 1840s was the so-called *Jerum*, an imitation of the popular carnival song of Cologne that included all kinds of jaunty foolishness.[43] As in early nineteenth-century Germany, where the civil carnival was mainly a matter of bachelors who liked to get into all kinds of mischief, Riensch and his friends introduced some of these carnival practices into Mazatlán's society. However, it seems that this kind of merriment was practiced not only during the pre-Lenten season. In general, carnivalesque gaiety and masked balls were common during the rest of the year as well. Riensch and other contemporary observers affirmed that in those years, Mazatlán's citizens were very sociable and amusements were plentiful. Carnival even took place in 1848 during the American occupation of the port.[44]

As on the Caribbean islands and in Brazil in the mid-1800s, the upper classes began to retreat from the street revelry to enjoy carnival as an indoor event fashioned around masquerade balls, house parties, and social club affairs. An American visitor to the port in 1856 noticed that the better classes of Mazatlán held private masked balls at the hotel:

Balls and evening parties and dinners are quite common in Mazatlán, and I have been much rejoiced to see the gayety and life manifested on such occasions. Shortly after my

arrival in this city [on 25 February 1856], I attended a masquerade ball at the French Hotel, where I have remained since my disembarkation. This ball was composed of nearly
fifty couples and a goodly number of spectators, among whom I was; they had passable
music, a rich repast at twelve o'clock, and then resumed the dance till broad day-light.
Several policemen were stationed about the house to preserve good order,—and the
head of the city police was in attendance at the ball, clad in his insignia of office, a military coat and hat with a sword suspended by his side. (Wheat 1857: 86)

The history of carnival in Mazatlán is better documented toward the end of the
nineteenth century because some of the affluent began actually to participate in
popular carnival celebrations—a behavior, however, that was not approved of
by all notables.[45] Though the upper class in general withdrew from carnival and
the newspapers disapproved of it, a new social order was in the making, one
which found affective expression in carnival. In an attempt to control the carnivalesque excesses of the proletarian revelers, the city councils passed new laws.
Regardless of these prohibitions, the masses continued to celebrate carnival as
it was accustomed to for another two decades. In Mazatlán, the elite eventually
appropriated the revelry in 1898 by making it "official."

Because urbanization was a recent phenomenon in late-nineteenth-century
Sinaloa, carnival was a mixture between rural and urban fiesta. For one week
every year, the jubilant and ecstatic masses conquered the public space. Although members of the upper classes engaged in carnival celebrations, they
believed that they still distinguished themselves from the common people,
because "among the high society, the amusement does not manifest the vices
that can be noted in the madness of the people" (El correo de la tarde, 15 February 1893). Generally, popular carnival celebrations were criticized as "sanctioned public excess disguised by masks." As advocates of "the public morality," some well-to-do families requested that masked balls be abolished because "this excess of evil passions" spoiled not only their servants' morale, but
also the youths' purity. Their worries were repeatedly voiced in Mazatlán's
newspapers.[46]

But masked balls were only one of carnival's manifestations. The real thorn
in the notables' side was the so-called juego de harina, in which opposite parties
would throw eggshells filled with flour at each other. In the opinion of the
urban notables, the flour game corrupted the morale of the common people,
whose amusement allegedly became more boisterous each year—"a barbarous
game that causes much annoyance and even misfortune, especially among the
people from the villages" (El correo de la tarde, 27 January 1893).

The flour battle was in fact a source of violent conflict, since it was the preferred game of rivaling neighborhood gangs: La Pólvora (the factory work-

ers) versus El Hueso (the suppliers) in Culiacán, and El Muelle (the dock-workers) versus El Abasto (the suppliers) in Mazatlán. The street encounters between the two parties were planned beforehand. Barricades were erected from which the disguised opponents attacked each other verbally and with eggshells filled with colored paper, flour, ink, ashes, or even less innocuous material. The verbal compositions of the mock battles, ranging from parodies to travesties to obscene insults, and the accompanying music were called *papaquis*. Under the influence of alcohol and stirred up by the *papaquis*, these encounters had a potential for violence. Indeed, what started out as mock battles fought with words and eggshells would often turn into bloody combats in which stones and sticks were used to harm the opponents and with the police interfering in a brutal manner. Mazatlán's daily newspaper summarized the last "unofficial" carnival laconically: "Carnival is over. The flour has just dispersed from the atmosphere, but it will take more time for the bellicose notes of the popular bands which make a profound impression on the ears to completely die away" (*El correo de la tarde*, 6 March 1897). Launched by the Porfirian establishment in Mazatlán, the Junta Patriótica aimed at organizing an orderly carnival by disciplining the *pelados* of the two rivaling parties and by prohibiting the most popular attractions of the festival: the mockery and the flour battles. The reaction of the populace was hotheaded. There was a rumor that *los del muelle* [the dockworkers] intended to blow up the municipal market, the symbol of Mazatlán's economic progress (Rodríguez 1997: 13).

Despite this fierce response and much to the people's regret, the *juego de harina* was eventually prohibited by decree in 1898, the flour replaced by confetti and streamers. The spontaneous exuberance of the popular carnival was transformed into a graceful spectacle, organized by the social elite and observed by the masses.[47] Except for the parades of floats of decorated carriages and masquerades, the now-official carnival resembled the celebrations of civic holidays, including regattas, enactments of the 1866 naval combats between the French and the Mazatlecos, artillery salvos, firecrackers, and fireworks. Kings and queens were elected by a carnival committee consisting of respectable citizens. The coronation of the queen, a privilege given only to the "distinguished young ladies of the city," was primarily an upper-class spectacle held in Culiacán's elegant Teatro Apolo and in Mazatlán's Teatro Rubio, respectively.[48] The popular *papaquis* continued to reverberate:

Por aquí pasó la muerte	Death passed here
con su aguja y su dedal	with its needle and its thimble
preguntando, ¿dónde vive	asking: where does
la reina del carnaval?	the queen of the carnival live?

Once a licensed and sanctioned affair, carnival no longer undermined the authorities. Rather, it became a form of social control of the subordinate by the ruling elite and thus served the interests of the very official culture it apparently opposed. Although the world still might have appeared to be turned upside down during carnival, the fact that kings and queens were chosen and crowned actually reaffirmed the status quo—even more so because the candidates were chosen from among the elite only.

After the success of the first official carnival in 1898, the committee planned the following year with much enthusiasm and rigor. Instead of "punches, drunkenness, high expenses for flour, and headaches," carnival was to be celebrated in a "good and healthy way" and in "peace and harmony" (El correo de la tarde, 26 November 1898). House-to-house visiting, street promenading in decorated carriages, and musical entertainment by military bands completed the "new carnival," which was characterized by fancy court dress. The street masquerade was under control: those who wanted to wear a mask had to ask for prior permission. Everybody in possession of a noisemaker was invited to participate in the monstrous parade. The noisy revelry, however, was limited to a few hours.

Mazatlán's professional musicians—the military band and the orchestras of Enrique Navarro and Eligio Mora—participated in the parade of 1899 masked and disguised as animals. Among the sumptuous allegorical floats inspired by progressive and republican ideas, the float "Entierro de la harina" [The Burial of the Flour] with the two banners of war of the now-vanished parties "El Muelle" and "El Abasto" paraded through the streets.[49]

Dance and music were central to carnival celebrations. Unfortunately, most newspaper comments refer to dance and music in general terms only—that is, without describing or specifying them. What kind of bandas populares produced that warlike sound? What did these energetic popular dances look like? What kind of ensemble was the banda de música that performed the merriest pieces of its repertory? Who were the musicians strolling through the streets during the early morning hours?[50] Was it the military band, as on other occasions, or was it a popular band from one of the surrounding villages?[51]

It was not until the turn of the century that a village band and its director's name were mentioned repeatedly in one of Mazatlán's newspapers.[52] Somewhat detached but well disposed, one of the reporters commented on the happenings on Mazatlán's main plaza where Banda del Quelite was entertaining the cheerful crowd: "The Plaza Colón appeared in a very extraordinary way as one would watch the popular dance event in the plaza . . . . The steps, the platforms, and the railings were entirely occupied by spectators in a good mood. . . . In the square, they were dancing to the sound of the music of the powerful [banda from] Quelite, and masks appeared from everywhere."[53] It seems that at the beginning of the twentieth century, Banda del Quelite was firmly established in Mazatlán. Newspaper reporters noted its arrival and departure and acknowledged its performances. When it visited Mazatlán during the patriotic festivities in 1900, the band's name was mentioned in the same sentence as that of the renowned military band: "The band of the 17th Battalion played in the Plaza Machado, that from Quelite in the Plaza Hidalgo. . . . The night of the 15th, the banda del Quelite strolled through the streets of the city, playing in front of some houses the best pieces of its repertory" (El correo de la tarde, 17 September 1900). The village band had conquered the bandstand, thus, winning a major battle—it was finally acknowledged by the social elite (here represented by the newspaper reporter): "It must have been around ten at night when a banda assaulted the bandstand. Since the fortress is suffering under deterioration, not much effort was needed to take control of it. Combative sounds and loud drumbeats announced the triumph of the war-inured musicians" (El correo de la tarde, 17 February 1904).

These documents indicate that the upper classes, at least, had started to become aware of the people's cultural expressions. In the opinion of the elite, the tambora was still only a shabby imitation of their sophisticated military bands. They were not yet able to hear that the popular bands had made this music their own, investing it with a new and lasting identity. It would still take many decades for Sinaloa to recognize its own cultural resources and take pride in its regional band music.

Musical Entertainment in the Countryside

While newspaper commentaries and travel reports offer a sketchy picture of urban life and musical entertainment, primary source material on music in nineteenth-century rural communities is very meager. However, it seems that toward the end of the century brass bands and ensembles with violin, guitar, and accordion had become a prominent and ubiquitous feature of Sinaloa's musical life. Since at that time all music was necessarily live music, people in rural areas had far fewer opportunities than city people to hear professionally played music.

In isolated villages and towns, the band was one of the few recreational organizations available to townsmen. These people were more or less illiterate and hence did not leave written records of their thoughts and life experiences: their legacy was as elusive as their bands were ephemeral. Once again, we have to satisfy ourselves with accounts from outside observers to learn about rural musical tradition. One of the most detailed descriptions of life and customs in the Sierra Madre Occidental was written by John R. Flippin, an American mining engineer who spent five years in Guadalupe y Calvo, Chihuahua. He noted: "The games in this section of the country are limited in number. The classes of amusements are few, and inferior in quality. . . . Here there are no theaters and operas. The love for them may indicate high culture, but these mountains are too high for such aesthetic entertainments" (1889: 248–249). Indeed, Guadalupe y Calvo, situated in the heart of the Sierra at an altitude of 2,400 meters, was quite isolated. The nearest large cities were Parral, three hundred kilometers away to the northeast, and Culiacán, three hundred kilometers to the south. There were only trails on which this mining town could be reached, and one had to travel on foot or mounted on mules. Despite the distance from urban culture, Flippin observed:

Here all classes are fond of music. I might truthfully say, inordinately fond of it. There is scarcely a village but that has one or two bands, and there is scarcely a week but on one or two occasions they do not parade the streets and make the welkin ring with their music and noisy demonstrations. Like the brass band everywhere it draws to itself in its march all the straggling loafers in town, not excepting the inevitable small boy, who either heads or skirts the procession in its aimless marches and countermarches. Their open air soirees, with their attendant crowds, present in dress and appearance a grotesque sight. Some Mexican, with a few dollars in his pocket, gets drunk and he immediately wants a band of music to go up and down the streets and stop in front of the houses and stores and play for glory, the glory of his being drunk! It is then or never he relaxes his purse strings, and his soul floats out on the wings of the song, or it finds its heaven in a band of music. Night and day he will keep up the performance, and keep the village awake until his funds are exhausted, or music no longer soothes his tired nature. The authorities of the place seem to catch the spirit of the occasion, and however annoying and detrimental it may be to others, they never think of abating the sweet nuisance. Liquor of some kind generally starts the *trouble*, keeps it alive until it dies from sheer exhaustion after the lapse of some days. In the meantime it must be borne by all as the free musical treat of some eccentric drunken villager. Sometimes I have almost wished for the power to abolish brass bands, even at the risk of incurring the charge that I was "fit for treasons, stratagems and spoils". (1889: 149–150)

Brass instruments were not only able to carry a melody, they were also loud and durable, and therefore ideal for outdoor performances. Technical improvements in the manufacture of brass instruments in the 1840s were the principal reason for the evolution of instrumental-ensemble music making outside the professional, middle-, and upper-class environment in which such activity had previously been centered. Valve mechanisms made it possible for amateur players to master the instruments after practicing for a short time. Moreover, most of the brass instruments could be played interchangeably with similar mouth-

INSTRUMENTOS DE MUSICA

TROMBONES
CONTRABAJOS
BARITONOS
TENORES
ALTOS
CONTRALTOS
CORNETINES
TAROLAS
FLAUTAS
CLARINETES
REQUINTOS
GUITARRAS
VIOLINES

LOS MEJORES
PRECIOS DE PLAZA

FCO. ECHEGUREN Y CIA. SUCS. Mazatlán

10. Advertisement for musical instruments in Mazatlán's daily
newspaper El *correo de la tarde* (1926). Photo by Helena Simonett.

pieces and identical fingerings, and thus could be shared among bandsmen according to the needs of the ensemble.[54]

Mazatlán's important foreign merchant houses had established retail stores in the smaller market towns, where they sold mass-produced imported instruments at attractive prices and allowed purchase through installment payments.[55] As instruments became easier to obtain and less expensive, the number of bands in rural areas multiplied.

There is no evidence that early bands relied upon municipal patronage. Rather, these bands were small, independent, and self-governed amateur organizations that controlled their own business. Playing in a band was not only a leisure activity but also an opportunity to earn an additional peso. Hardly any of these instrumentalists were musically literate and, thus, aural musical practice dominated. Musicians memorized entire pieces of music or learned simple harmonic patterns and played *ad libitum* to support the melodic lines. Because the musical conventions of village bands were generated within this "plebeian" musical tradition, educated outsiders such as Flippin necessarily perceived the village band music as "annoying" and "detrimental." Perhaps aware of his harsh judgment, Flippin added later: "I don't think I undervalue music and its harmonizing influences. . . . But a Mexican can make too much of a good thing out of the best thing, by heroically overdosing at inopportune intervals his surfeited listeners" (1889: 251).

Village brass bands were not a direct offshoot of military bands, but rather a group of locals who would chose their instruments, repertory, and engagements according to their own preferences and abilities, and who played what the local audience demanded. Despite "cultured" people's complaints about the continuing "noise," the economic survival of such bands probably depended much on "eccentric drunken villagers." The custom of hiring a band to stroll through the streets and get drunk, as described by Flippin, is still practiced by Sinaloans with rural and working-class backgrounds.

Both the settings and the band itself, with its powerful instrumentation, were indisputably the men's domain. "The men take to the violin and brass band, the noise from the latter of which we seldom fail to hear in the busy hours of the day or the tranquil hours of the night." Girls were taught softer instruments, if any: "The cultured young ladies discourse sweet music with guitar and harp" (Flippin 1889: 251). One of the amusements in rural areas in which both genders would engage was popular dance:

If there is one thing which the Mexican enjoys more than another it is the dance. . . . He looks upon life as one great big frolic, to be filled up with Mescal, music and dancing, and the end of life as some elysian ball-room where he may sip heavenly Mescal and dance the eternities away. . . . Sometimes they will begin a dance here in the evening, continue it all night, the next day and the next night, rest a few hours, and continue it until everybody is broken down, and nature refuses to take another step. They generally commence these dances on Sundays. . . . The music continues unbroken during the long hours, and until the campaign is ended the little fiddles and big fiddles, the little horns and big horn are tortured for their harmonies. They spend their money freely for the music, for this wafts them towards the ecstatic land. (Flippin 1889: 255–256)

There were few opportunities for relaxation and recreation, but celebrations were held whenever a pretext existed. Festivities with music and dance helped to break the monotony of everyday life. *Fandangos*, bull- and cockfights, horse racing, gaming, and drinking seem to have been common diversions on weekends in villages and towns. In the 1850s, a Prussian traveler witnessed such an occasion in Pánuco, a silver mine in southern Sinaloa: "The day we arrived was a Sunday, and the miners, having received their week's wages, were enjoying themselves in crowds on the *plaza*, where, as is common in Mexico, music, drinking, and eating-shops had been established by the owner of the mine, in order that the money laid out by him in wages might return to him, before the new week commenced" (Tempsky 1858: 22). Near the end of the nineteenth century, Owen W. Gillpatrick, a reporter for the *Mexican Herald*, spent two years traveling in Mexico, including the mountains of northwestern Mexico. He reported on his stay in San Dimas, Durango (on the border with Sinaloa), at that time a mining town of 1,200 inhabitants. Like other larger settlements, San Dimas was the center of festivities for people living in the surrounding pueblos and on the mountain ranches. Holidays attracted well-to-do families and working people alike. Gillpatrick, invited to attend Christmas Eve celebrations, noted admiringly: "It was hard to realize we were five days from the railroad. . . . The music was excellent. The favorite dances were waltz, polka, schottische and the Mexican danza. The latter, which is also known as the 'love dance,' is thoroughly characteristic" (1911: 324). When the party was over, the musicians accompanied the remaining participants to the square, where they would strike up a last waltz and continue to play until the last couple was out of sight. Gillpatrick had also observed this "pretty and complimentary custom" in smaller villages (1911: 324–327).

Gillpatrick observed, in addition to hurdy-gurdies, a string band playing for both the outdoor concert on the plaza and midnight mass at church, though he unfortunately failed to describe either instrumentation or music. He presumed that the piano he saw on a wealthy hacienda, three hours' ride from town, was "the only one on that side of Mazatlán, [and] was carried all the way from the coast on the shoulders of peones."

San Dimas could not boast a theater. If a touring opera company stopped in town, a stage would be set up on the street. The spectators had to bring their own chairs, but, according to Gillpatrick, "primitive comforts by no means interfere[d] with their enjoyment." Like other travelers, Gillpatrick noted the absence of lavish entertainment in rural areas.

Unfortunately, comments on popular music making are not only scarce, but also do not reveal much about the music itself. Who were the musicians? What instruments did they play? How did the music sound? Although these questions cannot be answered conclusively, memoires and official documents allow us at least a glimpse of nineteenth-century musical life in urban and rural Sinaloa, banda music's spawning ground.

Music in the Center,
Music on the Periphery

Se fue con el mariachi, me dejó
se fue con él que toca el guitarrón
porque lo que ella quiso no canté
como le canta ahora el barrigón.
José Luis Quiñones, Banda Degollado

When I told my friend's family who accommodated me in Mexico City that I was going to do research on banda music, they asked, somewhat embarrassed: "Why don't you study some *nice* Mexican music such as mariachi?" Evidently banda music was not to their taste. One of the musicians of Mariachi Los Camperos in Los Angeles reacted similarly when I explained that I was very much interested in banda music. He jokingly imitated a typical quebradita gesture and shook his head while smiling at me with pity. His opinion of banda music was not very high: why would anybody want to study such vulgar, low-class music?

Unlike mariachi, Mexico's national folk music, banda has never been considered an object of folklorists' study, although it was, like mariachi, the musical expression of a rural population. In fact, both regional ensembles, mariachi from Jalisco and banda from Sinaloa, originated in villages and small towns during the nineteenth century; both mariachi and banda musicians were *campesinos* in the first place; both interpreted *sones*, regional tunes, and other popular songs; and both ensembles included European as well as locally manufactured instruments. Thus the questions arise: Why was banda music so persistently ignored by folklorists? Why was banda excluded from their interest in "folk culture"? Whenever and wherever Mexico nowadays presents herself, there is a mariachi ensemble accompanying the event. How could mariachi overcome its social stigma of being a lower-class music? Why did mariachi, which was only one of many regional styles, succeed and eventually become ac-knowledged as "national music"? Why was mariachi better suited to represent Mexico than banda, even though they share a similar history and a similar musical repertory? What other musical factors played a role in mariachi's triumph? Why has it been so difficult for banda to gain recognition? How have changing economic and social relations and the music industry affected the development of both mariachi and banda?

As shown in the previous chapter, the nineteenth-century writing elite consigned people's expressive cultural forms in general, and musical creations in particular, to a notion of the primitive. This chapter will develop that argument in a slightly different direction by focusing on the sociohistorical development of both regional ensembles in the early twentieth century and, in particular, on the relationship between "folk music" and nationalism. Socially confined notions of culture were intrinsic to the consolidation of a class-based society, and they continued to be determining for modern Mexico, where a people's culture came to represent the nation-state.

Music and National Identity

Like other Latin American nations after independence, Mexico went through a painful process of detaching herself from peninsular influences. The *criollos* [Mexicans born to Spanish parents] denied their peninsular heritage in order to forge a new government and a new society. Yet, the upper classes continued to enjoy a musical life dominated by Italian opera and lighter musical theater, including such Spanish-derived genres as *zarzuelas, tonadillas escénicas,* and *sainetes,* as well as songs and romantic piano music. It was not until the last decades of the nineteenth century that a definable Mexican national style emerged (Béhague 1979: 96–101).

Mexicans' struggle to affirm their own cultural and political identity led them to turn to their "folk" and folklore in order to differentiate their national heritage from other nation-states. Like that of other countries, Mexico's national character was modeled from traditional cultural practices of the peasantry. The large, basically unlettered rural population, however, presented a potentially embarrassing contrast to the ideal image of the emerging *mexicano* which the political leaders and the dominant classes had in mind. Thus, the national character needed some correction, and eventually an articulated set of stereotypes was constructed from images that the elite had formed of the life styles of the peasant and the worker. As Roger Bartra has pointed out, "[T]he new nationalism that sprang from the Revolution employed the same figure of the *pelado,* but now as a revolutionary symbol" (1992: 93). The "vulgar Mestizo" had been transformed into the "superior Mestizo," the personification of

Mexicanness. Similarly, peasant music was so separate from the cultural attitudes of Mexico City's elites that the *sonecitos de la tierra*, the little national tunes, had to be harmonized and performed on the piano to please the ear of the "educated" urban audience.[1]

On a continental scale, Mexico still belonged to a peripheral zone, which means Mexico's upper classes were oriented toward what they viewed as the cultural center and tried to imitate cultural forms developed in those centers. Among the Mexican upper class, France was considered the archetype of modern civilization. Thus, the culture of the Mexican metropolis and the provincial cities was a distant echo of nineteenth-century France. According to Frances Toor, during the regime of Porfirio Díaz (1877–1911), "no one paid any attention to folk art, songs or dances" (1930: 33). The social elite and a growing prosperous upper-middle class self-consciously copied European modes of dress, education, and even language. The Mexican philosopher Samuel Ramos summarized: "The spiritual influence reaches its height in the epoch of Porfirio Díaz, when the cultured classes dressed according to the Parisian vogue and imitated its good and bad customs. . . . To be a cultured person knowledge of the French language was a *sine-qua-non* condition. The Mexican atmosphere was saturated with French ideas, to the point where domestic realities were ignored" (1962: 53).

Mazatlán's notables, too, had adopted more polished manners; they cultivated self-control and a sense of style that was influenced by European royal models. They had changed not only their behavior but also their language; and they stopped eating common beans and tortillas and dined instead on *volaille braisée aux champignons* and *haricots*.[2]

Mexico's upper classes and those who aspired to move upward socially were torn between adapting a "sophisticated European culture" and feeling pride in their own native culture. A large number of pianist-composers cultivated salon-music genres such as waltzes, polkas, mazurkas, and schottisches.[3] As the very concept of nationalism in the arts stemmed from European romanticism, it was with these romantic pianists that the very first vernacular elements appeared in Mexican music.

In the early twentieth century, Mexico's composers trained in the European classical tradition "discovered" the ancient Aztec legacy. They began to integrate not only reconstructed Aztec music but also mestizo folk idioms into their compositions.[4] Far from resembling the people's *sones* and *jarabes*, these nationalistic works were essentially stylized arrangements of popular material. Nevertheless, the composers' interest in people's music was seminal for the consolidation of folk elements and the establishment of folk styles.

The idea of a "Mexican nation" came from the intellectual leaders, and it was imposed on the people with whom they desired to identify. Members of the upper classes fostered their national consciousness by imitating the peasantry, wearing an urban version of the *charro* and *china* costumes.[5] To many nationalists, the rustic and the natural—free from the rules of European upper-class elitism—seemed very appealing. The attempts of nineteenth-century composers to integrate Mexican folk tunes into operettas as well as those of the "nationalistic composers" of the early twentieth century to trace their ancient Aztec heritage have to be seen in this light. Only a few intellectuals recognized the picturesque dimension of such national display. Ramos, for example, criticized: "But this Mexico of the *charro* and the Mexico of the *china poblana*, as well as the Mexico of the legendary savage . . . constitute a Mexico for export which is just as false as the romantic Spain of the tambourine" (1962: 103). As elsewhere, the discovery of the people and its cultural expressions was closely associated with the rise of nationalism. The emergence of folklore scholarship in Mexico was intimately related to the romantic nationalist movement that followed the Revolution of 1910. The image of folk tradition created in Europe was pursued by Mexican intellectuals. Their notions of "folk music" and "folk dance" carried implications of romantic, nationalist ideologies such as the following: "In the fiestas of our peasantry, like those in any part of the world, I recognize the simple life style of the laborers who sing and dance with noble souls. In the charro I recognize a graceful man, and the white breast of the china poblana wins my love" (Alfredo Ramos Espinosa, introduction to Campos 1946: viii). The musicologist Daniel Castañeda distinguished between two different types of Mexican music: the spontaneous expression of the rural population—the folk—and the conscious creation of educated urban men: "Until 1910, Mexican music—*Mexican in its ideology and in its form*—had been *a direct product of the sentiment of the people*, an exclusive manifestation of the humble classes. . . . Mexican music pours out of the fields, slides along the mountains, emerges from the small villages, takes shelter in our villages, hides in the provincial cities, and appears from time to time—stealthily—in our capital cities; but never before 1910 . . . does it emerge *as a creation* among the cultivated musicians of our cities as well as in the Republic's capital" (1941: 438–439).

According to Otto Mayer-Serra, mestizo folk music "is the most representative and most consistent expression of Mexican music." It is determined by three factors: two "external" (folk music of neighboring, migratory, or immigrant people, and art music) and one "internal" (particular methods of interpretation):

The "Mexicanness" of Mexican folk music should not be sought in the substance formed by what we have called "external" elements, often of inferior quality. . . . What produces the characteristic, unmistakable Mexican, flavor is primarily the method of interpretation. If ever a compilation of Mexican folk music is made, it will have to include not only all the elements that go to make up the interpretation (voices, instrumental parts, stamping, clapping, ejaculations, etc.), but particularly its phonetic peculiarities. Only the description of this atmosphere, never the mere transcription of the melodic line, will be able to convey an authentic picture approximating as nearly as possible the emotional and sound content of Mexican music. If the Spanish model reacts on certain aspects of the general musical and choreographic interpretation (effects on harmonic resonances on the guitar, juxtaposition of binary and ternary rhythms, tendency to create several harmonic planes), other aspects derive from a completely different combination, such as the composition of the *mariachi* band, the special technique of its violins and guitars, its sustained syncopated basses, the piercing sonority of its trumpet (a recent addition) and the way in which the brasses of the village band play slightly off pitch. (1946: 29–30)

At the root of the concept of uniting nation and musical style was the idea that a nation's folk music was bound to reflect the inner characteristics of that nation's culture, the essential aspects of its emotional life—its very self. Mexican musicologists and folklorists of an earlier generation invariably pointed out that the essence of Mexico's inner self—*el alma mexicana*, as they put it—was to be found in the nation's folk traditions. The Sinaloan folklorist Alfredo Ibarra, for instance, noted: "There are various roads to arrive at the soul of the people. One is through their sentiments which are expressed through dances, melodies, or in verses" (1944: 71); and "Folk music brings to light the people's character. The Sinaloans are gay, dynamic, and of great melodious feeling" (1960: 316). Musical expressions have often been used by scholars to make assumptions about the psychological disposition of the peasantry as a whole. Among intellectuals, such assumptions were, and continue to be, a premise of their romantic, bucolic view of the other. The Sinaloan scholar Héctor R. Olea, for instance, postulated: "At every peasant fiesta, the simple hearts of the people swell up in boundless delight when 'the Tambora' reverberates. The magic of the primitive sound captivates them. . . . 'The Tambora,' in its folkloric sense, is a music traditional in Sinaloa which was born in the womb of the *pueblo*, where it existed for centuries nourished from its spirit, and where it keeps the emotions of the people's subconscious afloat" (1985: n.p.).

Tradition is often defined as what is given to the present from the past. On the other hand, revolution, by definition, breaks with the past. It is therefore somewhat paradoxical that Mexico's revolutionary leaders believed that a specifically Mexican culture could be developed only on the basis of the traditions of the peasantry. Yet, the attachment to some past state or condition is pervasive in all nationalistic movements, and innovations are backed up by reference to a "people's past" (see Shils 1981: 209–212; Hobsbawm 1983: 13). Although the Mexican Revolution "uncovered a false Mexico, imitative of Europe and led by the Frenchified regime of Porfirianism," as Ramos had noted, "before the Revolution was over, the return to native values was corrupted by a false nationalism symbolized in the Mexican horseman and festive dresses à la china poblana" (1962: 176).

Existing traditional practices were modified and institutionalized for the new nationalism. The reason for selecting folk dances as one of "the traditions" was intimately linked to the political motivation of establishing a collective symbol of identity.[6] Folk dances were especially suitable for representing Mexico's regional diversity—a few distinctive steps with the corresponding typical attire were enough to characterize a regional dance—while simultaneously demonstrating the nation's unique character. Efforts were made to develop an "official" folklore that would help blur regional differences so as to create a more integrated society. The mariachi was established as the national musical ensemble. Cultural missionaries were sent out by the government to study and collect folk songs and dances throughout Mexico. The main task of folklorists was the codification and exhibition of the national folk heritage—in short, the creation of tradition awareness. The state increased its role in musical education through special programs. Toor noticed that in the 1920s the jarabe received special attention: "The Ministry of Education is establishing a new department of esthetic calisthenics in which folk dances will be taught and new ones worked out with the steps of Indian dances from all parts of the country serving as a foundation" (1930: 34). Folklore tradition was, and has remained, institutionalized, supported, and controlled to a large extent by the government. Folk dances were used to mobilize society for national goals and were preferably displayed at manifestations on national holidays such as Independence Day and Cinco de Mayo, as well as at other public events.

Mariachi: National Folk Music

Because mariachi has been considered Mexico's folk music par excellence, it has also been subject to the various ideologies folklorists have cultivated over the course of more than a century. Most of the literature on mariachi makes a distinction between the authentic folk mariachi and the commercial urban mariachi. "There are actually two kinds of mariachi band in Mexico," Geijerstam observed: "The original mariachi, consisting of string instruments only, belongs to the realm of folk music. String mariachi bands are still to be found in the countryside of central Mexico. Around 1940 a commercial type of mariachi began to develop, primarily in the cities. . . . In the last few decades the folk music mariachi has nearly disappeared, and the mariachi has come to belong almost exclusively to the field of commercial music in Mexico" (1976: 41–42). Shortly after the commercial style of mariachi began to develop, Toor observed a decay of the folk mariachi and lamented that "unfortunately, this popularity is degenerating the type of music the mariachis play" (1947: 307). Such comments are not surprising in the light of folklore studies from the first half of the twentieth century, when folklorists began to notice the effect of industrialization on the life style of the peasantry, regarded as the main carrier of tradition. It was feared that folk music would soon vanish and be lost forever if not perpetuated and rescued for the future. In accordance with prevailing notions of folk music and national cultural heritage, critics condemned contemporary innovations in mariachi music fervently.[7]

Paradoxically, while scholars deplored innovations that turned the "folk mariachi" into a commercial commodity in the 1930s and the following decades, mariachi succeeded in becoming internationally known as "the folk music of Mexico." Books, dissertations, and countless articles have since been published about mariachi music; newspapers print supplements on Cinco de Mayo with information on the history of mariachi and its importance for Mexican society. How could mariachi become such a highly regarded national symbol and how did this public acknowledgment affect the music itself?

"De Cocula es el mariachi, de Tecalitlán los sones" [The mariachi ensemble is from Cocula, the tunes are from Tecalitlán (both villages in Jalisco)] is a familiar quotation explaining where the ensemble and its music originated. During the early nineteenth century, in the villages and towns in the state of Jalisco, the instruments most commonly used to perform mestizo music consisted of a harp, a *guitarra de golpe*, and one or two violins. The ensembles became known as mariache or mariachi.[8] Nevertheless, there was no generally agreed upon designation of the mariachi ensemble until the beginning of the twentieth century, when indigenous musicians began to migrate to Mexico City. As the ensemble began to be more peripatetic, the *guitarrón* replaced the harp, since it could more conveniently be carried through the streets as the musicians looked for customers willing to hire them; it also supplied the ensemble with a stronger bass, and since it could be tuned to a variety of scales, it had a larger repertory.[9]

The first known mariachi performance in the capital was given in 1905 by the Conjunto Coculense de Justo Villa, a quartet from Cocula (Urrutia de Vázquez and Saldaña 1982: 454).[10] The musicians were brought to Mexico City for the celebration of President Porfirio Díaz's birthday and Mexico's Independence Day. According to Rafael Méndez Moreno, the quartet was admired "not only for the joy, emotion, and uniqueness of their *sones, corridos,* and *canciones*; but for . . . the unusual, folkloric appearance of their native garb: large straw *sombreros* with chin strap and hat band; red *poncho* or black wool blanket over the shoulder; long, baggy, straight-cut muslin pants; cotton shirt of the same material; red sash around the waist; and simple *huarache* sandals" (1961: 132–133). Actually, the musicians were dressed like ordinary peasants, except for the black wool blanket and the red sash around the waist, added in order to spruce up the outfit for the celebration.

When it became clear that Porfirio Díaz intended to give democracy no more than lip service, Mexican liberals decided that the only hope of improving Mexico was through armed revolt. Under Francisco I. Madero, small guerrilla groups from northern Mexico began to defeat federal troops, initiating the Mexican Revolution in 1910. What began as a simple political movement broadened into a major economic and social upheaval, bringing together "Mexican people" from all social classes. The postrevolutionary period was characterized by the rise of a strong national identity. The mestizos came to form a part of the longed-for "national spirit," and through them popular music experienced a renewed vigor (Urrutia de Vázquez and Saldaña 1982: 451).

During the 1920s, various mariachis arrived in the capital. Mariachi de Cirilo Marmolejo, for example, was invited by Luis Rodríguez Sánchez, a physician from Cocula and at the time director of Mexico's public health administration. He wanted a mariachi group to play for some evening parties in Mexico City. Rodríguez introduced the musicians into the new aristocracy of "revolutionary capitalists," many of whom shared the essentially rural, working-class background of Marmolejo and his mariachis.[11] Although some mariachi ensembles found affluent benefactors in the city for whom they played from time to time, most of them were less lucky.

Despite the revolution and its ideas of social equality, mariachi musicians were in general not highly regarded; mariachi was still considered the entertainment of the poor and of drunken men. The musicians who stayed in the capital used to gather in front of the cantinas in Plaza Garibaldi waiting for customers willing to pay for their music. Those who got a chance to play for an upper-class audience had to dress up in order to fit the romantic image of the peasant the elite still cherished. In the 1930s it became necessary to adapt a wardrobe that would not only characterize the mariachis, but also provide them with more elegance and prestige.[12]

Like the music they played, the costume for the musicians had to be a mestizo product in order to represent Mexico's national spirit. Charro, the type of clothing the *mestizo ranchero* [rancher or small landholder] used to wear, was considered the most suitable.[13] These rancheros were viewed as "the first real representatives of the new Mexican race of Spanish-indigenous blood; they were very patriotic and played a leading part in the struggles for Mexican Independence" (Toor 1947: 287). Interim President Abelardo Rodríguez, for instance, requested that the mariachis he invited to the capital in 1933 dress as charros for their performances.

In the 1930s and 1940s, many mariachis were featured in movies. The musicians' dress was changed from locally made rural cotton pants and shirts to the type of dress that would have been worn by estate owners. The tendency to emphasize the aristocratic origin of the costume became even more exaggerated in the movies of the following decades.[14] Less elaborate dress was worn only in melodramas that featured the urban poor—a stylistic device used to impart authenticity to the scene.[15]

The radio broadcasting and recording industries were influential in forming the "typical" mariachi ensemble. XEW emerged in Mexico City in 1930 as the most powerful Latin American radio station.[16] Advertised as "La Voz de la América Latina desde México" [Latin America's Voice from Mexico], it was even heard in the southern United States, the Caribbean, and South America. Nationalistic radio laws issued by the Mexican government privileged certain popular cultural forms in order to ensure that the medium would disseminate a uniquely Mexican culture and thereby promote a sense of national solidarity. Commercial broadcasters were required to include 25 percent "typical Mexican music" in all radio programs. This regulation had cultural consequences as it provided fertile ground for the construction and dissemination of a Mexican national culture (Hayes 1993: 35).

The expanding broadcasting activities attracted many musicians and singers, some of whom found work at XEW or some smaller radio stations. Mariachi instrumentation was becoming standardized. The trumpet was added to furnish the string ensemble with a sound that would carry. More violins and a guitar had then to be added to keep the overall sound in balance.

Although the movie industry influenced first of all the visual aspects of the ensemble, some of the sound modifications were consequences of developments in the movie industry too. Solo singing with mariachis, for example, excelled when Mexican filmmakers of the 1940s and 1950s responded to their mainly middle-class moviegoers' preference for melodramas and comedies. According to Carl J. Mora, "the predictable succession of love affairs, personal misunderstandings, conflicts, and spurious folklore—all liberally garnished with ranchera music—could not have retained the public's interest without the appearance of a 'superstar'" (1989: 58). When singers such as Jorge Negrete, called "El Charro Cantor" [The Singing Charro], and Pedro Infante became actors, the music shifted into the foreground and the musicians into the limelight. Singing in three parts became common practice and it largely replaced singing either in unison, in thirds, or in sixths.

Often traditions change because the circumstances in which they exist change. In the early twentieth century, when the peasant mariachis migrated to the cities selling their music to whoever paid for it, their songs became a marketable commodity: the music became separated from the social environment that had originally produced it. On the other hand, traditions also change because they contain the potential to change. As Shils has noted, "The creative power of the human mind in confrontation with the potentialities resident in traditions produces changes. Imagination of events and relationships not previously perceived or experienced, the invention of a technique not previously known or used . . . are all steps beyond the reiteration of the given. These steps are guided by traditions, they are extensions of traditions beyond the state of the transmitted. They are enrichments of the stock; enrichments are changes in tradition" (1981: 213–214). Changes in the mariachi tradition caused by the mass media, however, have more often been seen as decay rather than as enriching innovation. Philip Sonnichsen, for example, considered the recordings of Marmolejo's mariachi some of "the finest examples of early mariachi music . . . before the Mexican music industry and popular taste were able to impose the uniformity of style and arrangements commonly heard today" (1993: 5). The mass media, indeed, played an important role in the standardization of a once multifarious folk music. On the other hand, the most drastic changes in mariachi music were initiated by the radio, recording, and movie industries, as mentioned above. Moreover, by introducing female vocalists, the music industry even challenged conventional social roles.

Banda: The Development of a Regional Style

As one of Europe's most significant cultural exports of the nineteenth century, the brass band was introduced to every colony overseas.[17] It was modified over the years as it took root and developed in its new environment. The instrumentation of early village bands, however, was variable. Around the turn of the century, specific combinations of brass, woodwind, and percussion instruments evolved in different regions of Mexico. The revolutionary movement of the first two decades of the twentieth century was crucial in the development of bands' regional characteristics, inasmuch as it was a major impetus to both patriotism and regionalism. With time, these *bandas populares* acquired vernacular names such as *tambora* in Sinaloa, *tamborazo* in Zacatecas, and *chile frito* in Guerrero.

Around 1920, the lineup of *bandas sinaloenses* began to be more and more standardized. Band membership averaged from nine to twelve musicians playing clarinets (which replaced the *requinto*), cornets (trumpets), trombones with valves (replacing the *barítono* or *saxor grande*), saxhorns (*alto* or *saxor*; also called *armonía* or *charcheta*), *bajo de pecho* (also called *contrabajo*, upright-bell tuba), *tarola* (also called *redoblante*, snare drum), and *tambora* (double-headed bass drum).

While the wind instruments were imported, the drums were manufactured locally. The body of the tambora was made of wood; goatskin was used for the membranes which were tied and adjusted with *mecate* [maguey] strings. The large drumheads provided a perfect surface for publicity, and most bands painted their name, town, and perhaps a decorative emblem on the membrane. Placed on a wooden rack, the tambora was played with a soft-headed wooden stick. In the other hand, the drummer held a cymbal, which he struck on its counterpart attached on the top of his drum. These two concave disks of brass provided a brilliant clashing accent to band music. The tarola was made of the same material as the tambora. The bottom membrane of the tarola was fitted with several strands of gut. These strands were kept tight against the membrane, producing the characteristic crisp timbre of the drum. Sometimes, *cascabeles de serpiente* [snake rattles] were placed into the drum to increase the "snare" sound. The tarola was played with two wooden sticks.

Although increasingly standardized through the 1920s, bands did not become comprehensively uniform at that time. The instrumentation of bands varied as players left or joined. Not all groups achieved an ideal number and balance of instruments. Some continued to perform in nonstandard combinations and on ill-matched instruments of poor quality. Being small, informal, and voluntary organizations, individual bands generated little or no paper in their ordinary course of business. Hence, after the breakup of such bands, no documentation remained. Many ensembles disbanded during the rainy season, re-forming when called for social functions such as weddings, funerals, cockfights, or *fandangos* where music was needed. Enthusiastic individuals were crucial in the formation of local bandas. The village band was often a family affair, embracing several generations of musicians. Many band players began their musical careers as young boys. Sometimes family members split away from the main ensemble and started bands of their own. Family dynasties remain significant to the present day (for example, Los Rubios in Mocorito).

From the last quarter of the nineteenth century on, the Escuela Industrial Militar in Culiacán and its bandmasters played a seminal role in the training of future professional musicians. The Banda de Música del Estado recruited its members from the students of the school.[18] The rest of the students who wished to pursue a musical career would work in regional bands, orchestras, and, from the 1920s on, in jazz bands. Some would become accomplished bandmasters, music teachers, and composers, and a few would return to the Escuela as teachers.

11. Banda de Eldorado, directed by Gumersindo Hernández, 1924.
Photo courtesy of Manuel Flores.

One of the school's most outstanding directors was Angel Viderique, who was active as a musician and teacher in Culiacán around the turn of the century.[19] With their public performances in the late nineteenth and early twentieth century, military bands were vitally involved in spreading the aesthetic of classical music. State-employed bandmasters were seminal in the education of musicians and in the formation of regional bands. Proficient bandmasters and itinerant teachers had an enormous influence on village music making. Valente Vélez, a senior musician of the 17th Battalion, stationed in Mazatlán, for example, formed a band in the village of El Venadillo (*El correo de la tarde*, 11 February 1901). According to an elderly townsman of La Noria, "El Aparecido" was the nickname of a musician who one day showed up in the village (Alejo Salas, personal communication, La Noria 1996). He had a golden mouthpiece for his *bajo de pecho* [tuba]. Although the townspeople considered him the best musician in Sinaloa, "El Aparecido" could not live from music making alone: he also worked as a water carrier. Except for Refugio "Cuco" Codina, a professional musician who lived and taught in La Noria for many years, all the musicians had some other job during the week. Like Codina, and before him his uncle Genaro Codina, Feliciano Gómez, and Francisco Terríquez were active as music teachers in the southern part of Sinaloa around the turn of the century.

In 1910, as a result of the revolutionary turmoil, most municipal bands disbanded. From the forty to fifty musicians of the municipal band of Cosalá,

12. Band of the 8th Battalion, Mazatlán, 1922. Photo courtesy of Manuel Flores.

for instance, a reduced group of a dozen musicians remained in 1911 (Ibarra 1987: 8). Members of the "old guard" participated in the revolution, serving in the brigades of the revolutionary armies as bandmasters. The Banda de Música del Estado, Sinaloa's official band, assisted General Ramón F. Iturbe during the revolution. In 1913, General Rafael Buelna incorporated the municipal band of Concordia and its bandmaster, Sebastian Sánchez, into his contingent and took them to Mexico City. After the revolution they returned to Concordia, but disbanded in 1930. Many members of this band became indefatigable music teachers and acquired a reputation as composers. Manuel Páez, for instance, initiated several bands and taught various generations of musicians in Tepuxtla, Siqueros, and El Recodo. Wenceslao Moreno composed "El niño perdido" [The Lost Child], nowadays a standard of every Sinaloan band. Pedro Alvarez initiated a band in Elota in 1922 after he had served in General Iturbe's band. He then moved to La Cruz and later to Navolato, where he formed an orchestra (Los Diablos, 1933) that attracted many good musicians. In Navolato, Conrado Solís and his Banda Los Charoles had already made a name by the early 1900s. They competed with the Banda de Concordia and the military bands at the carnival in Mazatlán, and they traveled as far as Nogales, a U.S.-Mexico border town, to perform on national holidays. Los Alamitos, an accomplished "family band" led by the brothers Casimiro,

13. Banda La Rielera, Mazatlán, the official band of the railway company Ferrocarril Sud-Pacífico de México, ca. 1926. Photo courtesy of Enrique Vega Ayala.

Alberto, and Genaro Ibarra, traveled extensively in northern Sinaloa and in the sierra of Durango.[20]

In 1926 the Mazatlán's railroad workers' union initiated Banda La Rielera. The formation of this band was probably inspired by examples in the United States, where railroads were particularly energetic in sponsoring bands for their workers.[21] Among other duties, the Banda La Rielera had to cheer the railroad workers' baseball team during its games. Under the direction of the clarinetist Jesús "El Nango" Sánchez, La Rielera became a very prestigious band that aspired to high musical standards. Some of its musicians made a reputation after they left the band: El Nango formed a jazz band in 1938, Francisco Argote went to the United States to conduct a symphony orchestra; and Romeo Zazueta became the leader of Banda Los Guamuchileños, which, in 1952, made the first recording of Sinaloan banda music.

Work in a band was only one aspect of the musical careers of many early professionals. Only a few musicians played exclusively in one type of ensemble or setting. Severiano M. Moreno from Escuinapa, for instance, was skilled on a number of instruments. He directed an orchestra in 1889; served as organist and cantor; was the subdirector of General Buelna's military band during the revolution; taught music in Rosario, Concordia, Quilá, and Cosalá, where he also founded a student band; and was an acclaimed composer. Like Moreno, most professionals were able to move from band to band, or from brass band to orchestra. Even the conductors of the band of the Escuela Industrial Militar and members of the Banda de Música del Estado would play in other settings: both Rafael Lomelín and Refugio Soto, for example, played in orchestras and later in the jazz band of the Cine Royal, Culiacán's first cinema, which opened in 1927.

Photographic material dating from the 1920s on shows that tamboras or regional bandas were made up of ten to thirteen musicians—quite a large ensemble for a village, but small compared with military or municipal bands, which were often composed of forty or more musicians. The tambora was a civil but not a civic ensemble: its musicians did not depend upon the municipality, nor were they subsidized in any way by the government. At best, they were exempted from paying taxes for their respective business or occupation in exchange for playing serenades or carrying out similar civic duties.[22] The group usually bought the necessary musical instruments as a whole—single instruments did not belong to individual musicians. Whenever a musician quit the banda, he left without his instrument.[23] Sometimes, a high-ranking military person or a wealthy patron would donate an instrument—for instance, both Banda El Recodo and Banda Los Guamuchileños received a tuba from General Gabriel Leyva Velázquez in the 1950s.

Manuel Flores Gastélum's first contact with a village banda was in Los Mochis when he heard the llamada, a series of drumbeats calling the musicians back from work on their parcels of land to the rehearsal. In 1933, at age fifteen, Manuel was sent to the Internado del Estado de Culiacán (formerly the Escuela Industrial Militar). This school provided him, as it did other boys of poor families, with a solid musical education. He learned to play the cornet and to read and write music. The pupils of the school band, known as Los Azulitos (named for the color of their uniforms), had the opportunity to travel extensively, accompanying the governor on his official tours throughout Sinaloa. It was on these occasions that Manuel began to take notice of the popular repertory and to take an interest in who these other musicians were: "We played during the official part—classical and semi-classical music. After the cultural part there was a fiesta, there was dancing. A regional band would play. They played tunes from Sinaloa" (personal communication, 1996, Culiacán).

While the Azulitos performed Mascagni, Liszt, Wagner, Beethoven, Verdi, Strauss, and some national composers, Manuel Flores was enchanted by the rhythms of the regional bandas. Their repertory included sones sinaloenses such as "El coyote," "La cuichi," "La guacamaya," "El toro," "La ardilla," "El buey palomo," and "El palo verde."[24] Flores also admired individual musicians for their particular skills. When asked how they learned to master technical obstacles, they would point to their heart and reply: "Well, I feel it here." This was a typical answer of a musician who had grown up within an aural musical practice and hence was not accustomed to giving verbal explanations of his playing.

Village and town bands performed their music in a style that drew its conventions from traditional practice. The configuration of elements that made up the plebeian musical style was quite different from professional musical practice, which was based on literacy. Although some elements of elite musical practice were probably imitated and absorbed, musical standards and aesthetics were generated within the "plebeian" tradition.

As Manuel Flores witnessed in the 1930s, there was musical contact between "official" bands, such as the Azulitos from Culiacán, and popular bands, that is, between military or military-style and civilian bands. But except for a few arranged *aires regionales*, "official" bands had their own repertory.

Surviving as a full-time musician in the early 1900s meant being flexible and musically literate. Apart from professional and semiprofessional bands, whose members could all read staff and sol-fa notation, village and town bands of illiterate musicians who played by ear continued to flourish throughout the twentieth century. Musical notation never came to dominate the plebeian musical practice, although an increasing number of those who played by ear mastered basic musical notation and theory. Some of these musicians were self-taught. Margarito Lozoya from Mocorito, for instance, was an excellent clarinetist who supposedly had perfect pitch. Viderique's attempt to win over Lozoya for Sinaloa's premier band was futile. After years of playing in different smaller towns, in 1935 Lozoya returned to Mocorito, where he became a leading force in an SEP (Secretaría de Educación Pública) mission, propounding musical education among the rural population.[25]

Musicians' Social Stigma

At the time mariachi music began to gain a foothold in the capital, banda musicians in Sinaloa played a similar repertory: regional *sones* and popular tunes. Most of the former referred to the immediate environment of the peasant musicians; the latter included tunes, such as "Alejandra," that became popular and spread all over Mexico during the revolutionary years, and corridos dedicated to revolutionaries, such as "Valente Quintero" and "Juan Carrasco," and to other brave men, such as "Heraclio Bernal." In addition, they also performed pieces such as "Estrellita," "Sobre las olas," and "Cielito lindo" from the popular repertory of Mexico's salon composers.

The musicians were campesinos for whom musical activity was an economic sideline. With the passage of time, some of the peasant musicians gave up working the soil and began devoting their lives to music making, thus becoming professional musicians. They earned their livelihood by playing for dances and performing at private as well as public celebrations; they entertained *rancheros* and agricultural laborers, found an audience in the cities' bars and brothels, accompanied the men who built the roads across the state, and followed the railroad construction workers beyond the state of Sinaloa. According to Manuel Flores Gastélum, banda was the music of the *pueblo* and occasionally of a local boss or landowner who, on his sprees, got drunk together with his peons (1980: 6).

The press, which had become increasingly sensationalist since the 1920s, repeatedly reported that local fiestas usually would end in violence. As indispensable as music, dance, and alcohol were for the success of any local fiesta, so were the bloody consequences of the fiesta for the entertainment of the newspaper readers; hence, such gossip became an integral part of newspaper coverage.[26]

Although some folklorists exalted the peasantry in a romantic way and glossed over the crude realities, fiesta, music, dance, alcohol, and violence were all related. As a result, upper-class disapproval of people's leisure activities extended to their music—the musicians and the music themselves became stigmatized. Thus, despite the acknowledgment of mariachi as Mexico's official national music in the early twentieth century, its musicians continued to suffer under the low status that had attached to the music from its beginning.

Mariachi's low-class origins and its association with drunkenness and machismo are a stigma that many mariachi musicians keep struggling against—even in the United States, where cheerful mariachi performances glorify a "colorful" Mexican character, and where the general audience hardly knows anything about mariachi's darker past. Nati Cano, leader of Mariachi Los Camperos, one of the most successful mariachis in southern California, would like to see mariachi music get a little more respect in the United States. He was one of the first to take mariachi music out of smoky barrooms and introduce it to middle-class audiences in Los Angeles.[27] On the other hand, mariachis continue to perform famous *canciones rancheras* such as "Entre copa y copa" [Between Two Drinks] by Felipe Valdés Leal, "Llegó borracho el borracho" [The Drunk Arrived Drunk] and "El rey" [The King] by José Alfredo Jiménez, and "Me dicen que soy mujeriego" [They Say I'm a Womanizer] by Pedro Infante.

The drinking and womanizing charro cherished in numerous movies from the golden age of Mexican cinema not only modified the notion of the hardworking, honest, brave, and patriotic mestizo charro; his image also left its imprint on the mariachi musician. José Hernández, founder of Mariachi Sol de México, would like to see this stereotypical image change: "The mariachi is not a big-bellied individual with a huge mustache, hard-drinking and skirt-chasing, rather he is an elegantly dressed artist with a charro suit, capable of excellently interpreting a music pleasing to all."[28] Yet, the expression "mariachi" had already entered the everyday vocabulary, describing a person of weak character, someone who is unstable, unreliable, and frivolous. Even the musicians themselves seem to accede to this widespread image: "The sky is my roof, the sun is my blanket . . . ay, vagabonding heart! . . . They say I'm a mariachi and that I'm a have-not."[29] Banda singers may replace the word "mariachi" with "bandero," thus identifying with the same prejudiced stereotype.

Banda Degollado, a Sinaloan-style band from Jalisco, addresses the social status of mariachi and banda musicians and how they look at each other with a song titled "Se fue con el mariachi" [She Took Off with the Mariachi] by José Luis Quiñones:[30]

Ay, que pena que tengo, compadre, ¡imagínase usted!	Ay what pain do I suffer, *compadre*, imagine!
que la loca de su comadre pronto se me fue	your crazy *comadre* left me
a la Plaza de Garibaldi anoche la llevé	after I took her to Plaza Garibaldi last night
un mariachi contraté pa' cantarle una canción	and paid a mariachi to sing her a song
y la ingrata se ligó al viejo del guitarrón.	the ingrate banded together with the old guy of the guitarrón.
Se fue con el mariachi, me dejó	She took off with the mariachi, she left me
se fue con el que toca el guitarrón	she took off with the guitarrón player
porque lo que ella quiso no canté	because what she wanted I didn't sing
como le canta ahora el barrigón.	like the pot-bellied now sings for her.
Se fue con el mariachi, me dejó . . .	She took off with the mariachi, she left me . . .
Y ahora yo le canto pa' que vuelva	And now I am singing to make her return
esta vieja canción que dice así:	this old song which goes like this:
[en estilo de mariachi]	[in mariachi style]
"Yo lo que quiero es que vuelva	"What I wish is that she would return
que vuelva conmigo la que se fue."	that she who had left would return to me."
Y se fuera con un ingeniero, orgulloso estaría	If she'd have gone with an engineer, I'd be proud
o tal vez con un licenciado, eso me alegraría	or maybe with a lawyer, that would please me
mas la ingrata mi amor ha cambiado con él del guitarrón	but my dear ingrate has exchanged me with the guitarrón player

el hijo de Garibaldi a mi mujer me quitó	Garibaldi's son took away my wife
con su guitarra grandota todita la apantalló.	he conquered her with his giant guitar.
Se fue con el mariachi, me dejó . . .	She took off with the mariachi, she left me . . .

[en estilo de mariachi]	*[in mariachi style]*
"¿Qué voy a hacer si yo soy el abandonado?"	"What will I do now that I'm abandoned?"
Se fue con el mariachi, me dejó *[etc.]*	She took off with the mariachi, she left me *[etc.]*

This song is a mambo, a common rhythm for a banda ensemble but one never played by mariachis. When the singer refers to the "old song" that he now wants to sing so as to make his wife return to him, the accompaniment switches to mariachi style. The two lines of this section are a musical quote from a famous *canción* by José Alfredo Jiménez, "La que se fue" [She Who Had Left]. The refrain of that song goes: "What do I need wealth for / if my soul is lost and without hope / I wish that she would return / that she who went away would return to me." The second mariachi insert is a quote from the song "El abandonado" [The Abandoned] by José de Jesús Martínez, which sustains the common stereotype of the (mariachi) musician: "What will I do / now that I'm abandoned? . . . I have three vices / and I have them very much ingrained / to be a drunkard, a gambler, and a lover."[31]

Popular Music on the Fringes

By the end of the nineteenth century, many villages had a band that offered its services for public and private events. During the first decades of the twentieth century, particularly after the revolution, the demand for musical entertainment increased. As a result, bands began to mushroom. Mariano López Sánchez, born in El Recodo in 1913, remembered that the small village had three bands when he was a child. His father and his uncles were all band players. Like many other boys, Mariano joined them at a very early age. After moving with his father to Rosario and later to Villa Unión, he settled down in Mazatlán in the late 1920s where he first played in small *conjuntos* and later in *orquestas*.

In the 1920s, *orquestas* throughout Mexico began to adjust to music from the United States by replacing the traditional double bass with the tuba, integrating a percussion set, and adding instruments such as saxophone and banjo. This new formation came to be known as the jazz band (Flores Gastélum 1980: 4–6). Local bands, too, began to play the new rhythms: the fox-trot, the charleston, and the blues. The renowned musicologist Rubén M. Campos, for whom "the band was, and continues to be, the popular institution par excellence," criticized this tendency with sharp words: "In the city, which prostitutes even the dogs, [the popular bands] have degenerated; nowadays they play the American fox-trot as in the past they played the British schottische, and this is nothing short of imitating lowborn and cheap art" (1928: 200). The provinces, too, were swept by foreign musics. In Sinaloa's flourishing urban centers, particularly in the port city of Mazatlán, a dynamic and sprightly musical life unfolded. Influenced by new developments in jazz, some of the local orchestras began to modify their ensemble. Consisting of saxophone, trumpet, slide trombone, violin, contrabass, banjo, and percussion instruments, these jazz bands played mainly for upper-class ballroom dances, performing the fox-trot, charleston, and tango.

In 1926 a lengthy article with the title "La música de ayer y de hoy" [Yesterday's and Today's Music] appeared in one of Mazatlán's newspapers. In it the author enthusiastically embraced folk music as a refuge against the "Yankee invasion":

The winds from the North carry the raucous vibration of jazz and relegate to oblivion the sweet melodies of the romantic times, the danzas and the waltzes that bewitched the spirits of our grandparents during the formal soirées, the informal evening parties, and in the narrow streets of the suburb. . . . The conquest of the Yankee fashion . . . is part of the slow but firm advance of a convoluted army of civilization, the scorn and decline of our characteristic customs, of the timeless surroundings of the ranchers and the rural soul. . . . In the patios of the neighborhood and the salons of the aristocracy one hears nothing other than the foreign rhythms of a voluptuous and languid tango, the noisy gymnastics of a fox-trot, the annoying epilepsy of the charleston. . . . But on the dusty roads, in the humble one-horse towns, the echoes of those unforgettable melodies continue to float, the harmonies of the composers who formed a legion so much ours, so national, so Mexican. . . . And thus, it is not surprising that in the remotest and loneliest places one can hear the musical protest of a *canción*. (Armando Roque, El *demócrata*, 14 September 1926)

As in folklorists' writings of that time, Mexican music is both located within the peasantry and related to the revolution. (Apparently, the revolution also left its imprint on the kind of language used by the writer.) "Mexicanness" was viewed as endangered by the invasion of foreign fashions that, in the writer's opinion, were undermining the traditions that had shaped Mexico as a nation. The Mexican spirit, manifested in the people's music, was in retreat.

One would expect that by the late 1920s, after the experience of the revolution, Sinaloan intellectuals who cherished a rural life style, as the author of this text did, would think of regional bandas as characteristic of their people's cultural expression. Yet, the author went on:

The characteristic orchestras, the mariachis, and the marimbas make up the trenches in which the Mexican spirit has fortified itself, confronting the devastating offensive of the Jazz-Bands that triumph with their "Yes we have hot bananas" ["Yes! We Have No Bananas," a hit song of the 1920s by Billie Jones], with "Oh, Catarina," and the other fox-trots. At this time the hullabaloo of the saxophone, the banjo, the cymbals and tubas, or the ocarina, bells, and bass drum sound better than a guitar, a harp, a *salterio*, a *bandolón*. . . . It sounds better to the ears standardized by the vibrating vertigo of the locomotives and electric trains and of the machinery of the factories. . . . But among the sounds of the modern fox-trots, the acrobatic charlestons, and the sentimental, sensual tangos, one can hear the fine and harmonic echoes of the *canciones mexicanas*, a musical protest of our *pueblo*, the expression of the national soul. The *canciones* are surviving. . . . The *canciones mexicanas* still palpitate in the city and in the countryside, in the mountains, and in the valleys. . . . The national soul has not yet died. It fights heroically against the invasions of the modern music so distinct from that which moved our grandparents, and that which today wraps in its vortex today's generation from all countries. . . . Under the trees of Chapultepec [park in Mexico City], Lerdo's [Orquesta] Típica revives the National Aires, and in the outskirts, breaking the silence of the night, a hurdy-gurdy sobs a fashionable tune, while the languid and enervating sounds of the banjo, the saxophones, and the ocarina emanate from the cabaret. (El *demócrata*, 14 September 1926)

This text is in many ways revealing, for it shows that in the late 1920s urban Sinaloan intellectuals already considered ensembles such as orquestas típicas, mariachis, and marimbas as embracing Mexico's national spirit. Banda, on the other hand, the regional ensemble right on their doorstep, was ignored—and this despite the fact that some of the echoes in Sinaloa's countryside, mountains, and valleys were most likely produced by banda musicians. Since, in general, brass instrument players had and continue to have a lower social and musical status than players of string instruments, banda may not have been considered noble enough to "express the national soul." Maybe its instrumentation was too loud, too vulgar.[32]

In 1936 the local newspaper El *día* published an essay that was motivated by a call from the National University of Mexico for an artistic competition, a contest out of which the "true national music" would arise ("La Universidad Nacional de México motiva un certamen artístico de distintas regiones de México, un concurso del cual surgirá 'la verdadera música nacional'"). "El arte musical de Sinaloa," as the essay was titled, not only reflects the prevailing attitudes of urban intellectuals at that time, but also explains, indirectly, why banda music was never considered "true national music." It shows how urban intellectuals imposed their aesthetic judgment on village traditions: in their view, folk traditions had to be cultivated, that is, elevated to the level of art music. Moreover, only organized, "controlled" music was worthy of being called "good music"; spontaneous musical expression was disparagingly referred to as "murga, música corriente y populachera." In the elite's opinion, the lack of "nice Mexican music" was partially responsible for Sinaloa's not very flattering image in the rest of the republic. The commentator wrote:

I suppose that they will make a selection, let's say of tunes, to form a music that would encompass all the styles of the republic's regions. They will select from the proposed folkloric dances to generate one which would be comprised of the zapateado [heel dance] from Yucatán, the jarabe from Jalisco, and so forth, naturally, of course, without leaving out the typical indigenous dances which are still used in many places. Undoubtedly, Sinaloa will be the state that will present the least of all, because, unfortunately, in our confines the cultivation of the music has been neglected a lot, even more so the original [folk] dance. Although in all the important towns good musical bands exist which both entertain the public and introduce it to good music, the author of this [essay] suffered the experience of observing a group of schoolteachers in a nearby village who were dancing when the band was playing "Poeta y campesino" [Poet and Peasant, by Franz von Suppé]. This simply means that they have little exposure to classical music and therefore don't know that not every score is danceable.

In Culiacán, a band was recently founded under the direction of the indefatigable Maestro Cabrera, and it is certain that this organization will disseminate good music in the state's capital. On the contrary, in Mazatlán, the most important city of Sinaloa, there are nothing but murgas, which, instead of pleasing with their performance, make one sick when they ramble along the roads announcing movies. For in Mazatlán, musical performances are given only during the fiestas; but then the music played is extremely ordinary and vulgar. Only when orquestas add charm to particular fiestas can one from time to time hear a good selection, a piece of good provenience.

To hear a good band, it was necessary to spend many thousands of pesos in order to bring the one from the Estado Mayor [National Army Band]; but the circumstances under which it performed did not allow the whole public to enjoy its quality. The band's stay in Mazatlán is so short-lived that the public only gets the opportunity to hear it during the parades playing the papaquis [Carnival song].

When the Syndicate of Musicians was founded [in Mazatlán in 1920], we believed that the alliance of the musicians of the whole district would inevitably cause an improvement in the musical groups in general. The aforesaid Syndicate even announced the forming of a symphonic orchestra. . . . Yet, under the current circumstances, it is to be expected that Sinaloa can submit little or nothing to the competition for which the National University has called; and this is very deplorable, for in Mexico, a very poor judgment will be made again about our state which has gradually been shaking off its nickname of "the crude state" [el estado torpe] that was attached to it some time ago. (Don X, El día, 9 August 1936)

In 1920 the Sociedad Filarmónica "Santa Cecilia" was founded in Mazatlán with the noble aims of "contributing to the perfection of civilization" and glorifying morality and nationhood. The program of the society, posted on the wall of the office of the Sindicato de los Músicos in Mazatlán, reads in part: "By uniting us socially, by striving for good behavior in public as well as in private, by complying with the duties of a good citizen, and by taking into consideration that the art we practice puts us in intimate contact with the Cultivated Society that surrounds us, we will reach our goal, and our dreams will be fulfilled: one day we will enjoy the goods that will result from the inescapable change of our social situation." Village musicians, of course, were not part of the music society and its ideological program. The main purpose of village music making was to entertain and gratify the local public. The little extra money helped the musicians to support their families. Forced by economics, they became more and more mobile. The larger cities attracted many musicians from the surrounding villages in search of work. Many of them ended up playing in so-called bandas canasteras or bandas huiperas, bandas that were looking for clientele in cantinas, the domain of informal ensembles with little-educated musicians.

In Mexico, like elsewhere, concepts of folk culture were developed in the center, that is, in the capital, and by intellectuals. The distinction between center and periphery thus was both geographical and social (see Shils 1975). Mexico's urban elite of the nineteenth and the early twentieth centuries regarded folk culture as being located in the periphery and with the peasantry. Yet, the rural population of Mexico's northwestern states was too peripheral to be known in the center. In fact, it was twice removed from the central core. On the contrary, the state of Jalisco, although peripheral as well, is located in the heartland of Mexico—close enough to the center to allow for transculturation.

Sinaloan intellectuals had never considered regional banda music folk music. As a result, it never stood in the spotlight, it was never put onstage and exposed to the process of folklorization and standardization. It was never the focus of interest, never presented as a tourist article, and never used for national political purposes. Banda did not shun the light, but it evolved in the shadow of the periphery.

At the time mariachis accompanied celluloid singing heroes, all nicely dressed up in charro costumes, banda was still considered the music of the poor and of the ranchers.[33] Almost thirty years after the first mariachi ensemble was sent abroad to represent Mexico at the Chicago World's Fair (1933), the first banda crossed the border to the United States to play for a few countrymen who had emigrated.[34] In 1952, almost half a century after the first mariachi recordings were made, RCA Victor recorded four tunes performed by Banda Los Guamuchileños de Culiacán.[35]

The most prominent Mexican composer of *canciones rancheras*, José Alfredo Jiménez, recorded some of his most successful songs with Banda El Recodo in 1968. They included the "Corrido de Mazatlán," a composition dedicated to Mazatlán and its people. Germán Lizárraga believes that the line, "es necesario la Banda El Recodo para cantarle un corrido a Mazatlán" [Banda El Recodo is necessary to sing you a corrido for Mazatlán] stuck with the audience and thus helped to promote their band nationally:[36]

Hoy que el destino me trajo hasta esta tierra	Today the destiny brought me to this region
donde el Pacífico es algo sinigual	where the Pacific is like nowhere else
es necesario la Banda del Recodo	Banda El Recodo is necessary
para cantarle un corrido a Mazatlán.	to sing you the corrido for Mazatlán.
Yo sé que debo cantar con toda mi alma	I know that I must sing with all my soul
para esta gente que es puro corazón	for this kind-hearted people
a ver si llega mi canto a la montaña	let's see if my singing reaches the mountains
y hasta en el faro se escuche mi canción.	and one can hear my song even in the lighthouse.
Ay que bonito Paseo del Centenario	Ay how beautiful is the Paseo del Centenario
ay que bonita también su catedral	ay how beautiful also is its cathedral
aquí hasta un pobre se siente millonario	here, even a poor man feels like a millionaire
aquí la vida se pasa sin llorar.	here, life passes without tears.
Yo soy fereño, nací de aquí muy lejos	I am a stranger, born very far away from here
y sin embargo les digo en mi cantar	and despite that I tell you in my song
que tienen todos ustedes un orgullo	that all of you have a lot of pride
el gran orgullo de ser de Mazatlán.	the great pride of being from Mazatlán.
(¡No te rajes, Sinaloa!)	(Don't back down, Sinaloa!)
Esas mujeres que tienen por mujeres	These women you have as wives
ante las rosas las pueden comparar	you can compare them with roses
porque el aroma que tienen los claveles	because they have the fragrance of the carnations
lo tienen ellas y tienen algo más.	and they have something even more.

Y de sus hombres, pos que podría decirles	And of their men, well, what could I tell you
que son amigos y nobles en verdad	that they are friends and very noble in fact
y sin que olvide sus típicas arañas.	without forgetting their unique coaches.
¡Qué lindo es todo lo que hay en Mazatlán!	How beautiful is everything of Mazatlán!
Ay que bonito [etc.]	Ay how beautiful [etc.]

This musical homage to the city of Mazatlán has since become a standard of the banda repertory. Stylistically, the "Corrido de Mazatlán" is a *corrido ranchero*: it features the poetic, descriptive structure of the corrido, but it is sung in the characteristic (mariachi-)ranchera vocal style.

Although many famous Mexican singers made recordings with a banda, the banda did not become a standard ensemble for accompanying ranchera singers. It was too late: mariachi had already incorporated the *canción ranchera* in the 1940s, the heyday of the genre. Moreover, the mariachi ensemble served perfectly to accompany both *canción ranchera* styles, *el estilo bravío* [the fierce style], dominated by trumpets, and *el estilo sentimental* [the sentimental style], dominated by string instruments.

Banda music apparently had gone a different way from mariachi: whereas mariachi nowadays belongs to the realm of musical folklorism and has stagnated to a certain degree in its musical development, banda has become a highly popularized, commercialized music style keeping up with the flow of fast-changing fashions.

Tradition:
Sedimentation and Innovation

Tal como el río no corre pa' trás
así mi vida no puedo volver.
  José Felipe Hernández, Banda Flor del Campo

My primary goal when working in the archives and libraries was to find material that would enable me to "reopen the past." I wanted the documents—witnesses of the past—to become alive again. My acquaintances who saw me working at Mazatlán's archive day after day would sometimes ask whether I had found any useful material. Isidoro "Chilolo" Ramírez showed a special interest in my progress. He knew that I was trying to document banda's history, and he knew that documents were scarce. I had introduced him to my research objective, but without going into details. One day he asked me for more background information on what I was doing.

I thought about how to communicate my concepts, considerations, and hypotheses. I wanted to show him that history is where we place ourselves; that my digging for information in the archive was not to excavate dead material but rather to search for threads that would allow me to weave a past-present-future tissue. I also wanted to show him that most historical texts refer to the subject matter only indirectly, and that they had to be interpreted in order to become meaningful. Hence, I believed that one of the historical texts I just had discovered could serve to convey my ideas.

Weaving Threads through Past-Present-Future

The story I retold Don Chilolo was published on 12 October 1926 in Mazatlán's daily newspaper *El correo de la tarde*. The boldface front-page headline had caught my attention immediately. It read: "In San Marcos the director of the Banda del Recodo was fatally injured." The story went like this:

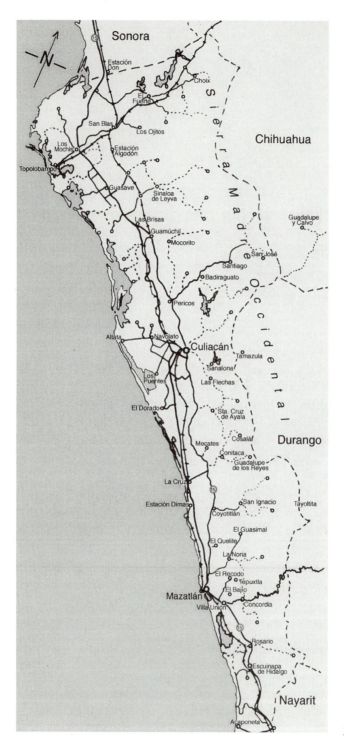

3. Sinaloa.

An impressive scene of blood was recorded last night at a place near the town of San Marcos, within the municipality of La Noria, caused by the bullet wounds of Señor Alfonso Lizárraga, the director of the Banda de Música from El Recodo, who at the present time is in the civil hospital struggling between life and death. The one to blame for the injuries of Señor Lizárraga is Benigno Sánchez, nearby resident of the cited town, who has always distinguished himself for his provocative and quarrelsome character. As it seems, the incident arose because of certain difficulties regarding the payment for several hours of music that Sánchez owed. One of our reporters . . . was able to interview the injured Lizárraga. . . . When asked by our representative, the wounded said that last night, shortly after ten o'clock, he met Señor Sánchez in San Marcos, who owed him one hundred pesos for playing a few days ago; when he requested the payment of that money, [Sánchez] replied that if he wanted the indicated sum, he would have to accompany him to a place which was known as the "Little Well," where he had the money with which he would pay him. Believing in good faith that Sánchez would pay him, Lizárraga accompanied him to the indicated place. Shortly before arriving and knowing that nobody would discover the crime, according to Lizárraga, [Sánchez] drew a gun without saying a word and shot four times, causing him three wounds, two extremely dangerous ones in the stomach and one in the right outer ear. The delinquent took off running and the unfortunate philharmonist remained thrown on the path until two villagers picked him up and carried him to the town of San Marcos, from where he was brought to this town on a passenger truck. . . . So far, the delinquent has not been apprehended. Allegedly, he headed for the sierra to reach the state of Durango.

On 20 October 1926, another long article appeared on the front page of the *Correo de la tarde*. Its title was a provocative question: "Could it be true that they wanted to attack the cargo of the mining company of Tayoltita?" This open question was already transformed into certainty with the first paragraph, which summarized the detailed account that followed: "A musician was organizing a group of bandits who were hatching the sinister plan to slaughter the muleteers at a particular place and to seize a great quantity of silver bars. One of [the group] missed the encounter, thus causing failure of the first attempt. Aware that the others considered him a traitor to be eliminated, he let the leader himself fall into a trap and wounded him severely." The journalist then repeated the incident of the shooting as described eight days before. In this new version, however, the roles of victim and perpetrator were reversed: instead of being the innocent victim of a brutal aggressor, Lizárraga himself allegedly had pressured Sánchez to take part in criminal activities. To evade such participation, Sánchez decided to kill the leader of the squad:

One of our reporters who had the chance to travel through the local villages heard different versions of the incident that contradict the reasons given by Lizárraga that he was injured by Sánchez. The comments about the incident that are made by the villagers are very presumptuous and we make them public without being liable for their truthfulness. . . . It is said that Alfonso Lizárraga had been traveling for some days through the villages of the district with his music band trying to recruit partisans for an overthrow, which we referred to as the attack on the cargo that brings the products of the mines of Tayoltita to the station of Dimas. The cargo of several hundreds of silver bars that are produced by the mines of San Luis every month is transported to the above-mentioned station by mules which are the property of Señor Francisco Bastidas, resident of San Juan.

What I found especially interesting, I told Don Chilolo, was how the reporter distinguished between "fact" and "fiction," that is, between the "truth" and the versions of the incident told in the villages. According to the reporter, nobody really knew what had happened in Los Pocitos except the fact that two people had found Lizárraga on the road and had brought him to San Marcos. Although the reporter dismissed these stories as "presumptuous," he made the whole incident something worth writing about. Moreover, he obviously enjoyed indulging in gossip: "[Lizárraga] said that [Sánchez] injured him over an overdue debt while the nearby residents speculate about the way in which the events developed, for everybody knows that Lizárraga could not have asked Sánchez for a sum that high; what calls their attention most is the manner in which the payment was made."

In the afternoon of the next day I was at home when Don Chilolo drove up to tell me the news: he had found the son of the aforementioned banda director. The story had kindled Chilolo's curiosity, and he wanted to learn more about the mysterious Lizárraga. So he went to see Francisco "Chico" Herrera, an elderly man who was said to be very knowledgeable about things past. It turned out that Chico Herrera himself was Alfonso Lizárraga's son.

Of course, I had never expected Don Chilolo to investigate the story himself, nor had I anticipated that this story would actually convey my notion of history so strikingly. Don Chilolo seemingly enjoyed my amazement as we followed the thread of the past to Mazatlán's market, where Chico Herrera was waiting for us in one of the restaurants on the upper floor.

Chico Herrera was born in El Recodo in 1922. He had been too young when his father died at the hospital as a consequence of the injuries inflicted by Sánchez to remember him. However, according to Don Francisco, the newspaper did not report the true cause of the incident. His father, he was told, was something of a joker. He allegedly told Sánchez that if he did not want to pay with money, he could pay with his wife. Sánchez agreed, but on the way to his house, he shot the musician. As a result of this tragic incident, the boy grew up without a father. The following year his mother passed away as well. Chico stayed with his uncle Teofilo, the father of the famous Cruz Lizárraga of Banda El Recodo, until he went to El Bajío, the native village of his late mother. At the age of twelve, he started to play in the banda of El Bajío under the guidance of Luis Ramírez, "El Gigante," Chilolo's uncle. He played in some well-known bandas in Mazatlán until, in the 1950s, he met Ignacio "Tata Nacho" Fernández Esperón and his legendary *orquesta típica* during carnival in Mazatlán. He joined the orchestra and went to Mexico City, where he was hired as a musician by XEW. In the late 1950s he accompanied José Alfredo Jiménez with the musical caravan La Corona and toured throughout Mexico for two months. He then started to compose songs, mainly for *conjuntos* [small ensembles] and trios, and he became known as "Chico" Herrera, "El Rey del Corrido" [The King of the Corrido]. In 1982 he and Cruz Lizárraga founded the Asociación de Autores y Compositores de Mazatlán [Union of Authors and Composers], for which he was still working in 1996 when I first met him.

Cultural life is always embedded in practical activity and is a reflection upon it. The very possibility of coming to understand cultural life flows from that life. This chapter, thus, will focus on cultural life, both south and north of the border, and on the actors that inhabit and shape it.

Tradition in Flux

Tradition does not just preserve and prescribe. As has been shown in the chapters on technobanda, the reinterpretation of a tradition is an innovative activity. Yet, so-called traditional music does not simply belong to the past either. When played and heard, it overcomes the temporal distance by virtue of its own meaningful presence. Hence, tradition can be understood only as something always in motion. In other words, tradition is always a *living tradition*. Rather than being a construct or "a dead deposit," tradition is constantly being created and recreated by individuals (Ricoeur 1988: 221).

Sinaloa's "traditional" musicians are both culture-bound and individual agents. They understand themselves very much as heirs of their culture, yet they do not think of themselves as tradition keepers in a strict sense. Their understanding of their activities as musicians is much more pragmatic than ideological, for their economic survival depends very much on their being flexible and innovative. In musicians' daily experience, their musical expertise and their own musical preferences are less important than what the audiences demand. Too often, the public requests what is popular at the time, regardless of whether or not the songs belong to the banda repertory. But since many musicians view their profession like any other craft, they seem to accept the "él que paga manda" [he who pays, orders] hierarchy willingly. Hence, everyday reality makes musicians conscious of the notion of a living tradition.

As Felipe Hernández expressed in his composition "Quiéreme siempre" [Love Me Forever], one cannot make past things unhappen: "Just as the river doesn't run uphill, I can't turn back my life."[1] Like a river, tradition is constantly in flux. We are part of it and we take part in it. To use Hernández's metaphor, one cannot leave the river either; yet, surrounded by the same water, one is being carried through an ever-changing landscape. Thus, most musicians understand and accept innovations as musical continuity with the tradition rather than as a change of tradition. Innovations, in general, are not viewed negatively. Rather, they are imperative for the survival of tradition.

Growing into the Tradition

The core of this section is the stories of a number of individual musicians of the Sinaloan tradition. Why did they become banda musicians? How did they grow into the tradition? There are as many stories as there are individuals, so there is no such thing as "the traditional musician." Whereas musicianship was put into the cradle of some of the individuals, others had to struggle for it. Whereas some of them dreamed of becoming professional musicians, others were forced to play. Each story unveils how the individual inherits, appropriates, and shapes musical practice. Yet, even the most personal or unique narrative reflects the worldviews prevalent in that particular society and shared by the other members of the community. Since each individual is part of his community, the following stories are more than just personal anecdotes. They also tell us a great deal about the development of banda music during the past half century.

ISIDORO RAMÍREZ SÁNCHEZ

Isidoro "Chilolo" Ramírez Sánchez was born in 1939, the eldest of three boys, in El Bajío, a little village in the municipality of Mazatlán. His father played in the local banda but died before he could initiate his sons into the music. Still, two of his sons became professional musicians: Isidoro learned to play the trombone and José Luis ("El Indio") the tambora. José Luis has led Banda Los Escamillas of Mazatlán since the 1970s. Before, the two brothers played together in Banda El Recodo. Chilolo stayed for twenty-some years with this renowned banda until he retired in 1992. In the early 1980s, he founded Banda Los Recoditos [The Little Recodos] to give the sons and other young relatives of El Recodo members an opportunity for learning and practicing. One of his sons is still playing with Los Recoditos, a banda that belongs to the best on the inter-

14. Chilolo Ramírez at his home in Mazatlán writing down a new piece to be learned by the young musicians of his band. Photo by Helena Simonett.

national music market. Tired enough to leave Banda El Recodo with its full travel schedule but not yet ready to give up music making, he now devotes his life to teaching young musicians. In 1992 he founded another banda, Los Chilolos, giving it his nickname. Sometimes, he says, he has to grapple with the youngsters—many of whom think that being a musician means having fun and making lots of money—and to remind them how important it is to learn the basics and to acquire the traditional repertory in order to be able to compete with the many other existing and emerging bandas.

The following is an account of how Chilolo remembers his youth, in particular his struggle to enter a tradition that, after the untimely death of his father, seemed to be out of reach:[2]

IR: My dad, Hijinio Ramírez Vizcarra, was a musician. He played the tuba with the local banda: the Banda de El Bajío. I also have an uncle who does know some music. But he is a local man, a man who doesn't know much music or how to express it outwardly. It's the culture: they were not educated, they just were from the village. Well, both were members of the same banda. They were the only [musicians] of my family. Later, my uncle's sons, too, played in the banda: El Bajío, conducted by Señor Luis Ramírez Vizcarra. He was the clarinetist, but he played various instruments.

It began like this: when I was five years old, my father began to introduce me to the music. There was an instruction book by Hilarion Slava, which is still in use.

This instruction book was used to teach the beginnings of music. It's very complete instruction, but at that age, I was not able to grasp it. My dad taught me out of the book only; he did not teach me to play an instrument. He taught me twenty lessons, but I didn't comprehend very well. [In those days] they wouldn't tell you: "Look, this way"—they hit you. He made me cry, and instead of singing in tune, I was crying. He vocalized the lessons, the sound of every note [*he sings*]: do-re-mi-fa-sol-la-si-do. This was the first lesson. In the next, the notes were not in order, and one had to intone them oneself. [During the day] he went to work, and when he came home at night, he made me study. He was a peasant. He worked in the fields and played during the weekends. They traveled, too. Back then, they didn't have connections by road. When they went to larger villages, they went by animal. They would leave without having a contract or anything. They just went on a venture. One day, my dad had an accident while working in the field. After heavy rainfalls, a big rock fell down and hurt him. He couldn't work anymore. The wound caused an infection, and after some years, he died. I was about eleven. Some years went by and nothing happened. And I asked myself how I could start again, now that I didn't have anybody to teach me.

HS: *Didn't he try to teach you music during the years he was ill?*

IR: No, he already was very ill. They were looking for a way to bring him to Mexico City. There was no other means of transportation than the railroad. They didn't have sufficient funds to cover the cost of his sickness. But there was a president of the republic whose name was Lázaro Cárdenas del Río, and he was very fond of the farmers. Well, when this president came into power, he expropriated the big landowners to give the land back to those who needed it to work on. He was very successful because the people liked him a lot. Well, my dad had a twin and his brother tried everything to bring him to Mexico. But for that, he first had to go to Michoacán—the president was from Jiquilpan, Michoacán. My uncle, the twin, first went to talk to a person who wrote a letter that gave the order to get him to Mexico. . . . I was very little. We stayed back without any support. My mom didn't have any economic resources, so she would work as a housekeeper, doing laundry, ironing. . . . We went through all that. We grew up, and I felt this anxiety because I felt that I liked the music, and that I could succeed. But I didn't have the support of anybody who wanted to help me.

HS: *Did you have any opportunity to listen to other types of music in the village, for example, in the chapel?*

IR: Yes. In those days they sent seminarians from the diocese of the cathedral of Mazatlán, and they started to teach Catholicism to all the children, as well as to sing. The all-boy choir was a murmur of one voice. I was the only one who sang the second voice! From very early on. But because I was a child who had no re-sources, they didn't listen to me, they didn't give me any attention. After some time I discovered that my uncle had gathered a group of boys in his house to teach them. He didn't know about my capability. He never called me, nor did he say: "Hey, come to study together with the other boys!" I approached him against his will. Al-though I had not forgotten what my dad had taught me, my uncle didn't want to teach me.

So I went to his house and saw that he kept instruments there, and since he didn't want to give me one, I had to steal one: it was the harmony [horn]. I was about thirteen years old, and I was already working in the fields. I hid the in-strument in my mom's room. When I returned from work at night, I started to blow on it for myself. My uncle wasn't aware that one of them was missing since he had more instruments that nobody used. They were forgotten; more, all of them were already perforated [damaged]. I remember that at that time some villagers who dedicated themselves to growing beans on a large scale and on huge territories were in Villa Unión. These people took my mom to Villa Unión to work for them. She was cooking. My uncle passed through Villa Unión because he went with his banda to a fiesta in a village called Pánuco. One musician was missing, the one that played the tambora. Well, he passed through there and took me with him to play the tambora.

But nothing happened afterward. After some time, I returned home. I didn't know what to do. I felt this anxiety to become a musician. So I went again to steal another instrument: this time it was the trombone. This instrument wasn't in use ei-ther because it was one of the old ones. That was in 1953. I was fourteen years old. This was when Banda El Recodo made its first recordings. I heard the recordings on the jukebox. It was a Wurlitzer. Here in El Bajío, at a place where beverages—beer and tequila—were sold retail, I used to listen to those records. There was no other mass media; very rarely would somebody have a radio. The jukebox had all kinds of music: mariachi, Pedro Infante, Javier Solís, Lola Beltrán—those artists of Mexican music. I liked banda most: it was a novelty. It was the beginning of banda in those years.

Well then, because I was listening all the time, because I loved the tunes recorded by Banda El Recodo so much, I began to dream of how the mechanism of the instru-ment worked, and of how I had to move [my fingers] so as to elicit those tunes. It was a dream. I was searching for that trombone sound in my own instrument, and I found it. That's how I began to play the instrument on my own; just by listening to Banda El Recodo's recordings.

HS: *Was this sound different from the sound of the banda of El Bajío?*
IR: Yes, it was different. It was more professional, more cheerful, more beautiful.

And we all tried to copy what Banda El Recodo was doing. Well, I asked my uncle again to give me a chance in his banda. So I played the harmony—for about two years. I remember that during that time they were building the main road from Mazatlán to Durango through the Sierra Madre. They brought us to the camps where the laborers stayed on weekends. We went, for example, to Copala, to Santa Lucía, to El Palmito, to Ciudad, which already belongs to the state of Durango, and to Salto Grande. We were transported by a truck that brought the mail from Durango to Mazatlán, a cargo truck. That's how we arrived there, we all were dizzy from the many turns the driver took while we were locked in the truck.

HS: *Were there no bandas in Durango?*

IR: No, but I think that they also listened to music from Sinaloa. For example, the mine of Tayoltita belongs to the state of Durango, and the bandas from here used to travel a lot over there. The miners liked banda music, and we did well. We went to the cantinas. The cantinas were frequented by people from the vicinity and there were some people with money, *hacendados* [estate owners], and others who dedicated themselves to the cultivation of apples, peaches, and avocados. Certainly, they could afford to pay the musicians' work. We worked for that kind of people. They asked banda tunes: "El Sinaloense," "El toro," "El coyote," "La ardilla"—genuine tunes of the *banda sinaloense* repertory—"El gavilancillo," "El palo verde," traditional tunes of the banda. It was with the Banda El Bajío, how I learned the whole banda repertory. After that, I didn't want to play the harmony any longer. I wanted to do something else. That's when I picked up the trombone. My uncle let me do so because he knew I was useful. We even made a recording. I don't know if I have a disk here from that time—very bad, very bad.[3] We recorded here in Mazatlán. It was around 1959. XEW, the radio station, had studios. The man who produced the records, Francisco Herrera, is still alive. The banda began to thrive. It was at an event in the village of Siqueros where we played, when Señor Cruz Lizárraga heard me for the first time. Later, we made a trip to Los Mochis where Banda El Recodo was playing too. It was already a *bandón* ["weighty" banda], a well-constituted banda. And there, he heard me again, but I didn't care much. As time passed, though, I recognized that the regional banda was not enough to make for a living. Moreover, they didn't have the same vocation as I had. I recognized that I didn't have a future in El Bajío. That's why I left for Mazatlán.

Since there was not sufficient work—the music didn't have the market that it has nowadays—every musician had to work another job. I first worked in Mazatlán as a bricklayer's assistant. I had to work on the top of the roof of the Copa de Leche [a restaurant on the Paseo de Olas Altas]. The technique for manufacturing concrete was not known then: we had to fabricate the shingles ourselves. I couldn't endure more than two days. I also worked at the brewery here—for a short time only. After that I went around in the cantinas with a band by the name of Banda del Pajarero, later with the Banda del Dandy from Mazatlán, followed by another banda which was called Banda del Borrego.

In those years, there were two very good bandas here in Mazatlán: one was El Recodo and the other was called Los Escamillas. Well, they heard how I played. Don López Alvarado, then leader of Banda Los Escamillas, invited me to play with his banda. When they heard back home that I was about to leave, they tried to hold me back, my mom and my uncle. My uncle counted on me, and he knew that he would miss me. So I went [to Mazatlán] to hide. They came searching for me. That's what happened, and I took off with Señor López Alvarado for a tour to Tijuana.

RAMÓN LÓPEZ ALVARADO

Ramón, born in 1928, was the only son of the musician and banda leader Ramón Alvarado, a native of Siqueros, in the municipality of Mazatlán. Ramón Jr. had all the prerequisites for becoming a qualified banda musician—prerequisites that Chilolo felt he was missing: Ramón Jr. was the son of a semiprofessional musician who wanted him to step into his footprints. Hence, the boy was constantly exposed to banda music and grew naturally into the musical tradition. He was encouraged to learn an instrument during his early childhood, and he was given the opportunity to practice it. In short, he got all the support Chilolo had to struggle for—what Chilolo considered the ideal condition for developing one's musical potential (which Chilolo tried to offer his own sons). Although Ramón eventually became a qualified musician and a distinguished *maestro* who taught generations of young musicians, his experiences were not that cheerful. From early on, he had to share the hardship of a musician's life. When asked whether it was his own wish to become a musician, Ramón said that he never felt a vocation for musicianship; rather, he was forced into it by his father. First he was made to learn the trumpet, but because his cousin wanted to play the trumpet, Ramón ended up with the clarinet.[4]

I started when I was very small, at the age of ten. What happened is that my dad was a musician, my uncles were musicians, and, well then, I come from a family of musicians. Logically, I was inclined toward that kind of life, and up to the moment I don't regret it, and I think I will never regret it. I remember my childhood as something very special because we were very humble. My father earned little—as musicians have always done—and to move forward, he combined his career with working in the fields. . . . My dad was a very energetic man who didn't let me play with the other children of my age, and, instead of giving me a little time off to relax, he began to teach me the clarinet. I started to play the clarinet when I was ten. For two years my dad taught me day and night, and when I got tired, he would scold me. When I was twelve, they gave me an opportunity to play in the banda. I played for two years without getting paid any salary. That's what they call *acamellar* [to slave away].

Ramón formed his first own banda at the age of fourteen. The following year they gave their debut at the Hotel Belmar, at that time Mazatlán's most refined hotel. Unfortunately, the day ended in tragedy:

They contracted us to play on carnival Sunday of the year 1944 at the Hotel Belmar. It was where the governor Rodolfo Loaiza would stay too. It was where they killed him. You are familiar with that story.[5] . . . After that, we went to El Dorado for three years [one hundred miles north of Mazatlán] and later to Culiacán. I remember that those were the times of the ballgames, of the Liga de la Costa del Pacífico and the great encounters between Mazatlán and Culiacán. Of course, we played in favor of our Venados [Mazatlán's team], and that's why we sometimes were showered with beer. That was a beautiful time. . . . We returned to Mazatlán, where we lived through a difficult period. Trying to make a living, we toured to San Luis Río Colorado, Mexicali, Tijuana, and Tecate, and we traveled through the state of Sonora. That's how we spent six years: struggling through ups and downs.

When they moved north, Ramón Alvarado Sr. gave his banda a new name: Banda Mazatlán (earlier, it had been called after his nickname, Los Pelillos). Life in Culiacán was not easy either: there were too many professional bandas competing for an audience. Los Sirolas and Banda Los Guamuchileños had already established themselves; and Banda Los Tamazulas from Durango came to stay, too. This competition was productive in the sense that it facilitated some drastic innovations: Sinaloa's bandas abandoned their old repertory with its military influences and its rural associations, and began to integrate the big-band mambo sound that was so popular during the 1950s. They already had a heavy brass section and reeds; all they needed was to add more percussion instruments such as bongo drums, *maracas*, and *cencerros* [shakers and cowbells]. As so-called banda-orquestas, they became very fashionable for middle- and even upper-class ballrooms. The first recordings gave banda music a new impetus, too, and many bandas started to travel extensively. After Alvarado's death, Banda Mazatlán disbanded in 1957.

Ramón Jr. formed his own banda in 1958. The following year he directed Banda Los Escamillas. That was when he invited Chilolo to join Los Escamillas. Ramón separated from Los Escamillas after a few months to continue with his own banda, which was not given a name until it made its first recording in 1964: Banda La Costeña. The same year they traveled for the first time to the United States.[6]

15. Author visiting with Ramón López Alvarado, Mazatlán, 1996. Photo taken by his daughter.

Ramón López Alvarado composed more than thirty pieces. Although his most successful piece, "El pato asado" (1964), was performed and recorded by many bandas, he considered his arranging skills his real strength. Singers agreed: Banda La Costeña had been their preferred banda. Luis Pérez Meza, "El Trovador del Campo," for example, made eighteen recordings with Banda La Costeña. It also accompanied Antonio Aguilar, Gilberto Valenzuela, Lino Luján, Victor Iturbe "El Pirulí," Federico Villa, Pepe Aguilar, Joan Sebastian, Juan Valentín, and many more. It was featured in the movie *Lamberto Quintero*, accompanying Antonio Aguilar. Because of a serious illness, Don Ramón retired in 1996, leaving the future of Banda La Costeña in the hands of his two sons, Ulises and Edgardo. He died in Mazatlán in 1997.

CRUZ LIZÁRRAGA

Sinaloa's other idol, Cruz Lizárraga, and his Banda El Recodo followed a similar path. Cruz grew up in a humble family as well, but his story of becoming a musician is very different. He was born in 1918 in El Recodo, a small village some thirty miles from Mazatlán with an active musical life. His father, Teofilo Lizárraga, was a peasant and discouraged Cruz from becoming a musician because he not only feared that his son would starve to death, he was also worried about the low status musicians had in society. Don Cruz recalled: "My parents were afraid that I would end up drunk and lost." Like most other farmers' children at that time, Cruz received only minimal formal education. Forced by their economic situation, he had to help his father cultivate the land. Later, he was working as muleteer, barber, and tradesman. Eventually—and despite parental objections—he decided to become a musician. Cruz secretly bought a clarinet and learned to play with the help of his cousin Carlos Rivera. He started his musical career at the age of twenty:[7]

I always liked the music, but in those times, men who dedicated themselves to music were looked at with disdain; they were considered drunkards and playboys. One day I made a decision, and I came to Mazatlán to meet with a man who traveled as a tradesman for a hardware store located at Angel Flores street, across from Hidalgo square, called the Mercería Alemana [in another interview he referred to the Mercería La Mazatleca]. I ordered a clarinet from Mexico City. It cost me seventy-five pesos—a huge sum— enormous for me in those times. One Sunday, I had just sold a sow for forty-eight pesos which I left as down payment for the clarinet, and I was notified that my aunt, who was going to lend me the other twenty-five pesos, had arrived. That's how I finally obtained the clarinet, which, hidden from my father, I started to practice—just by ear, because I never went to school. Fifteen days later, I joined the local banda, and for the first presentation we gave outside El Recodo, I got my first salary, consisting of seventy-five cents.

Because I never drank and was more or less serious, the clients for whom we played preferred to deal with me. Hence, my colleagues appointed me their representative, and being in that position, I suggested that they buy new instruments. We bought a tarola— because we still used some military drums—and one of those tamboras manufactured by Don José Cordero from El Quelite. They cost us 250 pesos. That was how the banda began to improve and to be hired by people from outside El Recodo.

The first trip we made led us to Magdalena, Sonora, for a celebration of October 4th, the feast of Saint Francis. Of course, we didn't know it would be that far away, and hence, we spent more than we earned. We saw ourselves urged to beg the Señor Municipal President to exempt us from paying the taxes—he agreed and thanks to that we were able to return. But on the way home we stopped in San Blas, Sinaloa, to play. The people like it so much that we got a contact in Choix.

Like many other young and adventurous musicians, Cruz Lizárraga had left his village to try his luck in the city. Overrun by bands, the musicians' union did not allow Lizárraga to form a new one. So he joined different ensembles. In 1951, he was asked by RCA in Mazatlán to put a band together to record a few traditional pieces for local distribution. Don Cruz recalled:[8]

It was at one of the many events we attended in El Quelite when Don Mariano Rivera Conde, the artistic director of RCA, heard us playing. It was he who helped us to record our first disc. After this first one, many others followed, and we got better contracts: not for fairs any longer, but for dance events. Cruz Lizárraga and his Banda El Recodo played in the Club Muralla and the Hotel Belmar—the prime social centers in the 1960s. We were also contracted to play in other cities such as Tepic and Durango. Eventually, I had to move to Mazatlán because, being in El Recodo, it was difficult to get into contact with the people who wanted to hire us.[9]

Well, then, I had to confront other problems with my colleagues. I suggested that we dress uniformly—because it looked awful to me that each of us had different clothes on. They started a hellish row with many protests. They thought I was foolish or insane. They couldn't picture tambora musicians in uniforms. However, I insisted, and out of my own pocket I bought them white shirts and marine-blue pants. That was the utmost they would accept.[10]

After the release of Banda Los Guamuchileños' recordings by RCA in Mexico City in 1952, the demand for banda music increased. Mariano Rivera Conde invited El Recodo to record in Mexico City in 1954. Although they had accompanied singers before—for example, Eduardo del Campo in 1953 (Radio XERJ, Mazatlán) and Luis Pérez Meza (repeatedly since 1957)—José Alfredo Jiménez was the first nationally acclaimed singer they recorded with (1968). Banda continued to be a purely instrumental ensemble and was seldom used as mere accompaniment. Yet, the music played by Banda El Recodo in the 1960s no longer had much in common with the traditional Sinaloan music.[11]

Cruz Lizárraga recognized the great commercial potential of banda music, and he set about improving the level of performance. The key to success, Lizárraga believed, was the musicians' ability to accommodate their music to an urban audience of the upper social strata. This meant that they had to adjust their performance in terms of sound as well as of sight. Lizárraga's quarrel with his fellow musicians about uniform clothing is just one example of his different viewpoint: while they could not picture a tambora musician in uniform, he envisioned an elegant, modern band, able to compete with other music groups in the world of popular music. To achieve this goal, some old-fashioned habits had to be sacrificed and new ideas had to be embraced.

Since danceability had always been banda music's strongest allure, Lizárraga and his musicians began to explore a musical terrain that appealed to the musical taste of middle- and upper-class urban audiences of the 1950s: the repertory of the American big bands (Glenn Miller, Benny Goodman, Tommy Dorsey, and Artie Shaw) and the great Mexican orchestras (Luis Arcaraz, Pablo

16. Banda El Recodo in the early 1950s with Cruz Lizárraga and his son, Germán (second and third from the right). Photo courtesy of María de Jesús Lizárraga.

17. Banda El Recodo, c. 1963. The popularity of American big bands changed the performance practice of aspiring urban bandas in Sinaloa: rather than standing and playing by ear, the musicians are sitting and reading music. The suits and ties underscore the new image of the commercially successful banda-orquesta. Photo courtesy of Isidoro Ramírez.

Beltrán Ruiz, and Ismael Díaz). Lizárraga ordered the scores from Mexico City and arranged them for his banda. The dance aficionados went crazy. Banda El Recodo, which used to play in the billiard saloon El Toro Manchado and at village fairs, got contracts to play at elite dance events.

GERMÁN LIZÁRRAGA

The oldest son of Don Cruz, Germán, was born in El Recodo in 1938. Although the boy dreamed of studying medicine, life turned out quite differently. When his father abandoned Germán's mother and her eight children to try his luck as a musician in the city, it was left to the boy to provide for the large family. After working here and there to earn a few pesos, he eventually picked up the clarinet to join a band. Soon after, he was integrated into the new band his father had formed in Mazatlán for the RCA recording. He has been playing with Banda El Recodo ever since. Germán's initiation into banda music, like Don Ramón's, was involuntary, but both have become important personalities in the world of banda music.

The following is Don Germán's memory of his childhood and his first years as a banda musician:[12]

I was thirteen years old when I began to play, as one says, by force. I had to work: in the morning, . . . I went to the river to gather five bundles of pigweed; I tied them at my waist, returned to El Recodo, took them off, and let them dry because when soaked with water, they were very heavy. I sold the bundles of pigweed for twenty centavos each. I made one peso. In those times, nobody had tap water. The people had to get the water from the Río Presidio. There were wells on the bank. I went to get water and sold the jar for five centavos—twenty jars. I earned another peso. In the afternoon, I went to cut wood, loaded our donkey, and sold it. I made another peso. I earned three pesos daily. But I needed three pesos and fifty centavos to buy food for my siblings, my mom, and myself. There was a man who had a little store, Enrique Páez. He was my godfather. He gave me the fifty centavos. . . . Before my dad left my mom, he gave me a few lessons out of an instruction book by Hilarion Slava. I practiced the clarinet together with another boy, Bernardo—he already played the tarola in the banda. One day, one of the banda's clarinet players got sick, and Bernardo told the band leader: "Take Germán."—"No, he doesn't know how to play."—"Take him, man." And they called me. We played the whole afternoon and part of the night. The musicians gave me twelve pesos. Twelve pesos! I made three pesos daily doing this and that, and I made twelve pesos playing music—well, here I am!

Since then I have dedicated myself to the music. I started to study music. I went to Mazatlán to study with a maestro whose name was Fraulio Pineda. Unfortunately, the maestro passed away soon. I continued my study with another maestro called Refugio

Ortega, Don "Cuco." And so I first played with a group consisting of accordion, guitar, and *bandolón* [a stringed instrument]. That's where I practiced until the day my dad was asked to make a recording for RCA Victor, with Mariano Rivera Conde acting as artistic director.

My dad had already moved to Mazatlán, but the Musicians' Union of Mazatlán did not allow him to form a new band. The union didn't want more bands in the city. So my dad had to solicit musicians from here and there to make the recording. He brought some musicians from El Recodo, and that's how the banda was initiated. He also took me along. Well then, on Constitución Street was a nightclub called El Recreativo. They turned the place into a studio, covering the walls with blankets, rolls of bedding, and bags. That's where we made our first recording. We recorded "Mi gusto es," "El sauce y la palma," "El sinaloense," "Que bonita es mi chaparrita," and other songs . . . but purely instrumental. That's how Banda El Recodo began, recording that year [late 1951]. And by 1952 the recordings came out.

They began to call us from different places. Tepic, Nayarit, was the first place we went to play outside the territory of our state. We surely did very badly because we weren't prepared at all to play at that kind of event—a *baile!* We alternated with the orchestra of the López brothers. We did very badly. The next day, the newspaper *La escoba* wrote about how badly the musicians of the Banda El Recodo played—and indeed, they were right! Then we traveled to Durango, to Guadalajara . . . and the people began to speak well of our banda.

The next recording was made in Mexico City, in the studios of RCA Victor, in 1954 and under the direction of Mariano Rivera Conde. Later, when Mariano left RCA, we continued to work with them for many years until RCA Victor recessed [didn't re-sign the group]. We then recorded with Discos Tambora in Mazatlán, an independent label, owned and operated by José Vicente Laveaga. We also made recordings with Gabriel R. Osuna here in Mazatlán. He had an agreement with RCA.[13]

Don Germán is one of the few musicians who have been loyal to Banda El Recodo since its beginning in the early 1950s. Most musicians of his generation have already decided to slow down: the fast pace of an internationally renowned band like El Recodo is murderous. A number of ex-members started their own band in Mazatlán in the early 1990s: Banda Los Pioneros, headed by Popo Sánchez and Simón Lamas.[14] These musicians not only play at a high professional level, they have also devoted themselves to continue the great Sinaloan music of the 1960s and 1970s, and they take the band's duty to teach the younger generation of musicians seriously. They have carved out a space where they can play what they like most, without the unrelenting pressure of the music business. Don Germán, on the other hand, has kept up with the rapid commercialization of banda music in the 1990s. After the death of his father in 1995, he took on the band's leadership. He and his father's widow, María de Jesús "Chuyita" Lizárraga, manage the band and its frequent concert tours and recordings.

FELIPE HERNÁNDEZ

Felipe Hernández was born in 1957 on his parents' ranch in Jacola, some fifty miles south of Culiacán. His mother gave birth to twenty-four children, all but eight of whom died at an early age. Timid and frail, Felipe did not live up to the image his father had of his sons, and he inevitably became the family's black sheep. At the age of six, he accidentally cut his toe with a machete while clearing weeds from the family's land. After his brother stopped the bleeding with a handful of dirt, the wound became infected, and Felipe had to be brought to a doctor in Culiacán. During his recovery, he stayed with his uncle José Quiñonez, a well-known banda musician (Banda Los Hermanos Quiñonez de Culiacán). Like most boys, Felipe was thrilled by the brass-band sound. He had wanted to learn the trumpet ever since he first heard and saw "El niño perdido" performed in his village.[15] His mishap on the ranch turned out to be his good fortune: his father left him in the custody of his uncle, under whose guidance little Felipe entered the world of banda music. After his initial years with *huiperas*, bandas that play in bars and brothels, he joined professional bandas such as Los Nuevos Coyonquis and Los Hermanos Quiñonez. He moved to Los Angeles in the mid-1980s, where he eventually formed his own banda in 1989, Banda Flor del Campo. Among the musicians is his seventeen-year-old son, whom he taught to play the clarinet. Felipe believes that the way he learned to become a musician is still very common in Sinaloa. Recalling his first memory of banda music and the mishap that turned his life around, he tells about his early experiences as a banda musician:[16]

Before a banda would go to a ranch to play for a dance, they would come to ask for permission. They would pay a girl to go from house to house to invite all the girls of the ranch: "There will be a dance. Tell your father to accompany you!" I had two older sisters. Although [my parents] didn't allow us to go, we went there for a little while anyway. I remember that the banda began to play. I liked the trumpet—an instrument I've never learned to play. I remember that they played "El niño perdido" and that one trumpet got lost and started: [*he sings*] Traa-ra-ra-ra-ra-ra-ra. I was flabbergasted wanting to learn the trumpet. . . . Only, if one is little, one also gets easily intimidated—I think that many boys are interested in music, but the others ridicule it.

I think it was about one year later when I cut myself in the foot. I was six years old. We were working in the field cutting the weeds to protect the parcel of land. On a ranch, a child of five years already knows how to sharpen his machete, how to cut wood, how

18. Banda Flor del Campo, Los Angeles. Photo courtesy of José Felipe Hernández.

to milk—everything a grownup does. . . . I didn't yet go to school when I cut myself in the toe with a machete. It was bleeding a lot and my brother took a handful of dirt to stop it. It was a very large cut and it got infected. It looked very bad. My father brought me to Culiacán. The doctor cured me and said that I could not return to the ranch since we had cows. I think the cattle dung is very dangerous for a cut. . . . My uncle [who was a musician and lived in Culiacán] told my father: "*Compadre*, why don't you leave the *güerito* here and I teach him to play? Wouldn't you like to be a musician, my son?" And I said yes. But I didn't really understand what it meant. So my father left me and returned to the ranch. That's how I ended up in Culiacán with my uncle who was a musician and who had a banda. I told my uncle: "I want to play the trumpet." And he said: "I don't have a trumpet for you, son." Because he played the clarinet, he said: "Here is a clarinet. You can have it."—"But I want a trumpet."—"Well. Practice it in the meantime."

My uncle began to teach me. The first couple of days, I remember, I was very enthusiastic, but then I lost interest. I stayed for two years and I didn't want to study. I was very lazy. My father arrived and he scolded me: "Look, if you don't learn I will take you back to the ranch." I didn't believe him. But when I overheard my father saying to my uncle: "It's pointless, *compadre*, why should I leave him here? I will take him with me so that he works on the ranch." I said to myself: "Oh, that's serious. . . . I hope my uncle can convince him." He did convince him and I stayed. It was at the time when we had three months of vacation. In those three months I learned everything a musician has to learn: I learned to read music, theory—not much, but I learned some theory. There is a method called *Solfeo de los solfeos*—one has to intone the notes. My uncle said: "No, you're singing completely out of tune. Better try the clarinet for you'll never be a singer anyway." . . . After two years [of resistance to learning], I finished the first, second, and third part [of the method] in three months and I learned some ten pieces.

The first piece I learned—well, I only blew and my uncle moved the fingers to elicit the melody of "Las mañanitas." The first song that I achieved to play on my own was "El mambo número ocho." I studied and studied because I liked it. That was when [this song] really hit. They played it on TV. . . . After that I learned a very difficult piece for the clarinet—the one I told you that Señor Guadalupe "El Sirola" gave me—called "Viva Guaymas" and written for me by [El Sirola], and I started to study it when I was very, very little. That's why all musicians said, "Oh, this little guy will become a very good musician. He'll be very good."

My uncle had something I believe very few people have. He never got angry. If you didn't understand, he didn't bother, he would say: "Calm down, calm down, look, listen well, focus on this. You don't have to worry. The music finds its way into your head alone. If you worry, your head will heat up, and you won't understand anything." . . . My uncle never told me, "You're stupid, you're an empty-head," never. On the contrary, he always told me, "Oh, my son, you're very keen. You're going to learn." That's how I began to know the music. And I really liked it.

All of my uncle's sons are musicians: Armando, Luis, Manuel, and Leonel. He has four sons and four daughters. All of them are professionals. Armando, for example, is a doctor and a clarinetist. . . . They had a great argument in my uncle's home. My aunt never agreed that their sons should become musicians. My uncle said: "And why not? If they've eaten till now, it's me who has maintained them."—"No, nobody likes musicians 'cause they are shameless, they are drunkards. . . . " My uncle replied: "Drunkards? What do you mean? I'm not a drunk, I'm not shameless. If they want to be like that, they will, but they don't have to be musicians to do so." And that's why all of them studied and graduated. But my uncle also taught them to play. . . . I, I didn't finish secondary school. I have always been very slack. I left to play and I never returned to my uncle's house. How ungrateful!

I went to play with a banda in the red light district. There are bars and they have dances. The banda arrives and asks whether it is allowed to play. . . . In Culiacán, this is called un *guipiar* [*huipiar*]. That's how I started in Culiacán. All the saloons are very near each other. The guests drink together with the women. The boldest of the banda approaches them and asks, "Do you want us to play a song? —"How much do you charge?"—"So much."—"OK. Play ten for me." Sometimes one can earn a lot in one night; sometimes one doesn't even play. That's where I started to work. At that time I was still very young. Believe me, even the musicians scared me. They called me "El Copechillo" [Little Glow-Worm] because I used to smoke a lot. I became [morally] loose there in Culiacán.

In Culiacán, that's how almost all musicians start [their career]. Usually, the bandas that work in *la huipa* are bandas made up by old people; people who no longer get work in one of the more organized bandas. But despite the fact that they have all the experience, they know all the songs, these old men don't want the responsibility of teaching either.

There are always musicians in a banda who care about playing better, more modern. That's why tensions arise: the young musicians don't want the old ones because they keep playing the old stuff. So the old ones start to gather together and then go for *la huipa*. But it is these old musicians who give the newcomers a chance. An organized banda would never give a chance to somebody who doesn't know to play.

I happened to start with a banda with musicians whose average age was about fifty. Everybody liked me. Well, there were two who didn't. Those who played the clarinet like myself didn't like me. Before I started to play with them, they lost a lot of work because one of these two men was sick very often. The other musicians wanted somebody to substitute for him. And when I joined them, they didn't care any longer whether he came along or not. Of course, he didn't like it. He got very mad when we took off while he stayed at home and, even worse, when we earned good money. There came the moment when he threatened the boss and said: "Well, *compadre*, get rid of this damn little guy or I leave." And the boss replied: "No, *compadre*, we won't kick out this little guy. He's just starting to learn."—"Then, I leave."—"If you wish so, *compadre*." He left. He managed to stay away for some ten days and then came back to work. I played for about three, four months with them and learned well. They never paid me what they earned. If they earned twenty pesos themselves, they would give me three or five. . . . When someone begins to play, he usually gets some money; it is thought of as a stimulus—to animate you. Because when I started in Culiacán, I didn't know more than some ten songs.

Felipe's uncle told him to write down the titles of ten songs and the keys they were played in each night when he went with the older musicians to work in the cantinas of the red light district. Later he would teach the boy those ten songs, helping his nephew to expand his repertory gradually.

The Era of Modern Technology

The cantina has always been the domain of the bandas and other small ensembles whose members have little eduction. The *orquesta*, on the other hand, the premier expression of an upper-class aesthetic, entertained the more affluent citizens in the dance halls of the hotels and nocturnal recreation centers. A deep economic crisis, however, changed the situation in the 1940s. For musicians, this crisis coincided with the assassination of the Sinaloa governor Rodolfo Loaiza at the Hotel Belmar during carnival 1944. At that time, this oceanside hotel with its most luxurious dance halls was an exquisite social center, for both the local elite and rich American tourists. *Orquestas* enhanced the ambience during dinnertime and played dance music until early morning hours.[17]

Mazatlán's carnival used to attract the most renowned orchestras from Guadalajara and Mexico City. After the murder of the governor, however, the carnival changed. Masks on the street and public masked balls were not allowed anymore, the hotel became quiet, business declined. With the fading sound of the orchestra, the ambience of the hotel was gone. The orchestra musicians split up into small groups looking for work—desperate enough to even enter the bars. But it was technological innovation that eventually finished off the *orquestas* in the 1950s. Mariano López Sánchez, at that time trombonist of the Hotel Belmar orchestra, recalled: "The wave of the new groups had arrived, there at the hotel: four, five musicians—voice, guitars, and percussion. Well, the audience liked these modern ensembles. It was very sad to see the complete *orquesta* playing in the dining room—playing music of Glenn Miller and all that beautiful music, and no one was listening. Five youngsters were killing us, as one said. All the good *orquestas* died in Sinaloa as well as in all of Mexico" (interview, 1997, Mazatlán).

Although pop groups replaced many of the *orquestas* in the upper-class dance halls, they did not threaten banda's domain nor its musical practice. On the contrary, some bandas slowly began to take advantage of modern technology: they played on local radio from the mid-1940s on and eventually caught the attention of the (inter)national recording industry, which was on the search for new, (that is, unfamiliar), sounds in popular music.

Airplay and recordings popularized banda music immensely. As a result, many of the job-seeking *orquesta* musicians in the 1950s ended up in bandas. Both commercial success and the incorporation of these new musicians caused the traditional tambora sound to shift. The appropriation of Caribbean and American music styles and repertories was facilitated by the radio, which had already shaped the public taste. The more commercially oriented bandas adapted the percussion instruments of the *conjuntos tropicales* to play the popular Cuban dance genres, and saxophones to interpret the music of the American big-band era. This modified banda became known as *banda-orquesta*. Yet, despite this pull toward popular international music, *banda-orquestas* always retained the Sinaloan core repertory.

While in earlier days ambitious town bands were inspired by military bands and their sophisticated repertory, one after another they turned away from classical music to interpret mainstream popular music, thus adapting to the changing taste of the larger audience. Teodoro Ramírez, looking at a photo of Banda Los Guamuchileños from 1947, noted about the change in repertory: "In those times, the way to play—and the music we played, too—was completely different. [Banda Los Guamuchileños] was very versatile: they played equally well 'Poeta y campesino' [*Poet and Peasant*, by Franz von Suppé], 'Trovador' [from Verdi's *Il trovatore*], 'Rigoletto' [from Verdi's *Rigoletto*], 'El sauce y la palma,' 'El toro,' or any other piece of Sinaloa's folklore. They played it equally well. When Pérez Prado came with his music, the banda was ready to play the mambos of Pérez Prado" (interview, 1996, Guasave). Pérez Prado and his mambo orchestra combined the syncopated rhythm of mambo with the brassy sound of the American swing band. The popularity of Pérez Prado's orchestra had a tremendous impact on Sinaloan bandas with a commercial emphasis. They started to play Pérez Prado's mambos and, as Mexican orchestras did, they experimented with new rhythms, combining mambo with *guaracha*, bolero, and *danzón*. Their repertoire also included the cha-cha-chá and the twist.

Although the big band and mambo era left their imprints, banda kept its distinct character, usually referred to as *sabor sinaloense* [Sinaloan flavor]. This character results from the contrast of clarinet and brass timbres, the juxtaposition of tutti and soli (that is, the alternation between the whole banda and the individual instrumental groups of the front line: trumpets, trombones, and clarinets), and the improvisation of countermelodies on one of the front-line instruments, a technique that is nowadays often used while accompanying vocalists.[18] There is a strong emphasis on volume and pulse. Dynamics are mainly generated by the alternation of tutti and soli sections, the latter executed on the front-line instruments.

THE FIRST RECORDINGS

During the 1940s, Banda Los Guamuchileños, directed by Romeo Zazueta, established itself in Culiacán. In September 1952 they traveled to Mexico City to support General Miguel Henriquez Guzmán in his candidacy for the presidency of the republic. Bandas had often been used in Sinaloa for political purposes such as campaigning. But this was the first time that a regional banda had been invited to the capital. The trip was organized by Enrique Peña Batíz, a Sinaloan who was politically active in Mexico City. Among his friends in the capital were the ranchera singer Luis Pérez Meza, the composer and actor José Angel Espinoza ("Ferrusquilla"), the singer Enrique Sánchez Alonso ("Negrumo"), and the artistic director of RCA Victor, Mariano Rivera Conde, all of them Sinaloans, and all of them contributors to the growth of banda music.[19] According to Peña Batíz:

Until 1952 the tambora music had dwelled hidden away. But on e day, at the end of September, the situation changed, and through the recording of two discs recorded by RCA

19. Banda Los Guamuchileños, 1947. The patron, a businessman from Culiacán, is sitting in the center. Photo courtesy of Teodoro Ramírez Pereda (tuba).

Victor and performed by Banda Los Guamuchileños from Culiacán, our musical genre became known nationally and internationally.

In 1952 I participated in a very important political movement: the candidacy of General Miguel Henriquez Guzmán for the presidency of the republic. On September 29, the day of his patron saint [Saint Michael], we brought the banda from Culiacán to boost the spirit of the festivity. The tambora was my contribution to the celebration.

After Los Guamuchileños's trip to the Federal District had been confirmed, I went on to speak with my dear friend and fellow countryman Mariano Rivera Conde, artistic director of the RCA Victor record company. "Mariano," I said, "the tambora from my native land is on its way, and I would like to know if you could arrange to record them as you had promised me." Mariano, who was known for his great musical sensibility, which led to his eventually becoming the president of RCA Victor, didn't hesitate: "We stand by what we said. When are they ready to record?" I responded: "They have their obligation with General Henriquez on Sunday. After that, they are yours." He said: "I expect you at ten on Monday morning at RCA."

The following day, we showed up at the studio of the record company. Mariano made me act as artistic director, and I had to select the four pieces that were to be recorded. I selected "La india bonita," "El niño perdido," "Grato dolor," and "La batalla de Tabasco." The recording was realized with great ease. There weren't many takes: one after another, after another, after another, and ready. It went very fast. Everything was done. In reality, however, it was at that moment when the great popularity tambora nowadays enjoys nationally and internationally was born.

[The musicians] returned to Sinaloa. The recordings came out. And from the very beginning, they were overwhelmingly successful. [RCA] sold sixty thousand records in a very short time. It was a hit. It was a big success. Mariano, of course, wanted to record the Guamuchileños again. But the success went to the Guamuchileño boys' heads because they had received plenty of well-paid offers. They already toured far away; they traveled a lot. When Mariano invited them a second time, they thought they could dictate the condition. . . . Well then, Mariano invited Cruz Lizárraga and his Banda El Recodo instead. Romeo Zazueta and Los Guamuchileños had less vision than Cruz Lizárraga had. . . . Banda El Recodo increased its prestige to such a degree that it is considered the best-paid banda and the one most liked by the great Mexican singers. (Interview, 1996, Culiacán)

Whatever the reason, the initial success of Banda Los Guamuchileños did not last long—they disbanded in 1958. I thought I had lost the trail of the story of this pivotal first recording from a musician's point of view, since none of the members of the current Banda Los Guamuchileños de Culiacán is related to any of the earlier banda members. But luckily, I located one former member in Guasave, where I got a chance for an interview in November 1996. The following narration reflects how Teodoro Ramírez Pereda, the tuba player for Banda Los Guamuchileños from 1946 to 1957, experienced the first recording:[20]

I was with them to make the first recording in 1953 [sic]. We were brought [to Mexico City] by someone called "El Güero" Sanz [Eduardo "El Güero" Sanz López was Peña Batíz's contact person in Culiacán]. He brought us to General Leyva Velázquez [sic]. Something like that. They were friends or something. Peña Batíz was there, too. He had the idea that the Guamuchileños should record two discs—these little 78 rpm ones. He made us record two discs—four pieces—and we did it. Banda Los Guamuchileños was the pioneer of recording discs with tambora music. It was in '53, I believe. . . .

Before that we played at the radio station here in the province, yes, at [XE]BL, at [XE]CQ, and later at XECA; at all three radio stations that existed in Culiacán. For six months I played for a program at a store by the name of "The Progress" twice a day: once in the morning and once in the afternoon. It was broadcast directly. We went directly on air. From 1945 on . . . they solicited [banda] music for commercial programs. The business would ask the banda to go to the radio station, a program of forty-five minutes. It just went on the air. They didn't record it.[21]

The Guamuchileños had a certain reputation even though in those days there was not a lot of publicity. Here in Sinaloa we created publicity through our presentations in different communities. But after the first recordings were released, they were disseminated throughout the whole country. Many records were sold—many, many records.

They were sold [with such success] that they continued to record later. The second time [we recorded] was in 1955.[22] They brought the equipment from the radio station and from the Columbia [record company]. They came with the equipment to the Autonomous University of Sinaloa. They prepared a room so that Los Guamuchileños could record there. This second time, they recorded twenty-something pieces. It was ranchera music, but of the healthy kind that doesn't glorify or apologize crime or contraband—it was pure music. And we also recorded *danzones*, other regional pieces, waltzes, pasodobles, tangos. The recording of the Guamuchileños was very much accepted in Cuba, because most of the records were sold there, in Cuba. In Puerto Rico, too, many records of the Guamuchileños were sold. At that time, no singer was used. Some little parts were vocal, but in a comical way. Singing didn't have any importance, only as an element of a comic piece. (Interview, 1996, Guasave)

For Teodoro Ramírez, it was not important to recall dates and names in detail. Rather, what was important was the impact that this first recording had on his life as a musician: it meant other work opportunities and better pay. Although the Guamuchileños had played before on local radio stations, their music was heard in a very restricted area. It was the records that helped to build a larger market for their music and for banda music in general, which at that time, was still largely unknown outside Sinaloa and neighboring states. With this new medium, the musicians could reach out to new audiences. They, too, were finally part of the modern world.

After the release of Banda Los Guamuchileños' recordings in 1952, the demand for banda music increased.[23] Mariano Rivera Conde invited Banda El Recodo to record with RCA Victor in Mexico City in 1954. Other recordings soon followed. As Banda El Recodo became more prolific and successful, its major priority was maintaining musical standards. Cruz Lizárraga was an ambitious leader, and he recruited only the best musicians. These musicians were able to play different types of music and to move between sight-reading and playing by ear from memory. Banda El Recodo was able to adapt to changes in popular musical tastes and habits, and its new musical style had a great influence on aspiring young musicians. The band set a standard that semiprofessional players could not match. With their interpretation of international popular music, they imposed an impression of what virtuosity on brass and woodwind instruments was. As a consequence, their recordings contributed to the standardization of the style and the repertoire.

TRAVELING IN SINALOA AND ACROSS THE BORDER

Traveling had always been an integral part of a musician's life. According to older village musicians, there was only minimal communication among rural villages and towns in the first half of the twentieth century.[24] On weekends and when there was little work on the ranch, *campesino* [rural] musicians would take their instruments and leave to look for work. Traveling was an arduous task, and sometimes a dreadful experience. Usually the musicians traveled by foot, their luggage carried by mule. They slept in the open fields. When they arrived in a village, they would play for a *baile* [dance]. If there was no festivity such as a horse race, a bull- or cockfight, a celebration of a local saint, a wedding, or a funeral, they would play one or two pieces in exchange for food and continue their travels. They might stay in the next town for one or two days.

Campesino musicians did not have the means to organize their travel in advance. They were taking a risk, leaving without any confirmed destination. Even though communication systems improved toward the middle of the century, local bandas still roamed around without firm contracts. They knew more or less where to find the clientele that could pay them adequately. The construction of the main Mazatlán-Durango road in the late 1940s, for example, attracted many laborers. Their camps provided an ideal opportunity for semiprofessional bandas. On the weekends, the laborers would spend their salaries in the cantinas, drinking and paying the musicians to play. There was not much else to do at such camps, and the musicians knew that they would find plenty of work.

Traveling was also part of the life style of professional banda musicians. Although enterprising bandas had better commercial opportunities and played in more refined environments than bandas that settled for lower musical standards, their lives were not much easier. Professional musicians lived most of their lives far from home. As the transportation system improved in the second half of the century, traveling became somewhat more comfortable. The tuba player Armando "El Serrucho" Bastidas went with Banda El Recodo through periods of economic hardship:[25]

We suffered a lot with the banda. On some occasions we were even abused. Sometimes, [instead of money] we got vouchers for food. Many people didn't pay us. Oh man, how we suffered to make the tambora popular! Nowadays it's easier. Everything is well organized, with buses, with good lights and everything. But not so before; we didn't have a sound system, it was only the sound that we produced by mouth. A musician's life is very harsh. It's a lot of work. It appears to be an easy life because one is among people. But something else makes [life] even harsher: those who don't dedicate their lives solely to music making become addicted to drugs, they start drinking too much, or they like women too much. That's not good. What is difficult is not to get there [to the top], but to stay there. We put a lot of heart into the music! (Interview, 1996, Los Angeles)

In 1957 Banda El Recodo was invited to join a traveling troupe, the caravan La Corona. Organized by the entrepreneurial impresario José Vallejo, the caravan

20. A village banda playing in honor of the patriarch of the rancho Los Llanitos, 1996. Together with the banda, the company walks over to the field to watch an *hulama* match, an ancient ball game in which a heavy rubber ball is kicked back and forth between two teams using the loins only. Photo by Helena Simonett.

featured Mexico's most famous vocalists and musical ensembles, such as José Alfredo Jiménez, Javier Solís, Luis Pérez Meza, Los Xochimilca, and Mariachi Vargas de Tecalitlán. Banda El Recodo accompanied Luis Pérez Meza, "El Trovador del Campo," an accomplished singer from Sinaloa, who knew the regional repertory by heart. Pérez Meza was a great force in popularizing banda music.[26] El Serrucho recalled him with much respect: "We had already accompanied Luis Pérez Meza a lot, because it was he who made the songs of Sinaloa popular. Nobody but him knew Sinaloa's music. He knew all the songs from Sinaloa with their words. Hence, when we came to accompany him on the tours, he would sing all these songs, and he became enormously famous. They called him 'El Trovador del Campo' [The Troubadour of the Country]. He could sing any type of music: boleros, waltzes, *huapangos*, rancheras. He was a well-prepared man. He had an extraordinary musical sensibility and a marvelous voice. That was when that whole thing with the tambora started. And we began to travel far away."

This tour helped Banda El Recodo get wider exposure. A few years later, they got an invitation to accompany Luis Pérez Meza at the Teatro Blanquita in Mexico City. Apparently the audience liked their music—their one-week contract was extended for another two weeks. Shortly after their engagement in the capital, they were called to California by a Sinaloan impresario, Manuel Cevallos,

21. Advertisements for upcoming events on a wall near the Mazatlán airport and in town.

who also arranged their visa. This first trip across the border in 1962 turned out to be a disappointment for the musicians. Germán Lizárraga remembered: "We played everywhere in California: in Modesto, Manteca, Fresno, Bakersfield, and Oakland. It did not go well for us. In fact, whenever we played, nobody came to listen—ten, twenty people. Nobody came to hear us. We didn't even make enough money for food" (interview, 1998, El Recodo).

Their next trip was organized by Arnulfo Delgado, an impresario and associate of the Million Dollar Theater in Los Angeles. Built by Sid Grauman in 1918 on Broadway and Third Street and originally used as a movie theater and for stage shows in English, it became the most attractive entertainment house for visiting Mexican artists in the 1950s. Pedro Infante, Dolores del Río, Pedro Armendaríz, José Alfredo Jiménez, Agustín Lara, María Félix, Lola Beltrán, and many other famous artists performed at the Million Dollar Theater, which was well known throughout Latin America.[27]

Banda El Recodo's performance was such a success that it was booked again in the following years. Not only had it crossed the border, it had also conquered a new territory. Unquestionably, Banda El Recodo paved the road for the many bandas that would follow in the years to come.[28]

Aspiring banda musicians have often been accused of modifying or even betraying the tradition with their innovations, in particular the commercially profitable innovations. Germán Lizárraga told me: "Some people said that my dad did the musicians a very bad service by recording, because from then on nobody would hire a *banda*, because with twenty centavos and a jukebox, everybody could listen to banda. . . . But no, everything was getting under way." Although modern technology had an enormous impact on banda music and changed it in manifold ways, it did not take away the music's meaningfulness in people's lives. As it did a century ago, the tambora accompanies people from their first to their last breath. The music is intertwined with individuals' most memorable moments in life. Aside from highly commercialized bandas, including the recent techno version, one can still hear the throbbing tambora beat played by a *campesino* musician of a village banda, or the big-band mambo sound of the 1960s of a professional urban banda. Individual bands emerge and disappear, but the sounds will stay with us—be it a military march, a *guaracha*, a waltz, a bolero, or a cumbia.

A Bustling Tradition

Despite technological and commercial innovations, the traditional music is still very much alive. It is alive where those customs are practiced that have always included music. Yet, it is not necessarily the countryside that has preserved these customs; traditional music can be heard in the city as well. To illustrate this energetic tradition, the following paragraphs give some impressions of three events as they are celebrated nowadays: the *día de la música* [day of music] and the *feria ganadera* [stockbreeders' fair], both of which take place in Culiacán annually, and the carnival of Mazatlán.

EL DÍA DE LA MÚSICA

The daily life experience of musicians is a confrontation with the public's musical taste. In their workaday life, economic considerations have priority. But there is one day of the year where musicians collectively ignore the constraints of their profession, that is, the economic pressure to play for a paying audience: *el día de la música,* celebrated on 22 November, the feast day of Saint Cecilia, the patron saint of music. Asked why they commemorate her, banda musicians simply respond that it is an old custom to worship Saint Cecilia on that day. Among banda musicians in Culiacán it has become a custom to organize a procession through the center of the city on the afternoon of 21 November and to play the *mañanitas* for Saint Cecilia at midnight. "Las mañanitas" is a traditional Mexican song that is usually performed at birthday and saint's day celebrations in the early morning, thus the name.

The Catholic religion was introduced to Mexico by the Spanish conquerors, and with it all the saints of the Roman Catholic church. Cecilia was a Roman virgin martyr who died for her Christian faith in the third century. Early Roman sacramentaries, which contained allusions to the martyrdom and triumph of the appropriate saint for the day, honored the martyrdom of Saint Cecilia on 22 November. Ten centuries later, the story of her life and death was retold and embellished in medieval martyrologies, immortalizing her name and fame. According to these legends, Cecilia's voice was of such sweetness that even the angels descended from heaven to listen to her singing. Medieval artists provided Saint Cecilia with the emblems of music. Eventually, the whole Catholic world accepted her as the patroness of music. The first celebrations of Saint Cecilia's day by musical performances date back to the sixteenth century. After a musical society in England held a series of musical festivals on 22 November, similar musical celebrations became frequent throughout seventeenth-century Europe. Innumerable musical societies and other music institutions were and are named in her honor (Lovewell 1898).

In the late afternoon of 21 November 1996, around a third of the bandas located at Francisco I. Madero Boulevard prepared themselves for the annual procession in honor of their patroness. One by one, musicians showed up to get their instruments, which are usually stored in the banda's office or rehearsal room. Most of these rooms are rather small and sparsely furnished with a few chairs, a cooler, a little table, a phone, and, next to it, a blackboard announcing upcoming performances. Posters or photos of the banda decorate the walls. And there is, of course, the picture of Saint Cecilia. After socializing a bit in front of their offices, some musicians began to load the tamboras and other drums into the buses that were parked along the sidewalk. Finally the musicians were seated, and a convoy of six buses started to move. Escorted by policemen on motorcycles, they slowly drove down the street. The procession caused much attention, and not just because it made the traffic pause for a moment. Despite the cacophonous surroundings, the bandas succeeded in filling the narrow streets with their music. The sound blared through the open windows. For motorists, pedestrians, street vendors, storekeepers, and neighbors

22. Bus of Banda Mocorito de los Hermanos Pacheco parked in front of their office at Francisco I. Madero Boulevard, Culiacán. Photo by Helena Simonett.

alike, the procession was a musical reminder that Saint Cecilia's day was near. The convoy cruised for about half an hour through Culiacán's center. Finally, it returned to Francisco I. Madero Boulevard. Playing in a bus is not really pleasant. There is not enough space to hold a clarinet comfortably, not to mention a tuba or a tambora, and the sound level, especially during the tutti sections, is extremely high. Hence, many of the musicians seemed to be glad when the procession came to an end. After the buses stopped in front of the offices, the musicians got off, put away their instruments, and grabbed a beer.

When I returned to Madero Boulevard half an hour before midnight, nothing pointed toward the coming event. Some musicians I recognized from the procession were hanging around in front of their offices, chatting and drinking beer. The ambience was very informal. Los Guamuchileños invited me to enter their office. The rather scanty room was now immersed in a warm light. The altar with Santa Cecilia's picture was decorated with flowers and glittering paper; candles were burning, and little Christmas-tree lights were flashing. Red, turquoise, and gold dominated. The altars of the other bandas were decorated just as beautifully. Shortly before midnight, the musicians finally got up and gathered around their altars. Although some spectators were gathering in front of the doors and windows, the celebration was not aimed at them at all. At twelve o'clock the musicians intoned "Las mañanitas." The neighboring bandas began to intone the song, too. Some of them had to play outside their office

23. Musicians of Banda Los Nuevos Coyonquis waiting for customers in front of their office at Francisco I. Madero Boulevard, Culiacán. Photo by Helena Simonett.

due to lack of space. However, they also faced the altar to congratulate their patroness on her day of celebration:

Que linda está la mañana	How beautiful is this morning
en que vengo a saludarte	on which I come to greet you
venimos todos con gusto	we all come with pleasure
y placer a felicitarte.	and delight to congratulate you.
El día en que tú naciste	The day you were born
nacieron todas las flores	all the flowers were born too
y en la pila del bautismo	and at the baptismal font
cantaron los ruiseñores.	the nightingales were singing.

24. Banda Los Guamuchileños gathered at midnight in their office in Culiacán to play the *mañanitas* for Saint Cecilia, 1996. Photo by Helena Simonett.

Ya viene amaneciendo
ya la luz del día nos dio
levántate de mañana
mira que ya amaneció.

It is already dawning
and daylight has been given to us
get up in the early morning
look, it is already dawn.

Quisiera ser solecito
para entrar por tu ventana
y darte los buenos días
acostadito en tu cama.

I wish I were the sun
so I could enter through your window
and wish you a good morning
while you were still in bed.

Quisiera ser un San Juan
quisiera ser un San Pedro
y venirte a saludar
con la música del cielo.

I wish I were a Saint John
I wish I were a Saint Peter
I would come and greet you
with heavenly music.

De las estrellas del cielo
quisiera bajarte dos
una para saludarte
y otra para decirte adiós.

Of all the stars in the sky
I would like to give you two
one to greet you
and the other to say good-bye.

Con jazmines y flores
este día voy a adornar
hoy, por ser día de tu santo
te venimos a cantar.

With jasmine and flowers
I will adorn this day
today on your saint's day
we have come to sing for you.

Los Guamuchileños played the *mañanitas* with a passion that was different from anything I had previously heard. Some musicians had their eyes closed: their music making seemed to be an entirely personal and introspective matter. After their rendition of "Las mañanitas," they continued with waltzes played in an extremely slow tempo. Despite the waltz rhythm, these tunes were not danceable. The atmosphere was very contemplative: it was as if the slowly played traditional waltzes had created a sacred moment. Most of these men do not practice religion actively, and their motivation to worship Saint Cecilia is not religious in any ordinary sense of the word. Yet, the encounter with the music itself elicits deep emotions and hence is comparable with a profound religious experience. On the *día de la música*, musicians find themselves in a truly exceptional situation. On this one day, they decide that their only audience is their spiritual patroness. Hence, the payment they await to receive is not a material but a spiritual one: they trust that Saint Cecilia will guide them through the coming year.

One has to experience the *mañanitas* to understand that this popular belief in the help of a saint is more than superstitious. The celebration of the *mañanitas* allowed me to grasp the essence, to catch a glimpse of the soul of traditional music. It made me understand the *mañanitas* as a manifestation of a tradition's power for self-renewal. The music certainly moved the musicians as it did the audience that, despite the late hour, had appeared to listen to the music. The tradition once again had taken a hold upon its people.

LA FERIA GANADERA

I met most of the bandas that celebrated the *mañanitas* again at the fair that takes place each year on the grounds around Culiacán's bullfighting ring for two weeks in late fall. The *feria ganadera* is a festival that, apart from the exhibition of bulls for breeding, includes an amusement park with Ferris wheels and roller coasters as well as a marketplace with concession stands. Concerts and rodeo shows are held in the *palenque* [cockfighting ring] and in the bullfighting arena. Because such varied entertainment is offered, the fair attracts more than ranchers and cattle dealers. On the weekends, the grounds are crowed with families and young urban people. Although many of them pay attention to the cattle being exhibited, they are mainly interested in the various forms of entertainment. For the ranchers, naturally, the fair is an important place for business. Yet, as important as buying or selling is the possibility to gather together and have a beer. Hence, during the weekdays, the fair is mostly visited by ranchers, some of whom have come from far away.

Guadalupe "El Sirola" Ibarra told me that I could find most of Culiacán's approximately twenty-nine bandas on the fair ground between eight o'clock at night and four in the morning. He also mentioned that not only was there plenty of work at the fair for all of them, but it was also much better paid than the work in the cantinas where these bandas usually play. Indeed, they charge

25. *Banda de huipa* at the stockbreeders' fair in Culiacán, 1996.
Photo by Helena Simonett.

two, three, or four times more, depending on the deal they work out with their respective client. Since the fair only takes place once a year, the customers are inclined to spend more money to have a good time. Some of the ranchers—especially those who just sold their cattle—carry around wads of one-hundred-peso bills, and they seem determined to spend this money, be it on beer, music, or both. These men do not bargain very long about prices with the musicians. Hence, it is certainly possible for a banda to earn as much in one night at the fair as it does in ten days in the cantina.

Fascinated by the possibility of experiencing banda in yet another context, I spent several nights at the fair. Since it is located a little way outside the city, I went there by bus. After paying a small entrance fee, I could walk around the grounds as I pleased. The area nearby the bull exhibit, the rodeo arena, and the *palenque* captivated me the most because it was the bandas' territory. Standing in the midst of the crowd, I could spot the tuba bells reaching up above the heads of the masses. I counted at least half a dozen tubas and decided to stay close to one of them. Although the throng hindered the musicians from walking around easily, the banda was constantly in motion, trying to follow its patron, who was strolling down the square accompanied by some friends. He practiced a Sinaloan custom called *jalar la banda. Jalar* means to hire, but if used as a reflexive verb, *jalarse*, it means to get drunk. Usually, *jalar la banda* includes the the second meaning too. If practiced outdoors, it means to promenade through the streets, drinking and singing, accompanied by a banda. There are several songs that refer to this custom, for example, "Que me entierren con la banda" [Bury Me with Banda Music], composed by Melesio Chaidez Díaz:[29]

Mi vida siempre es alegre	My life is always cheerful
siempre andando de caramba	I always feel damn good
por eso quiero morirme	that's why I would like to die
paseándome con la banda.	when promenading with the banda.
La noche siempre es bonita	Nights are always beautiful
para andar en la parranda	for going on a drinking spree
llevándome por las calles	strolling through the streets
paseándome con la banda.	accompanied by the banda.
Al compás de un buen caballo	To the trot of a good horse
al son de la balacera	to the sound of the shooting
con diez cajas de cerveza	with ten boxes of beer
y la joven que yo quiera.	and the girl I love.
(¡Así se jala la tambora, señores!	(That's how the tambora gets going, Sirs!
¡Puro Sinaloa!)	Pure Sinaloa!)
Me encanta jalar la banda	I enjoy leading the banda
por todita la región	through the whole region
me gusta tratar amigos	I like to make friends
que les sobre corazón.	who have a lot of heart.

The refrain of Sinaloa's hymn, "El sinaloense," refers to the same custom:[30]

Ay-ay-aay, mamá por Dios	Ay-ay-aay, oh God, mamá
por Dios, ¡que borracho vengo!	oh God, how drunk I get!
que me siga la tambora	I want the tambora to follow me
que me toquen "El Quelite"	I want them to play "El Quelite"
después "El niño perdido"	after that "El niño perdido"
y por último "El torito"	and finally "El torito"
pa' que vean como me pinto	so that everybody can see who I am
ay-ay-aay, mamá por Dios.	ay-ay-aay, oh God, mamá!

Often, the patron goes on horseback while the musicians follow him on foot. Since horses are not allowed on Culiacán's fairgrounds, the patrons strolled along the food stands and between the bull exhibit and the palenque, followed by "their" musicians.

One night, after the rodeo show was over, one of the charros let his horse

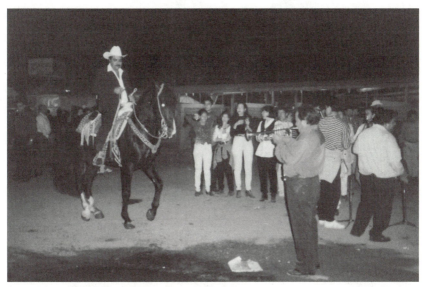

26. Disoc dancing to "El niño perdido" at the stockbreeders' fair in Culiacán, 1996. Photo by Helena Simonett.

dance to the rhythm of the banda that played in front of the stables. Dancing horses are a common sight in Sinaloa. I had seen ranchers with dancing horses before at village fiestas. Since these ranchers spend most of their life on horseback, they do not even alight at a fete. Having imbibed plenty of beer, but still sitting firmly in their saddles, they put on a show by letting their horses dance. The folklorist Frances Toor was obviously impressed by the manners of dancing horses when she wrote in 1930: "[The charros'] spirited horses are so well trained that at the sound of music they begin to dance. Then their masters ride them into the *cantinas*, where they put their front hoofs upon the counter and drink liquor from glasses. There is much drinking; often quarreling and shooting, and always singing and dancing" (1930: 29–30). Unlike his master, Disoc, the dancing horse at Culiacán's fair, did not guzzle liquor, but he shook his hoofs to the rhythm of the banda. The people stopped dancing themselves and made a circle around Disoc, who, to the amusement of everybody, even danced a fox-trot. The verses of a song that celebrates a horseman's nightlife and the fiesta came to my mind:[31]

Con la Banda Clave Azul	With the Banda Clave Azul
yo me quiero emborrachar	I want to get drunk
ique vengan Los Intocables	Los Intocables shall come
que cantan a todo dar!	to sing with vigor!

con la música norteña	Baltazar is going to get drunk
se emborracha Baltazár.	on *norteña* music.
¡Que le toquen una pieza	Let them play a piece
al caballo bailador!	for the dancing horse!
Baltazár es buen jinete	Baltazar is a good rider
y también hombre de honor	and a man of honor as well
para retar a su cuaco	to challenge his horse
de todos es el mejor.	he is the best of all.
¡Que siga el cuaco bailando	Let the horse dance
como el jinete lo manda	as the horseman orders
que me toque Clave Azul	Clave Azul shall play
para seguir la parranda	so the fete keeps going
que me canten mis canciones	my friends from the banda
mis amigos de la banda!	shall sing me my songs!
Andamos borrachos todos	We all get drunk
con tequila y con cerveza	on tequila and beer
unos porque traemos gusto	some because we are happy
otros porque traen tristeza	others because they are sad
¡que nos sirvan más bebida	Serve us more drinks
hasta que Dios amanezca!	until God wakes up again!

EL CARNAVAL DEL CENTENARIO

I arrived on Friday afternoon, just in time to join in the celebration of the famous Carnaval de Mazatlán. This year, the Mazatlecos celebrated its one hundredth anniversary, and one could expect five days of glamorous spectacles and ecstatic revelries. It was still quiet in the inner city, but busy hands put up stalls and tables, prepared the charcoal, stirred the atole, and put on the finishing touches. The anticipation of the great fiesta was tangible. By nightfall, carnival was fully under way. The streets leading to the Paseo de Olas Altas were alive with revelers of all ages. Music was blasting over the loudspeakers on the Paseo, and the bandas on the Plaza de Machado blared "Mi gusto es," "El sinaloense," and "Los papaquis," a carnival standard dating back a century. As always, Mazatlán's mild winter climate favored the open-air festivities. Immense crowds congregated in the center of the city to party, dance, eat, and drink. Booths were selling international food, snacks, and a lot of beer. Music flooded the streets. A few hours later, dizzied by the unaccustomed noise and motion, I decided to retire. Luckily, I did not have to walk far since I was staying at a friend's house just one block from the Plaza Machado. I felt asleep immediately. The banda continued playing all the beautiful traditional melodies of its repertory, and I was not sure whether or not I was dreaming.

Carnival, as it is celebrated nowadays, is the result of negotiations between dominant and subaltern groups that took place over a century ago.[32] Carnival was born of the conflict between the subjectivity of the different classes. Toward the end of the nineteenth century, the authorities sought to control the spontaneous and exuberant masses. In 1898 the "official" carnival celebration eventually replaced the popular revelry with the spectacle, and carnival—an attraction offered to the urban public—became part of the broader capitalist economy. Financed partially by local powerful individuals and commercial enterprises, the earlier critical aspect, the carnivalesque subversion, and the latent violence were successfully suppressed. The mocking verbal encounters, the *papaquis*, were transformed into the artistic *juegos florales*, a poetry and prose contest; the neighborhood rivalries were modified to the *combate naval*, ship-to-shore fireworks commemorating the battle between the Mazatlecos and the French in 1864. The official carnival celebration was dominated by the street parades of Mazatlán's upper classes. Introduced by wealthier citizens, floats decorated with allegorical figures, adorned bicycles, and *comparsas* (masqueraders) mollified the lower classes, who had been deprived of their uninhibited and boisterous street partying. Instead of participating in the popular flour games, they had to watch the reenactment of the game on an allegorical float. Celebrated in front of the masses, the coronation of the carnival royalty was an exclusively bourgeois activity. With the passage of time, the "master of ceremonies" turned into the "Rey Feo" [Ugly King], and the coronation of the genteel queen became a beauty pageant. Eventually, the local carnival became conceptualized as both industry and commodity within the national entertainment field. Under the direction of a central carnival committee, the annual pre-Lenten festival evolved into a series of staged, competitive performances for both adults and children (Vega Ayala 1991: 54).

It was at the carnival that the institutionalization of the beauty cult began.[33] Yet there is more to the carnival beauty peagant nowadays than smiling and waving; it means many hours of campaigning to raise money in the weeks leading up to carnival. Since the money from the sale of the votes goes to the Comisión de Promoción y Desarrollo Turístico (CODETUR), the organizers are interested in an profitable election system. In 1997, for example, the committee employed a method invented in 1961 by a publicist of Pepsi-Cola to end the predominance of the oligarchy and allow the middle class to participate in the competition. Sponsored by the soft drink companies, the so-called *corcholatazo* entailed that the public could vote for the candidates by depositing bottle caps in designated bins. Although this method was considered more "democratic,"

27. Jazz-Band Mutualista, sponsored by the local beer brewery Cerveza del Pacífico, at the Carnival parade in Mazatlán, 1936. Photo courtesy of Raúl Rico González, CODETUR (Comisíon de Desarrollo y Promoción del Turismo de Mazatlán).

money continued to determine the outcome of the beauty pageant. For the queen's contest of 1998, the committee came up with a new idea: to raffle a car for ten pesos a ticket and use these tickets as votes for the candidates.

The queen's selection had been passionate before, but the centennial celebration was marked by a new scandal—one that indicates how much beauty and power are intertwined. "The Drug Traffickers Like to Appoint the Carnival Queens," commented a national weekly magazine about the incident.[34] It was said that a girl who had actually placed second, the niece of an alleged drug trafficker, won the beauty contest because the leading candidate had had some of her votes withheld. Allegedly, this contestant and her family had been threatened by *narcotraficantes* if she did not withdraw from the contest. Everybody I asked in Mazatlán affirmed the rumors. Officials of the carnival organization, however, denied the murder threats, though they did not give a conclusive explanation of why the family of the leading candidate withheld votes so that her competitor could become the prestigious carnival queen. Instead, they pointed out that the queen's election had always been accompanied by controversies, and this was just one more and not to be taken seriously. After an initial outcry, the Mazatlecos became resigned to the outcome, and the carnival took its course as it had in years before.

Because of growing commercialization since the 1960s, carnival has evolved into a grand spectators' event. During carnival's centennial celebration, large audiences attended the competitive events held at the baseball stadium where huge screens transmitted the events onstage. The "Mega Show," the parade of the floats and the *comparsas*, was watched live by an estimated 500,000 spectators and on television by millions more. The show was for the eye rather than for the ear, although amongst the *comparsas*, the beauty queens, and the masked individuals riding on the floats, one could spot some musicians. In order to compete with the noise of the tractors that pulled the floats, the groups and recorded music had to be amplified through enormous speakers. Yet, contrary to the statement of the carnival organizer in its pamphlets that "tambora music remains a fundamental part of Carnival," bandas have vanished from the street parade: only one Sinaloan banda marched in the parade. Mazatlán's famous bandas were also conspicuous by their absence from the centennial celebration.[35] Banda El Recodo left town on carnival weekend to give concerts elsewhere, though they returned on Monday for a show at the Lienzo Charro in the Colonia Juárez, far from the center of the carnival celebrations.[36] The Paseo de Olas Altas reverberated with their recorded music only. A few members of Banda La Costeña were in town for a video production. The camera crew of Manoyo Productions, from Van Nuys, California, shot some pictures of La Costeña's vocalist singing in the bandstand in front of the cathedral.

On the part of the local banda musicians there was a growing reluctance to play at the carnival. Some banderos expressed their disappointment with the celebration in general. Others said that they lost interest in playing at the carnival because of differences with the organizers: not only could they not agree over performance fees, but the musicians insisted on receiving their compensation immediately after finishing their job.[37] José Luis "El Indio" Ramírez, the leader of Banda Los Escamillas, confirmed that bandas had had trouble getting their payment from CODETUR in past years. His banda thus preferred to keep its steady job at the Ostionería del Puerto.

Despite carnival's total commercialization, some aspects of the carnivalesque still palpitate in modern Mazatlán. The life-affirming and life-enhancing spirit continues to be carnival's main drive, for carnival's very idea is the celebration of the body, the senses, and the unofficial, uncanonized relations among human beings; carnival has to be lived (see Danow 1995). Thus, the "real carnival" takes place at the Paseo de Olas Altas, where thousands of revelers congregate every night to dance to the music that fills the air. Although the potential for violence increases in the densely packed streets as the night progresses, not many serious incidents were reported during the 1998 carnival.[38]

As in years before, the revelries extended from the Paseo de Olas Altas to the Paseo Claussen, but there was a clear division between the two sections: while staged bands (technobanda, norteño, banda, and recorded music) with powerful sound systems and expensive equipment were featured along the Olas Altas, a few local *bandas huiperas* strolled along the Paseo Claussen in search of paying clientele. This was also where some showily dressed, jewelry-clad, beer-drinking young men had congregated. Surrounded by their fellows and some young women in exquisite evening dresses, exhilarated by the banderos who played the corridos they had requested, they seemed to celebrate carnival in their own way. Their presence at Mazatlán's carnival as well as the *narcotraficantes'* alleged involvement in the carnival queen's contest were a conspicuous sign that Sinaloa's changing social reality has had some impact on its popular culture. The following two chapters will look more closely into how Sinaloa's contemporary popular culture and music have been shaped by both dominant and marginalized discourse. In particular, they examine how distinctive images and values perpetuated in folklore and songs have assisted the drug dealers' gaining acceptance, if not popularity. Following the flow of the illicit goods and the path of the traffickers, we return to Los Angeles, one of the urban centers across the border where the products are distributed and the traffickers enjoy their rewards.

PART 3

The Transnational Dimension of Banda Music
Narco Subculture and Contemporary Influences

The Music of a Transnational Subculture

De Sinaloa a California
me anda buscando la ley
más no han podido agarrarme
a pesar de su poder
sigo llevándoles polvo
no me ha tocado perder.
    Julio C. Preciado, Banda El Recodo

One afternoon in November 1996 I was lingering in front of the DIFOCUR bookstore in Culiacán.[1] A young woman who was also waiting for the store to reopen asked me what I was studying. I said, "Las bandas de Sinaloa." She then replied, "Pues, veniste al lugar justo para estudiar las bandas; tenemos muchos narcotraficantes aquí" [Well, you've come to the right place to study the Sinaloan bands; we have a lot of drug traffickers here]. I was a little bit baffled and hesitantly added, "Bandas de música." Whereupon she remarked: "Ay, es lo mismo" [Alas, that's the same]. Although I initially thought that this was only a minor misunderstanding—"banda" is a term used for both drug dealer gangs and music bands—it illustrates most tellingly a common image of banda and banda musicians in the minds of Culiacán's public. Since the 1970s, banda music has become more and more associated with and dependent on the subculture of Sinaloa's drug dealers, called for short *narcocultura* [narco culture]. Wherever drug bosses party, they hire a regional band—either an accordion-based *conjunto norteño* or a banda—to play their favorite music and entertain the invited guests. There are indeed plenty of newly composed songs, in particular corridos, that confirm this "custom," and the musicians themselves do not keep these "special events" a secret either.

The miscommunication described earlier is more than a simple anecdote.

Rather, it points to the very heart of a complex problem that involves questions about popular music and its relation to power, economic power in particular, and to violence. Luis Astorga asks in his book on the history of drug trafficking in Sinaloa, "Who in Sinaloa has not heard, or even danced to, a trafficker's corrido during some fiesta or in the street?" (1995: 139).[2] Despite the fact that many people still consider corridos that describe and apotheosize the deeds of drug traffickers both ethically and aesthetically deviant and morally and artistically depraved, the songs have become increasingly tolerated and accepted by Mexican society, notably in the rural areas of northwestern Mexico where they originated. Narcocorridos have entered public life not only in Sinaloa, but also in neighboring states as well as in the United States.

In this chapter, I would like to go beyond obvious factors such as the traffickers' economic power to coerce and coopt popular culture at large and ask why the general public has come to tolerate, and maybe even approve of, values and ideologies of the narco subculture. By relating the drug lords to Malverde, Sinaloa's most idolized bandit, I will show how subversive individuals may be transformed into folk heroes. Moreover, images of the Sinaloan character that have been perpetuated in folklore and songs facilitated the acceptance of certain subcultural values among a large public, even though the original values, shaped during the Mexican Revolution, were severely distorted. After a short historical survey of the drug trade in Sinaloa, I will focus on the image of the Sinaloan portrayed in regional songs and its recent shift as well as on the banderos and their alleged involvement with the drug traffickers.

The Bandit, the Hero, and the Narco

The Mexican Revolution of 1910 not only brought significant reforms in the national, political, and economic domains, it welded together diverse groups of people into one nation by forging a unique Mexican identity. "True Mexicanness" was found in the heroes of the revolution, whose struggle for social justice and equality laid the foundations of modern Mexico. Inspired by the revolutionary leaders and their deeds, a huge body of folklore grew up, which in turn served as fertile ground for popular culture, movies, and music. Despite personal tensions and violent battles between the revolutionary leaders (Zapata, Carranza, and Villa were all assassinated by fellow revolutionaries), the postrevolutionary regime laid them to rest in the pantheon of the national heroes. Mythologized and cultivated by the new government, the campesino leaders were transformed into "vehicles for applauding humility, endurance of suffering, and sacrifice for the Revolution" (O'Malley 1986: 132).

Although it was the revolution that generated the image of the brave man characterized by courage, presence of mind, generosity, stoicism, heroism, and bravery, ballads and stories of heroes were part of Mexican folklore long before the heyday of corrido production in the 1910s and 1920s. Many of these heroic men died for their ideals of social justice and thus are in some sense the precursors of the revolutionaries. Bandits, according to Eric Hobsbawm, "share the same values and aspirations of the peasant world, and as outlaws and rebels are usually sensitive to its revolutionary surges" (1969: 85).[3] Like the revolutionaries, nineteenth-century folk heroes opposed the ruling class and fought for the common people, the exploited and oppressed peasantry. Before the time of the mass rebellion against the regime of Porfirio Díaz in the early twentieth century, men who protested against oppression and poverty by disregarding law and order were called *bandidos*—criminals or outlaws. In the eyes of the common people, however, a bandido was not necessarily a bad person. Especially if he was a "social bandit" who committed crimes for the good of the community, he was a hero rather than a simple criminal. Activities regarded as unlawful by the authorities but originating from a concern for social justice may be considered rightful by the dispossessed. During periods of insurrection and reform, in particular, the unlawful may be conceived as legitimate and permissible action. Thus, categories such as good/bad and right/wrong are not necessarily antipodes. As we will see later, this same ambivalence also applies to a common attitude toward drug trafficking. Ethical categories are not as fixed as is often believed.

Like other regions of Mexico, northern Sinaloa has given birth to many brave men. One of the most celebrated is Jesús Juárez Maza, better known as Malverde, the "Generous Bandit" or "King of the Poor":[4]

Hermosa capital de Sinaloa
antes que todo te quiero saludar
para decirte la fama que tu tienes
que no cualquiera te la puede igualar.

Beautiful capital of Sinaloa
first of all I want to greet you
to tell you that your fame
is not matched by any other city.

Aquí existieron muchos hombres valientes
y uno la gloria ha logrado conquistar
Jesús Malverde, el bandido generoso
que allá en el cielo junto con Dios está.

You have brought up many brave men
and one of them has gained glory
Jesús Malverde, the generous bandit
who now is in heaven with God.

El fue un bandido mas nunca un asesino
cuando robaba era por necesidad
pues lo poquito o lo mucho que robaba
lo repartía con generosidad.

He was a bandit but never an assassin
when he stole it was out of necessity
the little or the lot he stole
he distributed with generosity.

Malverde allegedly was born in Las Milpas, in the municipality of Mocorito, in 1870. As described in the corrido above, Malverde was a Robin Hood–like figure rather than an ordinary bandit: hiding in the sierra, he robbed the rich and distributed the treasures among the poor. It is said that he even managed to let "his" people get the reward for his capture. Malverde, the noble robber, suits the image of the archetypal social bandit: what he stole "he distributed with generosity." The abstention from violence enhances his nobility: "he was a bandit but never an assassin." Although armed violence and killing were customary in Malverde's time and environment, it is understandable that the people would want their hero to be not only honest and respectable, but also entirely admirable (Hobsbawm 1969: 40). This desire is reflected in the following corrido, the story of the arrest of "El bandido generoso." An elaborate dialogue between Malverde and the official who has orders to execute him can be viewed as a kind of reconciliation between the opposed parties (law and outlaw), but above all, it allows for emphasizing again Malverde's noble character and his wit:[5]

Fusilaron en la sierra	They executed the generous bandit
al bandido generoso	in the sierra
murió amarrado de un pino	he died tied to a pine
con un pañuelo en los ojos	and with a scarf over his eyes
el gobierno lo mató	the government killed him
porque era muy peligroso.	for he was very dangerous.
En Durango y Sinaloa	He used to steal
donde seguido robaba	in Durango and Sinaloa
para ayudar a los pobres	to help the poor
o al que lo necesitaba	or whoever was in need
después hacía lo que el tigre	afterwards he would like the tiger
al cerro se remontaba.	withdraw to the mountains.
Cuarenta y ocho soldados	The forty-eight soldiers
que andaban tras de sus pasos	searching for him
todos le gritan aun tiempo	all shouted together,
—¡Sube las manos en alto	"Hands up and
y no trates de escaparte	don't try to escape,
porque te hacemos pedazos!	or we have to kill you!"
Le preguntaba el teniente	The lieutenant asked him
por que iba robando	why he stole.
—No robo porque me guste	"I don't steal because I enjoy it
tampoco me estoy rajando	or like to brag
me duele ver inocentes	it hurts me to see innocents
que de hambre andan llorando.	crying of hunger."

—No quisiera fusilarte
   por tu valor y nobleza
pero en toditos los bancos
   tiene precio tu cabeza.
—No se preocupe, teniente,
   cobre usted la recompensa.
	"I don't like to execute you
	   for you're courageous and noble
	but all the banks have put
	   a price on your head."
	"Don't worry, lieutenant,
	   redeem your reward."

—Vas a pagar con la vida
   tu buena acción con la gente.
—Eso yo ya sabía
   y no me asusta la muerte
en el infierno nos vemos,
   allá le espero, teniente.
	"You're paying with your life
	   for the good you've done for the people."
	"That's what I expected,
	   but death doesn't scare me
	we shall meet again in hell,
	   there I'll be waiting for you, lieutenant."

Malverde was hanged in Culiacán in May 1909, shortly before the outbreak of the revolution. Seventy years later a chapel was built by Eligio González León near the alleged place of his death:[6]

Vuela, vuela palomita,
   párate allá en aquella vía
cerquita de la estación,
   allí tiene su capilla
hecha por González León
   que es un hombre de valía.
	Fly, fly little dove,
	   stop on that track there
	near the railway station
	   where his chapel
	is made by González León,
	   a man of much prestige.

In Sinaloa, both the bandit and the bandit myth are important facts of life, impossible to overlook. Malverde's chapel is the most visible peculiarity of the bandido cult in Culiacán. It is evidence that people honor Malverde as a saint, although the Catholic Church has never made any move toward acknowledging him as one. People worship Malverde, asking him for all kinds of favors and miracles. In return, they show their gratefulness with gifts, including musical presentations for which they hire banda, norteño, or mariachi ensembles to play inside or in front of the chapel:[7]

De todo lo que robaba
   lo repartía entre los pobres
por eso es que hoy en día
   se le hacen grandes honores
con música y veladoras
   y ramilletes de flores.
	Everything he stole
	   he gave to the poor
	that's why nowadays
	   people honor him
	with music and candlesticks
	   and bouquets of flowers.

Malverde is omnipresent throughout Sinaloa. As the "Mañanitas a Malverde" assert: "They killed his body, but his soul remains with us."[8] People place little

28. Chapel and shrine of Malverde, "El bandido generoso," in Culiacán.
Photo by Helena Simonett.

29. Malverde's image imprinted on the silk shirt of a young patron at a performance of Banda El Recodo in Mazatlán, 1998. Photo by Helena Simonett.

altars with his figure, flowers, and candles at bus stations, in squares, or on street corners, or at home. If one looks at the different designs on the silk shirts of certain ranchers at the Feria Ganadera in Culiacán or of some of the clientele in Los Angeles's Sinaloan nightclubs, one will discover Malverde's portrait on the back, the front, or the sleeves of some of them. Many of these men carry a heavy golden medallion with Malverde's picture on their chest, next to a portrait of the Virgin of Guadalupe or the crucified Jesus.[9]

Malverde was originally the hero of the poor, but many rich people nowadays worship him too.[10] Narcos in particular are suspected of not only worshiping Malverde but also of identifying themselves with the generous bandit. Their deeds are known in Sinaloa as *narcolimosnas*, social works for the benefit of the community that are financed by drug charity. Narcos sometimes sponsor money allowing rural zones access to diverse services and commodities. Some remote dwellings in the sierra show evidence of narco charity: paved roads, schools, and even hospitals not financed by the government.[11] Because of their generosity, some narcos may be well respected and enjoy high social prestige and a good reputation in their native region. In the eyes of the rural poor, these modern Malverde-like bandidos may even acquire the mythic status of a folk hero.

Although a main source of their income is illegal, narcos are involved in many legal enterprises as well. Through their businesses, they have influential connections with bankers and politicians. The former may assist in laundering money, and the latter serve as protectors. Moreover, since most of the leading families are interrelated by marriage and/or by *compadrazgo* [godfather system], each drug lord has some relatives who are involved in official politics. Hence, without being legal, the drug traffickers' business is represented in the world of official politics, which means their business has a certain legitimacy, or is at least tolerated. Narcos play an influential role in the local culture patronizing leisure activities. They are employers and benefactors who build roads, introduce electricity and potable water, and loan money (see López and Prat Meza 1989; Trueba Lara 1995). Hence, despite activities that go hand in hand with drug trafficking—assault, robbery, kidnapping, and murder—they may be publicly respected men. In this sense, the narco unites the same two opposite personalities as the generous bandit: "Bad, but of noble hearts. Rude and unpolished, but loyal and upright. Murderers, but good-hearted. Various Sinaloans, past and present, have contributed to this value system and forged the collective imagination of a people. . . . It is not a hidden cult but rather a public, well-known, and openly celebrated one that unites and fuses folklore with delinquency and violence" (Córdova 1993: 39).

Picturing the Sinaloan: Boasters and Roosters

Songs, to put it somewhat generally, illustrate the character of the society in which they are created and for which they are designed. Sinaloa and its people are portrayed in the regional folklore, a folklore that reflects a collective mentality largely shaped by nationalistic ideologies arising after the revolution. This folklore appeals to its audience, which of course, has been shaped by the same ideologies.[12] As regionalist awareness grew, the sound of the tambora, the regional brass band, became representative for the state of Sinaloa.

Sinaloan composers came to consider the characteristic musical ensemble as the most suitable one to celebrate the state: "With the banda I will sing for the land I was born in and that I love from the bottom of my heart." Singers almost always mention their musical accompaniment. In some of the song texts banda's important mediating role is explicitly recognized. For instance, in "Los altos de Sinaloa" [Sinaloa's Heights], Cruz Lizárraga celebrated Sinaloa's natural beauty—its mineral wealth, its rivers, its panorama, its attractive women—and, as a representative of all Sinaloan bandas, Banda El Recodo:[13]

Que bonitos son los altos sinaloenses	How beautiful is upper Sinaloa
que colindan con la sierra occidental	that adjoins the Sierra Occidental
con sus grandes minerales de oro y plata	with its great gold and silver mines
y con vista de belleza natural.	and overlooking the [state's] natural beauty.
El folclor de nuestro estado	The Sinaloan bandas
son las bandas sinaloenses	are the folklore of our state
con la Banda de El Recodo	accompanied by Banda El Recodo
yo les canto esta canción	I sing this song to you
el orgullo de mi tierra	the pride of my land
está en mujeres bellas	is its beautiful women
que se entregan con cariño	who surrender with affection
y te dan su corazón.	and offer you their hearts.
Once ríos que también bañan su suelo	Eleven rivers bathe its soil
de los altos bajan todos rumbo al mar	from the altitudes they flow toward the sea
son millones las hectáreas que se riegan	the hectares they water are millions
para bien de nuestra gran humanidad.	for the good of our great human race.
De los altos se divisa el panorama	From the highlands unfolds the panorama
por las tardes cuando empieza	in the afternoons when the twilight
oscurecer	starts to fall
cuando el sol se va perdiendo entre	when the sun gets lost in
las aguas	the waters
regresando cuando vuelve a amanecer.	and when it returns at dawn.

Sinaloans are also proud of their history and their heroes. Fighting for social justice, these individuals have become examples of personal courage and moral integrity. "Los altos de Sinaloa" recalls Sinaloa's brave fighters and fosters their immortality:

Conocidos generales muy valientes	Famous and very courageous generals
Angel Flores, Juan Carrasco	Angel Flores, Juan Carrasco
y muchos más	and many others
que pelearon con las armas en las manos	fought with their weapons in their hands
solamente para darnos libertad.	only to grant us liberty.
Cosalá y su leyenda	Cosalá and its legend
forman parte de la historia	are part of our history
de aquel hombre sinaloense	that Sinaloan man
a su pueblo conquistó	who won over its people

y su nombre es eterno,
    lo traigo en mi memoria
lo apodaban como "El Rayo,"
    ése fue Heraclio Bernal.

his name is eternal,
    I will always remember him
they called him "El Rayo,"
    he was Heraclio Bernal.

Regional feelings are spurred similarly in the following song, authored by Alberto Chávez and dedicated to "Sinaloa":[14]

Al compás de la tambora
    le canto a mi tierra
a un pedazo de mi patria
    que se llama Sinaloa
y eso sí que satisfecho
    lo pregono donde quiera
que no hay tierra más bonita
    que mi lindo Sinaloa.

To the rhythm of the tambora
    I sing for my land
for the part of my native land
    that is called Sinaloa
I am very proud,
    I announce it wherever I please
no other land is so beautiful
    as my lovely Sinaloa.

Eres tierra de cantantes
    también de valientes
que figuran en la historia
    para nunca más morir
tiene fama donde quiera
    lo sincero de tu gente
que se apiada de cualquiera
    y también sabe sentir.

You're the soil of many singers
    and of many brave men
being part of history,
    they will never die
the sincerity of your people
    is well known
they take pity on anybody
    and also know how to feel.

Sinaloa, yo te canto
y en mi canto pongo todo el corazón
y en mi sangre vibra el gusto
y mi orgullo porque sinaloense soy.

Sinaloa, I sing for you
I put all my heart into my song
in my blood vibrates the delight
and my pride in being Sinaloan.

With folklore's increasing popularization, popular songs began to consolidate some of the existing stereotypical images. Under the commercial imperative, the idea or ideal of the *hombre valiente* [brave man] began to deteriorate slowly. Popular culture converted the kind of men the revolution had produced into mere *pistoleros* and *machos*. As Paredes has noted, the pistol is "a phallic symbol perhaps, but in a much more direct sense a symbol of power—and of the abuse of power as well. A symbol of the manliness of the bully, the macho of the movies, who guns his rival down in the middle of the street, lifts the girl to his saddle, and rides into the sunset on his faithful horse" (1993: 218). After the revolution, the brave man degenerated into the macho, whose courage is concentrated in his testicles, and into the pistol-toting bully, who commits crimes with impunity because he has power, money, and political influence.

In the following song, "Arriba mi Sinaloa" [Sinaloa Forever], by Jaime Peñoñuri, we learn about Sinaloans' negative image, namely as bullies and boasters. While the song's protagonist rejects these attributes, he shows pride in other, in his view apparently more favorable, images of "the Sinaloan": the stubborn fighter and the irresistible lover. The musical reference to two of Sinaloa's most typical pieces, "El sauce y la palma" [The Willow and the Palm Tree] and "El Quelite" [the name of a village in Sinaloa], evokes regionalist feelings:

Señores, pido licencia	Gentlemen, I ask for permission
para empezar a cantar	to sing you now
canciones que son recuerdos	songs that are memories
de Sinaloa y su capital.	of Sinaloa and its capital.
No soy matón ni bravero	I'm neither a bully nor a boaster
y nunca me sé rajar	but I never back down
si vienen buscando enredos	if you look for trouble
con mi pistola se las verán.	you'll get to know my pistol.
¡Arriba mi Sinaloa!	My Sinaloa forever!
Lo digo con toda el alma	I say it with all my heart
cuando oigo que la tambora	when I hear the tambora
me toca "El sauce y la palma."	playing "El sauce y la palma."
[música de "El sauce y la palma"]	[melody of "El sauce y la palma"]
Tampoco pido limosna	I never beg for charity
mi amor no es pa' cotorrear	my love is not to be taken lightly
a mí lo bueno me sobra	I have in abundance from the best
y hasta me vienen a procurar.	they even come after me.
En Mochis tengo un cariño	I have one sweetheart in Mochis
lo mismo que en Mazatlán	another one in Mazatlán
y me guardo los domingos	I reserve the Sundays
pa' ver los "mangos" de Culiacán.	to see the pretty ones in Culiacán.
¡Arriba mi Sinaloa!	My Sinaloa forever!
Mi pecho se lo repite	My heart repeats
cuando oigo que la tambora	when I hear the tambora
se arranca con "El Quelite."	playing "El Quelite."
[música de "El Quelite"]	[melody of "El Quelite"]

"Que retumbe la tambora" [Let the Tambora Resound], by Melesio Chaidez Díaz, is another song combining patriotic and patriarchal feelings. On the one hand, the tambora symbolizes the beloved Sinaloa, and on the other, it catalyzes this regionalist love: the tambora music serves to get one drunk and happy, to get one in the right mood to give the home state three cheers. Music, alcohol, pistols, horses, women, and friends belong to the image of the Sinaloan. Accompanied by the tambora, this man shows his qualities while on a spree:[15]

Soy sinaloense y me gusta la tambora	I am Sinaloan and I like the tambora
tomo el tequila, mezcal o bacanora	I drink tequila, mezcal, and bacanora
pues con la banda me paso noche y día	with the banda I spend night and day
porque me encanta de plano la alegría.	because I like to cheer happiness.
Soy sinaloense de hueso colorado	I am a hot-blooded Sinaloan
y tengo fama de ser enamorado	I've the reputation of being always in love
como jinete tener buenos caballos	as a good rider I have fine horses
y en las parrandas andar con buenos gallos.	and on a spree I'm always with good roosters.
¡Ay Sinaloa, Sinaloa, Sinaloa!	Oh Sinaloa, Sinaloa, Sinaloa!
Yo siento el alma	I feel my heart
que me pica y que me llora	that suffers and cries
con la pistola	with the pistol
que relumbra en la bola	that gleams out in the crowd
y con la banda	and with the banda
que retumbe la tambora.	that lets its tambora resound.
El sinaloense siempre vive muy alegre	The Sinaloan is always very cheerful
porque el bien sabe que pocas veces pierde	because he knows well that he hardly loses
en los amores se rifa con cualquiera	for romance he contends with anyone
y en las parrandas se vuelve hasta una fiera.	and when on a spree he turns into a wild beast.

The animal most often invoked in these songs is *el gallo* [rooster], a metaphor for a fighter, someone who is brave and aggressive in the face of danger. More specifically, the rooster stands for the valiant male hero with strongly pronounced sexual potency. His qualities may be characterized further as *valiente, bravo, fino, reconocido, afamado, jugado* [courageous, brave, fine, renowned, famed, experienced], or, in a phrase that encompasses all these attributes, as *un gallo muy sinaloense* [a very Sinaloan rooster]. His territory, of course, is the henhouse. Moreover, the brave fighter and gallant womanizer knows how to take pleasure in life. He distinguishes himself as chivalrous, noble, generous, and broad minded. His motto is to enjoy life and to spend everything as long as he can. "Vida prestada" [Borrowed Life], by Ignacio "Nacho" Hernández, for example, praises this attitude:[16]

La vida que vivo yo,	The life I'm living
yo la quiero disfrutar	I want to enjoy
y aunque digan lo que digan,	and whatever they say,
a mi no me va a importar	I don't care
porque cuando se me acabe	because the day it ends,
ya no volverá jamás.	it will never come back.
La vida que vivo yo	The life I'm living
nomás la traigo prestada	I have only borrowed
y el día en que me la quiten,	the day they take it back,
no voy a llevarme nada	I'll carry nothing with me
nomás un montón de tierra	only a pile of earth
con una cruz bien clavada.	with a well-attached cross.
De que sirve ser un santo	What is the good of being a saint
si a toditos por igual	if everybody's
se nos acaba el camino	life will finally
y se nos llega el final	come to an end
solo una vida tenemos	we have only one life
y hay que saberla gozar.	and that we'd better enjoy.

Ranchera music, Mexico's popular folk music genre, has served nationalistic purposes for many decades. Its passion-drenched singing style evokes patriotic feelings; its lyrics convey rural life as noble and romantic. Neither disillusionment over failed revolutionary ideals nor the socialist vision of the Cárdenas era (in the 1940s) manifested itself in popular music. Unaffected by political and social movements, ranchera music kept transmitting its idealized images of Mexico's rural world—and even the rural population itself began to believe in the stereotypes perpetuated by popular culture.

After the 1970s, however, Sinaloa's changing social reality began to have some effect on popular music. Although newer compositions did not really break with the entrenched ideologies, the picture of the idealized rural world began to crack, and the nasty reality began to creep into the song texts. As time passed, singers more frequently referred to Sinaloa as *la tierra de los narcotraficantes* [the land of the drug traffickers]. Saúl Viera, "El Gavilancillo," for instance, bemoaned Sinaloa and its people in "Los sinaloenses":[17]

Estado de Sinaloa,	State of Sinaloa,
¡cómo has agarrado fama!	what a reputation have you acquired!

con tus hombres de valor	with your men of honor
que trabajan en la mafia	working for the Mafia
trafican polvo maldito	they traffic the damn powder
y también la hierba mala.	and also the weed.

The vocabulary of the new songs about Sinaloa eventually began to include words such as "cocaine," "marijuana," and "trafficking," and tales of drug-related violence showed up in them. In "Sinaloa y su gente" [Sinaloa and Its People], Jesús Palma boasted:[18]

Desde que vine a este mundo,	Since I was born,
tú siempre has tenido fama	you've always been famous
de tener gente de acción	for having active people
y que la vida se gana	who make their livelihood
vendiendo la cocaína	selling cocaine
o sembrando marihuana.	or cultivating marijuana.

Rather than condemn the drug business, some singers seem to be proud of Sinaloa's international fame. In "El corrido de Badiraguato," for example, Chalino Sánchez announced with Sinaloans' typical bullheadedness:[19]

Señores, guarden silencio	Gentlemen, keep silent
y pongan mucho cuidado	and pay attention
voy a cantar un corrido	I'll sing a corrido
de un pueblo muy afamado.	of a very famed village.
Se llama Badiraguato,	Its name is Badiraguato,
es la tierra de los bueyes	it's the lands of the steers
apréndanselo despacio,	learn it slowly
pero apréndanselo bien.	but learn it well.

Este pueblo tiene fama	This village is famous
por todo mi Sinaloa	in the whole of my Sinaloa
porque nos echan la culpa	because they accuse us
que aquí sembramos la goma.	of cultivating narcotics.
Sólo les quiero aclarar	I only want to inform you
que aquí sembramos de todo	that here we cultivate everything
y si se enojan por eso pues,	and if you don't like it,
¡qué se enojen ni modo!	well so, who cares!

Sinaloa and the Drug Trade

Sinaloa is geographically and climatologically an ideal region for growing cannabis and opium poppies, and it has a long history of cultivating and trading drugs.[20] Since the nineteenth century, Mexico has produced and exported marijuana, which was primarily used for pharmaceutical purposes. In the early twentieth century, Chinese immigrants to Sinaloa and Sonora began to cultivate opium poppies. At that time, opium was legal and its flowers were even grown in Mazatlán's public gardens. After the prohibition of narcotics in 1927, the city's opium houses were closed. The government passed several antidrug laws in an attempt to control drug trafficking. But the cultivation of narcotics continued to flourish in the inaccessible and rugged Sierra Madre mountain states of Sinaloa, Durango, and Chihuahua. In the 1930s, northern Mexico was a transit point for drug smuggling bound for the U.S. market. However, Mexico was not an attractive partner in the drug trade until World War II interrupted the linkages of the heroin trade among France, Asia, the Middle East, and the United States. The production of marijuana and opium poppy plants in the mountainous area of the Sierra Madre was stimulated and financed by the United States, which needed to supply its and its allies' hospitals with morphine. By the late 1940s, Mexico's narcotics industry was well established despite national eradication campaigns such as the burning of opium poppy and marijuana fields. Encounters between the federal police and local drug gangs became more violent. An increase in U.S. marijuana consumption in the 1960s pushed Mexican marijuana production to new heights. Traffickers began to supply small-scale farmers with seeds, fertilizers, money, and weapons. "Many peasants [were] trapped in the dilemma of abiding by either the rule of law or the law of traffickers. Both law enforcers and drug traffickers [could] be violent, except that the latter [could] be a source of additional income" (Toro 1995: 42). Thousands of campesinos in poverty-stricken rural areas "reoriented their agricultural production" and got involved in the more lucrative enterprise.[21] When the heroin business in Europe and the Middle East collapsed in 1972, Mexico became the major drug supplier for the United States. Violence began to escalate. Because gunfights between rival gangs, drug-related murders, and execution-style killings were the order of the day, Culiacán became known as "the new Chicago of the huarache-gangsters."[22] By the mid-1970s, the narcos were a well-established social group within Sinaloa's society.

In a renewed effort to combat drug cultivation and traffic in the northern sierra, Mexico launched Operación Cóndor in 1976. The federal police, supported by the army, arrested hundreds of people involved in the drug business and burned a great number of the plantations. This large-scale eradication program helped control the situation for a while. Many of the drug traffickers had to flee Sinaloa. Their sudden departure had far-reaching consequences for the local economy. It also affected the musical bands that had become dependent on their well-paying patrons: "The years of the fat cows for the bandas and other ensembles were over; one could not hear the tambora anymore playing day and night 'El sauce y la palma,' 'Las Isabeles,' 'El torito prieto manchado,' 'Me importa madre,' 'El palo verde,' 'El pariente,' and all the other preferred melodies of those cheerful, naughty, and lively lads" (Figueroa Díaz 1991: 31).

In the early 1980s, however, drug trafficking and armed violence reappeared with greater intensity. *Corridistas* [corrido composers or balladeers] noticed the happenings in songs such as "La mafia vuelve" [The Mafia Returns] or "Han vuelto los pistoleros" [The Gunmen Have Returned]:[23]

Han vuelto los pistoleros	The gunmen have returned,
por ahí lo dice la gente	that's what the people say
vienen dispuestos a todo	they're ready for anything
porque son hombres valientes	because they're brave men
regresan a Culiacán,	they returned to Culiacán,
la capital sinaloense.	the capital of Sinaloa.
No vienen en plan de guerra,	They haven't planned a war,
son humildes parroquianos	they're humble citizens
vienen en buscar de aquellos	they've come to find those
que una vez los traicionaron	who once betrayed them
que les pusieron el dedo	who pointed the finger
y a la cárcel los mandaron.	and sent them to prison.
Las calles de Tierra Blanca	The streets of Tierra Blanca [*a notorious neighborhood of Culiacán*]
ya están muy bien transitadas	are already busy
ya se ven carros del año	one can see new cars
y se oyen rugir metrallas	and hear the roar of machine guns
y bonitas mansiones	and the nice mansions
ya no están abandonadas.	aren't abandoned any longer.
Se oye tocar una banda	One can hear a banda
por ahí con rumbo a las Quintas	from there by the Quintas
también un grupo norteño,	as well as a norteño group
corridos está tocando	playing corridos
a todos esos valientes	for all those brave men
que han venido regresando.	who've come back.

Operación Cóndor had an unintended consequence. The most powerful traffickers quickly adapted their organizations to the new enforcement climate. A good part of their huge profits was spent on protection, sophisticated U.S. weapons, and bribery of authorities. As a result, the drug trade grew more violent. Mexico's economic crisis in 1982, two devastating earthquakes, and the decline in oil prices in the mid-1980s gave the drug trade a major impetus. Moreover, the economic collapse coincided with both an increased demand for drugs in the United States and favorable weather conditions in northwestern Mexico. Mexico's high external debts and inflation rate had a profound impact on the country's social and political structure. Narcos became an important factor in the national economy by generating employment, bringing in foreign exchange, and investing money in infrastructure, companies, and the stock market.

Drugs are cultivated in rural areas where economic opportunities are few and a high percentage of the population suffers from chronic unemployment. Inflation and other adversities make life in rural Mexico difficult and have a debilitating effect even on the most law-abiding peasant. Traditional crops such as corn and beans are sensitive to drought. Thus, for many poverty-plagued farmers, intercropping illegal with legal crops is pivotal for their survival. These small producers are participating in clandestine activities not in pursuit of wealth and power, but out of pure necessity. As one corrido states: "He is of humble origin; he knows poverty well; he never presumes anything, wealth even less." For those involved in smuggling, risks are high, but the rewards are often worth it. Many poor feel that they have nothing to lose except life—a life, however, full of hardship and agony. In corrido lyrics, this gambler attitude is often given as an explanation for partaking in the drug business: "From very early on I understood how hard life is. That's why I decided that I wanted to raffle it off."

Small-time dealers and minor intermediaries who cross the border with small amounts of drugs every day dream of a better life, as a popular corrido remarks: "I don't deny that I was poor nor that I was a drudge [trafficking with small amounts], but now I'm a big shot." While there are corridos in which the protagonist boasts of being a narco because of self-interest, others reveal a social component:[24]

Cuando niño sufrió mucho,	He suffered a lot as a child,
a su mamá le decía:	he'd tell his mom:
—No más que crezca poquito,	"Just as soon as I grow a bit,
te van a tener envidio.	they will envy you."
Al parecer lo cumplió,	It seems he kept his word
porque le cambió la vida.	because he changed her life.

Or:

De plebe sufrió pobreza	He suffered poverty as a kid,
pero logró progresar	but he managed to progress

hoy es hombre de negocios	today he's a businessman
y le gusta trabajar	and he likes to work
pa' que a sus padres queridos	so that his beloved parents
nada les vaya a faltar.	won't lack for anything.

Corrido lyrics suggest that drug trafficking has a high correlation with poverty.[25] Indeed, young men from rural areas or disreputable urban neighborhoods are most likely to feel the tension between socially and culturally induced aspirations and their own inability to realize those aspirations in a legitimate way. A society in which economic progress is directly related to social progress and in which wealth is relatively easy to acquire entices men to opt for a quick, if criminal, way to make money in order to ascend socially. "Las dos hectáreas" [The Two Hectares], by Julio César Preciado, is one of many corridos that argue in this spirit:[26]

Las dos hectáreas de tierra	The two hectares of land
que me heredó mi padre	I inherited from my father
las sembraba con cariño	I cultivated with a lot of love
para salir adelante	to get ahead
más la realidad es otra,	but the reality was different,
me estaba muriendo de hambre.	I was starving to death.

Un amigo de mi infancia	One day a friend of my childhood
una tarde me propuso:	proposed:
—¡Vamos saliendo de pobres,	"Let's get out of poverty,
vámosle dando otro uso!	let's use the land differently!"
Les juro que en poco tiempo	I swear that in a short time
mi situación se compuso.	my situation improved.

Con aquellas dos hectáreas	With those two hectares
sembradas de hierba mala	cultivated with weed
inicié una nueva vida,	I started a new life
pues con dólares pagaban	because they paid with dollars
después ya fueron doscientas	I was able to cultivate
las hectáreas que sembraba.	two hundred hectares more.

El que se mete al negocio	The one who gets into
de traficar con la hierba	the trafficking of weed
vive rodeado de lujo	lives surrounded by luxury
y la gente lo respeta	and people respect him
bandas y grupos norteños	bandas and norteño groups
tocan en todas las fiestas.	play at all his parties.

In this corrido, the narco is portrayed as a respected, even admired person because he is an individual who has achieved important goals: power, status, and wealth. Many narcocorridos suggest that social acceptance is of prime importance to drug traffickers: "My father's friends admire and respect me because of the business I'm involved in, I walk wherever I please." If we assume that these texts mirror the public's view and represent narcos adequately, traffickers have gained not only social status but also an important cultural position within Sinaloa's larger society: they have become the new patrons of the regional music groups.

Narcomusic and the Image of the Banderos

Sinaloans in general, and narcos in particular, are known for their habit of throwing lavish parties. According to Astorga (1996: 105), during the heyday of the "narcoterror" in the 1970s, shoot-outs were often credited to *gomeros* [drug dealers] who got drunk while listening to tambora music. The connection between the banderos and the narcos was no secret: those years were the "ten fat years" in banda's history. Figueroa Díaz, for example, mentioned that "the tambora of the Coyonquis resounded for five days and nights in the house of a well-known and wealthy *gomero* in Culiacán who celebrated an extraordinary shipment to the border" (1991: 17).

Many banda musicians commented to me that they used to play for drug lords regularly. One of them proclaimed that I would not find a single musician who did not do such jobs. Since drug trafficking is affiliated with violence, the stories told to me reflect the milieu of violence. Often musicians themselves became the target of drunk patrons or clientele. Some banderos played at gunpoint until their lips started bleeding. Others were threatened and not paid for their performance. And others were left behind in the sierra after they finished their job, days away from the nearest dwelling or road. Yet, as newspaper reports from earlier in the century attest, violence has always been part of a musician's life. Thus, the circumstances under which musicians in the 1970s were playing had not changed so much. Musicians thought that the influence their new patrons had on the music itself was worse. As one banda musician explained: "Drug trafficking came to mess up the music. Unfortunately, we now depend on playing for the drug traffickers because it's they who pay for the music best. We are obligated to play what they ask for. And what they ask for is only music that justifies and upholds crime and trafficking. All that music is in corrido rhythm with a vocalist" (interview, 1996, Sinaloa). Mazatlán's chronicler Miguel Valadés certainly expressed the view of many older people who grew up with the sound of the tambora and now look at the recent changes:

The only thing I lament is that the new bandas are so contaminated. They dress like clowns, like eccentrics. Banda musicians didn't use to be like that! The garb of the former musician was that of a peasant. But now they put . . . it's the American influence! Those of us who like the original tambora do not accept this clowning. Cruz Lizárraga was the first to popularize the banda, but he also corrupted the banda. . . . Out of the need to survive, they do whatever pays well.

Nowadays, the music has changed to so-called narcomusic. Nowadays, the majority of the bandas play narcomusic . . . corridos about drug dealers. Why? Because the drug dealers pay them. During these last years, drug trafficking has been an important factor in the modification of banda music, for it is [only] the drug trafficker who is able to pay one, two, or three million pesos [old currency; roughly US$200–400] for a banda.

[With the increasing consumption of drugs in the United States] money began to roll in, a lot of money, and the drug dealers began to spend it on their *parrandas* [sprees]. That's how narcomusic began. What makes bandas so attractive is the noise they make. I remember when I was little . . . the drunkard, the *parrandero* [one who goes on a spree] liked to show off by making himself heard by the volume, the decibels of the wind music. Later, with the help of electricity, [bandas] didn't need so much force to dominate anymore. Bandas started to compete with each other to see which one could play louder. But rather than using the pure instruments, they use the new technology: potent, high-watt amplifiers. Nowadays, the bandas are 100 percent electrified. The original banda didn't have a vocalist [now they have]. And how they dress! They look like bullies, like clowns—no, no, that's something else. There are still two or three original bandas such as Banda Los Pioneros [Mazatlán]. Yet they live in misfortune because they aren't selling. (Interview, 1994, Mazatlán)

The power of the narcos also became noticeable in traditional practices such as the *jaripeo*, a rodeolike event. Jaripeo organizers began to announce the performance of the bandas as "la guerra de las bandas" [the war of the bands/gangs]. According to Valadés, the use of such vocabulary shows how much popular entertainment and music have come under the influence of Sinaloa's narco subculture.

In the early 1990s, commercially oriented bandas began to include more narcomusic in their programs and recordings. As narcomusic developed into a flourishing transnational business, Sinaloa's popular bandas felt compelled to expand their repertory. In 1992, Banda El Recodo hired Julio César Preciado as their lead singer, replacing Conrado Calderón, a professional singer from Nayarit. According to Germán Lizárraga, they exchanged the voice tracks on recordings already made to conform to the audience's shifting taste. In contrast to Calderón's refined voice, Preciado has a so-called ranchera voice. It has the same piercing, high-pitched, nasal quality as the voices of Sierra ranchers and

Sinaloan drug dealers.[27] Preciado's natural inflection is thus considered ideal for the performance of narcomusic. As one fan in Los Angeles observed: "His voice sounds *sinaloense*. He exaggerates [the twang] in the narcosongs. His voice gives you that mental click—it connects to dope dealing, it adds realism to the song" (interview, 1996). As could be expected, banda's commercial exploit of the narcomusic triggered some controversies. Confronted with the ambiguous image and message of the musicians, young fans in particular were torn between blunt admiration and attentive wariness: "A lot of people are saying that the quality of El Recodo has gone down a lot. Now, they even include a little bit of rap. They try to appeal to a younger audience. . . . The older generation doesn't agree with a lot of the changes. They know Banda El Recodo, but if they heard it now, they'd say: 'That's another Banda El Recodo.' [My friend's mom] says that they are playing trash right now; they didn't have a vocalist before; it was just pure, strong music; and now, they are playing a lot of trash—narcomusic" (interview, 1996, Los Angeles).

After it became known to a wider public that the ties of some bandas with drug traffickers were more than just musical, even Banda El Recodo, jokingly called "Banda El Recoco," felt compelled to defend itself. Poncho Lizárraga called the rumors lies scattered by envious minds and evil tongues. Yet, when the *Furia musical* writer Gonzalo Escudero asked him whether it was true or not that they had friends involved in drug trafficking, he affirmed: "Yes, but we also know politicians, lawyers, villagers, and many other people; [the narcos] are like any other audience. . . . We played many times [for narcos], and we don't mind admitting it, for they too like our music" (*Furia musical* 4, no. 7 [1996]: 22–23).

The controversy around narcomusic even made front-page headlines in the *Los Angeles Times* in January 1997. Critics were quoted as saying that "the ballads are the soundtrack to a nihilistic cult of automatic weapons and cocaine traffickers that is seducing their young," while defenders insisted that the ballads "are not the siren call of cocaine kings, but an artistic reflection of an undeniable reality . . . , a mirror of the contemporary Mexican political drama and part of a tradition as old as Mexico itself."[28]

Corridos Inherited by the Subculture

The corrido is a Mexican folk ballad that stems from the *romance español*, a long, often epic ballad introduced by the Spanish colonizers. Its transformation into a distinct Mexican form occurred during Mexico's struggle for independence in the early nineteenth century.[29] The corrido flourished during the Mexican-American war (1846–48) and reached its heyday during the revolution (1910–20). Corridos handed down on leaflets are an important source for the

30. Cover of the fan magazine *Furia musical* (April 1996) featuring Banda El Recodo. Cover story: "Banda El Recodo [musicians] Aren't Drug Traffickers!" © Furia Musical/Editorial Televisa. Used by permission.

documentation of Mexico's unofficial history. They comment not only on political events, national affairs, and natural disasters, but also on crimes, family feuds, and romantic entanglements. The corrido was so deeply embedded in rural society that after the revolution, the Ministry of Education used specially composed corridos for their so-called cultural missions.

Some corrido scholars limit the production of the "true" corrido to the period from 1880 to 1930. According to the Mexican musicologist Vicente Mendoza, after this period, the corrido lost its authentic folk character, its freshness and "spontaneity that emanated from the pen of mediocre writers"; it became "cultured, artificial, and often false." He concluded that "everything points to the decadence and the near death of this genuine folk genre" (1954: xvi).

The corrido is a song with a rather declamatory melody in either 2/4 or 3/4 time. Its harmony is based on the tonic, dominant, and subdominant chords. Whereas in earlier times the *corridista* [balladeer] used to accompany himself simply on guitar, singers are nowadays accompanied by norteño groups or bandas. The corrido is usually constructed of a number of stanzas of four or six octosyllabic lines. The melodic phrases are repeated for each stanza; occasionally, the corrido has a refrain, which may be in a different rhythm. Corridos used to be long story ballads, but nowadays they have to fit the three-minute format of popular songs.

The corrido style is extremely detailed and abounds in dates and names. Yet, as John McDowell has argued, "the purpose of the corrido is not, as some scholars have supposed, to convey news. . . . The corrido depends on a prior transmission of news; its purpose is to interpret, celebrate, and ultimately dignify events already thoroughly familiar to the corrido audience" (1981: 47). In contrast to the emotional style of ranchera singers, the corridista uses a deadpan language and performance style. Even the most melodramatic incidents are described in this matter-of-fact manner. Although the language employed in corridos is mostly simple and direct, the meanings of the texts are difficult for outsiders to understand. Not only do they feature the everyday language of the local ranchers or, in the more recent corridos, the drug dealers, they are also full of double entendres and allusions to local events, places, and individuals. Since the recounted story is usually put in the first or third person, the narrator pretends to know and to vouch for the protagonist. However, the narrator does not necessarily have to know the protagonist or observer, nor does the singer. This observation is particularly important for the analysis of commercial corridos.

In oral tradition, folk tunes exist in a array of versions or variants. On the other hand, folk tunes are essentially combinations of prefabricated elementary forms such as scheme, motif, theme, and formula. The creation of new tunes is largely based on permutations of more or less ready-made elements. Corridos, too, are largely based on formulas: the opening statement of date and place; the introductory reference to the singing of the corrido; a reference to the singer, the audience, or the song; dramatic speech events; journeys; certain words, exclamations, proverbial expressions, metaphors, and allegories; the bird messenger; and the farewell and so forth. According to McDowell, "The presence of a certain number of these familiar formulas establishes the outlines of the world of the corrido. A hero is present; his steed is honey-colored; a pistol gleams in his hand. . . . Many formulas in the corrido signal the corrido world; on this stage the particular story unfolds" (1972: 215). Moreover, formulas introduce the central and peripheral themes and facilitate the metric and rhyme requirements of the genre. Consequently, the corrido may be analyzed not only as a social document, but also as a literary text.

One of the most widespread, but somewhat romantic, views recognizes the corrido as a genre that expresses the people's feelings—their grief and happiness, their victories and defeats: "That is why [the corrido] only flourishes when a grand idea or profound grief takes possession of the collective soul; when profound grief or a grand idea consolidates collectively. . . . [Thus] the subjects of the songs are those men who have fought the most for those grand ideas during times of armed upsurge [Independence, Reform, and Revolution]" (Henestrosa 1977: 9).[30] The folk heroes of the late nineteenth and early twentieth centuries were individuals fighting against Porfirio Díaz's cruel regime. They raised arms against the established social order and the representatives of the ruling class, the *federales* [federal soldiers]. It is no surprise, then, that the production of corridos in which the deeds and deaths of such heroic men were extolled culminated during and immediately after the revolution. The protagonists of these corridos fit the image of the hero whose actions show courage, boldness, and strength. Defending one's honor through armed combat is more than legitimate: it is virtue in a man for him to protect his dignity, his pride in his maleness.

By 1930, however, "the sense of manliness typical of the Revolution is converted into exaggerated machismo," as Paredes has so pointedly observed. "Machismo betrays a certain element of nostalgia; it is cultivated by those who feel they have been born too late. . . . The Mexican macho behaves as if he is still living in the times of Pancho Villa" (1993: 234). Whereas the heroes of the revolution fought on behalf of all lower-class Mexicans for a more dignified life, the heroes of the more recent corridos are fighting private and less ethical battles. In these corridos it is common for "two rivals [to] confront each other publicly—in a *cantina*, a dance, or a similar popular meeting place—and the encounter will help define the merits of the individual and, implicitly, the values of the community. . . . [T]hese conflicts very often result in death" (G. Hernández 1995: 32). Such duels are often provoked by seemingly insignificant matters such as excessive eye contact. Conflicts may arise anytime a man feels disrespected or dishonored. Where a notion of manliness dominates that connotes virility, pride, and a particular self-concept of personal worth in one's own eyes as well as those of one's companions, physical violence is easily justifiable, for it is considered the only way to reestablish one's honor. Not only are men apotheosized and their deeds immortalized in corridos, but Mexican ballads are generally written by men and hence abound in patriarchal ideology. But is it still the "peasants or newly transplanted campesinos living in the city . . . who compose, buy, hear, and sing corridos," as Herrera-Sobek (1990: 14) argues in her feminist analysis of the Mexican corrido?

No doubt the corrido tradition is alive despite industrialization and urbanization. Contrary to predictions in the 1950s that the genre would not survive the decade, "the recorded radio performance has been a major factor in keeping these musical traditions alive. The corrido song style is thriving not only in Mexico, particularly in rural areas, but also in such large urban centers in the United States as Los Angeles, Detroit, and Chicago" (Herrera-Sobek 1990: ix).[31]

Indeed, the escalating sales of the recording industry and the popularity of radio stations that broadcast narcomusic in the United States suggest that the corrido is no longer confined to a rural and semiurban population or to a specific social class. The current boom of the corrido genre indicates that the music industry has succeeded in generating a music that speaks to very heterogeneous audiences—both south and north of the border. The following chapter, thus, will focus on Los Angeles, the center of narcomusic production, its agents, and its protagonists.

Another Sound in "Nuevo L.A."

En Los Angeles radica
de la vida ha disfrutado
se pasea por Las Vegas
Washington y Colorado
tomando con sus amigos
con la banda por un lado.
      Chalino Sánchez, Banda Flor del Campo

Antonio Aguilar's interpretation of the corrido of Lamberto Quintero was a big hit in the mid-1980s among a Mexican radio audience north of the border.[1] The corrido "Lamberto Quintero" (and a movie by the same title), performed by one of Mexico's foremost ranchera singers and actors, not only increased Quintero's fame posthumously, but also immortalized his name. This young Sinaloan man was supposedly a notorious drug trafficker and one of the many victims of the rivalry between the Quinteros from Badriaguato and the Lafargas from San Ignacio. Triggered by a random murder in 1971, the vendetta between the two mafioso families stretched over several years. In January 1976, Lamberto was gunned down in El Salado. Two days later, the families and their *gatilleros* [hired gunmen] had a half-hour shoot-out in the center of Culiacán in which between twenty and thirty people were killed. The vendetta eventually ended with the total extermination of the Lafarga clan (Figueroa Díaz 1991: 47). Lamberto Quintero allegedly had a passion for horses and alcohol, and he enjoyed going on his sprees accompanied by banda music. Because of his fondness for "las hembras, el chupe y la tambora" [women, drinks, and banda music], Quintero is "an authentic Sinaloan." Quintero's Sinaloan attributes and his dramatic death provide the fabric from which corridos are traditionally made. Although Quintera was nothing but a drug trafficker, the acclaimed composer Paulino Vargas turned him into "un hombre fuera de serie" [an extraordinary man] and bestowed upon him the status of a hero. "Chito" Lafarga, who was also killed during the lethal encounter in El Salado, was honored with a corrido composed by a local corridista, a cousin of the victim. It is said that the corrido was made quite well, yet the influence of the mighty Quintero clan impeded it from being performed and recorded (Figueroa Díaz 1991: 115). While the corrido of Lamberto Quintero, performed by Aguilar and the venerable Banda La Costeña, soon conquered the airwaves and immortalized Lamberto's name, Chito Lafarga's corrido, and hence his name, will be lost forever in anonymity. The successful suppression of Lafarga's corrido by the Quintero clan not only shows how hegemonic forces work within the subculture, but also points to the corridos' significant function within the subculture.

In recent years, music related to drug trafficking or traffickers has become very popular among a predominantly young Spanish-speaking audience north of the U.S.-Mexico border. Commercial narcomusic is a fast-growing business, especially in the United States. Considering the current popularity of narcocorridos among young Latino audiences, we may assume that some, if not many, listeners indeed regard dope-dealing as a gratifying shortcut or a magical path to personal empowerment, even if they are not personally involved in the illicit business. After all, norteño groups that represent this music, such as Los Tigres del Norte and Los Tucanes de Tijuana, are among the most successful transnational bands, as measured by sales figures and official recognition such as Grammy awards.[2] Associated with commodified structures and incorporated into the network of the superculture, they have reached a visibility that evidently validates the music they play. Although frowned upon by the authorities and banned from the airwaves in Mexico, narcocorridos nowadays get significant airplay, especially in the Los Angeles area.[3] Tracking profitable "ethnoscape markets," major record labels have signed and are promoting narcobands.

In the late 1980s, the influence of norteña music on the banda repertory grew stronger. In order to be competitive in an international music market that embraces principally the United States and Mexico, renowned bandas began to focus more and more on the reinterpretation of the narcocorrido repertory.[4] Banda's gowing popularity north of the border, thus, was not only triggered by the technobanda craze, it was also a result of its appropriation of norteña hits.

Although "narcocorridos are to dance to, to listen to, but not to live," as a prominent narcocorrido composer has asserted, there are an increasing number of aficionados who commission narcocorridos for themselves. In Los Angeles, the center of the corrido industry, such songs have become a status symbol among drug traffickers, as well as among those who seek to imitate them, that substantiates success, wealth, and power. The flourishing business with narcocorridos in Los Angeles nightclubs and recording studios began around 1990. Largely responsible for this development was the Sinaloan corridista

Chalino Sánchez, who, immortalized with and through his songs, embodies like no one else the narco subculture that encompasses both the United States and Mexico. This chapter will explore both the overarching and the local music systems, as well as their interplay.[5] In comparing the body of commercial and commissioned narcocorridos, special attention is given to the differences between the two types.

Música norteña and the "corridos prohibidos"

Los Tigres del Norte is indisputably the most popular and the most influential norteño group. The group's members originate from northern Sinaloa, but they have lived in San Jose, California, since the late 1960s. After Los Tigres del Norte launched its first big hit in the early 1970s, it became one of the top-selling groups in the Latino market, and it figures among the most influential binational bands.[6] Although the group succeeded in capturing with its bittersweet immigration songs the imagination of hundreds of thousands of Mexicans living in "el otro México," it initiated its career with "Contrabando y traición" [Contraband and Betrayal], a corrido about drug smuggling. This hit song also established the band in Mexico. Using a clever marketing strategy of fabricated censorship, Los Tigres produced an entire album about drug trafficking in 1989 with the title *Corridos prohibidos* [Forbidden Corridos]. In the decade since, hundreds of norteño bands have emerged on both sides of the border taking advantage of the narco theme. Los Tigres' bold but successful marketing strategy to turn "forbidden corridos" into a desirable commodity has also found imitators: recently, Los Tucanes de Tijuana released an album named *Tucanes de plata: Catorce tucanazos censurados* [Silver Toucans: Fourteen Censored Tucano Smash Hits]. Although Los Tigres del Norte distanced itself explicitly from the violence and drugs that mark most norteño lyrics nowadays, the majority of the songs on its Grammy-nominated 1997 album *Jefe de jefes* [Boss of Bosses] exploit the narco theme again. In the title song the Tigres defend their decision in a spoken dialogue: "—I like the corridos because they describe the real events of our village/people. —Yes, I like them too because they sing of the pure truth."[7] The claim to truthfulness seems to be a clever strategy to disguise what really counts in the music business, namely, the number of records sold. Moreover, it is a simple excuse for the exaltation of drug trafficking in popular music.

Los Tigres' lasting success suggests that its migration-related corridos and border-crossing themes express widely shared experiences and views among Mexican immigrants and hence appeal to many of them. Yet, the production of its songs is based not on emotional and sentimental considerations but rather on unrelenting calculated commercial interests. Los Tigres and the composer

Enrique Franco know how to take advantage of the market. According to the musicians themselves, their selection of the themes for new compositions "depends on the stories of new happenings. We do some marketing research to find out what people feel, and according to the results we use the vocabulary that the people understand, depending also on the countries we are touring. We make sure that all the stories are entirely truthful. Who ever brings us a magnificent idea, we try to round it off so that it fits our market."[8] In Los Tigres' opinion, this is exactly what technobandas and bandas have neglected: they have not been creative enough in launching new songs, instead repeating the same themes over and over again. Because banda lacks market strategies, Los Tigres predicts a decline in its popularity. So far, however, bandas' incorporation of "prohibited corridos" into their repertory has catapulted them to the top of the regional Mexican music market. Norteña and banda now coexist as favorite musical ensembles to interpret corridos and narcocorridos respectively.

Although Sinaloa has a long history of cultivating and smuggling drugs, corridos about the illegal trade are a relatively recent phenomenon. María Herrera-Sobek supposes that these corridos grew out of the smuggling tradition of the Lower Rio Grande border. In her analysis of the drug corridos of the 1960s and 1970s, she observes a strong moral stance among the border communities against drug trafficking despite the prevalent view of smugglers as "culture-conflict type heroes" (1979a: 53). Yet, if the corrido indeed expresses the moral view of a community, as many corrido scholars believe, we would have to avow a major change in people's attitudes toward drug trafficking since the 1980s. With a few exceptions, the more recent corrido production is an apotheosis of the narco and his life style. Although the way of life narrated in narcocorridos may be part of the everyday life of many inhabitants of various cities and regions in Mexico and across the border, these corridos can no longer be considered folk ballads in which the common folk express their sentiments and points of view regarding their social reality. Commercialized and mass-mediated narcocorridos call for a redefinition of this genre. Contemporary corridos not only suffer from a commercial mystification of the drug trafficker, they also succumb to the hegemonic power of the popular culture industry. The current popularity of the corrido genre indicates that the music industry has managed to generate a music that speaks to an audience that is not confined by social, regional, national, or gender boundaries. But it also blurs the fact that there exist distinct corrido audiences.

Commercial Narcocorridos

There are basically two types of narcocorridos: the commercial corrido and the noncommercial or commissioned corrido. Whereas the former type is recorded on compact discs and made available to a mass audience, the latter may be heard in nightclubs frequented by drug traffickers. Some of the non-commercial corridos may be obtained on cassettes sold in small record stores or at swap meets throughout Nuevo Los Angeles. Since the boom in commercial narcocorridos in the 1990s, noncommercial corridos too have been discovered as a profitable commodity by major record companies such as Capitol Records (EMI Latin) and Balboa Records (Musart).

Commercial and commissioned narcocorridos have much in common. Yet there are a number of noticeable differences, created by the proficiency of the composer and the target audience. Corridos aimed at the general public are usually composed by a professional songwriter and reflect an outsider's view. They retell happenings already published in newspapers and spread by radio and television; they narrate fictitious stories about drug traffickers' adventurous lives, worries, victories, aspirations, and deeds, usually in the voice of the narcos themselves; they justify and gloss over unlawful actions associated with the drug business; and/or they mirror the fantasies of personal potency and virility. "Clave privada" [Private Code], composed by Mario Quintero Lara, lead singer of the norteño group Los Tucanes, is representative of this type of corrido:[9]

Dicen que me andan buscando	I heard they are looking for me
que me quieren agarrar	that they want to catch me
ruéguenle a Dios no encontrarme	pray to God that they don't find me
porque les puede pesar	because they could regret it
mi gente se me enloquece	my people get crazy
cuando le ordeno matar.	when I give them orders to kill.
Ya mucho tiempo fui pobre	I was poor for a long time
mucha gente me humillaba	humiliated by many people
empecé a ganar dinero	I started to earn money
las cosas están volteadas	everything has changed
ahora me llaman patrón	they now call me boss
tengo mi clave privada.	I have my private code.
Yo me paseo por Tijuana	I promenade through Tijuana
en mi cheyene del año	in my latest Cheyenne
dos hombres en la cajuela	two men in the back
con un cuerno en cada mano	with a rifle in each hand
de vigilancia dos carros	two cars as vigilance
por si sucede algo extraño.	just in case anything strange should happen.

Voy a seguir trabajando	I continue to work
mientras tenga compradores	as long as I have customers
en los Estados Unidos	those in the United States
allá existen los mejores	are the best of all
compran cien kilos de polvo	they buy one hundred kilos of powder
como comprar unas flores.	just like they would buy some flowers.

Quiero mandar un saludo	I wish to greet
a toditos los presentes	all of the persons present
amigos que están conmigo	my friends who are with me
y también a los ausentes	and those who are absent
brindemos por las mujeres	let's toast to the women
las traigo siempre en mi mente.	whom I always have in mind.

Mi orgullo es ser sinaloense	My pride is to be Sinaloan
lo digo donde yo quiero	I say it wherever I want
Estado de muchos gallos	State of many roosters
que se encuentran prisioneros	who are now imprisoned
pero este gallo es más bravo	but this rooster is braver
les canta en su gallinero.	he's singing in their henhouse.

Tengan cuidado, señores	Be careful, gentlemen
andan buscando la muerte	you are looking for death
el miedo no lo conozco	I don't know what fear is
para eso no tuve suerte	in that I wasn't lucky
soy cerca de Mazatlán	I'm close to Mazatlán
tierra de puros valientes.	region of the brave men.

This corrido is narrated in the voice of a drug lord who is intimidating law enforcement and bragging about his power, his wealth, and his cleverness. The way he acquired his affluence is no secret, but he does not even think of taking any responsibility for his illegal business. Rather, he tries to win sympathy from underprivileged people. They will understand because they too have experienced the humiliation of being poor. He suggests that for people like him (and them) there is only one way to gain respect: to get rich. Money not only buys respect but also luxury articles as well as other people, including bodyguards, gunmen, friends, and women. The modern corrido hero has replaced horse and pistol with the Cheyene del año [lastest-model Chevrolet Cheyenne] and the cuerno de chivo [AK-47 rifle]. These two objects are the most distinguished items of the modern hero who still boasts of his pride in being Sinaloan and the bravest of all brave roosters. In traditional corrido manner, the narrator greets his audience (verse 5). The greeting is a refined tool the composer employs to make the actual audiences believe that they too are part of the narrator's exclusive circle of friends. Hence, the corrido speaks directly to us listeners, inviting us to sympathize, if not identify, with the drug lord whose generosity embraces all of us.

The following corrido, "La clave nueva" [The New Code], also composed by Mario Quintero Lara, is fabricated after the same model:[10]

Ya descubrieron mi clave	Now they've discovered my code
pero no me han agarrado	but they couldn't catch me
mátenlo con todo y gente	to kill me and all my men
mil veces han ordenado	a thousand times they've ordered
pero mis cuernos de chivo	but my rifles
todo tienen controlado.	have everything under control.
Saben que soy sinaloense	They know that I'm Sinaloan
pa' que se meten conmigo	why do they meddle with me?
mi herramienta de trabajo	my working tool consists
son puros cuernos de chivo	of pure rifles
y dejan de disparar	and they only stop to shoot
cuando ya no existen vivos.	when no one is alive anymore.
Donde quiera me paseo	I walk around wherever I please
pero muy bien escoltado	but well escorted
yo sé que corro peligro	I know that I risk danger
no puedo andar descuidado	if I go around without protection
mis ordenes son matar	I've already shown
ya se los he demostrado.	that my orders are to kill.
Mi nombre ya lo conocen	My name is well known
el falso y el verdadero	the false and the real one
yo sigo vendiendo polvo	I continue to sell powder
nunca he conocido el miedo	I've never known fear
¡cómo he repartido kilos	How I have distributed kilos
aquí y en el extranjero!	here and abroad!
Como amigo soy amigo	As a friend I'm a real friend
como galán soy un gallo	as a gallant I'm a rooster
como enemigo cuidado	as an enemy, be cautious
pa' disparar soy un rayo	I shoot very fast
y para quitarme el sueño	to keep sleep away
[otra versión: para darme un perico]	[other version: to take a parakeet]
no necesito ir al baño.	I don't have to go to the restroom.

La muerte a mi no me asusta	I don't fear death
todos vamos a morir	everybody has to die
por eso hay que divertirnos	that's why we have to enjoy ourselves
antes de que llegue el fin	before it's too late
—Primo, en el carro está el kilo	"Cousin, bring the kilo from the car
¡tráetelo para repartir!	so we can share it!"
Yo sé que me andan buscando	I know that they're looking for me
por cielo, mar y por tierra	in the air, on the water, and on the land
ya descubrieron mi clave	they've already discovered my code
pero mi clave primera	but only my first one
van a pelarme los dientes	they can't beat me
ya tengo mi clave nueva.	I already have a new code.

Norteño hits such as these were widely reinterpreted and recorded by bandas. Eventually a few songwriters emerged from the camp of the banderos, among them Julio C. Preciado, at that time lead singer of Banda El Recodo. His narco-corridos, "El Cheyene del año" [The Latest-Model Cheyenne] and "De Sinaloa a California" [From Sinaloa to California], show significant similarities with Quintero's corridos above: the trafficker is too smart to be apprehended by the law; he is surrounded by weapons, luxury goods, friends, and women; he insults and ridicules the police; and he boasts of being a true Sinaloan, that is, a honorable man and a brave rooster:[11]

De Sinaloa a California	The law is hunting me
me anda buscando la ley	from Sinaloa to California
más no han podido agarrarme	but despite their power
a pesar de su poder	they couldn't catch me
sigo llevándoles polvo	I keep bringing them powder
no me ha tocado perder.	so far I've never lost.
Me han visto por Sinaloa	They've seen me in Sinaloa
y por tierras michoacanas	and in Michoacán
en mi cheyene del año	in my latest Cheyenne
y mi pistola fajada	and with my pistol in the holster
mientras que los federales	while the federal police
buscan mi clave privada.	is looking for my private code.
Les voy a dar una pista	I'll give my friends
a mis compas federales	from the federal police a hint
soy sinaloense hasta el tope	I'm Sinaloan to the brim
y no hay perro que me ladre	and no dog dares to bark at me

la mujer es mi delirio	women are my delirium
y mi cuerno es mi compadre.	and my *cuerno* is my companion.
Tengo amigos donde quiera	I have friends everywhere
porque soy hombre de honor	because I'm an honorable man
él que llega a conocerme	I show my values to those
le demuestro mi valor	who get to know me
no importa cual sea el terreno	this brave rooster doesn't care
este gallo es muy entrón.	whose territory it is.
Adiós amigos sinceros	Good-bye my sincere friends
de Sinaloa a California	from Sinaloa to California
mi nombre no se los digo	I don't tell you my name
se me borró en la memoria	it is erased from my memory
digan que soy un mendigo	just say I'm a beggar
que no figuro en la historia.	who does not exist in history.
Adiós a los judiciales	Good-bye also to the criminal police
y federales también	as well as to the federal police
si se terminan los narcos	if you finish up with the drug dealers
¿quién le va a dar de comer?	who's going to feed you?
Mejor ya déjense de eso	You'd better give that up
yo los puedo mantener.	and I will support you.

The lyrics come with subliminal messages that glorify the drug business and are often encoded. Yet poetic devices such as the *doble sentido* [double entendre] have always been very popular among Mexico's lower classes. Hidden and ambiguous meanings not only subvert the dominant use of language, they also allow prohibited or censored topics to enter the popular discourse. For example, the rooster, parakeet, and goat stand for marijuana, cocaine, and heroin, respectively. The protagonist of the Tucanes hit song "Mis tres animales" [My Three Animals], composed by Mario Quintero Lara, boasts that he makes his living with the three fine animals: "My animals are selling better than the hamburgers at McDonalds." And in "La piñata," the same norteño group sings about "the most expensive piñata in recent years": instead of candies, the piñata at the party of an influential narco was filled with the brave animals.[12] I frequently heard children and young teenagers request these two songs at Los Angeles radio stations, probably still unaware of the implied meaning.

Not all commercial narcocorridos glorify the lives and deeds of the drug traffickers. On the contrary, the plot often takes its own course: destiny hits and the trafficker recognizes his wrongdoing, usually too late. In "La carga del diablo" [The Devil's Cargo], for instance, the protagonist deplores his cruel fate:[13]

Maldito sea mi destino	Damned my destiny
maldita sea mi suerte	damned my luck
maldita sean las drogas	damned the drugs
maldito aquel que las vende	damned those who sell'em
ojalá y que los quemaran	if only they would burn
a todos con leña verde.	all of those with the green bills.
Yo también soy asesino	Me too, I am a murderer
envenené a mucha gente	I poisoned many people
pero ahora quiso el destino	but then destiny
pegarme un golpe de muerte	struck me with death
me arrebató a mis dos hijos	it robbed me of my two sons
por culpa mía solamente.	it's all my fault.
Por ambición al dinero	Because I sought to be rich
me dediqué al contrabando	I dedicated myself to contraband
mis pobres hijos murieron. . . .	that's why my poor sons had to die. . . .

Although the protagonist of the corrido "El destino cobra" [When Destiny Charges] does not moralize, the message rings through:[14]

Juro que daría a la vida	I swear I'd give my life
por volver a Sinaloa	to return to Sinaloa
poder andar por sus calles	to stroll through the streets
paseando con la tambora	followed by the tambora
de Mazatlán a Los Mochis	from Mazatlán to Los Mochis
de Culiacán a La Noria.	from Culiacán to La Noria.
Se acabaron los amigos	All my friends
y aquellos carros del año	and those latest-model cars are gone
también los cuernos de chivo	so are the *cuernos de chivo* [AK-47s]
con los que hice tanto daño	with which I did so much harm
hoy me encuentro detenido	now I'm in jail
nada dejó el contrabando.	the contraband left nothing.
Hice dinero a montones	I made piles of money
y hoy no tengo ni un centavo	and now I've not even a penny
ya no hay coñac ni canciones	there is neither cognac
ni más viajes a Chicago	nor music, nor trips to Chicago
tampoco mis plantaciones	nor my plantations
en Culiacán y Durango.	in Culiacán and Durango.
Adiós linda Tierra Blanca	Good-bye beautiful Tierra Blanca
adiós Lomita querida	good-bye beloved Lomita

adiós a todas las bandas	good-bye to all the bandas
que me alegraron la vida	that have made my life happy
cuando yo tenía "palancas"	when I had power
y daba buenas mordidas.	I was known for giving good tips.

Si un día salgo de la cárcel	If one day I'll be released
y mi Dios me lo perdona	and if my God forgives me
quiero volver con mis padres	I'd like to return to my parents
a mi lindo Sinaloa	and my lovely Sinaloa
a levantar mis maizales	to pick up my cornfields
y no volver a la droga.	but never do drugs again.

Como me duele aceptarlo	How it hurts to admit
qu' envené a tantos niños	that I intoxicated so many children
nunca me puse a pensarlo	I never thought
que un día se cobra el destino	that one day destiny might collect
hoy otros son millonarios	today others are the millionaires
envenenando a los míos.	intoxicating my beloved.

Narcocorridos do not present a complete picture. As they give voice to different experiences of reality, they stir up various conflicting reactions. Similar to the different views of the *bracero* experience in elitelore and folklore described by Herrera-Sobek, people not involved in the narco culture judge it from a different position than people directly affected by it. Critics who want to ban narcocorridos from the airwaves in the United States forget that a music forced underground will gain power rather than disappear. The ban of narcocorridos from Sinaloa's radio program certainly did not dam up the production of narcomusic; and Los Tigres have sold a record number of copies of their album *Corridos prohibidos*. Defenders, on the other hand, often forget that corridos are no longer "the artistic expression of a people," but a million-dollar market with enormous profits for which multinational labels are competing.

Composers such as Mario Quintero Lara, Teodoro Bello, Paulino Vargas, and Julio C. Preciado certainly know how to fabricate a commercially successful narcocorrido. This type of corrido is, as Astorga (1995: 37) suggests, a kind of oral retranslation of the already visible—cars, weapons, clothes, attitudes, and gestures—and an assertion of the already articulated. Indeed, most of what these corridos reveal has either been published in newspapers and spread by radio and television, or is part of a collective myth. A closer look at commercial corridos shows that they hardly ever mention names, nor identifiable locales or events. Rather than specific individuals, the persons described are characters or prototypes of the narco, very similar to the archetypal bandido-hero. Although narcos are far from being "noble robbers," they benefit from the bandido myth. Like the bandits, they "are heroes not in spite of the fear and horror their actions inspire, but in some ways because of them. They are not so much men who right wrongs, but avengers, and exerters of power; their appeal is not that of the agents of justice, but of men who prove that even the poor and weak can be terrible" (Hobsbawm 1969: 50). Men who dare to oppose the authorities have always earned the respect of the underprivileged. Audacious individuals such as highwaymen, poachers, brigands, hoodlums, smugglers, desperadoes, and other outlaws have captivated the imagination of many people all over the world. In contrast to the official (governmental) representation of these criminals, however, the image painted in folklore is more favorable. It is no surprise, then, that modern folklore (the commercial corrido) portrays the modern bandit (the narco) in a sympathetic manner as well.

Commissioned Corridos

The same is, of course, also true for noncommercial narcocorridos. Commissioned corridos reveal the customers' desire to present a colorful self. Moreover, since these ballads are based on firsthand information provided by their customers, they also contain forthright statements about the protagonists' worldview. From the narcos' point of view, drug cultivation and trafficking is a way of life, often the only way of life with which the narcos are acquainted. The world of the drug traffickers is not anarchic at all; rather, it follows a set of established rules that are based on a deeply ingrained value system. Narcos' value judgments, as deduced from their corridos, overlap considerably with traditional Sinaloan virtues such as honor, sincerity, generosity, courage, endurance, uprightness, and intrepidity.[15] As mentioned above, their corridos are not originally intended for a mass audience. Rather, they are commissioned by individuals who find pleasure in having their own corrido, or by relatives or friends who want to honor and remember a deceased person:[16]

Baudelio Chaydez y Nacho	Baudelio Chaydez and Nacho
también su hermano	also his brother Juan Luis
Juan Luis lo recuerdan con cariño. . . .	remember him with affection. . . .
Sus hijos y sus hermanos	His children and his brothers
sufren mucho por su ausencia	suffer very much because of his absence
lo extrañan y le echan de menos. . . .	they miss him a lot. . . .

Or:

Ya me voy, ya me despido	I'm leaving, I bid farewell
fue mi triste cantario de brindo	I sang this sad dedication song

porque su hijo mayor   because his eldest son
le manda hacer el corrido. . . .   requested a corrido. . . .

Such corridos are usually made by insiders—a friend, an acquaintance, or a local singer or bandleader—who are intimately familiar with the world of the narcos. Many corridistas share the essential moral standards and ideologies of the patrons who request corridos. Thus, in spite of their references to atrocious deeds, such as killing rivals, commissioned corridos often convey a tone of innocence and of normality.

The majority of the people involved in the cultivation of narcotics come from rural areas of the Sierra Madre. Thus, they are familiar with the typical local music: the norteño corridos and the banda tunes. As mentioned in the preceding chapter, narcos are known for their habit of throwing extravagant parties. With abundant money but few years to live, traffickers spend much of their drug profits for personal consumption: "He returns with a lot of money, and he is looking for ways to spend it"; "He spent the money for banda music."

The custom to have live music playing at a party is often mentioned in commissioned narcocorridos. The following verses are just a few examples:[17]

Cuando Jaime anda en su tierra	When Jaime goes around
con sus amigos tomando	with his friends drinking
siempre un conjunto norteño	there is always a norteño group
o esta banda está tocando	or this banda playing
por una mujer bonita	what you hear now
es la que se esté escuchando.	is dedicated to a beautiful woman.

Or:

En Los Angeles radica,	He resides in Los Angeles
de la vida ha disfrutado	where he enjoys life
se pasea por Las Vegas,	he shows off in Las Vegas,
Washington y Colorado	Washington, and Colorado
tomando con sus amigos,	drinking with his friends
con la banda por un lado.	and with a banda at his side.

Or:

. . . Es el corrido de Lalo	. . . This is the corrido of Lalo
como todos lo llamaban	as he was called
alegre y muy parrandero	cheerful and on a spree
en California gozaba.	he enjoyed life in California.
Gozaba con sus amigos	Partying with friends,
ya que así se divertía	that's how he amused himself:

—¡Toquen "Los amarraderos"!	"Play 'Los amarraderos'!"
al conjunto le decía.	he said to the band.

This type of corrido is usually composed on request by an individual who, as is sometimes suspected by the audience, wants to immortalize himself and/or the person to whom the ballad is dedicated. Since the composer and the customer often know each other, have mutual friends, or frequent the same locales, the relationship between the first person singular (corridista) and the third person singular (narco) in commissioned corridos coincides with the actual relationship between the corridista and the client.[18] The customer usually provides the corridista with a list of biographical data that he wants to have mentioned: names of friends and places, his car model and favorite weapon, details of his deeds, and so forth. The composer accommodates his client's wishes. He puts the information in rhyming octosyllabic lines, garnishes it with formulas borrowed from the traditional corrido repertory, and sets it to a plain melody based on a simple chord progression.

New compositions may be heard live in particular nightclubs in Nuevo Los Angeles that feature local bandas and norteño groups. For the musicians, such nights may be very lucrative. The regular clientele of the nightclub dances to the music of the patron, whose presence is anything but a secret. Obviously, private corridos are also intended to be heard in live performance and by a larger audience, as the following corridos suggest:[19]

No voy a hablar de tragedias	I won't speak of tragedies
ni de difuntos famosos	nor of famous dead men
el corrido le dedico	I dedicate this corrido
al buen hombre de negocios	to a good businessman
él que quiere escucharlo en viva	who wants to hear it live
para sentirse orgulloso.	so that he can be proud.

Or:

En viva quiere el corrido	He wants the corrido live
para poder escucharlo	so that he can listen to it
tomando con sus amigos	and enjoy it together
quiere a la vez disfrutarlo	with his friends drinking
y también pa' que se piquen los	but also to annoy those
que han querido tumbarlo.	who wish to bring him down.

If a client wants to have his corrido as tangible proof of his aptitude and his "heroic deeds," he may arrange to record the composition with the musicians of his choice in one of the recording studios in the area.[20]

Commissioned corridos are significant for both the creation and the perpetuation of a narco's self-image. Narcos are inclined to brag about their courage, coolness, capability, and efficiency. As characterized in their own ballads, narcos favor the sphere of danger and violence that allows them to act out a masculine ideal of manliness and an aggressive will to power. Despite this bravado, narcos seem to depend greatly on being accepted and loved. Hence, they surround themselves with loyal friends and beautiful young women:[21]

Trae una súper bonita	He carries a super beautiful one
con el cartucho cortado	that is loaded and ready
la quiere pa' perdonar aquel	he has it to pardon the one
que lo ha traicionado	who betrayed him
sus amigos lo respetan,	his friends respect him,
las muchachas lo han amado.	women have loved him.

Or:

Tiene amistades muy buenas	He has very good friends
porque sabe respetar	for he knows how to respect
le toca mucho la banda	the banda or this musical group
o este grupo musical	often play for him
las mujeres lo procuran	the women seek him
porque es hombre especial.	for he is a very special man.

Commissioned narcocorridos also contain candid statements about the protagonists' worldview. Since most of them are living a rootless life in a temporary, precarious, and insecure environment, drug traffickers have strong feelings for their home, their kin, and the ranch where they grew up. Many commissioned ballads contain a poignant nostalgia for this lost idyll:[22]

Al rancho Los Vasitos	He has a lot of affection
le tiene mucho cariño. . . .	for the ranch Los Vasitos. . . .
La colonia Sinaloa	He always remembers
el siempre le ha recordado	his neighborhood Sinaloa
allí fue donde creció	where he grew up
y se enseñó hacer honrado.	and learned how to be respected.

Or:

Ya con ésta me despido	With this I bid farewell,
se me ha llegado la hora	the time has come
de terminar mi corrido	to end my corrido
pa' mi lindo Sinaloa	for my beautiful Sinaloa
lugar donde yo he nacido	where I was born and raised
y creado entre la amapola.	in the midst of the poppy plants.

In contrast to commercial narcocorridos which favor fierce encounters between narcos and law enforcement, commissioned corridos pay much less attention to lawmen than to the narcos' real enemies: fellow narcos, in particular *soplones* [traitors] and *gatilleros* [hired gunmen]. Although the government, the police, and the drug enforcement agents are the drug traffickers' natural opponents, commissioned narcocorridos suggest that their protagonists respect them as part of the game. Agents and soldiers are considered brave as well, because they too know how to die with honor. In-group traitors, on the other hand, are regarded as dishonorable because they neither respect nor adhere to the local moral system of which they are also a part. Within this moral ideology, the narcos' illicit business and bloody deeds do not contradict such self-ascribed virtues as being respectful, honorable, generous, hardworking, and trustworthy. Moreover, narcos have a strong sense of justice: "He is an upright and loyal man"; "He always liked to do everything in a just way." In practice, however, this justice is often likely to take the form of vengeance and retribution. Vendettas are passed from father to son and may last for generations:[23]

Le mataron a su padre	They killed his father
en una forma cobarde	in a very cowardly way
Amador siguió adelante	Amador continues
buscando a los criminales	to search for the criminals
para cobrarles la deuda	to collect the debt
de esos falsos federales.	from these false federal agents.

Drug cultivation, processing, and distribution are accompanied by high homicide rates. Revenge killings and blood feuds rage. Deadly violence is so common in certain communities that it affects everyone:[24]

El rancho se está acabando	The ranch is getting smaller
el panteón se está agradando	the graveyard is growing larger
año por año es lo mismo	year after year the same happens
en esos meses de mayo	in these May months
uno, dos o tres que dejan	one, two, or three who leave
viudas y madres llorando.	widows and mothers crying.

Despite the corridistas' newspaperlike reports on these happenings and their traditional matter-of-fact narration style, narcocorridos do not tell the magnitude of the problem. Yet, many of them express its human side.

Chalino Sánchez

I learned about Chalino Sánchez's death when I first heard a corrido on the radio telling of the brutal assassination of this well-known singer. I was

31. Chalino Sánchez, a fervent admirer of Pancho Villa, dressed up as a Mexican revolutionary. On this recording, Chalino is accompanied by Banda Santa Cruz de Irineo Pérez (Los Angeles). CD produced by Pedro Rivera, who firmly believed in Chalino's talent and who recorded and promoted Chalino Sánchez on his Long Beach–based label Cintas Acuario. Photo by Pedro Rivera (1992). Used by permission.

shocked because I heard him singing "Nieves de enero" [Snows of January] or "Alma enamorado" [Heart in Love] whenever I tuned in to the Los Angeles FM station KBUE. Thus, it had never occurred to me that Chalino might already be dead. His voice was ubiquitous in Mexican Los Angeles, but not only there, as one of the many corridos composed in his memory suggests:[25]

Te oigo cantar	I hear you singing
en Monterrey, en Sinaloa y en Nayarit	in Monterrey, in Sinaloa, and in Nayarit
tú ya no estás	you are no longer
pero tu voz todos la escuchan, verdad de Dios.	but, by God, we all continue to listen to your voice.

Chalino Sánchez was a key figure in the musical landscape of Mexican Los Angeles in the early 1990s, but his impact was still noticeable at the end of the
decade. His legacy is the numerous corridos that he recorded, accompanied by
bandas and norteño groups. Part of his legacy is also the approximately 150
corridos that have been composed in his memory since his assassination in
1992. Never before had so many corridos been devoted to a single person.
Chalino's success was partly due to his ability to fabricate his own image by
drawing from Sinaloan folklore, the bandido-hero myth, and the corrido tradition. But more important, Chalino lived the corridos he sang, or, as one corridista expressed it: "Vivió cantando el corrido y el corrido fue su muerte" [He
lived singing the corrido; the corrido was his death].

Sinaloa's newspapers reported Chalino's death the day after his brutal assassination in Culiacán. Apparently Chalino's car was stopped on one of the city's
main streets shortly after he and some friends had left a nightclub called Los
Bugambilias, where he had performed until after midnight. His friends reported that Chalino was "arrested" by men who appeared to be agents of the
federal police. The next morning, Chalino was found dead, shot four times execution style. According to the newspaper reporter Luis Lim, Chalino's violent
death was like one more of his corridos, which were full of stories about
vengeance, assassinations, excessive passions, and even sentence of death.
"Crimen en Culiacán" [Crime in Culiacán], one of the corridos on his latest album, Lim believed, was a foreshadowing of Chalino's own fate.[26]

The police investigation apparently brought to light two contradictory versions of the events that resulted in Chalino's death and raised many questions.
Version 1 states that Chalino left the nightclub accompanied by his brother and
a woman, but without his five armed personal guards. On Insurgentes Street,
close to the Cuauhtémoc intersection, they were cut off by two cars, a Tsuru
and a Suburban. Version 2 claims that Chalino and his friends were followed by
his escort when heavily armed agents in a Suburban stopped them on Madero
Boulevard. The agents apprehended Chalino and drove away before his bodyguards could interfere. It was never learned whether the kidnappers were real
or disguised police agents, nor who had ordered the execution of the famous
singer. The files were closed, and Chalino's case rests with all Culiacán's other
unsolved crimes.

"La muerte de Chalino" [Chalino's Death], composed by José Quiñonez and
performed by El Bronco de Sinaloa, is representative of the many corridos that
narrate Chalino's death:[27]

(Descanse en paz, mi amigo Chalino
    Sánchez.)
	(May you rest in peace, my friend Chalino
	    Sánchez.)

Sinaloa está de luto	Sinaloa is in mourning
también en México entero	as well as all of Mexico
por la muerte de un cantante	because of the death of a singer
lloran en el extranjero	they even cry abroad
su nombre, Chalino Sánchez	his name, Chalino Sánchez,
amigo fiel y sincero.	a true and sincere friend.
Año del noventa y dos	In the year of ninety-two
tu le acortaste el destino	his destiny was changed
a principios del presente	at the beginning of the present
alguien le pegó unos tiros	somebody shot him
en Culiacán, Sinaloa	in Culiacán, Sinaloa,
le acortaste su camino.	his path was shortened.
Mayo 15 era la fecha	May 15 was the date
viernes por cierto ese día	it was certainly a Friday
cuando salía de cantar	when after singing he left
del salón Las Bugambilias	the nightclub Las Bugambilias
fue en la glorieta Cuauhtémoc	it was at the Cuauhtémoc square
le taparon la salida.	where they stopped him.
Un Tsuru y una Suburban	A Tsuru and a Suburban
el paso le habían truncado	cut off his path
dizque era la federal	it was said they were the federal police
y que iban a interrogarlo	and that they wanted to question him
cuando lo vieron confiado	after they had persuaded him
lo llevaron secuestrado.	they kidnapped him.
Entre las cuatro y las cinco	Between four and five
al despuntar [un] nuevo día	when the new day began
ya con los ojos vendados	with the eyes covered
a él lo hincaron de rodillas	they thrust him on his knees
en una forma cobarde	in a cowardly way
Chalino perdió la vida.	Chalino lost his life.
"Tanto va el cántaro al agua	"The pitcher goes often to the well
que se tiene que quebrar"	but is broken at last"
Después de varios intentos	After several attempts
por quererlo asesinar	to kill him
la muerte ya lo buscaba	death sought him out
sin dejarlo descansar.	without letting him rest.

Su muerte un rompecabezas	His death is a puzzle
muy difícil de juntar	very difficult to put together
Chalino no era dejado	Chalino could not rest
alguien lo mandó matar	somebody wanted him dead
por envidia o por venganza	because of envy or revenge
o un coraje pasional.	or a passionate anger.
En este mundo rodamos	We roam this world
como se rolan los dados	like rolling dice
y algunos que son mañosos	and those who are clever
¿bien saben cuando pararlos?	know well when they have to stop
mas cuando hay tramposo	but one day even the villain
q' un día tarde tendrá que pagarlo.	has to pay for it.
En un panteón solitario	In a lonely pantheon
lejos de la sociedad	far away from society
se encuentra una tumba triste	one can find a sad grave
donde ahora descansa en paz	where he now rests in peace
mi amigo Chalino Sánchez	my friend Chalino Sánchez
siempre lo he de recordar.	I will always remember him.
Vuela, vuela palomita	Fly, fly little dove
no te canses de volar	never stop flying
avísale Abel Orozco	notify Abel Orozco
él del famoso Parral	the one from the famous Parral
también dile a sus amigos	also tell his friends
que no volverá a cantar.	that he'll never return to sing.
Ya se fueron las flores de mayo	The May flowers are gone
y con ellas ha ido un gran amigo	and with them a great friend has left
cuando lleguen las nieves de enero	when the January snows arrive
su recuerdo estará siempre vivo.	his memory will always be alive.

This corrido is molded in the traditional corrido style. Verse 1 introduces the subject of the corrido; verse 2 specifies the date and place of the crime; verses 3 through 5 give details of the occurrence, largely corresponding with the facts reported by the newspaper; in verses 6 through 8, thoughts about the bloodshed are expressed, and about violence and death in general; with verse 9 Chalino's story ends; verses 10 and 11 add the assurance that he will never be forgotten. To understand every detail of this corrido, some previous knowledge of the events and the localities is necessary. Moreover, this corrido draws from the pool of formulas traditional corridos are made of. Verse 10, for example, uses one of the most common lyric formulas: "vuela, vuela palomita" [fly, fly little dove]. The dove or some other bird is usually asked to deliver the message of the corrido to named individuals. In this corrido, the dove shall bring the sad message of Chalino's death to the owner of the "famous Parral," a nightclub in South Gate, Los Angeles, where Chalino used to sing. Verse 11 contains poetic allusions to Chalino's own songs.

The following corrido, "Recordando a Chalino" [Remembering Chalino], written by Alma Martínez and performed by her brother Rogelio Martínez and Banda Los Guamuchileños (from Los Angeles), refers to the many corridos that have told Chalino's story and hence does not repeat it. Instead, Chalino and his work shall be remembered: "Quitillo," the "Hermanos Mata," and "Pelavacas" are people for whom Chalino composed corridos. "Alma enamorada" and "Nieves de enero" are the title songs of the last albums Chalino produced, and "Las golondrinas" [The Swallows] is a farewell song traditionally played at burials:

Siento un nudo en la garganta	I feel a knot in my throat
y muy triste el corazón	and my heart is very sad
al recordar a un amigo	when I remember a good friend
que mataron a traición	who was killed by betrayal
él era Chalino Sánchez	he was Chalino Sánchez
cantante y compositor.	a singer and composer.
Varios corridos se escuchan	Several corridos could be heard
ya de su muerte fatal	about his fatal death
yo no contaré la historia	I won't tell the story
muchos la han contado ya	which has already been told by many
solo quiero recordarlo	I only want to remember him
sin llanto y sin falsedad.	without weeping or falsity.
Era un hombre muy famoso	He was a very famous man
también muy enamorado	and always very much in love
rodeado siempre de amigos	all the time surrounded
y mujeres a su lado	by friends and by women
Sinaloa fue su cuna	Sinaloa was his cradle
y ahí también fue sepultado.	and there too he was interred.
Se escuchan "Nieves de enero"	One can hear "Nieves de enero"
también "Alma enamorada"	and also "Alma enamorada"
el corrido del Quitillo	the corrido of Quitillo
y el de los hermanos Mata.	and the one of the brothers Mata.

Vamos mis Guamuchileños	My Guamuchileños
a hacerle honor a su alma	let's go and praise his soul
que retumbe la tambora	let the tambora resound
pa'l famoso "Pelavacas."	for the famous "Pelavacas."
Fue gallo de Sinaloa	He was a Sinaloan rooster
que jugó en muchos palenques	who played in many rings
era un hombre decidido	he was a determined man
y siempre fue muy valiente	and always very brave
a traición le dieron muerte	they killed him by betrayal
porque no podían de frente.	because they couldn't do it from the front.
Cantando en Las Bugambilias	When he sang in Las Bugambilias
él no presentía la muerte	he didn't feel that death was waiting
vivió cantando el corrido	his life was to sing the corrido
y el corrido fue su muerte	the corrido was his death
Dios ya lo quería a su lado	If God didn't want to have him at his side
si no, aquí estaría presente.	he would still be with us.
Ya me despido de ustedes	I bid you farewell
con un dolor muy profundo	in deepest sorrow
con el alma destrozada	my soul is shattered
por la muerte de Chalino	by the death of Chalino
no toquen "Las golondrinas"	don't play "Las golondrinas"
¡tóquenle un buen corrido!	play him a good corrido!
Se escuchan "Nieves de enero," [etc.]	One can hear "Nieves de enero," [etc.]

"La tristeza de Chalino" [Chalino's Sadness], a corrido composed by Emilio Carrillo and performed by Hilaría Rey, uses Chalino's sad end to accuse a society in which violence is prevalent. Rather than retelling the circumstances and the unfolding of Chalino's assassination, the corridista reveals character and personality traits:

"Perder sin jugar las cartas	"To lose without even having played the cards
es tristeza de un valiente"	is sad for any brave man"
La historia que he de contarles	The story I have to tell you
ya la sabe mucha gente	a lot of people already know
la tragedia de Chalino	the tragedy of Chalino
un gallo muy sinaloense.	a very Sinaloan rooster.

Hay hombres que son muy hombres	There are men who are very manly
y no por eso hacen ruido	but without making a big deal of it
Chalino les dio las pruebas	Chalino has proven
de ser hombre decidido	that he was a decided man
cuando anduvo en Sinaloa	when he went around in Sinaloa
y en los Estados Unidos.	and the United States.
Estado de Sinaloa	The state of Sinaloa
tiene fama por su gente	is famous for its people
[la] capital Culiacán	its capital Culiacán
vio morir a otro valiente.	saw another brave man die.
Chalino Sánchez decía:	Chalino Sánchez said:
—Morir a mí no me pesa	"I don't care if I have to die
que no pueda defenderme	but not being able to defend myself
ésta si que es mi tristeza.	that would make me very sad."
Los pendientes de familias	The members of the families
también los del contrabando	as well as of the contraband
siguen sembrando la muerte	continue to sow death
y sangre van derramando	and they will shed blood
dejando más viudas solas	leaving behind more lonely widows
y escuadras que van sobrando.	and squads that will be superfluous.
—Llegó la hora de que cantes	"The hour you sing of has come"
le dicen los criminales	the criminals say to him
—Yo solo canto corridos de hombres	"I only sing corridos for men
que son muy cabales	who are very upright
ya no pierdan más el tiempo	don't waste time anymore
que al gatillo han de jalarle.	let the gunman pull the trigger."
Se oyen disparos de muerte	One can hear deadly shots
han matado a un sinaloense	they killed a Sinaloan man
sus hazañas y corridos	but his deeds and his corridos
los recuerda mucha gente.	will be remembered by many people.
Adiós mi "Rancho de flechas"	Farewell my "Rancho de flechas"
adiós mis "Nieves de enero"	farewell my "Nieves de enero"
adiós toda mi familia	farewell my family
en el cielo los espero.	I will wait for you in heaven.

Imaging "the Sinaloan"

In the days after his murder, Chalino's recordings sold like hotcakes.[28] Yet, according to sales statistics, Chalino had already sold more cassettes and discs in Culiacán during the early 1990s than any other artist, including leading international Hispanic idols such as Luis Miguel. Chalino had been a controversial singer during his lifetime. Hence, it was no surprise that people started to wonder about his death. Wild speculation arose along the lines of a Sinaloan saying: "Ese cabrón es capaz de dejarse matar para que le compongan un corrido" [This pimp is able to let himself be killed only if they compose a corrido for him]. When I asked Marisela Vallejo, Chalino's widow, whether it was true that Chalino became famous through his death rather than his singing, she replied: "No. I don't believe that he got famous because of his death. For a singer who didn't have a record company, a singer who didn't have any advertisement—he never spent a cent for radio broadcasting, advertising, or the like—he made himself with the sale of his cassettes. . . . For somebody who already has such very high sales of cassettes . . . he was already on the top. Then the tragedy came and many people thought that [his success] was because of his death" (interview, 1996, Los Angeles). Chalino was indeed a controversial singer. Many believed that he did more than just compose and sing narcocorridos. Chalino never said anything to clarify these allegations. Thus, his widow had to defend his reputation after his death: "Chalino was neither a [hired] gunman, nor a gangster, nor a drug trafficker."[29] People like the banda leader and composer Felipe Hernández, who knew Chalino closely, attribute the singer's success to his charisma, not to his particular clientele:[30]

Adiós al Rey del corrido	Farewell to the King of the Corrido
siempre fuiste muy valiente	you were always very brave
y aunque te costó la vida	although it cost you your life
tu moriste entre tu gente	you died amongst your people
y te siguen recordando	and they will always remember you
aunque ya no estés presente.	even though you're no longer with them.
Tuvo muchos enemigos	He had many enemies
la mayoría por envidia	the majority for envy
y ahora los que éste cantan	those who are singing this [song]
porque todavía te admiran	do it because they still admire you
por tu carisma tan fuerte	because of your compelling charisma
[eres] de los que nunca se olvida.	you are one of those one will never forget.

The owner of Cintas Acuario, Pedro Rivera, another of Chalino's acquaintances, reveals in his corrido "El gallo de los Sánchez" [The Sánchez's Rooster]:[31]

Chalino era muy valiente,	Chalino was very brave,
más cuando tenía razón	more so when he was right
odiaba las injusticias,	he hated injustice,
muchas veces [lo] demostró	that he proved many times
porque él se rajaba el cuero	by jumping into the fray
sin medir la situación.	without heeding the odds.
Ese gallo que mataron	That rooster they killed
nunca se supo rajar	never knew to back down
porque arriesgaba su vida	because he risked his life
hasta por una amistad	even for a friendship
por eso lloran y extrañan	that's why they cry and miss
al gallo de Culiacán.	the rooster from Culiacán.

All of the above corridos disclose important features of Chalino's character. They picture Chalino as a brave and determined man; a sincere and true companion; and a famous and adored singer who is always surrounded by friends and women. Ascribed to him are the virtues of the corrido hero: to be *un hombre valiente* [a brave man] and *un gallo muy sinaloense* [a very Sinaloan rooster].

Yet, it cannot be only the Sinaloan attributes that made Chalino the singer he was. Many people, including some famous Mexican artists, were quite irritated by Chalino's wide acceptance and popularity (Luis Lim, *Noroeste*, 23 May 1992). Chalino's voice was not considered a good singing voice. On the contrary, he did not have a singing voice at all. He said himself: "I know that I can't sing, but the people like it and one has to give them what they ask for."[32] His widow recalled:

MV: At the beginning there was a lot of controversy because he wasn't a common singer like anybody else. Everybody expects from a singer a clear voice, a trained voice, a clean voice. His was not. His was the contrary. He was all original: from his way to singing to his timbre. . . . Chalino had a kind of voice like turbid water, like something that is not very clear. . . . Chalino Sánchez was born and brought up on a ranch and, hence, is a rancher by origin. These [other singers who emerged after Chalino's death] are not ranchers. They imitate and try to speak like a rancher, but they aren't.

HS: *José Alfredo Jiménez, "El Hijo del Pueblo" [Son of the Common People], for example, had a different voice. He too came from a ranch, but he had another singing style.*

MV: He had another style, yes, because I think that each region has its own style.

Chalino has the classical style of Sinaloa: very impulsive by nature—very crude. In other regions, for example, they are more educated and the way of expressing oneself is very different. In Sinaloa, those who are brought up on a ranch are very boorish. [But] that's exactly what [the audience] likes. They like the boorish, the original, the crude, the so-called classic *ranchero* style. (Interview, 1996, Los Angeles)

Chalino's voice certainly did not fit the accepted idea of how an educated voice should sound. Yet, José Alfredo Jiménez, one of Mexico's most prominent singing idols, did not have "a trained voice" either, and he was not precisely what the Mexicans of his day envisioned as a popular singer. According to Gradante, everybody agreed "that he never had a beautiful voice, that he was not an actor by vocation, and that he certainly was not good-looking. It seems that it was exactly this 'ordinariness' that made him the beloved poet and singer he became, for it was for the Mexican masses, the 'ordinary' people, that he composed and sang" (1982: 53). Despite his untrained voice, Jiménez became one of the most successful Mexican vocalist of his time. With reference to Jiménez, the ranchera singer Amalia Mendoza noted: "The most important thing is to live what one is singing" (quoted in Gradante 1982: 53). Like Jiménez, Chalino sang his own songs and only rarely recorded songs he did not compose himself. His candid statement about his own voice reminds one of a verse from the traditional Sinaloan song "El Quelite":

Yo no canto porque sé	I don't sing because I know how to
ni porque mi voz sea buena	nor because I have a good voice
canto porque tengo gusto	I sing because I like to
(*otra versión:* yo canto porque soy alegre)	(*other version:* I sing because I'm cheerful)
en mi tierra y en la ajena.	at home as well as abroad.

Chalino was one of the people he composed and sang for: like Jiménez, he shared the ordinariness of his audience. Born in 1960, Chalino grew up in a large family in Sanalona, a village some twenty miles east of Culiacán. At the age of eighteen he immigrated to California like many other poor Mexicans, hoping to find a better future in the north. (It is said that he had to leave Mexico because he had avenged his sister, who had been dishonored by a local *valiente*.) After working different jobs that brought him into close contact with the narco world, Chalino began to compose corridos on commission and later, from 1989 on, recorded them for his clients with norteño groups and local bandas. That was how he began to realize his dream of being a professional singer. Marisela Vallejo assured me that his modesty was one of his most valuable characteristics, and that Chalino's determination to succeed was rooted in his humble origins:

He comes from very humble roots. I think that is also where his career was rooted, because that's where he began to sing. He started to sing at the age of twelve. He would sing for people who paid for it. He grew up with the idea of doing it on a professional basis. When he began his singing career [in Los Angeles] there were not many singers, neither with banda nor with norteño accompaniment. At that time [1988] banda was almost totally dead. There were no banda singers and only a few norteño singers. There were some groups, but they weren't outstanding. It was a completely different ambience than nowadays. . . . When he began to sing, people liked it and he excelled. [His success helped to] convert him into the idol of many singers. That is how the banda movement emerged—at least here [in Los Angeles]. In Sinaloa there were many people singing with bandas, but [they weren't prominent]. [Chalino] was the one who excelled. (Interview, 1996, Los Angeles)

Chalino started his career on the streets, selling cassettes he had produced all by himself, from the song texts and music to the recording and reproduction. Marisela Vallejo recalled that people in the streets would look down on him and laugh when he went around in his cowboy hat and boots, selling his cassettes. But he would say: "I don't care. That's how I like to go around. I'm Mexican and I'm proud of being Mexican. Why should I dress in a different way?" Chalino created his own label, RR (Rosalino Records). Only when he was no longer able to handle the growing sales of his cassettes, and when he could no longer dedicate enough time to the development of his career, did he decide to sell his material to other labels such as Discos Linda, Cintas Acuario, Kimo's, and Musart (Balboa Records). Although there are only twelve original Chalino records, reissued by the various companies, the number of new compact discs is steadily growing. Modern recording technology allows new recordings to be created by stripping the vocal track from the original recording and adding other voices and new musical accompaniment. Six years after Chalino's death, there were more than twenty ersatz recordings on the market on which Chalino sings in duets and with groups he had never met when alive. Despite the fact that thousands of bootleg cassettes are sold in the streets, Chalino continues to be good business for the record producers. According to Musart, in 1998 Chalino's royalties were worth several million dollars.

Because of Chalino's humble origins, his artistic career, and his death at the peak of his professional life, a promoter of local events in Sinaloa compared Chalino Sánchez to the other prominent Sinaloan singing idol, Pedro Infante. Indeed, Chalino fits the concept of the idol that was created by the Mexican mass media earlier this century. Almost all the singing Mexican idols came from the poorest classes. Having the same inclination and taste as the majority of Mexicans, actor-singers such as Pedro Infante, Jorge Negrete, and Javier

Solís were able to generate immediate identification with the public through their mere appearance. According to the musicologist Yolanda Moreno Rivas, Pedro Infante, the former carpenter and driver from Guamúchil, preferred to eat home-cooked Sinaloan food sitting on the floor of the recording studio like a laborer or a bricklayer (1989: 200).

Chalino was buried in the village Los Pocitos, El Salado, Sinaloa, in the presence of his family and friends. A banda was playing some of Chalino's most popular compositions. They fulfilled Chalino's last wish, expressed in the corrido "Que me entierren cantando" [If They Will Bury Me Singing]:[33]

Ahora sí ya estoy solo en el mundo	Now I am alone in the world
solo, solo en el mundo vagando	roaming alone, alone through the world
no me importa si algún día me muero	I don't care if one day I'm going to die
nada más que me entierren cantando.	if they only will bury me singing.
He pasado mi vida sufriendo	I went through my life suffering
he pasado mi vida rodando	I went through my life roaming
pero juro que de hoy en adelante	but I swear that from now on
me verán solamente tomando.	you'll see me only drinking.
Un día voy pa' arriba	One day I will go up
y voy a entregar lo	to give back
que un día el Señor me prestó	what the Lord has loaned me
un día voy pa' arriba	one day I will go up
y nada me importa el día en que muera yo.	and I don't care about the day I will die.
Y ese día que yo ya me muera	And the day I will die
yo no quiero oírlos llorar	I don't want to hear you cry
lo que quiero es que lleven la banda	but I'd like you to bring the banda along
para oírlos a todos cantar.	so that I can hear you all singing.
Si es que cierto que un día me quisieron	If you really loved me once
y que salga de su corazón	and if it comes from your heart
quiero oírlos a todos muy fuertes	I'd like to hear you all very clearly
que me canten mi humilde canción.	singing my humble song.
Un día voy pa' arriba [etc.]	One day I will go up [etc.]

This corrido is one of many that disclose a Sinaloan's last wish, that is, to be buried with the sound of the tambora.[34] The music comforts the mourners and pleases the deceased. For those who have enjoyed the tambora during their lifetime, a paradise without banda music is unthinkable. The last wish reflects what was valued most during their lifetime.

Since Chalino's death, dozens of youngsters in the Los Angeles area have emerged imitating Chalino—his voice, his singing style, and the particular tough-guy image of the Sinaloan sierra rancher that he had celebrated and that, ironically, also led to his early death.[35] Despite the fact that Chalino's corridos composed on commission did not get any airplay, neither in the United States nor in Mexico, they were, and still are, in high demand. Although Chalino's career lasted only four years, his impact on Nuevo L.A.'s micromusical world cannot be overlooked. The part of the business that involves commissioned corridos barely exists in Mexico; the center of its production is Los Angeles. According to Quiñones, "The corrido has adapted to the new Mexican reality of having to live and work away from Mexico. Immigrants use commissioned corridos as tangible proof—like a new car or Nikes—that they've made it in the U.S.A."[36] The demand for new compositions and for recordings has generated income for composers, singers, and musicians alike. Norteño groups and bandas are now thriving in Nuevo L.A.

Technobanda's Lasting Influence

Mira que sabroso es este ritmo, mamá
ésto que se llama brincaíto, caray
bailan las muchachas tu lo vas a gozar
ándale Costeña que no existe otra igual.
        José A. Sosa, Banda La Costeña

Forty-three thousand people were present at the annual "Viva México" festival in Chicago in 1993 when Banda Machos was crowned "La Reina de las Bandas." Ironically, Banda El Recodo, the venerable and indisputable "banda queen," which also performed at the Chicago festival, went unnoticed. Cruz Lizárraga was upset when asked by a local journalist about the distinction with which Banda Machos was honored: "Some groups or bands—I won't mention names—pretend to be 'La Reina de las Bandas' [The Queen of the Bandas]. But 'La Reina de las Bandas' is Banda El Recodo, because we play you any music including waltzes, cha-cha-cha, *sones* from Sinaloa, Jalisco and Michoacán, pasodobles, the music of Glenn Miller, of Pérez Prado—all in Banda El Recodo's own style."[1] For Lizárraga it was not the number of records sold that entitled a band to be called "queen," but solid musicianship and a long-standing career. How could a "bunch of unskilled musicians" from Jalisco who produced a meager, synthesized sound that lacked the dashing brass, the piercing clarinets, and the pounding tambora even be called "banda"? Although many Sinaloan banderos dismissed technobanda as "something completely different that has nothing to do with *banda sinaloense*," they deeply resented the fact that these other groups also called themselves "banda." In the competitive world of musicians' economic survival, such name appropriation is taken seriously. Ramón López Alvarado, leader of the renowned Banda La Costeña, pointed out the difference: "Well, not every group that calls itself [a banda] or that plays banda music is a banda. I call them 'technobandas' because they use technology, electricity. We don't. We use only wind and percussion instruments. Those others are purely imitators."[2] And Cruz Lizárraga mocked the technobandas: "I even dare to say that the majority [of them] aren't bandas at all. . . . All of them are technologically advanced, but if the electricity goes out—their little number is over."[3] By using the designation "banda," technobandas consciously placed themselves within a specific tradition. Raúl Ortega, at that time lead singer of Banda Machos, freely admitted that they "took the Sinaloan sound, updated and modernized it."[4] Why not? In the modern world, music has become a commodity of which anybody can make use. In the eyes of traditional musicians, however, the techno musicians not only trespassed upon their confines by appropriating their name. Worse, they achieved success on the international music market by imitating (badly) the traditional Sinaloan sound.

The crowing of a "pseudo-banda" at the 1993 festival in Chicago hurt the pride of many loyal Sinaloans. Years later, the affront was neither forgotten nor forgiven, as one could read in a local Sinaloan newspaper:

Sinaloa has many bandas and very good ones. . . . That's why we think it is unfair and arbitrary that grupitos [little groups] such as Banda Machos pompously call themselves "The Queen of the Bandas" only because they are popular right now (but fashions, as we all know, are transient). They might be very macho, but they are not so much banda to monopolize a title that does not belong to them. . . . [All technobandas] are the same. Not one of them has its own style. All are copying each other. [It's] a music without soul that totally distorts the true music. There are signs that the fashion has already outlived itself. If only it would! Maybe that is how we Sinaloans can recuperate our venerable wind music again, with its sones, its melodies, its memories, its eternity which is not worn out by remorseless commercialization.[5]

Banda Machos, however, was more than just a fad: as the 1990s ended, the group was still able to fill a stadium with its fans, and it continued to launch hits on Billboard's Hot Latin Tracks. People who expected technobanda to pass quickly believed that it was nothing but an ephemeral fad, a "disproportionate commercial boom." Obviously, they ignored the deeper significance of technobanda as a music and dance phenomenon able to transcend geographical distances and borders. They also ignored the fact that innovation keeps a tradition alive. This last chapter, thus, looks at how technobanda and other contemporary trends in Latin music have influenced, transformed, and revitalized Sinaloan banda music.

Smoke, Lights, and Amplifiers

Beneath the fervent resentments cited above lies the serious question that always arises in discussions about tradition—the question of how much innovation is acceptable. Opinions on this matter, of course, diverge greatly. It was not the first time in history that banda had transformed itself and, as a result, received harsh criticism, mainly from purists. Half a century earlier, when upwardly aspiring bandleaders catapulted banda out of the bawdy cantinas into plush dance halls of urban Sinaloa and neighboring states, and later into the theaters of Mexico City and Los Angeles, purists expressed indignation at the more progressive bandas, also called banda-orquestas to distinguish them from their "more authentic" counterparts. In order to reach a broader and a more cosmopolitan audience, members of progressive bandas adjusted their outward appearance by putting on a nice suit and tie; they modified the makeup of the standard ensemble by expanding the percussion section with tropical instruments such as gourds and conga drums; and they diffused the regional style by branching out in diverse stylistic and repertorial directions.

Like other urban popular musics from the 1960s onward, progressive urban bandas were caught up by a culture industry that left very little outside its sphere of influence and that introduced styles increasingly defined by the transnational market. Advances in mass communications and other technologies in the 1980s intensified transnational musical interaction between Mexico and the United States. International labels discovered "local musics" and began to transform them into a profitable mass-market commodity. Technobanda's sudden popularity marked a lucrative new phase in the transnational dance-music business. If Sinaloa's commercially oriented, high-profile bandas wanted to get their share, they had to adjust to the standards set by the mass media and culture industry, in particular to the predominance of the visual and the verbal.

The advent of synthesizer-driven bandas affected Sinaloan musicians in manifold ways. High-wattage sound systems, smoke, and light shows enabled technobandas to attract new and youthful audiences. With the fast-paced quebradita rhythm, the newcomers reinvigorated and energized the dance floor. Young but relatively unskilled musicians with a handful of catchy songs were able to make people move. This certainly shook up the more traditional musicians, who relied upon solid craftsmanship and a vast musical repertory. Moreover, technobanda adhered to modern ideas of musical professionalism, not so much in terms of musicianship, but in terms of marketing and visual appearance.

Technobanda owed its sudden popularity, in Cruz Lizárraga's opinion, to public-relations campaigns rather than to the musical quality of the new bands. At that time, however, Banda El Recodo itself had already embraced much of technobanda's innovations. Lizárraga had long hesitated to make the necessary changes that would allow the venerable Sinaloan banda to compete successfully with the popular technobandas on the growing international music market, but in 1992 he eventually engaged Julio C. Preciado, then lead singer of Banda El Limón from Mazatlán.[6] Maricela Contreras, her father's right hand at Fonorama, the Guadalajara-based record company, summarized: "When Julio Preciado joined [Banda El Recodo], it began to change its style. Because somebody new came, somebody who had a vision of a new banda. So Banda El Recodo began to change from its traditional style to the one that is now called technobanda"[7] (interview, 1994, Guadalajara). Banda La Costeña's leader, Ramón López Alvarado, did not show much enthusiasm for the new musical style either. On the contrary, López Alvarado expressed dismay at the contemporary developments, as Manuel Contreras recalled: "I tell you right away: at first, the people from the Sinaloan bandas didn't want to accept this [new] music. They didn't want to accept the innovations. Señor Don Ramón López Alvarado is a good friend of mine. Once he got very angry and told me—you can imagine how many things! 'You overthrow our Sinaloan music. You overthrow our tradition. Why are you doing that?' He scolded me [laughs]. Don Ramón López Alvarado scolded me! And now he plays in that style as well. That's what sells. That's that market. That's the business" (interview, 1994, Guadalajara). Indeed, in the mid-1990s, a "renewed" Banda La Costeña returned to the dance halls to create a furor.[8] Their up-tempo tropical rhythms captivated and enlivened thousands of young dancers on both sides of the border. Songs such as "El brincaíto" [Little Jump] showed that Banda La Costeña once again had found its distinctive sound:[9]

Mira que sabroso es este ritmo, mamá	Look how savory this rhythm is, darling
ésto que se llama brincaíto, caray	the one that's called brincaíto, confound it!
bailan las muchachas, tu lo vas a gozar	the girls're dancing, you're going to like it
ándale Costeña que no existe otra igual.	go on Costeña, there is no one like you.
¡Anda, déjate llevar	Come on, let youself be carried away
mira, sé que te gustará	look, I know that you're going to like it
solo un poco sudarás	you'll only sweat a little bit
mira, lo tienes que probar!	hey, you must give it a try!
Y no importa como lo goces	It's not important how you enjoy
el chiste es nunca parar de brincar	but that you never stop jumping
no castigues a tus pies	don't punish your feet
solo déjate llevar. . . .	just let yourself be carried away. . . .

Since its beginning in 1958, Banda La Costeña had always interpreted a great range of musical genres. Among López Alvarado's favorite rhythms was the cumbia. In the 1960s he composed several cumbia-style pieces himself, among them "El pato asado" and "Ven a Mazatlán." The commercial cumbia style that had developed in Colombia's coastal towns around 1960 featured, besides brass, electric bass, drums, and shakers, the clarinet as the main melody instrument. Based on the similarity of instrumentation, Sinaloan bandas soon embraced the style. By the late 1960s cumbia had become one of the hottest dance rhythms in Mexico's middle- and upper-class ballrooms. At that time, however, the music was purely instrumental.

Although Banda La Costeña had accompanied various Mexican ranchera singers in the 1980s, including Antonio Aguilar, whose cover of "Tristes recuerdos" got heavy airplay on Los Angeles's Spanish-language radio stations, it was not until technobanda's phenomenal breakthrough of fast-paced danceable songs that López Alvarado decided to integrate a vocalist into his banda as well. In 1993 La Costeña made a recording that contained a combination of rancheras, cumbias, and quebraditas. The latter was a potpourri of four technobanda hits. As its title, "Popurri tropical," suggests, Banda La Costeña appropriated the novel rhythm by giving it a more tropical twist.[10] Similarly, Banda El Recodo took advantage of the quebradita dance craze in 1993 with "Bailando quebradita" and "Pegando con tubo," and later with hits such as "La quebradora" and "El chilango quebrador."[11] While the earlier songs are in quebradita style, the latter may be better described as Mexican cumbias with a distinct Sinaloan tinge.

Nowadays, Banda El Recodo's onstage performance does not lag behind Banda Machos's in extravagance. The venerable Sinaloan banda of fifteen musicians employs more than one hundred men to set up the sixty tons of equipment and to run the show. It features sophisticated sound and light systems, smoke machines, and special effects: while highly amplified sound blares out of the 180 speaker boxes, pictures of the dancing musicians in garish outfits flicker over the twenty video screens. The production culminates in a dazzling pyrotechnics show that demonstrates the tens of thousands of fans who regularly throng the arena: *banda sinaloense* represents the height of technology—it is modern, and it is international.[12]

Blurring Borders

With their decision to enter the international music market, Sinaloa's high-profile bandas had to conform to certain trends imposed by the culture industry. The shift in their musical repertory toward the more universally appealing, danceable cumbia and the romantic balada enabled bandas to compete with other popular Latin musics. Although they continued to play rancheras and corridos, CDs such as Banda El Recodo's *Tributo a Juan Gabriel* (1996), whose

32. Banda El Recodo, with lead singer Julio César Preciado, captivates thousands of young fans with an energetic onstage spectacle in Guadalajara, 1998. Photos courtesy of María de Jesús Lizárraga.

success was echoed with *Juan Gabriel con Banda El Recodo* (1998), paid tribute not only to one of Mexico's most acclaimed balada composers, but also to the record industry. Banda La Costeña's *Secreto de amor* (1997) indicates a shift in musical style toward romantic songs.[13]

The driving force of Sinaloan banda music and its strength in coping with changing fashions and cultural trends can be ascribed to its versatility and adaptability. As a popular dance music, it has always had a tendency toward eclecticism. From waltz, fox-trot, and danzón to mambo and cumbia, banda has appropriated every foreign rhythm that was fashionable in the dance halls throughout the last century. To suit the dancing public, banda's repertory has always consisted of a mixture of fast- and slow-paced pieces. When banda entered the new phase of international commercialization in the mid-1990s, regionally rooted *sones* and old-fashioned waltzes eventually had to give way to the internationally more marketable cumbia and balada.

Banda's recent musical shifts, including its incorporation of a vocalist into the group, are related to general trends in the music business. Although bandas have accompanied ranchera singers for half a century, their core repertory remained instrumental. When performing in traditional settings, bandas played either pure dance music or songs whose lyrics were already known to the local audience and thus did not need to be sung. With their new emphasis on recording for a mass market and on performing stage shows for a transnational mass audience, however, the music had to become less community centered and more universally appealing, and a vocalist had to be added.

Romantic songs have always enjoyed great popularity among Mexican audiences. Emerging in the 1930s, the *comedia ranchera* [ranch comedy], the most enduring genre of Mexican cinema, helped to establish the *canción ranchera*, performed by mariachi and the singing charro. After World War II, the *canción romántica*, a more refined version of the canción ranchera, arose and gained in popularity, in particular among middle-class urbanites. Popularized by the trios, the bolero and the *canción-bolero* flourished for more than a decade until they were forced to give way to the new musical developments that enraptured Mexico's youth in the early 1960s: rock and roll and an international ballad type popularized by the famous crooners Frank Sinatra and Julio Iglesias. No new styles surfaced in the following couple of decades. Composers largely drew from previously popular styles (see Moreno Rivas 1989). In the 1990s Luis Miguel, a young Mexican pop star, was instrumental in reintroducing the romantic bolero to a new, transnational generation. Romantic songs continued to enjoy enormous popularity in the international Latin music market.

Banda's response to this commercial trend in Latin music was *banda romántica*. Although intimate feelings and marching-band instrumentation seem to contradict each other, banda managed to create a sound that was perceived by its audience as emotional, expressive, and romantic. This spirit was captured in a balada titled "Música romántica." Composed by Pancho Barraza and performed by Banda La Tunera, this hit song was widely played on Los Angeles's ranchera-format radio stations.[14] By the mid-1990s, *banda romántica* had emerged in full force. On both sides of the border, bandas were expanding their repertory of sentimental love songs and romantic baladas, often covering songs by prolific songwriters of previous eras and other styles. A number of young banda composers made a name specializing in love songs, among them Pancho Barraza. First the lead singer of Mazatlán's Banda Los Recoditos and later of his own Banda Santa María in Guasave, he was one of Sinaloa's most devoted advocates of *banda romántica*.[15] Other young bands such as the Sinaloan-style Banda Pelillos, Banda El Chante, and Banda Caña Verde (the last advertised as "la banda más dulce" [the sweetest banda]), followed the trend toward combining sentimental baladas and danceable cumbias.[16]

Local Sinaloan singers on both sides of the border, such as Saúl Viera "El

Gavilancillo," El Puma de Sinaloa, El Monarca de Sinaloa, and Bulfrano Moreno "El Lobito de Sinaloa," began to peform more and more love songs and thus gradually disassociated themselves from violent narcocorridos and the tough-guy image they had built up previously.[17]

Music making is a rigidly masculine activity. No women play in bandas or norteño groups, and only a few female musicians have joined the technobanda movement.[18] It is very rare to hear female singers perform in nightclubs. Adriana Galán, a young singer who at age thirteen recorded with Banda Los Pericos de Culiacán, is an exception. After her family moved to California, she began singing in nightclubs and touring the United States. Like most female singers who have recorded with banda, she has experimented with other styles as well.[19] Asked whether she thought there would be more female singers or musicians in the future, she replied: "I do think so. [But] there are very few women who are able to endure this lifestyle because it is very tough, very fatiguing. The majority of women wants to get married and have children. I too think of that, one day. . . . There are indeed very few [women] singing with banda. Maybe three or four. And most of them do not exclusively sing with banda. Most are versatile. We want to stay with the fashion" (interview, 1996, Los Angeles). Galán and other young female singers in Los Angeles, as well as experienced singers in Mexico who have recorded with banda, tend to perform romantic songs of the bolero and ranchera repertories.[20] But rather than singing in a soft, crooning voice, these women employ the typical bravía ranchera voice popularized by Lucha Reyes (1906–44), a ranchera singer who personified the fierce, vivacious Mexican woman and who set the standards for all generations of female singers to come. In contrast, many men sing in the estilo sentimental [sentimental style] and feature a rather soft, nondominating "bolero voice," even when accompanied by banda.

The musical landscape of Mexico since the mid-1980s has been marked by the onda grupera. Led by the prolific singer and songwriter Marco Antonio Solís, Los Bukis dominated the romantic pop grupero music scene and inspired dozens of other groups: Los Temerarios, Liberación, Los Fugitivos, Bronco (a grupo-norteño fusion), Los Yoncis, Bryndis, Ladrón, and others. With their keyboard-driven romantic pop baladas and tropical pop cumbias, grupos have had an enormous influence on various succeeding styles, in particular technobanda and tejano. Both styles have made consistent use of the synthesizer and have incorporated the cumbia and the balada into their repertories. According to Manuel Peña, tejano's new emphasis on these transnationally appealing genres reflects a shift of Texas-Mexican society from a community-centered one to a "fragmented, heterogeneous mass with a 'decentered' sense of ideological purpose" (1999: 189).[21] Indeed, Mexican American identity, which throughout the century had been rooted in regional cultural contexts, particularly in musical forms, shifted in the 1990s. Like other contemporary (post)modern societies, Mexican Americans are experiencing a rapid cultural decentering, which Jesús Martín Barbero (1998) rightly attributes to the hegemonic power of the mass communication systems, in particular their audiovisual products.

Tejano musicians who wanted to be competitive on a mass market had to "decenter" themselves, to disassociate themselves from the community-rooted polka-ranchera conjunto style and fuse with "mainstream" genres such as rhythm and blues, country, and pop (successful fusions were made by Mazz, La Mafia, Selena, and Emilio Navaira). Variety became the key to the international market.[22] Similarly, technobanda, designed by Manuel Contreras as a "grupoversion of Sinaloan banda with norteño flavor," increasingly fused with other styles, including rock, country, rap, and reggae. Technobanda recordings typically comprised a vast range of rhythms from technobandas' own quebraditas to grupos' cumbias and baladas, trios' boleros, and norteños' rancheras and corridos. But despite the eclectic mixing, the stylistic and repertorial borrowing, and the blurring of borders in general, despite their efforts to expand from a regional, yet sizable, to a more global market, both tejano and technobanda remained rooted in local identity, categorized by the record industry as "Regional Mexican."[23]

Technobanda's Influence on Local Bandas

When technobanda hit Southern California in the early 1990s, there was no question among banderos working in the Los Angeles area that this new musical trend would have a lasting impact on their own music, their repertory, as well as their economic situation. How it would affect their musical lives depended on the type of the banda (local, regional, or transnational), place of residence (Mexico or the United States), orientation (mass market or small-scale live performance), ambition, and other, individual, factors. The clarinetist and bandleader Felipe Hernández, who settled down in Los Angeles in the 1980s, summarized technobanda's influence on the local Sinaloan banda: "The technobanda movement did not help *banda sinaloense* at all. It ruined it. Banda already had a name before. [Technobanda] was a new style that emerged and that hit. But the only thing they accomplished was to ruin what we used to earn. They are six or seven musicians, we are a banda of fifteen. When I formed my banda, I charged $1,500–1,600 for two sets. Nowadays they pay me $800. Why? Because when [the technobandas] came out, it was what people liked. If they get $100 for each [musician], that's a good salary" (interview, 1996, Los Angeles). Relying on synthesizer and electric instruments, technobanda was able to downsize its ensemble to half or a third of the personnel of an acoustic banda. The "downsizing" set new economic realities. Technobandas, however, not only deflated the prices local bandas used to charge for performing, they inflated the market in such a way that the few established Sinaloan bandas had to fear for their future. Fresh young bands such as Banda América from Los Angeles jumped on the bandwagon; they stormed the nightclubs and record studios. The majority of these newcomers played for fun. Since they either had a regular day job or still went to school, they did not depend economically on their music making. The explosion of new bands aggravated the situation of local banderos who depended on their full-time jobs as musicians.

Moreover, the technobanda boom and the high demand for live music in Los Angeles's nightclubs attracted hundreds of musicians from south of the border, and many of them came to stay. The local market was soon saturated. Thus, in spite of expanding performance opportunities for all musicians, the technobanda movement ruined the small business that local bandas had built up in Los Angeles since the mid-1980s. In Hernández's opinion, only bandas rooted in Mexico were able to benefit from the movement—bandas such as El Recodo, La Costeña, Los Recoditos, Los Nuevos Coyonquis, Los Tamazulas de Guasave, and others. Banda La Costeña from Mazatlán, for example, spent almost eight months of 1996 touring throughout the United States. It was indeed easier to attend a performance or to schedule an interview with any of these bandas in the United States than in their native land.

Shortly after technobanda erupted onto the scene, proficient musicians realized that most of the rising techno musicians did not have the necessary foundation for a long-lasting musical career—the benefit of a solid musical tradition. Hernández and his colleagues in Los Angeles were convinced that the spark and ingenuity that ignited the explosion would soon die down, the craze would gradually lose steam, and the novel sound would dwindle. They expected that it would be only a matter of time until the market went back to normal. In the meantime, however, they played technobanda's novel songs to please their audience because, as they said, "we cannot close our eyes." As much as banderos trusted their own musical skills, they believed in the strength of their tradition rooted in Mexican culture and history: "*Banda sinaloense* is the basis; like mariachi, it is the original." Felipe Hernández analyzed the situation as follows:

The old repertoire is the basis because people come and ask you: "Play me 'El Quelite'!"— "OK." It's one of Sinaloa's regional songs, [*sings*] "How beautiful is El Quelite. . . ," but instrumental. The people are happy. They ask you: "Play me 'La huigerita' . . . 'El huizache'!" [*sings*]. [Technobandas] play only what they have recorded. Once we were playing at an event where Banda Maguey played as well. They repeated two songs during their presentation: one because the people ask them to, and the other because they didn't know anything else to play. With the type of banda I have it's the contrary! There are so many songs one knows, at the moment they are requested, one knows how to play them. For example, if a banda of the type Banda Maguey goes to play at a *quinceañera* [coming-of-age party for a girl], they will be asked: "Play the *quinceañera* waltz!" They can't play it. They go to a wedding, they don't know what to do. A regional banda plays "Alejandra," "Julia," "Sobre las olas," "Dios nunca muere." It's the old songs that are played at *quinceañeras* and at weddings. (Interview, 1996, Los Angeles)

As long as traditional customs continue to be practiced "the old way," the musical repertory that has been constitutive for ceremonies in the past will continue to be constitutive in the future. In this sense, old songs have an immense power over the future. It is therefore crucial for any musician to know the vast traditional repertory if he is to partake actively, and in the long run, in his culture. As Hernández emphasized, this also holds true for Mexican musicians working across the border. In sum, it was not the new music style or repertory that gave the local bandas a great deal of trouble but the economic aspect. Even though local bandas picked up the new songs quickly and adapted to other innovations as well, they were never able to successfully compete with the emerging technobandas because of their large number of personnel. Paradoxically, "banda music" was booming like never before, but banderos could hardly survive.

As in other folk traditions, music making in Sinaloa has traditionally been regarded as a trade. Musicians are craftsmen, like saddlers, carpenters, or mechanics, who distinguish themselves by their musical ability and by their skills. Since proficiency is reached through years of consistent hard work, a musician's reputation is based on his musicianship, his musical abilities and skills. Consequently, not much attention is given to visual appearance or showy performance. This still holds true for Sinaloan banda musicians who migrated to larger cities and across the border. Yet, when technobanda emerged and began to intrude upon their confines, banderos saw themselves compelled to reconsider both their outward appearance and their stage performance.

For techno musicians, visual aspects and onstage image have been pivotal from the very beginning. They liked to display glamorous and flashy dress and to dazzle the audiences with energetic onstage spectacles involving elaborate dance routines carried out in the midst of dry-ice smoke and light effects. Moreover, the technobanda musicians were young, energetic, fresh, indefatigable, and enterprising, and they lived their youthfulness and exuberance to the fullest on stage. Their music and their outfits reflected their dash. One of the probably most influential figures was Ezequiel "Cheque" Peña, lead singer of Banda Vallarta Show, who enraptured his audiences with his extravagant costumes and erotic pelvic dance gestures. His onstage performance helped create technobanda's unmistakable showy image. For years, his pictures and stories filled the pages of popular fan magazines. Peña's pretty-boy looks were packaged and sold together with his life story. For many of his fans, Peña embodied the American success story. The youngest of twelve children, he grew up on a ranch in Nayarit. At the age of eighteen he moved to California, where he worked in a variety of menial jobs. He joined Banda Vallarta Show as its lead vocalist when the band was formed in 1988. At the peak of the technobanda craze, thousands of fans would flock to stadiums, arenas, or parks to see their idol.[24]

The idea of incorporating a vocalist into the Sinaloan banda is a recent phenomenon that was encouraged by technobanda and norteño alike (and, as already pointed out, by general tendencies in the popular music market). Both ensembles rely on a vocalist to sing the song lyrics. Indeed, the central figure in both ensembles is the vocalist. Sinaloan bandas, on the other hand, have always had an egalitarian character, which can be traced to the conventions and aesthetics of nineteenth-century plebeian musical practice. The music they traditionally played impeded single musicians from standing out. Only with the commercialization of urban bandas in the 1960s did some bandleaders begin to add their own names to that of their bandas, which were typically called after the village or town of provenance.[25] The leader or *representante*, as Sinaloan musicians say, has a great responsibility since he manages everything from scheduling the banda's performances to negotiating the payment with the patrons, from arranging songs to keeping an eye on his musicians. It is secondary whether one plays the clarinet, the tuba, or the tambora as long as one has the proficiency to represent a banda, which, of course, also means being an outstanding musician. In local settings where everyone knows each other, traditionally banda representatives blended visually with the rest of the musicians. In the mass-media world, on the other hand, there seems to be a need for differentiating roles, for having a recognizable leader or a star with whom the audience can identify. The recent idolization of Cruz Lizárraga as "The Father of Banda Music" and his representation on record covers, and the celebration of lead singer Julio C. Preciado in fan magazines, are examples of singling out individual artists.

Technobanda's visual innovations had some lasting impact on local Sinaloan bandas as well. Forced by relentless competition, banderos began to enhance both their appearance and their presentation. Nowadays, the minimal requirement is to wear matching outfits, or at least shirts and/or pants of the same color, and to perform some synchronized dance steps while playing. The representative of the banda may dress differently in order to be recognizable as such. Owing to their economic situation and their aspirations or commercial sophistication, some bandas have incorporated a vocalist. In others, however, one of the musicians is designated to sing the lyrics.

Bandas and the Nightclub Circuit in Los Angeles

Because of the high density of nightclubs in certain areas of Los Angeles, they began to diversify by attending to different segments of the Latino population. Those catering to a general Mexican-Latino audience featured music with a more universal appeal such as technobandas and grupos, while nightclubs frequented by immigrants from Mexico's northwestern coast contracted local and touring Sinaloan bandas and norteño groups.

When I began to attend nightclubs in Los Angeles in 1994, all of them featured live music. Bands were hired to play for one or two sets, alternating with each other. As in any discotheque, the sound volume was just at the bearable limit. Some of the more progressive bands produced a flashy and energetic spectacle, executing elaborate dance routines. Technobanda was in high demand. Yet, like any fashion, popular music and dance styles become outdated after a while. In 1996 technobanda's popularity began to decline, and norteño groups and a new style the nightclub-goers simply called *el sonido* ["the sound," music with a tropical flavor] took over. The former was very popular in nightclubs frequented by recent immigrants from northwestern Mexico, while the latter was preferred by people from other parts of Mexico and Central America.

Nightclubs featuring Sinaloan music usually have a *banda de planta*, a band that is contracted to play on all nights.[26] In general, nightclubs save money if they have one or two groups playing on a regular basis because they can avoid paying the high prices bands are charging on the well-attended Saturday nights. For the musicians, to play *de planta* has both advantages and disadvantages: on the one hand, they have a steady job in one establishment; on the other, it prevents them from pursuing more lucrative Saturday jobs elsewhere. Usually *bandas de planta* perform for the same salary as on the other nights of the week, that is, between $800 and $1,500, depending on how many sets they play. If bandas procure a Saturday job, they may earn $3,000 or more, depending on the nightclub and the number of paying dancers, because they *ganan por la puerte*, that is, they receive 40 to 60 percent of the cover charges.

Banda musicians are highly mobile. Many work on both sides of the border, living a rather transient and unstable life. After the peso's devaluation in December 1994, Mexico's soaring inflation forced more musicians to go north and seek an income in the United States. Many of these men, however, do not remain in one place long enough to establish a household or settle down permanently. Their migration is temporary and, most often, circulatory. These seasonal musicians send money home each week and make periodic visits to their hometown. While in Los Angeles, they may live together with other banderos in an apartment rented by the banda to accommodate their itinerant colleagues.

Like other transnational migrants, banderos established in Los Angeles tend to keep close ties with their families and hometowns, and they hold on to their native culture and traditional networks. For established banderos, itinerant colleagues are thus of importance in a variety of ways: they are a direct link to their home society; they help to maintain, reinforce, and forge social networks that span borders; and they engage in the exchange of musical ideas and expression so vital for any music tradition. Moreover, itinerant musicians allow established bandleaders to exercise some control over the local music market, enabling them to react and adjust to the fluctuating demand. One musician who travels back and forth between Mexico and Los Angeles told me that there are simply more opportunities in a big city like Los Angeles. Although he spent $400 monthly to pay his phone bill, with his income of around $2,000 he was able to support his family of four children and his mother, who were living in Mexico. For someone with little formal education, he thought, it paid well to be a musician.

The fluid and complex existence of transnational musicians, on the other hand, also poses special problems to bandleaders. Felipe Hernández spoke about the difficulty to keep fifteen or more individuals together. In order to maintain a banda over the years, he said, it is important to find the right balance in leadership and to cultivate personal loyalty and friendship with and among all musicians. Despite such attempts, bandas are subject to fluctuations in personnel as players drift from one to another or return to Mexico. Asked why bandas emerge and disappear, Hernández explained: "Let's say the representative of a banda starts to work here. He notices that there is plenty of work; he goes back home, invites musicians, maybe even teenage musicians; he brings them over here and he forms a new banda. Or there was already a banda here, but because of financial or other problems the musicians abandon the leader and he, since he has already established a clientele, solicits musicians from Mexico to come over; they arrive and, there, we have another banda. They work for some years, the same happens again; they leave him and, there, another banda will be formed. . . . It has always been like that" (interview, 1996, Los Angeles).

In general, local musicans know each other well and frequently realign in new groups drawn from their previous rivals. When Hernández formed his own banda in 1989, there were four other Sinaloan bandas residing in Los

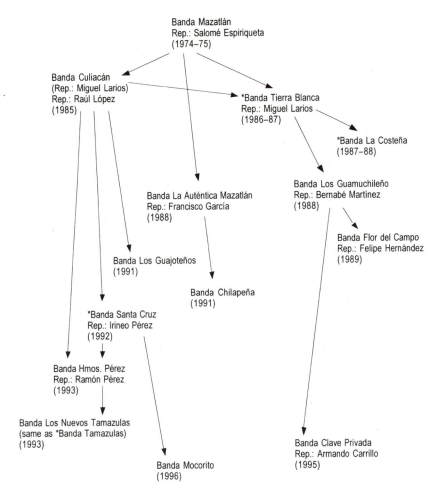

Banda Mazatlán
Rep.: Salomé Espiriqueta
(1974–75)

Banda Culiacán
(Rep.: Miguel Larios)
Rep.: Raúl López
(1985)

*Banda Tierra Blanca
Rep.: Miguel Larios
(1986–87)

*Banda La Costeña
(1987–88)

Banda La Auténtica Mazatlán
Rep.: Francisco García
(1988)

Banda Los Guamuchileño
Rep.: Bernabé Martínez
(1988)

Banda Flor del Campo
Rep.: Felipe Hernández
(1989)

Banda Los Guajoteños
(1991)

Banda Chilapeña
(1991)

*Banda Santa Cruz
Rep.: Irineo Pérez
(1992)

Banda Hmos. Pérez
Rep.: Ramón Pérez
(1993)

Banda Los Nuevos Tamazulas
(same as *Banda Tamazulas)
(1993)

Banda Clave Privada
Rep.: Armando Carrillo
(1995)

Banda Mocorito
(1996)

* Banda no longer exists.

4. Development of Sinaloan bandas residing in East and South Central Los Angeles (1996).

Angeles. He recalled that until the appearance of the technobandas, they all had plenty of work. Then the market tightened. In addition to the mushrooming technobandas, new Sinaloan bandas had developed in the area and aggravated the situation of the established local bandas. Moreover, other bandas emerged that played in Sinaloan style—Banda Perla Azul, Banda La Costera, Banda La Auténtica Zacatecas, Banda Hermanos Ventura, and Banda Río Grande—and that competed with the Sinaloan bandas in the local market. Last but not least, there were a growing number of touring Sinaloan bandas and Sinaloan-style bandas, many of which were contracted by local nightclubs for a series of performances. Banda Los Recoditos from Mazatlán and Banda Caña Verde from Bellavista, Jalisco, for example, had extended stays of several months.

Another problem Sinaloan bandas in Los Angeles are confronted with is of an internal nature: probably none of them consists of pure Sinaloan personnel. Rather, they also employ musicians from other states such as Nayarit, Michoacán, and Jalisco. Musicians and other insiders, of course, notice the difference in playing style. Aesthetic discrepancies may lead to internal conflicts and even to separation.

Continua

In 1994 technobanda was at the zenith of its phenomenal rise. The radio station it had driven to the top was still number 1 in Los Angeles. Concerts held in huge sports arenas would regularly draw tens of thousands of fans. At that point, however, only a few realized that technobanda had reached its limits. Manuel Contreras, who launched the first technobanda in the mid-1980s, did not hesitate to predict its future: "Of course [technobanda] has to pass! Also the charleston passed, the boogie-woogie, the fox-trot, the cha-cha-chá, rock and roll, heavy metal rock, and many other things that came and went! . . . But there is music that has stayed for many years and continues to stay. I think banda will not come to an end completely. Why? Because it is part of a music culture, tied to many performers, to very good musicians. Banda is part of the custom. Hence, it cannot die, and it will never die. It will stay at a [certain] level. Another music for the youth will arise. Maybe some strange noise, but one that fits the youth, right? Or maybe some of the rhythms that have already passed. . . . But banda will not die" (interview, 1994, Guadalajara). Two years later, *banda sinaloense* indeed was on the upswing while technobanda gradually lost steam. Like any popular music style, as Contreras predicted, technobanda would not last forever. Yet it was not drawing to a close either. Banda Machos, Banda Maguey, Banda Arkángel R-15, and others who have shaped the identities and sensibilities of so many youths in the 1990s continue to make music and to move their audiences in the new century.

Technobanda is more than a footnote in the history of Mexican and Mexican American music. Its popularity in the United States had a legitimizing effect on the music as a whole, opening the door for traditional banda to enter mainstream Mexican culture. Technobanda broke the hegemony of Mexican common-denominator popular music by catapulting a regional music onto center stage.

At first reluctantly, traditional (acoustic) bandas began to incorporate certain elements of the technobanda style. Banda now has its own idol, a lead singer, with whom the audience can identify. It makes use of sophisticated technology for both recording and performance. With its new onstage style, the regional music has been able to win over young audiences used to MTV and music videos; with its fast-paced cumbia rhythms, it appeals to dance-loving youth; with its romantic baladas, it speaks to yearning and loving hearts. While the big-name Sinaloan bandas have the economic ability to successfully compete on the international Latin music market, local bandas are thriving as vehicles of popular expression independent of, though not completely unaffected by, the commercial recording industry. What Mark Slobin has attested to regarding subcultural music making in general is particularly true for bandas: they encompass "the full range of communal enterprise, from the mundane commercial life to the hired band through the transcendent fellowship of song, including links to local and intercultural industry, diasporic and intercultural contact networks, cross-subcultural rapport, and a sweeping sense of history that can bridge centuries or can almost instantaneously invent a tradition" (1993: 106–107).

As the musical scene in Nuevo Los Angeles shows so strikingly, local cultures are always in flux. Musicians are constantly urged to mediate between accommodation and resistance, between remaining loyal to their tradition and appropriating innovations. Throughout the twentieth century, bandas played a wide range of genres; a diversity that has helped ensure its vitality. Although Sinaloan bandas in general have become showier and make use of amplifiers and light effects, they have remained faithful to their knowledge of traditional music. The established bandas continue to thrive and attract audiences across all generational and occupational divides. Indeed, the traditional banda sound is powerful because it is so different from the sleek, smoothly produced mass-market sounds floating around us. Banda sinaloense is a strong and vibrant tradition that continues to affect many people because, as musicians say, "viene del corazón" — it comes straight from the heart.

Epilogue

¡Ay Sinaloa, Sinaloa, Sinaloa!
Yo siento el alma que me pica y que me llora
con la pistola que relumbra en la bola
y con la banda que retumbe la tambora.
     Melesio Chaidez Díaz, Banda El Pueblito

More than a decade after an ingenious record producer in Guadalajara created technobanda and half a decade after this novel sound conquered southern California and other parts of the United States where Mexicans have moved to find work and maybe a better future, I spent a couple of weeks in Mexico City, where I attended a conference organized by the National Association for Chicana and Chicano Studies. In its twenty-five years of existence, it was the association's first conference in the capital of Mexico, and my contribution to this unique event was a paper titled "*Que retumbe la tambora*: The Cultural Power of a Regional Music." I somehow anticipated that only a few in my (mostly Chicano) audience had previously heard about the banda phenomenon; after all, it was not the typical crowd that danced away its leisure time in underprivileged neighborhoods' obscure nightclubs. Nevertheless, I was still stunned how little this blue-collar movement had touched the academic Chicano community. My Mexican audience as well seemed to favor its safe and quiet ivory tower over dubious and noisy nightclubs. None of them could tell me where to find the city's banda nightclubs. Actually, it was not so difficult. I spotted an advertisement for El Salón Pacífico painted on a huge wall right in the neighborhood where I was staying. I went there on Friday night with some of my Mexican friends to look for *el chilango quebrador*, the quebradita-dancing Mexico City native, humorously portrayed in one of Banda El Recodo's hit songs. What we found was amazing: the nightclub was filled with exuberant youths, quite a few of them in their twenties, dancing in a style that had been in fashion in Los Angeles in the early 1990s. The music was live and loud and featured alternating sets by a technobanda and a Sinaloan banda. El Salón Pacífico had been in business for more than twenty years, as I learned from the present manager, who was himself from Sinaloa. In former years, Banda El Recodo used to play in this nightclub which was predominantly visited by Sinaloans living in the capital. When the Los Angeles banda craze swept back to Mexico and into Mexico City in the mid-1990s, the nightclub began to contract technobandas, and young Mexicans from the capital and all the provinces began to throng the dance floor.

Technobanda's challenge and the detour to the United States were necessary for banda music to eventually enter mainstream Mexican culture. The use of modern communication technology enabled commercial bandas to at last strip off the social stigma attached to them over a century ago by Sinaloa's bourgeois urbanites. Although brass-band music had long served as one of the educated classes' favorite pastimes, bands eventually became associated with lower-class music making and were rejected by the elite as a crude imitation of their venerable military bands by ignorant peasants who could not do any better. While the rural population and the lower-class urbanites continued to enjoy brass-band music, people from the upper social stratum found pleasure in orchestra music featuring soft-sounding, and thus "cultured," string instruments. Worrying that their loud and vulgar regional music not only affirmed but reinforced the already widespread prejudice of Sinaloa as *el estado torpe* [the crude state], Sinaloa's patriotic elite developed a profound disdain for banda's musical as well as textual crudeness. Banda musicians' low social status was related to the allegedly low quality of their music and to the rather disreputable locales where some of them had found work.

Urbanization, capitalism, and, eventually, the culture industry altered Sinaloa's society, lifestyles, habits, and popular-music tastes. Naturally, these changes mainly affected the cities. Rural areas and the sierra in particular lacked other attractions and newer pastimes. Thus, banda music continued to play a major role in the lives of the inhabitants of small towns, villages, and ranchos. In the cities, on the other hand, music bands faced competition from radio, phonograph records, motion pictures, the automobile, and other technological advances that led to the growing sophistication and mobility of the urban dwellers. Moreover, the hybridizing force of the urban environment had a tremendous impact on all musical ensembles, though less so, of course, on *bandas huipera* than on upwardly aspiring bandas, as attested by the course Banda El Recodo and Banda La Costeña took from the late 1950s on. In the cities, the pattern of local culture within which banda had grown up was gradually being superseded. As urban bandas became more proficient and absorbed a repertory and musical tastes shaped by middle- and upper-class aesthetics, they were able to acquire a certain respectability, at least in the province.

Recordings popularized banda music beyond its regional confines; the sound conquered new territories and crossed borders before any banda musician had even set foot on the new ground. But the recordings also contributed to the standardization of style and repertory within Sinaloa. Regional differences gradually blurred.

When pop music enraptured Mexico's youths in the 1960s and records became affordable for the majority, bandas lost their immediate attraction as a dance band. Only a few of the mass-market-oriented bandas managed to survive this new trend toward amplified music. Although the microphone enabled singers to be heard over the fifteen-man band, banda remained a predominantly instrumental music. In the countryside and in the less affluent neighborhoods of the cities where electricity was not available or musicians could not afford to buy an amplification system, banda continued to be the preferred musical entertainment of the people. It did not need amplification to fill the town square, the arena, the *palenque*, or the cantina. While the few remaining commercially oriented bandas played international popular dance music and toured the country and the United States, village bandas were largely unaffected by the popular music industry. Their music continued to adhere to a regionally based aesthetics and plebeian musical practice.

Banda's history is certainly not simple, as implied by one journalist who claimed that "had it not been for a radio station on Sunset Boulevard, just off the Hollywood freeway," banda would have continued to be merely a constituent of small-town Mexican life. It is correct that KLAX's success, and maybe even more its threat to the established English-language radio market, made banda visible to a larger society for the first time. Yet statements such as the above deprive this music and those who have practiced and lived it of a large and significant part of their history. This book, thus, is a contribution to the recovery, though partial and fragmentary, of a music's history and its continuation into the present. It expresses the need to recognize the historical continuity of local culture as it becomes part of our modern, transnational world.

Only a few years ago, Robert Walser (1993: 21) had good reasons to criticize academic writings on popular music for their lack of historical perspective. Since then, a number of outstanding books on popular musics have been published that emphasize the historical roots of contemporary mass mediated styles.[1] The need to study a popular music's rootedness in tradition became immediately apparent to me when I recognized how Mexicanos felt about the novel sound. Their notion of technobanda as inherently Mexican and intrinsically traditional called for an analysis that included the music's historical dimension. That was also when I began to realize the deeper significance of tradition as a way of conceptualizing the fragile communicative relationships across time and space that are the grounds for identifications (Gilroy 1993: 276). Tradition is not a lost past, nor does it stand in opposition to modernity.

Throughout this book, I have been concerned with music as a key to understanding social and cultural processes and, within them, forces that shape identity. Music, especially popular music, has an important social and political dimension. Thus, it is no coincidence that the banda phenomenon popped up in metropolitan Los Angeles during the early 1990s, nor that it became a major movement within the Mexican American communities in southern California. Technobanda was able to meet the needs of thousands of young Mexicanos longing for a way to express themselves culturally. As Peter Manuel has pointed out, "[I]ndividuals and communities have sought to reconstruct ethnic identities as reactions against the pervasive disenchantment, commodification, rationalization, and disorienting globalization of world culture" (1997–98: 22).

Although the flowering of technobanda was nourished by a profound sense of uprootedness or unrootedness caused by globalizing and transnational processes, its songs did not address issues such as the inequality, discrimination, and dislocation that result from these processes. Almost none of technobanda's new songs included overt political statements or direct social criticism. As a music for dancing, its main appeal lay in its power to make people feel that they were "in touch with an essential part of themselves, their emotions and their 'community'" (Stokes 1994: 13). Cultural enjoyment of identity, however, is neither innocent nor apolitical. Banda events provided the means by which its participants constructed, asserted, and mobilized their ethnic particularity at a time when their community was under attack. The music allowed Mexicano youths to reclaim a part of their history and to recover values shared with their parents and grandparents and rooted in their homeland. It is a people's past that makes the present livable and the future imaginable: "Ultimately, history is the root of all people. It is what gives them foundation. The individual (hi)story of each person is what defines them, what gives them projection, gives them direction. A person without history, without a past, does not exist and has no future. . . . People without history cannot advance, cannot exist as a people. They must grab on to something, a root which holds them to the earth, which is their history, their past."[2]

Holding on to a way of life informed by custom and history has become increasingly more significant to anyone trying to resist the uprooting and dislocating forces of our time. George Lipsitz thus urges us to see music as a part of the collective historical memory and of the continuing social dialogue, for "one reason for popular music's powerful affect is its ability to conflate music and lived experience, to make both the past and present zones of choice that serve distinct social and political interests" (1990: 104). Among younger Mexicanos, technobanda was valued because it sprang from Mexican roots and because it made them feel *orgulloso* [proud]. For once, their presence in the United States was acknowledged by the media in a positive way. Their love for dancing to banda music had been transformed into an important tool of cultural politics. Not only had they become visible, they were also audible. Cruising around in their cars that vibrated with the rhythm of the new sound of Los Angeles was both a powerful statement of identification with their Mexican heritage and a forceful reassurance that they too belonged to this city. The vibrant and youthful new style was relevant to both their lifestyle and their cultural needs. With technobanda, the Mexicano youth of the 1990s had finally found its voice.

Yet, after more than a decade of enjoying high popularity among Mexicanos, banda has still not entered the musical mainstream. A *Los Angeles Times* review of the 1999 Cinco de Mayo Festival at the Whittier Narrows Recreation Area in South El Monte, sponsored by Bud Light and attended by 120,000 people, read: "The third act featured Mexican pop singer Graciela Beltrán fronting a rowdy banda group. Banda, a relative newcomer to the Mexican music scene, takes the trumpets of mariachi and the tubas of polka to the extreme, mixing them with other blaring instruments and a pounding bass drum. The result sounds like the circus coming to town, and many at the festival said banda was a taste they had yet to acquire."[3] The reviewer's comments about the other Latin musical genres featured at the festival were less judgmental, stressing instead the universal appeal of artists such as the Colombian rock singer Shakira, the Dominican bachata singer Juan Luis Guerra, or the Spanish ballad queen Rocío Durcal. Rather than featuring exclusively Mexican music, as in former years, the 1999 festival presented a variety of Latin musics from Iberia to the Caribbean and Central America, so that heterogeneous cultures from different geographical locations converged. Is the festival's musical diversity an indicator that "musical tastes are opening up," as the reviewer claimed, or is it just another symptom of postmodern eclecticism? Shall we cherish music's seemingly uniting power if what is most successful are "hot fusions" of common-denominator popular musics? Whom does this music unite, and for what purpose?

Technobandas and the commercially oriented acoustic bandas have made many efforts to enter the mainstream Latino music market. They have adopted the international repertory of baladas and cumbias; they are armed with equipment that can compete with any international pop group; they have signed with multinational record labels; and they tour the world indefatigably. Yet, the music has kept the strong local identity that distinguishes it from other music styles. It is this specific Sinaloan tinge that makes it unique and, at the same time, incompatible with the musical taste of a global mass-market audience.

Their efforts, however, had a great effect on the banda tradition. Bandas in the most remote ranchos in the sierra know to play every single hit of Banda El Recodo and Banda Machos, and young banderos learn these popular songs before they have been properly introduced to the traditional repertory.

During my fieldwork in Sinaloa, I found banda music performed in a vast variety of settings: from a patriarch's birthday celebration on a rancho to the discotheque in Mazatlán's tourist zone; from the cantina in the harbor area to the highly promoted *guerra de bandas* in the city's arena; from the rehearsals at a banda's office to the stage show at Mazatlán's Carnival. Since music and life intermingle in complex ways, some of my encounters were rather unexpected. I remember that I was most impressed to find bandas established in the city of Culiacán commemorate the day of music's patron saint with a selection of *música antaña* [music from long ago] played in a most intimate setting, while the population of a small rural settlement danced to the highly amplified sound of a banda in celebration of Semana Santa, or Holy Week. Particularly striking at this rural fiesta was the contrast between high technology and poor environment: before the arrival of the banda, with its equipment worth the gross annual income of the whole village, the locals had watered the dusty soil that was to serve as a dance floor and placed a few strings of colorful paper cutouts to give the site a festive look. While women were busy preparing chickens for barbecue, men on horseback returned with the cattle from the field. As I sat and observed the village getting ready for its fiesta and the musicians and their crew setting up the stage, the microphones, the console, the speaker boxes, the cables, and the lights, and testing the sound system, I thought about the apparent incongruity between and the coexistence of the traditional and the modern. Yet the appearance of the traditional way of life was deceptive: the village had long ceased to be a bounded, coherent space. Its population was mobile; many had migrated to the cities or to the United States.[4] Thus, although many of the fiesta participants no longer resided here, they had taken Holy Week off to visit with their families. The fiesta was for them too. The banda had also been hired for them—maybe to show those who had left that this place too was catching up with the modern world.

A Mexican fiesta without music and dance would be a very sad fiesta, wrote the folklorist Erna Fergusson in the 1930s. Nowadays one may be tempted to add: a fiesta without a dozen heavy speaker boxes, a mixing console, and at least two sound engineers is a very poor fiesta. As Néstor García Canclini (1990: 200) has pointed out, one reason for the growth of local culture is the market's need to include traditional symbolic structures and goods in the mass circuits of communication in order to embrace the population least integrated into modernity. In our interdependent world, contrasting pairs such as urban and

33. Banda Machos has become part of the popular entertainment. Shooting gallery at the fair during Holy Week of 1997 in the village of San Miguel, northern Sinaloa. When a target button is hit by a bullet, music of Banda Machos and flashing lights would go on and last for a few seconds. Photo by Helena Simonett.

rural, modern and traditional, and progressive and backward are gradually losing the validity they once had (or we believe they had).

Banda continues to be deeply rooted in local culture, and the cultural forms in which banda music has been embedded have not vanished. Although some of the customs have been transformed considerably over time, most of them are still celebrated with banda music. People's lives literally are accompanied by the tambora from birth to death. Banda's versatility has helped to ensure its vitality for over a century, and it promises to carry the rhythm of the tambora through the twenty-first century. "Que retumbe la tambora"—let the tambora resound!

Appendix: Dancers' Voices

After dancing through nightclubs in the San Fernando Valley and in East Los Angeles, I decided to focus my ethnographic research activities on four nightclubs in Nuevo Los Angeles, the area in which technobanda first gained a foothold: El Lido and El Parral (South Gate), El Potrero (Cudahy), and El Farallón (Lynwood). They are in close proximity to each other: El Lido is only a quarter mile from El Parral, and three miles from El Potrero and El Farallón. Although there are other large clubs nearby (for example, El Palacio San Fernando on Pacific Boulevard, Huntington Park), I selected these four because most of the dancers I interviewed in 1996 went to all of them, depending on the day and on the bands playing. Featuring Sinaloan bandas and norteño groups solely, El Parral and El Farallón were, and, at the time of this writing, are predominantly frequented by Sinaloans. El Lido and El Potrero, on the other hand, feature more diverse bands and are preferred by people from Jalisco and other states. With capacities of 1,000 and 1,700, respectively, the latter are quite spacious. With an admission between five and ten dollars, El Lido is the best deal for dancers with a small purse and hence attracts especially young people. During "La noche del Lido" [The Lido's Night], as Thursday night is called among the youth, dancers enter free (women often enter free on the other days too). The other nightclubs charge between ten and thirty dollars, depending on the night and on the band that is playing.

Since the dance event is a site of social action, with multiple meanings for its participants, I decided to present the voices of a number of dancers I interviewed in early 1996. They all responded to a questionnaire I distributed at El Lido in January 1996 and agreed to share their experiences.

The interviewees presented here are eight women between the ages of eighteen and twenty-five. Six of them are second-generation Mexican Americans; the other two came to the United States as children. All of their parents are foreign born. Two of the U.S.-born women identify themselves as Mexicana, the others as Hispanic or Chicana. Although they are all bilingual, most of them consider Spanish their primary language. Besides bandas music, most of them listen to norteña, Spanish rock, and rap. Most of them go to nightclubs up to twelve times a month and spend an average of three hundred dollars for their preferred leisure activity—dancing.

The dance experiences of these young women—Victoria, Christina, Elydia, Lotty, Irma, Marina, Veronica, and Elena (pseudonyms are used for those who requested it)—are very similar, although their ideas about dance and dancing vary quite a bit. Victoria is the only among them who belongs to a quebradita club. She joined Los Chicos Banda y Quebradoras [The Banda Boys and the Quebradoras], a group of twenty young people who used to hang around together. Like other clubs, they named themselves after song titles: "Los chicos banda" is a song interpreted by Banda Los Pelillos, and "La quebradora" is one of Banda El Recodo's hits. Victoria tried several nightclubs such as the Zona Rosas, Leonardo's, La Sierra, and El Viejo Oeste, but then decided to frequent El Lido (Thursdays) and El Potrero (Saturdays and Sundays). Fridays are reserved for special events for which she would drive up to an hour and a half, depending on the banda playing. Being from Guadalajara, she hardly ever goes to El Parral or El Farallón. She does not like to dance in Sinaloan style and considers norteña music, which is frequently played at Sinaloan clubs, dull and lacking in energy.

Christina and Elydia are best friends, and they always go out together, "to keep an eye on each other," as they say. They dance about fifteen hours each weekend and consider it "a lot of fun and a good workout." In addition, the dancing keeps them out of trouble. They are both U.S. born (their parents are from Guadalajara and Durango, respectively) and aver that they are more into Mexican music than their parents.

Lotty prefers to dance "the old-fashioned way" and hence frequents the Farallón. She grew up listening to Mexican music, including banda sinaloense. Since her father and mother are from Zacatecas and Durango, respectively, she also likes the tamborazo, the regional band music from Zacatecas. Lotty has fully embraced Mexican culture and calls herself Mexicana, although she has been to Mexico only once (ten years ago). Irma's favorite places are El Lido and La Jalpa. The former nightclub she attends with a group of friends of the same age (eighteen), the latter with older friends who are more into norteña music. Although she had been familiar with banda music, she did not like Mexican music before technobanda started to become popular in Los Angeles, but since then, it is all she listens to.

Marina was born in Michoacán and moved to the United States at the age of five. She remembers that back in Mexico, her family had parties with live bandas playing. Although she has kept close contact with Mexico, she is strongly involved in American music. She likes to dance to banda music, but prefers norteña because it is easier to dance to.

Both Veronica and Elena used to listen to some Mexican popular music before banda caught their attention. They both attended college when the banda movement was in full swing. Sensitized by happenings on and off campus that affected the Latino communities, they became more interested in political issues and decided to take Chicano history classes to learn more about their roots. Veronica graduated in 1995 (with a double major in psychology and Spanish) and is now working with Latino teen mothers in the Pomona area.

The dancers' voices are all female, for two reasons. First, my emphasis on female voices is intended as a counterbalance to the male-dominated discourse of popular culture. Second, although I occasionally talked casually with male dancers, I did no formal interviews of any of them. Men were either too lazy or too shy (or maybe cowardly) to respond to my questionnaire. The few who did preferred to maintain their anonymity (putting their phone number on the questionnaire was optional). Men's voices nevertheless are implicitly present, be it in the women's conceptions about society, their assumptions about the other gender, or their conformity with or objection to the male-dominated world of popular culture. To fill the gaps created by their silence, I selected the lyrics of popular songs that respond to the same questions I asked the young women.

HS: *What do you like most about banda music and banda events?*

Victoria: This past week I wasn't able to go out. Now I feel desperate. What draws me [to the nightclub] is the energy of the music. I dance banda because it's so fast and there are live instruments: it's a complete band. On the contrary, if a conjunto norteño plays a cumbia, it doesn't sound the same as with banda. It doesn't sound as energetic; it sounds generic to me. Norteño is dull, whereas banda is very energetic, very complete. El Recodo, Los Pelillos, and Banda Limonense [a new banda from Jalisco] are my favorite bandas because they all are very complete, in the sense that even if they play romantic songs, you can feel a lot of energy in these songs. My favorite song is "La quebradora." I like it because of the name. The first time I heard it, it was not played by El Recodo, but by an air band from Sinaloa, Clave Privada. The one thing about this song that caught my attention is that it has four or five changes of rhythm: it's like four, five songs in one. The rhythms change so drastically, you can put all kinds of steps in there. It's a very, very danceable song. Also, I am from Guadalajara, Jalisco, and Banda El Recodo is very much associated with people from Guadalajara. Since there are many, many dancers from Guadalajara, Banda El Recodo always takes them into consideration when they play that song and they send a lot of greetings to Guadalajara. They say: "From Sinaloa hasta Guadalajara, Jalisco."

Christina: Banda El Recodo is my favorite banda because of the rhythm they have. It's good to dance to *el caballito* or *el brinquito*, and the lyrics are pretty good. They are older than any other banda. They have quite a background. They've been there longer. But that's not really important, because if I heard an old band that has a lot of tradition and I didn't like the music they were playing, I wouldn't listen to them, no matter what tradition they have. [The ones I like] are all similar: Banda Maguey, Los Recoditos. I've heard they're the sons of Banda El Recodo, but I'm not quite sure.

Lotty: El Recodo is my favorite banda. They also play quebradita music, but their beats are real fast. And they use other instruments, no synthesizers. I've seen them play. They are real good. There are a lot of them. Lots of them are young. What I like most about their music is the fast beat. What adds to the music is the tuba. The tuba has a strong sound.

Irma: The rhythm and the volume are most important. If you dance, that's what you listen to. I hardly listen to the lyrics; sometimes I do, but most of the time it's just the rhythm. Makes you just get up and dance. Banda El Recodo—I like the rhythms of the songs they play. The brass gives life to the song . . . without it, it wouldn't be the same, since it is the loudest. If I go to the Lido, I like to listen to the polka rhythm or cumbia. I like salsa too, but I don't like to dance it. I've been twice, because my mom's side [of the family] is from El Salvador. They like cumbias and salsa. [The purpose of] dancing is to forget about everyday life, to feel good, to clear the mind. And it is a good workout.

Veronica: I like the tambora. When the song goes to its full power, that's what I like, when all instruments play. You get into it, you want to dance, you want to party more. I like to listen to an older banda, especially when it is in the context of an activity. I remember once in Mexico, they had a quinceañera, and they couldn't find a band, so they hired the banda junior from the small town. They were about fifteen years old. They had the old instruments. I liked it, we were dancing to it. It was good.

HS: As a dancer, do you feel part of the music?

Victoria: As dancers, we are responsible for expressing what we want. The deejay has to hit the taste of the crowd—it depends on the day of the week, what kind of music they play during the intersection. We make the statement, request the music. It starts with us—it's like an echo. Punta and lambada, for example, came from the musicians and therefore [those dances] died shortly after they became a hit.

Christina: Yes, if there weren't listeners and dancers, I don't think there would be bands. We have to be there to make them popular, buying their cassettes. If it wasn't for us, [the bands] wouldn't exist.

Elena: Sure. Good musicians react to the dancing crowd. They don't just play a fixed program. If the crowd wants more cumbias, they'll play it [sic]. I think they can tell from watching the dancers, [seeing] what they like, from the energy that is going out from the dancers. The advantage of having a live-banda playing is that you can go and ask them to play a specific song. They usually do it right away. You really feel part of the event when they play "your" song and when they greet you.

Lotty: If they didn't play live music in nightclubs, I probably would not go so often. It's not the same. I like the live bands. During the break, the deejays play records, but it's not the same. It's not because they mix in all different songs, it's not the same feeling—you just feel it, the live band.

HS: *What other musics do you like and how did you get into banda and into the nightclub scene?*

Irma: Before it started with Banda Machos, I didn't like Spanish music. My dad listened to it. He is from Zacatecas, so he listened to tambora. That's what he likes. I listened to English music, techno, et cetera. Then banda became popular and everybody started liking it. All these songs came out. . . . And when the clubs started, that's when I started too. And since then, that's all I listen to. . . . The nightclub itself is a safe place. That's why they let me go out. It's safe. There is security everywhere. If you are underage, they don't let you drink. My parents would not let me go otherwise. . . . Both my parents went to the Lido. They checked it out. They know what it is like. They also went to this other place, El Jalpita, where my friend and I go to dance.

Victoria: My sisters listen to Spanish rock music. I listen to banda and I like K-Rock a lot. At work, when I'm alone, I listen to banda. My boss doesn't like it too much; he likes K-Rock. I had to defend the music and explain to my colleagues and friends that banda is beautiful. I also thought before that banda was low-class music. The music has that stigma. Before I started to listen to banda I was into heavy metal a lot. It was my primary choice. I had to listen to banda for all my life because my dad is from Michoacán and he is a big, big music person—to the point of having a big sound system in his car and a very loud stereo at home. But it wasn't my choice at the beginning. I grew up with it, but I didn't like Mexican music. I was one of those dumb girls—you go to a family party and you don't like Spanish music. It was not until I turned eighteen that I started liking banda. When you come to the United States at an early age, you get kind of dumb. You develop a different taste. I used to be into heavy metal—I used to wear long, black hair, boots, platforms. At eighteen I wasn't yet clubbing much on weekends, I would just go on Thursdays with my sisters. We are eight girls, eight sisters in the house. I have gone out with them since I was fifteen. I used to go to Leonardo's right there on Manchester and Vermont. [At that time] they played *tropical*, they had salsa. In the [intermission] it was very usual that they played English music like hip-hop. The reason why I started listening to banda music was that I was forced into it. Banda was coming on so strong that I found myself going to family reunions, *quinceañeras*, and everybody would look at me just very weird because I was dressed in that particular way [in which] I would go to the parties with English music. [Banda] was so in that they were all playing the music and wearing the music: leather vests, *cuartas*. It got to a point where I wouldn't dance the whole night because nobody would take me up to dance. They must have thought that I wouldn't dance [banda]. So I kind of mellowed down on that kind of dress. But I still don't dress in pants and boots.

Lotty: I grew up around Spanish music. I always liked it. My parents like banda but not the quebradita. They say: "Why don't they dance the way they used to back then?" They see me dance and say: "She dances the way we used to. But the quebradita— What happened? They are breaking with all these other things, they throw the girl around, they're spinning them, lifting them up in the air." My friends' parents say the same. I'm not embarrassed to like my parents' music. But I have friends that don't like Spanish music. They: "I don't want to listen to that!"—"Why not, we used to listen to it when we were small, and you never complained back then. You used to dance around when you were small and now, all of a sudden, you are embarrassed to listen to it in public."—"Naw, I won't go to this kind of party." They are embarrassed. They are set on one type of music, that's their style: like deep house. They do dance, but I have a lot of friends who don't know how to dance to Spanish music. I used to listen to them, I still like some of their music. . . . I started [to go to nightclubs] when I was seventeen. My mom would ask: "You are going *where?*" But my parents trusted my judgment on what I would do there and what I wouldn't do there. Some of my friends' parents don't let them go because of what is going on, like dealing and shooting. The problem is that they check the men but not the girls, or only the purse. They should check [better]—it's for the protection of other people. But I feel safe. The worst I saw was two girls fighting, they were pulling [each other's hair], ripping each other's shirt. At Farallón some months ago . . . we were inside and we walked out. There were a couple of people there and the cops. A guy was shot or they stabbed him. Things like that happen because of disrespect, or because of drugs, or because one cheated another with someone or something, or just because one gave another a wrong look or said something.

Christina: My parents are Mexican, so I grew up with that music. When I was small, I wasn't so much into it, until a couple of years ago—actually, when the quebradita started about seven years ago, I started listening to Spanish music, I started getting into it. And I still listen to it every once in a while. First I would go out to quinceañeras. My parents thought I was too young. My parents did not check out the places where we were going. But I have an older brother—he is the one who would tell my parents: "Don't let her go there." They didn't want to let me go. But then they would hear from other people, "Ah, that's a nice place." Whenever I go to El Potrero or El Lido, they know that there is security there. It is better than going to parties like house parties, where they don't know what you're doing there. At least in clubs, they know that you're not smoking pot or doing other illegal stuff. There is security, there is protection, even in the parking lot there is security. I feel safe for them and for me. I would rather go to a club than to a house party.

Banda Zeta, "Muchachas modernas" (Ze Luis): "Las muchachas modernas solo quieren bailar / ya no quieren quedarse en la casa a estudiar . . . / chicas, chicas modernas, chicas de hoy" [Modern young women only want to dance / they don't want to stay at home studying anymore . . . / girls, modern girls, today's girls].

Marina: Banda music has been around forever. I grew up with banda music. At that time, not very many people liked it. At least in Mexico, only the poor listen to that type of music. The rich do not listen to [banda]. They have Spanish pop-rock music, romantic music such as ballads. You go to a club, and it's divided: the rich and the poor. Even on TV shows and Spanish soap operas, when they make fun of the poor, the poor characters listen to banda. And you have the rich characters that listen to another, more sophisticated type of music. Here in California, it cuts through the classes. Here it doesn't matter. The way I see it now, quebradita and that type of music [technobanda], it's a fad. You remember how hot lambada was? [Banda] has stayed longer since it's been there lot more. When we were young, we always knew about banda music, but it was not popular, it was even embarrassing.—Whoa, that's old music, you wouldn't listen to that! But in Mexico it's really used in the rodeos. Where I come from, the banda has to be there for the rodeos, or else it's not a rodeo. A lot of the songs the bandas are playing are old music. Even my mom says, "Eh, that was when I was young!" In a while, young people who follow the trend will forget about it. But people that have always listened to it, there is no way you could forget about it.

Veronica: I think it has a lot to do with college. When I was in high school, I wasn't very much into Spanish. I would come back to my parents' country, Mexico, Jalisco, twice a year. I never stopped because that's my roots. I have a lot of family there. Both my grandmothers are there. My father's family is there. My mom's family is also there. What helps is that they're both from the same small town, El Chante. Now I like the tambora more than technobanda. It's the real stuff. Technobanda appeals mostly to the young crowd. Older people don't really like it. My dad feels that they are degrading it. He says, "Se la hechen a perder la banda." He doesn't like that mix. It should be banda—brass and that's it.

HS: Is it important for you that banda is a Mexican music?
Christina: It is important, I guess, because it is what your parents tried to hand down to you—the culture, the tradition. It reflects what my parents went through. Earlier I would say to my mom, "I don't know why you're listening to this kind of music." And now you catch yourself listening to it and you think, "Oh, my God, it really reflects what your parents did, what they listened to." I never really asked my parents about the music. They didn't grow up listening to the same kind of music. We are

listening to the same songs, but they fixed them up and made them banda. I'm more into [Mexican music] than my parents are right now. I listen to KBUE, while my mom is listening to oldies in English.

Lotty: Not really. It's more a personal style, of being Mexican. I know that in some bandas there are people from South America, Central America playing. It's OK, but you can tell—it's not in them as much.

Veronica: I like the music, but it is also political. To me, a lot of it has to do with my parents' history. It is knowing my history. I like a lot of the lyrics, especially the old songs—the older lyrics talking about growing up in a small town. Banda Machos's "Sangre de indio" talks about moving away from the hometown, about being an Indian. They're talking about being proud of who you are. I know how it is to live in a small town because of my parents. I feel proud of listening to this kind of music. It reinforces what I was taught to believe. My parents always said: "You have to be proud of who you are." That's why my parents always took us back twice a year. When we were little, they would take us the whole summer. It brings back those memories for me, when I was little. I like hearing [the songs]. It's a statement about my parents' history and it validates the history, what they have been through. It also shows, in a political sense, "Yeah, we're also here and we are proud of being here. We're strong people." . . . The cowboy outfit is more like a fashion statement. When I go down to Mexico, I never see them dressing like that. They dress like that more here that they do in Mexico. Many Chicanos are dressing like that to say: "I'm Mexican." . . . Have you noticed that the more that things turn against the immigrants and the more laws they make against the immigrants, the more they come out, they dress more expressively, they like to turn up their car radios more. They're proud of who they are; they are not intimidated any longer. The banda movement helped young people to address the issue of being Mexican. To tell who they are or to fight against injustice and discrimination. Definitely. . . . I have friends who were ashamed of their roots, they didn't want to admit that they are Mexican. And now I see my cousins' friend, they're going to dance banda: "Yes, I'm Mexican!" Young people are aware of a lot of things—at a younger age.

HS: *Why and how have technobanda and quebradita changed?*

Veronica: I started going out about three years ago—to La Hacienda [in La Puente]. It was very powerful when that article came out in the L.A. Times [*Magazine*, by Rubén Martínez]. I remember I was reading it at school. Three years later, it's still the same big crowd. In terms of clothes, it is different. It depends on where you are going. If you're going to La Hacienda or to El Lido, the dress code is to wear jeans, boots, and a nice shirt. That's it. Girls can go dressier. But if you're going to El Farallón or El Parral, there girls go dressed up: long dress, nice hairdos, high heels. They are now dancing more caballito and holding, I don't know how it is called. A cumbia, a love song, a norteña, a corrido—they always try to dance it together. The new thing is having more contact with your partner. All these accessories are gone, but they still react to the *saludos* [greetings to Mexican states]. It's not so territorial anymore. Just Mexico. Maybe there is an unconscious influence because there are so many things going on against Mexicans [in the United States] recently—they became the scapegoat for political reasons. It becomes secondary what state you're from.

Elena: If you are in it, you don't really notice the changes. It changes slowly, but it has changed a lot. Technobanda and quebradita are not so hot anymore. Now the real *banda sinaloense* is strong. They are very versatile—they play anything from quebradita to *tropical* to norteña. I think when the studios started to make these techno-mixes, that's what killed technobanda. It was the wrong direction. People wanted to go back to their roots, to hear the real music, played by real musicians—not by synthesizers and computers. The strange thing is that the dance went the other direction, toward techno. Before, people dressed in *rancho* style and danced *zapateado* to a techno-version of banda. Now that the music is authentic, they dance techno steps and dress techno.

Banda Arkángel R-15, "Nicolasa" (*Lourdes Pérez*): "Y bailamos zapateado y bailamos quebradito / la quebraba pa' un lado, bailamos de caballito / la tomé de la cintura y bailamos con sabrosura / ay, Nico Nicolasa, que bien bailas tú la cumbia" [And we danced zapateado, and we danced quebradito / I bent her to the side / we danced caballito / I took her by the waist and we danced with flavor / ay, Nico Nicolasa, how well you dance the cumbia].

Victoria: Technobanda was very strong. They dressed [according to] the music that was playing. Yes, they listen to it, they dressed it, and they drove it. Have you seen the trucks with the hats? That was very in, the trucks with the hats, with the ropes on the mirror. But right now they are more elegant, the trucks. Before, when *rancho* was in, [they drove] old trucks, and now, they are getting. . . "higher class," the *narco*-truck. The trucks now have spoilers. Their prime trucks are going to the paint shops. So has the dress changed: from cowboy shirts to silk-cream shirts—that's what they call them, *crema de seda*. The style of clothes is very much connected with the music. If I see you wearing Wranglers and if I see you wearing one of those Wrangler shirts, I know you are into conjunto. It would make no sense for you to wear that to dance banda. You can dance both, but I can tell what kind of music you prefer. Like my boyfriend . . . he is very much into norteño: from his belt to his boots, they have to be Wrangler. He knows how to dance banda very well; he is a very good dancer, but he loves norteño. You can tell by the way he dresses. You can also tell that most of the guys in our crowd dance caballito: their clothes are very baggy, they wear comfortable shoes, not boots. It's much easier to dance and move a girl with those kinds of shoes and *botines* than with boots because for caballito, they slide their feet, [while] for norteño, they hop. Boots are not uncomfortable for norteños and they wear them a lot. Our guys that dance *brinquito banda* [the fast style] like to dance caballito or *suelto*, loose. They don't wear hats. The girls jump so much that it becomes a bother for them; none of them wears a hat. They have a very short haircut. They are there to dance. The people that dress like that are usually also the people that were into English music before, that adopted some kind of dress style [and wouldn't change it when technobanda hit]. If you were not so much into that and someone would tell you "banda," what would you think? Hats, boots and, sadly, a little bit of ignorance. Stereotypes of that. [We] already went to another kind of experience with another type of music. We don't follow the stereotype. We have been through a transition.

Marina: You remember how quebradita was at first? You'll never catch anybody doing that again. I don't know why. What they do now is the jumping around, it's called caballito. Now they are more separate and they dance more techno. A lot of these people also go to English clubs and they dress like those techno people. They have these crazy haircuts: real short and just a bit on the top. They are dressed more casually. They don't dress like cowboys anymore, even the girls. You would look at them and you would not even think that they were interested in dancing Mexican music. In the Potrero, the style is miniskirts, and they wear shorts underneath. Some of the dance moves are techno.

HS: *What is the difference between quebradita, caballito, and brinquito?*

Ritmo Rojo, "Las caderas" (Gerardo Franco): "Sigue bailando de caballito / quebradita o de brinquito / que para el caso es igual" [Keep dancing caballito / quebradita or brinquito / which, by the way, is the same].

Victoria: Quebradita is the first style, when banda started coming in with the technomusic. *Quebradita* means "break." Before they would get the girl on a very low level, and that's why it was called breaking. "Caballito" says it. They also have another name for it, *brinquito*: that is what we do. It's trotting, what horses do, they trot [*shows the step*]. Right now, we're mixing quebradita with caballito. Specially at the contests in Lido's. Quebradita is acrobatic. Caballito doesn't have a lot of acrobatics. We did a step that's called "caballito," my dance partner and me. You probably saw it. He gets me and he flips me over. We call it "caballito" because it [looks like] saddling the horse. We do mix a lot of tango and steps borrowed from everywhere. But when there is a zapateado, it always has to be done the same way. I would never change a step in zapateado. It's the imitation of the way animals dance . . . A lot of people that wear the *avestruz* [ostrichleather] boots love *bandas sinaloenses*. They hate technobandas. And they might also hate the way we dance, because they say that's not the way it is supposed to be danced. You are supposed to dance it together and in a hugged style. I have talked to a lot of guys when I go out alone. They take me out to dance, and if a good song is played, say "La quebradora," I want to dance it separate. They say: "No, that's the way you're supposed to dance, only crazy people dance it separate." They find us who jump around too innovative, too modern; they think it's clownish. But both groups, the guys that are wearing the *botas de avestruz* and we who like to dance brinquito, we all love banda. A lot of us go to Banda El Recodo [concerts], but also the people who drive the fancy trucks will go. We both like the same music, but they disapprove of the way we dance. We think it's too boring they way they're dancing. It's peculiar. They do criticize us a lot. If you go to Farallón dancing the way we dance in Potrero, everybody will criticize you. We don't go there anymore. On Sundays, before, they used to have some caballito teaching lessons in El Farallón. But this crowd started bombarding El Farallón so much that we moved out. Since they were the ones with the money, the place accommodated everything to them. It's even open seven days a week. It's one of the few places that are open seven days a week, but they can afford it.

Banda La Costeña, "El brincaíto" (*José A. Sosa*): "Mira que sabroso es este ritmo, mamá / ésto que se llama brincaíto, caray / bailan las muchachas, tu lo vas a gozar / ándale Costeña, que no existe otra igual / anda, déjate llevar / mira, sé que te gustará / solo un poco sudarás / mira, lo tienes que probar. / Lo [que] importa es como lo goces / el chiste es nunca parar de brincar / no castigues a tus pies, solo déjate llevar" [Look how savory this rhythm is, darling / the one that's called *brincaíto, caray* / the girls are dancing it, you're going to enjoy it / go on Costeña, there is none better / come on, let yourself be carried away / look, I know you're going to like it / you'll only sweat a little / look, you have to try it. / The important thing is how you enjoy it / the trick is to never stop jumping / don't discipline your feet, just let yourself be carried away].

Lotty: They call it "caballito" because of the way they dance it. I don't really dance it, but I go to places where they dance it. It's more jumping. They have a lot of acrobatics, a lot of turning and flipping around. Caballito is influenced by American dance. They lift the girl, they spin her. If you see the movies from the '50s, that's the way they do it. With banda it's more like the old fashion. At one of the places I really go to they do the zapateado—El Farallón. They don't play quebradita music [techno-banda]. They have banda and they have conjuntos, small versions of banda. You could dance caballito to banda, but there are other ways—the old-fashioned way.

Christina: I would say that it was with quebradita when they really started with all [these movements]. Caballito is more jumping up and down—not so many stunts. *De brinquito* is the same as *el caballito*—because of the jumping. The acrobatics is something that's new. There is also a difference in dressing up: to *música de banda con norteño* they are dancing close to each other, but jumping, [they have] the hats, boots, belts, and everything. For *el caballito*, they're dressing more like hip-hop or reggae. The [girls] go with their short skirts, high heels.

> Banda Machos, "La bailera" *(Gilberto Díaz, Raúl Ortega, and Arturo García):* "Le gusta bailar la cumbia de brinquito con sabor / le encanta bailar los sones, quebradita es lo mejor" [She likes to dance the cumbia in brinquito (style) with flavor / she is delighted to dance the sones, quebradita is the best].
>
> Banda El Mexicano, "Nena, vamos a bailar" *(Casimiro Zamudio):* "Vamos a bailar de caballito, de quebradita, es lo mismo" [Let's dance caballito, quebradita, it's he same].

Irma: There is a big difference between quebradita and caballito. Quebradita started off when the clubs started. I don't think that they dance that anymore. That was a long time ago. That's pretty much out. I hardly do that, quebradita. Well, sometimes you can still see the *quebrar* or the zapateado. Caballito you can dance separate or *agarrados*, but mostly jumping. For girls it's easier, you just have to hold on to the guy. They do everything. They have to learn the steps; [for us] it's very easy. The new style that's now in at the Lido—they throw them up in the air and twist them everywhere—no, I don't really like that. That's for *el concurso* [dance contest]. It's fine, to win.

HS: *What does dance/dancing mean to you? What makes a good dancer?*

Elydia: It's a lot of fun and it's good exercise. It is also very relaxing, although on Monday you are very tired. There is a lot of pressure on male dancers to be good dancers. It's much easier for women.

Victoria: A good dancer is a guy who has confidence, confidence in the way he dances— say, a guy with a firm grip around your waist. If he tries a new step for the first time, if he is experimenting, he must have a picture in his mind and good control of you. He is also going with the rhythm of the music. He'll know where to switch when there is a change in the rhythm. I know when I'm dancing with a guy who feels the music, I can probably anticipate where he is going to make a change. I've heard the song before and most probably he's heard the song before, so he knows when there is a fast spot in the music and I can be more flexible too. So a good dancer is a guy who is confident of the steps and who is a little bit strong to control the girl. He has to have a firm grip on the girl so that he is able to move her. And he also has to feel the music, the changes. When dancing together, his [left] hand is very important. It can guide you on how to move your feet; it can guide you on how to move your hips. It is very tiring to move your waist when he keeps your [right] hand above the head because then he has to hold you very tight to make you move your waist. Sometimes, I would have brown marks on my back because [my partner] would hold me so strong to do what we call the *gusanito*, the worm, the way we move our hips. If they move their hand like that [circling on the side], the waist follows naturally, your body is going to go like that to accommodate to the hand movement. With the arm [moving] they get the necessary energy, they impel themselves with their arms. At the beginning they would dance quebradita with the left hand above the head all the time. If the guys get very tired in their arms, they just put their hands on your shoulder to rest, or they put both hands on your waist and they try to guide you like that. It's much more difficult for a girl to follow the step with both his hands on her waist than with the hand at the side. And it gets them tired too because you don't know where they are going to move, they have to use their strength. Sometimes, if they run out of energy, they prefer to dance separate.

Ritmo Rojo, "Las caderas" (Gerardo Franco): "Mueve la cadera par' allá, haz tres brinquitos par' acá / siente todo el ritmo que te toca la banda / es que no es difícil de bailar / solo es cuestión de practicar" [Move your hips over there, make three little jumps this way / feel the rhythm that the banda plays for you / it's not difficult to dance / it's just a matter of practicing].

Lotty: I have often thought about how men feel if they have to concentrate all the time on what comes next. How do they know what to do? They are leading, so they have to [watch out] not to bump into too many people. They do have to concentrate. You just have to listen to the music, follow it. It comes naturally. They have to watch out constantly. For men it is a lot of pressure. Sometimes we go out with guy friends. But we don't always dance with them. So they go to ask other girls. "Oh, that girl is pretty, I want to dance with her."—"Well, go ask her!"—"What if she says no? I can't dance all that well."—"Just go!"—"No, I can't." I heard that from guys I was dancing with: "I didn't want to come asking." I: "Why not?"—"Because I was afraid you'd say no because I don't dance so well." I do see that they're real pressured. The guys have to go up to the girls and ask them to dance. For women it's less pressure.

Irma: Guys are under a lot of pressure to dance well. I don't think it should be that way, but I think they are. They are challenging each other, to see who knows the better steps. They compete but they don't let each other know. Usually the guys who apologize for not dancing well are the ones that know how to dance. They know how to dance and they tell me: "Oh, I'm sorry I can't dance as well as you probably want me to dance, but these are the steps I know." But they are dancing very well. Sometimes, even if they are good dancers, I just don't get their steps and I tell them. If I step on them, I go: "I'm sorry, I don't get your step." And they go: "Oh, it's OK. We just learn together—to learn each other's steps." It's much less pressure for women.

Banda El Mexicano, "Nena, vamos a bailar" (Casimiro Zamudio): "Me gusta bailar pegao / me gusta bailar sudao / con mi sombrero de lao / al bailar de caballito" [I like to dance tight together / I like to dance sweating / with my hat sloppy at the side / to dance the caballito].

Elena: Dancing is a way of living in the imaginary world of the music. A good dancer feels the music and he must be able to transmit this feeling to you. The music has to be in his body. You can relax, lose yourself, close your eyes—just feel his body moving. If he isn't a good dancer, it's no pleasure because you have to concentrate too much. You can't relax because you have to figure out what he'll do next. You get all cramped and you're glad when the band changes the rhythm so you may dance separate, or say "Thank you" and go have a seat. With a good dancer, you just hope the music doesn't stop and he doesn't get tired of you. . . . A good dancer also knows the rules: he knows how tight he can hold you without making you feel uncomfortable; he changes positions at the right moment so that you don't get tired, and he never forces any movement upon you. Well, the "rules" are: if you don't know each other, you start dancing in pretty normal position, not too close. You hold his left hand, your left is on his shoulder blade. He puts his right hand on your lower back. If you feel good and find the rhythm, you get closer. He might put his cheek against yours. This position actually helps to stabilize the upper bodies and your head doesn't bang around. It makes it easier to follow his moves. Then he might turn around faster and you have to grab him firmer. If you feel comfortable, you stay tight together, if it's too close, you always keep your right hand on his shoulder or between your bodies, so you can make some space. If you want to encourage him, you put both your arms around him. It's up to you. If the body language doesn't work, you have to tell him [verbally]. But usually every guy understands your gestures. I think most of them just want to dance, to be close to somebody else, to be hugged—to feel good.

Banda América, "A mover las pompis" (T. Romeo, M. O. Iacopetti, and A. Pastor): "Quisiera que salga afuera lo que tu guardas adentro / bailando este ritmo nuevo, sentir lo que yo siento" [I wish you would let out what you're keeping inside / dancing this new rhythm, feeling what I feel].

HS: *What happens on the dance floor? Are there any situations when you don't like to dance? How do you decline an offer to dance?*

Victoria: That's what happens: we always sit at the little corner. . . . No guys go there to take us out, unless it is two of us girls or one of us alone. Even though I wear comfortable clothes, I still like to look nice or even provocative. If a friend of mine and I sit on the other side in Potrero's, people don't know us, maybe a norteño guy will come up to me and he'll take me out to dance. I'm the kind of person that says yes, not unless the guy is very rude in asking me or has very bad alcohol breath. I dance to the rhythm of the guy. If the guy has seen me dance before, he'll tell me that maybe he doesn't know how to dance the way we do it. Sometimes, they feel intimidated. But I tell them, "I just move however you move me"; that's what I say. Guys usually apologize for the way they dance. They apologize for not knowing how to dance, yeah. You know, I never talk about it with my girlfriends, but guys always apologize about the way they dance. So that's when you can tell them: "No, you're doing pretty good!" Encourage them. But usually I accept everybody unless they're rude or very insistent. Most of the time I will [say yes]. If we're dancing together and the musicians are playing a really good cumbia, I will tell them [I want] to dance it separately.

Christina: If I don't want to dance I just say no. Maybe four or five times out of ten, I say no. It's hard for the guys. I hear from my friends: "Oh, I don't want to take her out, because if she isn't dying for me, she is not gonna dance with me. She lets me down because I don't know how to dance." . . . They are embarrassed to dance. If you're going out on a regular basis like us, you start knowing people, you make friends. So usually they know you or they can tell from the way you're acting if they can approach you. If you're not holding hands with a guy, others come up to you to ask you for a dance.

> Banda Vallarta Show, "Esa chica me vacila" (Alston Becket Cyrus): "Cómo me mira esa mujer, cómo me aprieta esa mujer / le pregunté yo por su nombre y me salió con un, ieh!" [How this woman looks at me, how this woman hugs me! / I asked her for her name, but she let out an eh!].

Elydia: Usually I dance with people regularly, so I don't have to refuse them. But it is OK to say no. Sometimes they would insist: "Just one song."—"Well, if I say no, it is no. You should understand a no from a girl." You learn that you can do it your way, that you don't always have to be sorry for the person and think, Oh my God, you have to say yes. Sometimes guys can't take a no. They get rude: "Isn't that what you came here for?" I don't see the point of getting mad, because they are not gonna get their way. It's a good way to show them that they are not the only ones who are in demand, that they can't do what they want, that they don't get what they want all the time. To decide whether to dance or not, the first impression is important. We observe. If we want to dance with a guy, we try to make eye contact. . . . Sometimes it works.

> Banda Vallarta Show, "Provócame" (John Van Katwijk and Marcel Schimsheimer): "Pero tus ojos se clavaron en mí / te miré y te hice sonreír. / Provócame, mujer, provócame / provócame, a ver, atrévete, provócame / acércate, provócame así de piel a piel" [But your eyes riveted on me / I looked at you and made you smile. / Provoke me, woman, provoke me / provoke me, let's see, dare to provoke me / come closer, provoke me skin to skin].

Lotty: I like to dance, but I usually say no when I'm tired, when I don't like the type of music that's being played, or if I see a guy coming up who thinks he is real macho, or if he is real rude: "Let's go dance!" No matter how good he looks or how well he dances, I say no and turn around. But some girls say no with an attitude, it makes the guy feel bad. If you want to meet someone, you have to be polite. But you also have to set boundaries. You learn how you want to be treated by men, with respect. The same outside the club. In a relationship you want somebody who has respect for you. If they are real nice inside the club, you expect them to be the same outside. . . . I say no fewer than half of the times I'm asked to dance. From the way they are looking at girls, you can tell how they are. If I don't want to dance with someone, I won't make eye contact with them so that they won't get the idea that you want to dance with them. They try to make eye contact. So, just glance over them. If you really want to dance with someone, you try to make eye contact. Well, you can also walk by a guy and say: "Why aren't you dancing? Well, why aren't *we* dancing." Just trying to be funny. The guy would be like: "OK, then let's go to dance?"—And I: "OK." That's one way to approach a guy. Or you are sitting there with a guy and ask him: "Why aren't you dancing?"—"Oh, I don't know. I'm embarrassed to go ask that girl to dance."—And I: "Oh, come on!"—"You wanna dance with me?"—"OK." Some guys just go to nightclubs to drink. Usually these guys stand around and look at the dancing. A lot of men just sit around having their bottles. If a woman goes to a nightclub, she usually wants to dance.

Banda América, "A mover las pompis" (T. Romeo, M. O. Iacopetti, and A. Pastor): "Para bailar este ritmo que a todos los pone locos / no importa si eres un genio, sino que bailes un poco" [To dance this rhythm that makes everybody crazy / it's not important if you are a genius, but that you dance a little].

Irma: If somebody turns out to be a bad dancer, I continue to dance with him. Sometimes you can tell if a guy knows how to dance, mostly by the way they are dressed. You prejudge. I observe them when they are dancing on the dance floor and I'm sitting down. I check them out to see how they dance. . . . If they don't know how to dance, I just say, "No, thank you." I usually say yes to guys that are dressed nicely, that present themselves in a pleasant way. It's not mostly if they are cute. It's the outfit. I usually say yes if I know them or have seen them around or if I've seen them dancing. I say no if they smell like they've been drinking or if I just don't like the way they look. Four out of ten times I say no. But I really feel bad about saying no. In my experience, 98 percent of the guys are very polite. "Would you like to dance?"—"No, thank you."—"OK." And they just leave. Some of them insist: "Come on, let's dance! Why did you come? Just to sit here?"—"I came to dance, but I just don't want to dance with you." They kind of expect for a girl to dance with anybody, or just because it's them. Some guys that know how to dance and that know that they look good, they expect that any girl would dance with them. Sometimes I say no to those guys, because they expect you to say yes.

Ritmo Rojo, "Las caderas" (Gerardo Franco): "Si estás feo no importa si bien bailas / si te escondes te encuentran las muchachas / vente al baile conmigo, con la raza / pues lo feo se le quita al bailador" [It doesn't matter that you are ugly if you dance well / if you hide, the girls will find you / come to the dance with me, with the raza / a dancer's ugliness is taken away].

Marina: Banda, like they dance it at the Lido's [the more acrobatic style], is kind of hard. You have to have a very good dancer to do that. When I was there this guy asked me to dance. I just followed him, I told him, I'm sorry if I can't dance. He says, "Well, you're doing pretty good." When I go to dance, I want to have a good dancer, I don't wanna have just a . . . . It's kind of mean, but I want to have a good time. I never tell a guy no. Whenever he comes and asks me to dance, I go dance. I don't care how he looks or what he is wearing because that would be kind of rude. Maybe some other guy might see it: "Oof, she doesn't want to dance with him, she thinks she is all that." So I always go dance, and I'll dance once or twice, depending on if I feel comfortable. If I don't like him, I just tell him, "That's it." I go back to my seat. At least I did the courtesy of dancing with him because he asked me to. If I ask these guys, "How come guys here don't ask and are just sitting there?"—"Well, girls look you up and down and you made the effort of asking them to dance, and then: no! You go back and your friends make fun of you." They take it pretty bad [if they are rejected], they won't ask again. I had about three, four guys telling me that. They always go in a crowd with other guys, and when they go back after they see them rejected . . . the whole night they make fun of them. I'm always going out in a crowd. I'm just out there to have some fun. They're doing the same thing.

Elena: I don't like if I can't check them out before, if I don't see their face because it is in the shadow of the hat, or when they approach me from behind. I want to see the guy. I almost always say yes. I know that they are embarrassed if you say no. Only if I'm tired or if I just ordered a drink I'll say no. And of course, if I'm there with another man. Usually they observe you long enough to figure out that you're accompanied.

HS: Does dance embody gender ideas and gender relations? Is dance about sexuality?

Banda América, "La quebradita" (Vélez-Ramírez and Germán Wilkins): "Si porque ando sensible, si porque traigo el alma alborotada / y me atreví a decirte que desde que te ví no entiendo nada / cuando bailamos juntos un baile que se llama la quebradita / me lo enseñaste tú y así fue que sentí tu cinturita" [If because I'm sensitive, if because my heart feels hasty / and I dared to tell you that since I saw you I don't understand anything anymore / when we dance together a dance that they call quebradita / you showed it to me and that's when I felt your waist].

Banda Zeta, "*Echando los perros*": "Me gusta bailar contigo / me gusta besar tu cuello y morderte la orejita / me gusta cuando te veo bailando la quebradita" [I like to dance with you / I like to kiss your neck / and to bite your little ear / I like when I see you / dancing the quebradita].

Victoria: It has a lot to do with that. For example, why does the guy lead and not the girl? It is always the guy who invites the girl to dance. The guy is in charge. The only one good thing is that the girl decides if she wants to stop. She can say no. But most of the time when a girl decides to stop too early, the guy is embarrassed. It's very embarrassing for a guy to go up to a girl and the girl says no. He won't go back to his table; he'll just continue to go around the circle. It reflects the culture. . . . The *machista* guy is embarrassed to say, "I'm tired." How can he get tired before the girl? In our little crowd—since we went to a transition—you'll find that a guy gets tired before a girl. It doesn't matter. He would say something like, "You know, you're heavy today!" And he would dance separately with you.

Christina: My parents don't like [techno]banda, but they didn't reject it either. Just when la quebradita came out, some of the moves, like when they would throw the girls around—[my parents] were totally shocked: "What are they doing there?" Like, when [the male dancers] were moving the girls back and forth: "Oh my God! They are having intercourse!" Or something. That's a question a lot of people ask that are older: "The guys, don't they get excited dancing so close to the girls?" It's a question that comes up a lot. To me, if you are into dancing, why should you be somewhere else? But also young people . . . some American friends I have, I took them to a nightclub one time, and they said, "Oh my God! You're dancing with them for the first time and you're already hugging them." Totally shocked that guys just come up to you, they just hug and start dancing back and forth [quebradita movement]. See, it has nothing to do with sex, it's just dancing. You can tell from the way a guy hugs you, if it's too tight. . . . This new hip movement, I like it, there's nothing wrong with it. Older people who see it for the first time may be shocked. My grandmother would probably pray for me or something.

Banda América, "*La quebradita*" (*Vélez-Ramírez and Germán Wilkins*): "Con la quebradita, tus pasos, tus manos, mi pierna en el medio / así fue que empecé a enamorarme de toda tu forma de ser / fue la quebradita la que hizo acercarme y sentir tus latidos. / El ritmo te envuelve, los cuerpos se quiebran muy suave / esta noche con la quebradita yo te enamoré" [With the quebradita, your steps, your hands, my leg in between / that's how I began to fall in love with your way of being / it was the quebradita that made me come closer and feel your heart beating. / The rhythm entangles you, the bodies bend very gently / tonight I will make you fall in love with the quebradita].

Lotty: I don't think that the dance gestures embody, let's say, machismo. It's just dancing. Obviously the man is bigger. I can't really imagine the woman picking up the man. So I think it kind of fits their roles. When it comes to dancing, I don't think it has anything to do with machismo. The breaking is just their form of dancing, how they like it. If a guy wants to dance quebradita with me, I say no. The dipping back, I think you can take it as a sexual gesture. I personally don't like it. That's what I don't like about the quebradita, some of the moves that they make. . . . But the men with the fancy shirts, they just show off. They have their shirt unbuttoned halfway down their chest and they have their big gold chains. If they try to come up to you like they know what they want and they know that they're going to get it, that's a sign of machismo. You can tell just by the way they walk. It looks a little bit too macho. The way they carry themselves, I would say they're machos.

Irma: Do I associate dance gestures and dress with macho behavior? No. I haven't even thought about that. Well, some guys buy some shirts that are called *crema de seda*, silky shirts, bright like yellow and black, all sorts of colors. They are really expensive, some run up to like $200, $300. I guess they wear them to show girls that they have money; the same with the gold chains. I don't even think it looks right. I prefer guys with regular jeans and a nice shirt. . . . I don't think that dance gestures are sexually suggestive . . . hm, maybe. But I don't think about that when I'm dancing and do those gestures. I just like it. It's not intimate, no. It's just the style of dancing there, in the Lido. All the guys dance like that. Actually, I have some friends I dance with. When I'm dancing with somebody that I don't know, they usually start up dancing pretty much normal, then they ask me, "Do you know how to dance like this?" I say, "Yeah, a little." — "Let's try a step." That's always like that, if I dance with somebody that I don't know, they usually ask me if I know how to do certain steps. So, we just start dancing. They teach me new steps. . . . Actually, I never got why the man has to lead. It just has always been like that. So, since that's the way you learned it, I guess, I never questioned that. But I'm not sure what it means. I never really thought about that, why the man always has to lead. I don't know how they lead! Because when a guy says: "OK, if you don't get my steps, you lead me." I say, "No, it's OK." Because I wouldn't know how to lead since I've never done it. Sometimes when I'm dancing, I don't even know. . . . There are certain steps that just go the way they go because they just do. So, you just feel it — you feel how to turn this way, to turn that way. Different guys have different steps. They have different patterns of going to certain songs: one guy would go one step back and forth; another guy would go two steps to the back and one to the front, or two and two. When you mess up, they usually tell you: "I'm doing two to the front, one to the back." They usually tell you what they are doing. So I concentrate for the first couple of steps. After that you don't even think about it — it just happens. They are the ones who happen to do the work: they lead you. You just follow them, and that's it. It's easy.

Marina: The roles are defined. As a girl you never go ask a guy to dance. Though we wish we could do that! . . . Certain moves are sexually suggestive. My mother would interpret it like that. Older people would say: "Oh, look what she is letting him do!" But to me, it's not a sexual contact. I don't know how the guy may take it, but to me, it's nothing. And I'm sure all these people are just dancing. Sex doesn't even come to their mind at that time. . . . Have you seen how the norteña is danced in El Parral, El Farallón? They all practically squeeze your ribcage like you have no idea. And some of the guys get offended if you tell them to stay back. They feel like you're thinking that they are coming on to you. But that's just the way they dance. When they first started to dance like this, I wanted to dance the old way. They would say: "No, we have to dance like this." They would leave me on the dance floor because I wanted to dance the old way. To them, it's nothing. But if you never experienced it you're like, how I am gonna be all tight with this guy. I don't even know him. Why should he touch me like this? But now everybody has got used to it. It's like your brother touching. You're dancing—that's all. I can dance with anybody, I won't get offended if he holds me like this. That's the way they dance. Outside the dance floor, you can't be so close. I've always thought: Why can you hold someone and it's OK to hug someone while you're dancing, but outside the dance floor you can't hold someone like that? How come you can hold a stranger on the dance floor but not outside? Where I come from, if you dance consecutive dances with someone, that means a lot. It's not like here where you're just dancing. It's the kind of society you're in. Here people don't get scandalized over little things. Most Hispanic people come from small towns, rarely from the city. If they are from the city, they're more open minded. Here you have more freedom. It all depends on how you're raised and what values you have. For some it's decent, for others not. In my family, we had to go with my mom's values. Even though we were in the United States. Even now, when I go to the nightclubs she gets upset. She says, "That's not right. You're a mother of two. You shouldn't be in these places." And I get a whole story. But I tell her, "We are in America. I'm old enough now to know what I'm doing."

Elena: Of course, dance is about sexuality. That doesn't mean that you're going there to be picked up, no. The dance expresses feelings. You can't really separate form and feeling—at the moment of intuition, at least, you can't separate them. To dance also means to explore your body and to explore your partner's body [in couple dances]. It's beautiful to feel another warm body that moves to the same rhythm. On the dance floor you feel secure. The touching has no consequences. It is just a very agreeable feeling to be hugged. Then you drive home—you still have the music in your ears, your body remembers the warmth, the touching, the music. . . . You wake up the next morning and the memory is still there. The whole week you can feed on that feeling, that happiness, until you return to the dance floor the next weekend. To dance is like taking drugs, just better—it heightens your senses and makes you happy. You wish the music would go on forever.

Banda Pelillos, "A mover el guayín" (José de Jesús Meza): "Baila este ritmo si quieres estar feliz . . . / moviéndolo, bailándolo suelto o agarradito / bailando quebradita, cachondo de brinquito / moviendo todo el cuerpo o solamente las caderas / que debes de gozar tú bailarlo como quieras / pero goza este ritmo desde el principio hasta el fin" [Dance this rhythm if you want to be happy . . . / move it, dance it loose or together / dancing quebradita, sexy brinquito / moving your whole body or just your hips / you have to enjoy it no matter how you dance it / but enjoy this rhythm from the beginning to the end].

HS: *How important are song lyrics to you?*
Lotty: I sing along. When it is a catchy song, I'm very quick to [learn] the lyrics. Some of the lyrics I don't like—Mafia, drugs, shooting. OK, you just hear the song, you don't think about it, but it really does happen. I prefer the songs that don't have that stuff. A lot of the songs they play now, I don't like. I prefer more romantic songs. There are a lot of songs that have a fast beat and everything, but they do talk about romantic stuff. Those are nicer. They are not setting a [bad] example for younger kids.
Victoria: I memorize some of the lyrics, especially from El Recodo songs. Very few songs are poetic; most are short stories or the lyrics do not go anywhere. A lot of the cumbias don't really have a point. Have you heard "Cuando los hombres lloran"? That's a very, very nice song. The short stories [corridos] talk about reality. I know for a fact that a lot of these things are based partially on real stories, but they are very fictionalized to make them more interesting. They change a lot of things, they multiply the numbers; if it was one, they say it was ten. But I know that a lot of those things do happen, like they talk a lot about transporting illegal things, drugs, et cetera.
Christina: Sometimes I do listen to the lyrics. It depends on the song. I don't pay so much attention, more to the rhythm. Sometimes you hear totally awkward songs. . . . You're asking: What are they playing? Actually you do pay attention to the lyrics in some way. I think the stories do happen to somebody, or at least they knew of somebody it happened to. Sometimes you immediately connect to the song. Like the song "Triste recuerdos": it reminds me of something I went through. The song becomes prettier to you. That's why you make it your favorite song. Because it reminds you of something that happened to yourself, or to your friend, your mother, your father.
Irma: I'm pretty sure that lyrics are taken from real life. Because to some of the songs I can relate, but not to all of them. Some of them just make fun of people, they are

just funny. Some of the lyrics I don't like, because I don't agree with what they are saying. For example, "La niña fresa" [by Banda Zeta] or "También las mujeres pueden" [a corrido by Los Incomparables]. They talk about narcotic women from Colombia and Sinaloa. I don't approve of things like that. The reason I still might like the song is because of the rhythm. Or you just get used to it, listening to it on the radio, because they play it so much. . . . I don't think that guys sit down and try to listen to the lyrics. I think it's more girls. Sometimes I write down the lyrics. I record the song from the radio and I write out the song. Takes me a couple of minutes. Then I learn it—play it back and sing to it. When I really like a song, I write it down. I learn the lyrics.

Veronica: Banda El Chante is one of my favorites. They are from my parents' hometown. They're really good. They are a real banda. They just came out with their second CD, *Mi tierra*. I especially like their lyrics—what they say. I also like the romantic stuff. Sometimes it's all machista, but it's very traditional: they treat the lady right. The lady is first. It's nice to remember that.

HS: *Why are there so few female musicians in this music tradition?*

Victoria: It would never have occurred to me to be a musician. It has a lot to do with the culture. You're brought up hearing the men sing, sitting down clapping for them, waiting till they take you out to dance. So it really takes a very strong woman who has the talent and is willing to go for it. Our culture doesn't teach women that. The men are pushed to be public, to be strong, to achieve their goals. There are a lot of women out there—they might have the talent, they might like it, but they were not brought up with the sense "you want it—go for it." . . . I think musicians don't have a great job. It's miserable, unstable. The music they play is beautiful, but the poor guys can't dance and enjoy the music as the crowd can.

Elydia: There are only a few female singers. There should be more. Their songs are different. It's a different point of view.

Lotty: I would like to hear more women singing. Actually I have heard some female banda musicians at Potrero. They played there a couple of times.

Irma: I like listening to male vocalists. But it depends on the way they sing. Some female vocalists are a little too whimsical . . . not with a lot of feeling. And most of the male vocalists put a lot of feeling into their songs. They really mean it from their heart. The songs reflect mostly a male point of view. It's always their side of the story. And sometimes it gets me mad, because some things are not true. It makes it too general, and it's not. . . . There are no female musicians because banda is connected with physical strength: to blow a trumpet like that, you need a lot of strength. Also traveling is easier for men. Women are more complicated, they wouldn't like to put up with the inconveniences of that lifestyle.

Veronica: One of my favorite banda artists is Graciela Beltrán. I love her voice and what she says. A lot of songs are about *yo soy hembra*, you left me but I don't care, I'm moving on. I like that.

Elena: There are some female banda musicians. But only a few brave girls. I think it is very tough to stand there and to play. Specially in nightclubs where bandas usually play. Maybe it's just because we are not used to seeing any female musicians. With singers it's different. Female singers have a long tradition in Mexico. There are many famous mariachi singers. It must have to do with banda's past, with the whole tradition.

Many of the young Mexicanos and Mexican Americans I met during the time I was doing fieldwork in Los Angeles expressed the desire to know more about their traditions, particularly to better understand why things were as they were. Some of the dancers I interviewed asked me explicitly to keep them posted about my research. They too were eager to know more about the origin and history of banda music and to understand the power of this music to bewitch and entrance so many people—including themselves.

Notes

INTRODUCTION

1. Most settlers of Alta California originated from the areas of Sonora and Sinaloa. The newcomers were an ethnically diverse assembly consisting of Indians, mulattoes, Spaniards, blacks, and mestizos. Early Los Angeles resembled in its social and cultural patterns the towns from which its first inhabitants had come. In a seminal sense, they set a pattern, a precursor of things to come; see Nakayama Arce 1980, Ríos-Bustamante and Castillo 1986, and Romo 1983. Even today, in a seemingly anonymous and drab city like Los Angeles, it is the people who give life and color to their neighborhoods, some of which are unmistakably *sinaloense*.

2. "Ya llegó la banda" by Salvador Sandoval, *Banda América*, Sony Discos CDA-81246.

3. The article by Loza (1990) on contemporary ethnomusicology in Mexico turned out to be a useful guide for Mexico City, where I visited all the institutions that could possibly store any information in regard to banda music: CENIDIM (Centro Nacional de Investigación, Documentación e Información Musical), INAH (Instituto Nacional de Antropología e Historia), INI (Instituto Nacional Indigenista), Casa de la Música Mexicana, the libraries of the Colegio de México and UNAM (Universidad Nacional Autónoma de México), and MNCP (Museo Nacional de Culturas Populares), as well as museum stores and antique bookstores.

4. Although the MNCP is dedicated to research on popular urban music, I have not found in it any material regarding *banda sinaloense*.

5. Such enforcement activity tends to evoke unpleasant overtones of earlier, much resented operations, such as "Operation Wetback," which resulted in the expulsion of hundreds of thousands of Mexicans during the 1950s. Immigration raids—or "surveys," as the INS terms the operations—are commonly done in immigrant neighborhoods and at places where INS agents suspect large numbers of undocumented people: factories, hotels, street corners, and commercial parking lots where day laborers gather. During the increasingly incendiary immigration debate, some groups welcomed such roundups and called for massive deportations of undocumented immigrants.

6. See also *Cinco siglos de bandas en México* [Five Centuries of Bands in Mexico], published by the Archivo Etnográfico Audiovisual del Instituto Nacional Indigenista. Band music is presented on three LPs in chronological order (pre-Hispanic roots, colonial heritage, indigenous and mestizo music, military genres, and classical music), suggesting a development of brass-band music in Mexico along this course.

7. The multiple meanings of the term *banda* cause particular problems in studying the literature. It is often difficult, if not impossible, to figure out to what kind of ensemble the term refers. Often there is even a lack of coherent labeling within the work of one author. Flores Gastélum (1980), for example, did not clearly distinguish between military and civilian bands; he referred to both as *bandas populares*. This vagueness might be a result of the fact that some of the latter actually functioned as official military bands during the revolution. When designating military bands, Flores Gastélum employed either the term *banda de música y guerra* [music and war band] or the very vague expression *banda de música*. He only made a sharp division between the two civic ensembles, the *orquestas* [orchestras] or *música de cuerda* [string music] and the *bandas nativas* [native bands] or *música de viento* [wind music].

8. In Sinaloa, for example, El Recodo, El Limón, Los Escamillas, El Quelite, Mazatlán, Culiacán, Guamúchil, Guasave, Mocorito, Los Mochis, Santa Rosa, Tierra Blanca, and so forth.

9. For example, Los Mochis de Porfirio Amarillas, El Recodo de Manuel Rivera, El Recodo de Cruz Lizárraga, Los Hermanos Urías de Guasave, Los Hermanos Rubio de Mocorito, Los Sirolas, and Los Chilolos. Technobandas, on the other hand, do not identify themselves with specific communities or music dynasties and hence use catchy names that relate to the modern world: Machos, Vaqueros [Cowboys], Móvil [Mobile], Vallarta Show, Toro [Bull], Míster Lobo [Mister Wolf], Maguey, Cascabel [Little Bell], Tequila Band, Borracha [Drunk], Súper Charro, Pachuco, Olé, Guadalajara Express, Arkángel [Archangel], Súperbandido [Super Bandit], Ráfaga [Flurry of Bullets], M-1, X-1, MR-7, R-15, M-45, 38 Súper Band, and Súper K-47.

10. Although aware of the general neglect of the northern states, Manuel (1988) went only so far as to include *norteño* music in his survey on Mexican popular musics. Others simply subsumed the northwestern states within the vast north; see Moreno Rivas ([1979] 1989) and Claes af Geijerstam (1976). In *The New Grove Dictionary of Music and Musicians*, Stanford (1980) summarized the music of the northwest in a few sentences.

11. For details about how journalistic writers managed to back up their stories with alleged historical data, see chapter 1. An additional problem journalists were confronted with was the use of the term *banda*, which, in general, may be employed for any group of musicians. In the early 1990s, the connection between the emerging technobandas and Sinaloa's musical tradition was apparently not yet obvious. After all, technobandas called themselves simply "banda." Thus, sources often do not distinguish between the modernized banda and the acoustic banda. For those that do, the term *banda* refers to the acoustic Sinaloan banda, while *technobanda* has become the standard designation of the modernized banda that integrates electric instruments, although other terms such as *banda contemporánea*, *banda moderna*, *banda sintetizada*, or *neobanda* [contemporary, modern, synthesized, or neo-band] may still be in circulation. The fan magazine *Furia musical* uses *tecnobanda* and *banda* interchangeably. When referring to the acoustic Sinaloan banda, however, writers would either use *una banda completa* or *una banda hecha y derecha* [a complete band].

Other common designations for *banda sinaloense* are *banda natural, banda de viento,* and *banda banda* [natural band, wind band, "banda band"].

12. The works of Gadamer (1994) and Ricoeur (1984, 1985, 1988) are particularly engaging.

13. See, for example, Ricoeur 1970 and 1971. On the consequences of Ricoeur's notion of text for ethnomusicological inquiry concerned with the cultural power of music, see Savage 1995.

14. McDonald 1996 presents a brief but useful review of how "tradition" has been understood within the fields of folklore, cultural anthropology, and ethnomusicology.

15. Savage (1994: 30) has pointed out that the reality of culture is itself nothing other than the unfolding of a cultural self-understanding in the life of a historical community and its enduring traditions. Cultural self-representation is based upon the self-understanding of a historical community in the face of its own cultural works. Moreover, cultural self-representation is affected by the work of cultural imagination, that is, the depicting of a cultural identity.

16. Bourdieu 1977 focuses on individuals or classes of individuals as producers of action, conduct, and history. Practice is absorbed, learned, or imitated by observation and not by rules or models, and it is given back not by discourse but by action. The key to any understanding of human action is, according to Bourdieu, the habitus: "[B]ecause the habitus is an endless capacity to engender products— thoughts, perceptions, expressions, actions—whose limits are set by the historically and socially situated conditions of its production, the conditioned and conditional freedom it secures is as remote from a creation of unpredictable novelty as it is from a simple mechanical reproduction of the initial conditioning" (1977: 95). Practice theory has been employed by Cowan (1990), Ness (1992), Turino (1993), Rice (1994), Averill (1997), and others.

17. For a detailed critical review of the major trends of reader-response criticism in the United States, see Freund 1987. For a discussion of German reception theory, see Eagleton 1983: 54–90 and Holub 1984 and 1992. For a concise survey of both contemporary American and Continental theory and criticism, see also Suleiman 1980: 3–45.

18. There are still very few studies on popular music that include the voices of the audience; see, for example, Walser 1993 and Aparicio 1998.

19. *Journal of the IFMC* 7 (1955: 23). Note that this model of music proposes three categories: folk, popular, and art.

20. Nettl 1975: 74 summarized recent developments in ethnomusicology: "In the past, ethnomusicologists regarded urban music as something exceptional, as an unusual kind of rural music which required adjustments in the standard model for the field. . . . Rather than maintaining the substance of the field as rural, we now accept urban venues of music and musical culture and we even accept popular music, because its tradition is essentially oral." Some ethnomusicologists dismiss folk music as a separate category of music; others have made attempts to save the category by redefining the term. The emphasis on oral transmission, however, is shared by most scholars as well as "folk musicians."

21. Ethnomusicologists with a training in sociology in particular took a strong interest in the sociocultural aspects of music and music making. The title of the first scholarly journal to be dedicated to popular music, *Popular Music and Society* (first published in 1972), reflects the concern with studying popular music as a social phenomenon.

22. See Bausinger [1961] 1986 and Paredes and Stekert 1971. There have been previous studies, however, much in the spirit of earlier musicology; see, for example, Campos 1930.

23. The Mexican musicologist Yolanda Moreno Rivas ([1979] 1989: 41) suggests making a distinction between *canto popular* and *canto folclórico*. According to her, popular songs that turn out to be more than a fad become part of the folklore repertory. Thus, every folkloric song (*canto folclórico*) was once a popular song (*canto popular*). See also Béhague 1985: 3–38 and Reuter 1980: 14–20.

CHAPTER 1

1. KLAX moved from no. 21 in summer 1992 (Arbitron rating 2.0) to no. 1 in the fall with a share of 5.3. For the fall survey 1992, see "Spanish KLAX-FM Surges to Top in L.A.," *Broadcasting and Cable* 123, no. 2 (1993). For the following surveys, see Donna Petrozzello, "Competitors Gain on Top-Rated KLAX in L.A.," *Broadcasting and Cable* 124, no. 18 (1994); "Spring Ratings Show Age-Related Choices," *Broadcasting and Cable* 124, no. 28 (1994); and "Top Stations Hold Their Own," *Broadcasting and Cable* 124, no. 30 (1994).

2. Phyllis Stark, "L.A. Spanish Outlet KLAX Tops Fall Arbitron List," *Billboard* 105, no. 3 (1993). While Arbitron ratings are published only four times a year, Arbitrend reports on tendencies monthly.

3. Kathy Tyrer, "Confusion Reigns in L.A. Radio Ratings," *Mediaweek* 3, no. 3 (1993); Bradley Johnson "Spanish Radio Is Tops in L.A.," *Advertising Age* 64, no. 2 (1993); Claudia Puig "Buenos Diiiiiias, Los Annnnngeles!" *Los Angeles Times Magazine*, 12 June 1994. With a share of 6.5, KLAX was also leading in the morning. Howard Stern's morning show got only a 6.3 share. Other Spanish-language stations lost a significant number of listeners (KLVE dipped a full point and KTNQ 0.6 point). KLAX's share translates to over one million people who tune in for at least five minutes in any quarter hour between 6 A.M. and midnight.

4. Phyllis Stark "Winter Arbs Tell Significant Radio Stories: KLAX Holds Tight, Stern Takes a Tumble," *Billboard* 105, no. 18 (1993).

5. Elena Oumano and Enrique Lopetegui, "The Hottest Sound in L.A. Is . . . Banda?!" *Los Angeles Times* (Calendar), 1 May 1993.

6. In the spring of 1995, KLAX dropped from 5.6 to a 4.5 share, down from first to third place (*Billboard* 107, no. 18 [1995]). Judith Michaelson, "More Radio Stations Say Adios to English," *Los Angeles Times* (Calendar), 17 March 1997.

7. Eric Boehlert, "Banda Machos Takes Old Sound to New Heights," *Billboard* 105, no. 16 (1993).

8. Margy Rochlin, "Loud and Proud," *New York Times*, 25 July 1993.

9. Cristine González, "Banda Rides Wave of Hispanic Pride," *Wall Street Journal*, 4 October 1993.

10. David E. Hayes-Bautista and Gregory Rodríguez, "Technobanda," *New Republic*, 11 April 1994.

11. "La Banda: Dance of a New L.A.," PBS (Public Broadcasting System) series *Life and Times*, produced by Isaac Mizrahi and Martin Burns, hosted by Rubén Martínez, broadcast on KCET, 14 April 1994.

12. In June 1995 *Billboard* published the following list of the most successful genres along with their most famous progenitors: 1989, *flamenco*, Gipsy Kings; 1990, *lambada*, Kaoma; 1991, *bachata*, Juan Luis Guerra; 1992, *bolero*, Luis Miguel, and *punta*, Banda Blanca; 1993, *banda*, Banda Machos; 1994, *vallenato*, Carlos Vives; 1995, *norteño*, which was just emerging.

13. *Banda Kora de Puerta de Mangos*, Fonorama FR 1052 (1982); the cassette contains traditional pieces such as "El sinaloense," "El tilichi," "El cuervito," "Niña perdida," "Toro mambo," and "Rosita de olivo"; *Banda Kora de Puerta de Mangos*, Fonorama CA-FR 10-101 (1983), features *música tropical* and contains the hit song "Carola," a cumbia. In Mexico, the term *música tropical* is used for all African-influenced Caribbean music.

14. *Vaquero's Musical*, Fonorama FR-10-200. This cassette contains the first technobanda hit, "El ranchero chido," covers of traditional pieces such as the corrido "La tragedia de Heraclio Bernal" and "El toro mambo" (a potpourri of different songs), and corridos from the *norteño* repertory.

15. "Los creadores de la tecnobanda," *Furia musical* (USA) 2, no. 21 (1994). For the lyrics of the quebradita song "A ritmo Vaquero's" by Vaquero's Musical, see chapter 2.

16. Quoted in Gonzálo Escudero, "Banda El Mexicano: ¡La envidia de todos!" *Furia musical* (USA) 2, no. 6 (1994). See also Escudero, "Ahora seremos un caballito pop: El Mexicano," *Furia musical* (USA) 4, no. 15 (1996).

17. Mi Banda El Mexicano, *Fuera de serie*, Musart-CMP 1318 (1995).

18. Quoted in "Banda Machos se hace oír," *La opinión*, 24 March 1993.

19. For a discussion of these terms, see Slobin 1993.

20. Scotty Dupree, "Know What the People Want," *Mediaweek* 3, no. 7 (1993).

21. In 1992 Fidel Fausto left KWKW-AM to join KLAX-FM as a programmer and deejay. In March 1995 he became program director of KBUE 105.5 FM (see below).

22. "Lamberto Quintero" by Paulino Vargas, *Antonio Aguilar con tambora*, 1994 (Disco de oro, vol. 2), Musart CDN-1157; "Tristes recuerdos" by Catarino Lara, *Antonio Aguilar con tambora*, 1995 (Disco de oro, vol. 1), Musart CDE-1245.

23. For more information on Mexican and Mexican-U.S. mass media, see Santamaría Gómez 1996: 195–209.

24. Eric Boehlert "Contemporary Mix Makes Market-Toppers," *Billboard* 105, no. 14 (1993).

25. Luis Manuel González "Radio a la medida," *La opinión*, 2 February 1993. See also Henry Muñoz Villalta "Música de banda acapara audiencia de la radio en el Sur de California," *La opinión*, 30 April 1993.

26. Carlos M. Haro did a series of interviews with KLAX personnel for his joint article with Loza (1994). He kindly allowed me to make use of the interviews for my own purposes.

27. Peter Viles "Spanish KLAX Cruising in Los Angeles," *Broadcasting and Cable* 123, no. 15 (1993).

28. Maria Zate "Don't Touch That Dial!" *Hispanic Business* 16, no. 8 (1994); Rick Mendoza, "Back from the Brink," *Hispanic Business* 16, no. 12 (1994).

29. Claudia Armann, "The Audience Is Listening," *Hispanic Business* 17, no. 12 (1995). KKHJ-AM and KWIZ-AM also belong to Liberman, a Hispanic-owned media company. KTNQ-AM and KLVE-FM belong to Heftel Broadcasting Corporation, which also owns strong combos in Miami, New York, and Dallas. KLVE-FM, with its romantic international music, gained ground again in 1995.

30. Lucrecia C. Molina, "Ondas radiales: Fidel Fausto, 'Las voces de pito de calabaza son la base de mi éxito,'" *Onda musical* 1, no. 2 (1996).

31. Quoted and translated from an introductory text that promotes the magazine, "¿Por qué nace Furia musical?" *Furia musical* 1, no. 0 (1993).

32. For more information on Televisa's business interests, see Trejo Delarbre 1985; on Televisa and on Hispanic television in the United States, see Santamaría Gómez 1996: 77–101.

33. The record unit of Televisa expected to sell more than $26 million worth of banda music in 1993.

34. Polo López Alvirde "Bandas + grupos = pachangón ¡en serio!" *Furia musical* 1, no. 2 (1993).

35. Pacini Hernández 1993: 57 suggests that besides economic logic and social ideology, Latinos' efforts to resisting the assimilationist melting pot and to maintaining an independent, separate identity contribute to the marginality of Spanish Caribbean musics in the United States.

36. See, for example, Barnet and Cavanagh 1996. Contrary to what the title of the book suggests, the authors argue in their essay that economic globalization accelerates the standardization of entertainment markets and, in the process, outrages local sensibilities.

37. Henry Muñoz Villalta, "Juventud latina en EU parece preferir la música ranchera," *La opinión (Suplemento especial publicitario)*, 30 April 1993.

38. Banda Machos, *Sangre de indio*, Musical MCM CD-5104 (1992).

39. According to Anderson 1983, an "imagined community" is a group of people that develops a sense of common membership, yet without direct interpersonal relationships. Since members of an "imagined community" are linked primarily by "a common identity," they may constitute a very large collectivity (for example, nations). Contemporary broadcast media play an important role in constituting "imagined communities." Music, in particular, offers a potential for furthering the creation of collective self-consciousness.

CHAPTER 2

1. Joan Easley, "Strike Up the *Banda*," *Los Angeles Times Supplement*, 29 October (1993); Michael Quintanilla, "¡Que cool!" *Los Angeles Times*, 16 June 1993.

2. Cristine González, "Banda Rides Wave of Hispanic Pride," *Wall Street Journal*, 4 October 1993.

3. Jerry Adler and Tim Padgett, "'MexAmerica': Selena Country," *Newsweek*, 23 October 1995.

4. Margy Rochlin, "Loud and Proud," *New York Times*, 25 July 1993.

5. Quoted by Luis Manuel González, "Banda Toro expresa una fuerza musical arrasadora," *La opinión*, 3 May 1993. The original song, performed by Paper Lace, was a hit in American popular music in the 1970s. Banda Toro's interpretation is included in *Toro mix*, Musivisa Tune-1240.

6. "La quebradita" by Rubén Ramírez and Gervacio Rodríguez, Banda Arkángel R-15, *La quebradita*, LMC JUCD-9085 (1992), and Banda Arkángel R-15, *Cumbiando con la mera, mera*, Fonovisa (LMC) LFCD-7006 (1996).

7. Excerpt from "A ritmo Vaquero's" by Toreko; Vaquero's Musical, *A ritmo Vaquero's*, Musart CDP 1142 (1994).

8. Quoted by Lupita Franco Peimbert, "Movimiento musical que ocupa las pantallas de la TV," *La Opinión*, *Teleguía*, 23 May 1993. Galindo, however, agreed that "it was Banda Vaquero's Musical with its theme of 'El ranchero chido' who opened the doors to the new banda rhythm."

9. "¿De dónde es la quebradita?" by Rubén Ramírez and Gervacio Rodríguez; Banda Arkángel R-15, *De dónde es la quebradita*, Fonovisa (LMC) LXCD-4019 (1993).

10. The *zapateado* is the characteristic dance of the Veracruz region (eastern Mexico). The word *zapateado* is derived from *zapato* [shoe]. It refers to a type of dance with virtuoso footwork and seems to have evolved from the Andalusian flamenco. Since the zapateado was (and still is) performed on a wooden platform with a good resonating body, the dancers produce with their fiery stamping the same rhythmic pattern that is played by the musicians—a sesquialtera rhythm that characterizes the *son jarocho*.

11. At nightclubs, for example, it was approved behavior for women to show off with gestures such as "the horsetail." The nightclub scene is an environment that attracts *chicas modernas*, self-assured women with rather modern ideas about gender roles, and Chicanas rather than working-class Mexican women. At working-class Mexican parties, on the other hand, women would not perform excessive dance gestures. In fact, I was once invited by a friend of mine to attend a private party held in the backyard of his house in East Los Angeles. The party was organized by "The Club of the Carpenters"; they had hired a technobanda to play for the around 150 guests. The multigenerational crowd and was composed of singles, couples, and families. I did not dance much because most of the time my friend was occupied with organizational matters. After midnight, a stranger invited me to dance—apparently he was unaware that I was in company or already too tipsy to care. In any case, I agreed to dance with him. When the band struck up a fast-paced piece, I started to perform some of the fancy footwork I would usually dance at the nightclub. My dance partner was amused and he danced along, but after a while he told me I was dancing "like a man."

12. Quoted and translated from "Opinas sobre 'las quebraditas'," *La opinión*, *Teleguía*, 15 August 1993.

13. Excerpt from "No bailes de caballito" by Casimiro Zamudio; Mi Banda El Mexicano, *Fuera de serie*, Musart CMP-1318 (1995).

14. See the compilation of interviews in the appendix, from which the excerpts used in this chapter are taken.

15. "La estrella de los bailes" by Ernesto Solano; *Banda Maguey*, Fonovisa FPCD-9266 (1995).

16. "El vaquero güero"; *Banda Súper Zapo*, Fonovisa (MCM) MPCD-5261 (1994).

17. Excerpt from "Báilame quebradito" by Lourdes Pérez; Banda Arkángel R-15, *Cumbiando con la mera, mera*, Fonovisa (LMC) LFCD-7006 (1996).

18. Excerpt from "El jaripeo" by Julio C. Preciado; Banda El Recodo, *Desde Paris, Francia*, Master Stereo CDBGE-512.

19. Rubén Martínez, "The Dance of Nuevo L.A.," *Los Angeles Times Magazine*, 30 January 1994.

20. "Presumidas S.A." by Ze Luis; Banda Zeta, *Presumidas S.A.*, MCM RH-C 6005.

21. "También las güeras bailan banda" [Light-Skinned Women Dance Banda Too] by Juan José Caro; Banda Arkángel R-15, *Cumbiando con la mera, mera*, Fonovisa (LMC) LFCD-7006 (1996).

22. "El brincaíto" by José A. Sosa; Banda La Costeña, *De puro arranque*, Musivisa TUL-1606.

23. Diane Seo, "Dancing away from Trouble," *Los Angeles Times*, 3 February 1994.

24. "Banda pa' ti" by Benito Miranda; Banda América, *Muévanse todos*, Sony Discos CD-81529 (1995).

25. Cowan 1990: 23 gives an excellent introduction to the inherent problems of verbal approaches to tackling the meaning of dance. Addressing the dilemma of interpreting nonverbal forms, she recognizes that writing about nonverbal forms of action is a problem partially created by the very logocentricity of Western discourse.

26. Admittedly a nondancer, Limón (1994: 141) reveals about his dance experience at El Cielo Azul Dance Hall, San Antonio, Texas: "[A]nd most of the time, I'll be holding you or Beatrice and wondering what I'm doing here so focused on bodies after spending so many years on my mind" (1994: 161). While fieldwork for him means "more observation, less participation," dance scholars believe that dancing "ultimately requires an observing participant rather than anthropology's orthodox participant observer," as has been pointed out by Daniel (1995: 21).

27. In an earlier paper about the quebradita phenomenon (Simonett 1996–97), I referred to the concept of play as developed by Gadamer (1994: 101–134). Because the dancing masses on a nightclub's dance floor evoke the image of a sea with hats floating on its waves, and because the quebradita dance style has a playful character, Gadamer's notion of play serves as a useful conceptual framework to recognize the primacy of dancing over the consciousness of the dancer and, hence, to understand dance not as a "thing" but as an activity, as *dancing*.

28. Excerpt from the cumbia "Conga"; Banda Súper Zapo, Fonovisa (MCM) MPCD-5261 (1994).

29. Excerpt from "Banda pa' ti" by Benito Miranda; Banda América, *Muévanse todos*, Sony Discos CD-81529 (1995).

30. For a cross-cultural analysis of machismo in Hispanic cultures, see Gilmore 1990: 30–55; on machismo and its influences on Mexican male-female relations, see Castillo 1994: 63–84. González 1996 contains sixteen essays written by Latino

men. In a very personal way, each of them expresses how he deals with the cultural legacy of machismo and the stereotypes that have emerged in Latino and non-Latino cultures. Rudolfo Anaya, in "'I'm the King': The Macho Image" (57–73), claims that the cult of machismo is as ambiguous and misunderstood as any aspect of Hispanic or Latino culture. Omar Castañeda, in "Guatemalan Macho Oratory" (35–50), points out that machismo is a complex and multifaceted phenomenon that is unjustly often reduced to "self-aggrandizing male bravado." And Martín Espada, in "The Puerto Rican Dummy and the Merciful Son" (75–89), observes that "before this term came into use to define sexism and violence, no particular ethnic or racial group was implicated by language itself. 'Macho,' as employed by Anglos, is a Spanish word that particularly seems to identify Latino male behavior as the very standard of sexism and violence." See also two early, rather problematic studies on the psychology of the Mexican man: Ramos 1962 and Paz 1959.

31. "El bigotito de Tomás"; Banda Móvil, *Cuando los hombres lloran*, Fonovisa (Disa) FPCD-9353 (1995). "El bigote" by Luis Santi; Banda R-15, *15 grandes éxitos*, Disa CD-484. "Bigote mojado" by Joan Sebastian; Vaquero's Musical, *A ritmo Vaquero's*, Musart CDP-1142 (1994).

32. "Bigote mojado" by Joan Sebastian.

CHAPTER 3

1. The characterization of Los Angeles as "capital of the Third World" was popularized by Rieff (1991).

2. Seth Mydans, "Opposition to Immigration Mounting," *Daily News*, 27 June 1993. For a contrasting view, see Richard Rayner, "What Immigration Crisis?" *New York Times Magazine*, 7 January 1996.

3. In reaction, opposition among Latinos grew. Young people in particular were shocked, upset, and hurt by these hostilities. Student activists emerged with an intensity not seen since the 1960s, analysts noted. The new wave of Latino activism was first activated by Proposition 187 and later fueled by the California Civil Rights Initiative, Proposition 209, to dismantle affirmative action programs. The increased activism among young Latinos manifested itself in marches, rallies, and greater participation in campus politics. In 1996 California's governor Pete Wilson urged the Republican candidate for the presidency of the United States, Bob Dole, to campaign for the so-called Gallegly amendment in California which demands that children of undocumented immigrants be excluded from public school. For a competent overview on Chicanos and Latinos in contemporary Los Angeles, see Acuña 1996.

4. Quoted in Claudia Puig, "Buenos Diiiiiias, Los Annnnngeles!" *Los Angeles Times Magazine*, 12 June 1994.

5. David E. Hayes-Bautista and Gregory Rodríguez, "Technobanda," *New Republic*, 11 April 1994.

6. David E. Hayes-Bautista and Gregory Rodríguez, "L.A.'s Culture Comes Full Circle," *Los Angeles Times*, 5 May 1994.

7. Transmigrants are migrants who maintain active involvements with the people and places they left behind, thus, they create new kinds of communities that span the international border. See Schiller, Basch, and Blanc-Szanton 1992.

8. See note 6.

9. Rubén Martínez, "The Dance of Nuevo L.A.," *Los Angeles Times Magazine*, 30 January 1994.

10. This tendency is also observable in Europe, where young second-generation immigrants have begun to articulate their ethnic particularities through new styles of popular music. For British-born Indians, see Banerji and Baumann 1990; for German-born Turkish youth, see Greve 1997.

11. Quoted in Luis Manuel González, "A gusto con la quebradita," *La opinión*, 18 August 1993.

12. See Takaki 1994, a collection of essays on ethnicity, identity, culture, class, race, gender, and public policy whose authors reflect the multiracial diversity of U.S. society. For an analysis of the complex relationship between ethnicity, acculturation and assimilation among Chicanos, see Keefe and Padilla 1987. The authors observe that rather than assimilating into the melting pot, most Chicanos and Chicanas participate in both Mexican and Anglo culture. The authors call this group "cultural blends," replacing the term "bicultural."

13. Berger and Luckmann 1967: 173–180 noted as early as the 1960s that identity is a phenomenon that emerges from the dialectic between individual and society. Because identity is formed by social processes, any analysis of identity has to consider the social reality (subjective realities) out of which these specific identities emerge.

14. "Ethnicity is not something that is simply passed on from generation to generation, taught and learned; it is something dynamic, often successfully repressed or avoided" (Fischer 1986: 195). Reflecting the dynamic character of the cultural, the social, the psychological, and their interplay, the term "ethnic identity" is flexible rather than fixed, as Roosens (1989) has pointed out. While he argues that "ethnicity can only be manifested by means of cultural forms that give the impression that they are inherent to a particular category or group of individuals" (19), Fischer emphasizes that individuals have to find a voice or style that does not violate their several components of identity.

15. This is yet another possibility for second-generation youths attempting to resolve identity issues not accounted for by Suárez-Orozco and Suárez-Orozco 1995. As possible means of identity formation among second-generation Latino youths, the authors list total assimilation into and wholesale identification with dominant American values; a new ethnic identity that incorporates selected aspects of both Latino and American culture; and loyalty discord with and rejection of both ethnic groups.

16. See, for example, Waters 1990. It has been argued by postmodernists that identities are fluid, shifting, and malleable, and that one is free to choose one's own identity. These claims, however, are overstated. Identities are not "a private consumer construct from available elements," as Preston has pointed out. Rather, identities are socially made because every individual "will confront a dense sphere of relationships with others, and in the background will stand the collectivity" (Preston 1997: 5). Notions of sameness and difference emerge only through identification with larger collectivities.

17. See, for example, Feld and Basso 1996, Gupta and Ferguson 1997, and Stokes 1994. The latter volume contains an interesting collection of ethnomusicological essays that address questions of how music is used by social actors in specific local situations to construct and mobilize ethnicities and identities.

18. For a short but thorough summary and critique of Chicano literature on culture and ethnicity, see Sánchez 1993: 3–14. His observations about historical and sociological studies are also valid for cultural and ethnomusicological studies, respectively.

19. See, for example, O. Martínez 1994 and García 1994: 72–81.

20. Like other Chicano scholars of the 1970s who focused their attention on the retention of Mexican culture throughout the American southwest, Peña (1985) has placed the development of Texas-Mexican conjunto in its sociohistorical context, employing a bipolar model of opposing cultures, assuming that music necessarily reflects socioeconomic conditions, and, hence, restricting musical practice among Texas-Mexicans to two opposed inclinations: cultural continuity (*conjunto* music as a working-class musical style) and gradual acculturation (*orquesta* as the musical style of an upwardly mobile Mexican American middle class). Peña views the retention of the conjunto style by working-class *tejanos* [Texas-Mexicans] as a symbol of resistance to American cultural hegemony, as a "counter-ideological" alternative to the *jaitón* [high-tone] pretensions of the increasingly Americanized *tejano* middle class, and as a conscious attempt to preserve some level of cultural autonomy within the host culture. See also Peña 1980.

21. In *Barrio Rhythm*, Steven Loza presents a vivid picture of the heterogeneity of Chicano music making in Los Angeles. Many Chicano musicians went through what the author calls "the process of reinterpretation"—a process characterized not only by innovation but also by maintenance of particular musical styles. The East Los Angeles band Los Lobos in particular reflects the musical diversity and the processes of change, maintenance, and adaptation among the Mexican and Chicano people of Los Angeles. After the musicians had found their distinct style, they were able to revert to traditional musical forms. Los Lobos' international recognition as a Mexican-style rock-and-roll band and the Grammy award they received in 1984 and again in 1990 demonstrate that the group has moved from an originally risky position as a promoter of traditional music in a nontraditional setting to its current role as a definer of a new style. "However," Loza concludes, "a distinct genre has not actually emanated from Los Angeles. Although Los Lobos [and other East Los Angeles rock and R & B groups] exhibit a group style, they do not represent a particular genre, instrumentation, or repertoire representative of Los Angeles" (1993: 271).

22. For the complete definition of the "postmodern condition" from which this quote is taken, see Grossberg 1984: 107.

23. Multiculturalism asserts that people with different roots can coexist and learn to tolerate each others' culture. It proposes that some of the most fascinating things in history and culture happen at the interface between cultures.

24. Frameworks of thinking in such broad terms have been proposed by Appadurai (1996) and Slobin (1993). Appadurai's more theoretical writings on global

economy and cultural flows and Slobin's concrete suggestion that subcultural musics or "micromusics" be studied as small units in big systems are most helpful in understanding phenomena such as (techno)banda.

25. Prejudices cut both ways. See Richard Estrada 1995: 94: "Along the border, a Mexican American who is unfamiliar with the culture and language of Mexico is likely to be saddled by his fellows with the pejorative term *pocho*. . . . [A] Mexican American who dares to speak or write English too well . . . is derided as *agringado*."

26. Michael Quintanilla, "The Great Divide," *Los Angeles Times*, 17 November 1995.

27. "Canción mixteca" by José López Alavez; performed by technobanda on *Banda Súper Zapo*, Fonovisa MPCD-5261 (1994).

28. "Los machos también lloran" by Mariano Franco Moreno; Banda Machos, *Los machos también lloran*, MCM CDER-8001 (1993).

29. Banda El Chante de Jalisco, *Un amor como el mío*, Fonorama FRCD-2070 (1994).

30. "Yo nací pa' cantar" by Ismael Gallegos; *Banda El Chante de Jalisco*, Fonorama FCCD-4010 (1996).

CHAPTER 4

1. Also quoted in González Dávila 1959: 525.

2. Voss's book is an excellent study of Sonora's and Sinaloa's economic and political struggle from the independence war up to the Porfiriato (1870s). See also Ortega and López Mañón 1987.

3. For detailed information on Mazatlán's gowth, see Beraud 1996. According to Weidner (1882), Sinaloa's population was estimated at around 200,000, distributed over thirteen towns (between one and two thousand inhabitants each), seventy-one *pueblos* or Indian reservations, and over one thousand *ranchos*, farms, and mining settlements. Mazatlán was the capital of Sinaloa at that time, with twelve thousand inhabitants, twice as many as Culiacán. Ten percent of the imported goods came from the United States, the rest from Europe: machinery, dry goods, porcelain, glass, hardware, iron, mercury, gunpowder, wine, liquor, beer, paper, books, furniture, candles, medicines, and spices. Mexico exported silver, gold, copper, wood (mahogany), cotton, and fruit. Whereas the maritime commerce was mostly carried on German, French, English, and North American vessels, the coastal trade was done by Mexican crafts. The single port of Mazatlán hosted about one hundred foreign and four hundred coast vessels per year. See also López Alanís 1991, in particular the essay of Alarcón (153–163), which focuses on foreign merchants and their economic and political impact on Mazatlán. Although the port of Mazatlán was opened to international trade in 1820 by the Spanish court, the bulk of foreign merchants arrived in the 1840s. In 1846, eleven merchant houses owned by foreigners were operating in Mazatlán (six German, two Spanish, two North American, and one French).

4. This information is based on letters written by Cincinnatus, a pseudonym used by Marvin Wheat (1857), and refers to the conditions of Mazatlán in 1856.

5. See Riensch 1960. Adolph Riensch was a young German clerk who wrote in

his memoirs about theatrical acting, medley singing, carnival amusements, and other improvised diversions among Mazatlán's urban youth in the 1840s. The German nobleman von Württemberg credited the foreigners for Mazatlán's theater: "The actors, of course, do not belong to a regular troupe and their performance is rather average, but the beautiful Spanish language and their spirited acting make up for the other deficiencies" (1986: 141).

6. Mayer was the secretary of the U.S. legation to Mexico in 1841 and 1842. His comments refer to Mexico City. See also Widenmann and Hauff 1837: 331–333.

7. Foreign travelers often compared the Mexican *léperos* to the Neapolitan *lazzaroni*: "Léperos are thieves and liars by profession. . . . In Mazatlán they were more precocious. Eating, sleeping, drinking, they could easily dispense with, for a handful of beans and the open air was an economic mode of life, and cost little or nothing: but a few *rials* [coins] were absolutely indispensable to game with on feast days; and as the Léperos, as a body, are not fond of work, they exercised their ingenuity in appropriating property of others" (Wise 1849: 191–192).

8. El *Pacífico*, 29 June 1890: For the popular classes, a fiesta without music and dance, and, according to the educated class, without violence, would have been incomplete. El *correo de la tarde*, 29 April 1895: To attract the population from neighboring villages, Rosario announced special entertainment during Holy Week of 1895: "There will be bulls, cocks, tight-ropes, dances, various kinds of games, big and small taverns [alcohol], and the famous mariaches [music]." Indeed, people arrived "from Santiago, Acaponeta, Escuinapa, and other nearby villages with their small amounts of supplies for the fiesta."

9. It may be of interest to note that the U.S. navy's bands included many bandsmen of foreign birth. Foreign-born musicians were extremely important in the development of music in the United States in general. The reputation of European musicians was established early in the nineteenth century and continued for decades. As late as 1870 the U.S. Census listed more foreign-born performing professionals than native American players.

10. The first event took place in the harbor of Mazatlán on 16 February 1846, the second on 21 March of the same year. Watson was serving on the sloop *Portsmouth* where two musicians were employed, a fifer and a drummer.

11. *Huellas de Sinaloa* (Culiacán: Diario de Sinaloa, n.d.), 410; no references are given.

12. There is evidence that military bands had been quartered in Mazatlán's garrison earlier. According to González Dávila 1959: 60 (with reference to Eustaquio Buelna [1924]), Sinaloa's military contingent (La Brigada de Sinaloa) left Mazatlán in 1864 with its two music bands to rush to the defense of Mexico City against the French.

13. Under the baton of José Encarnación Payén, the Mexican military band performed at the World's Fair in New Orleans in 1885, and in Minneapolis in 1895, where they successfully competed with military bands from the United States and Germany.

14. El *Pacífico*, 23 February 1890: The garrison band played at the bullfight under the direction of Don Lorenzo Santibáñez. El *correo de la tarde*, 18 August 1898: The

military band played at the opening celebration of the pavilion in Plaza Hidalgo. El *correo de la tarde*, 10 May 1901: They played at the opening celebration of the Jardín Hidalgo.

15. Completed in 1842, the Iglesia de San José remained for many years the only church in town. Unlike parish churches in colonial towns which were located on the side of the main square, Mazatlán's first church was built on the slope of Cerro de la Nevería ("Ice Box Hill," where ice used to be stored for more-affluent citizens), at least five blocks from Plaza Machado, the city's main square. The weak presence of the Catholic church in Sinaloa was a result of the late settlement of the northwest and the Jesuit mission society, which prevented the formation of an ecclesiastical establishment.

16. El *Pacífico*, 2 December 1888: Visiting zarzuela companies not only performed at the theater but also sang at church on holidays. The division between sacred and secular music was apparently not very strict.

17. The foundry in Mazatlán was owned by German merchants, among them the Melchers Brothers. For further information, see La *fundición de Sinaloa: Talleres de construcciones mecánicas* (Mazatlán: Catálogo Ilustrado, 1904) and *Melchers Sucs., 1846–1921* (Mazatlán: Casa Melchers, Sucs., 1921).

18. These notes were taken by Buelna during 1881–82, but not published until 1924. Buelna was a historian and the elected governor of Sinaloa in 1871.

19. Before Riensch resided in Mazatlán, he spent two and a half years in Tampico, a port city on Mexico's east coast. With respect to the life style of German immigrants, Riensch's narration of those years is also very interesting and revealing.

20. Riensch described the music ensemble vaguely as "die Musik" [the music] and "das Orchester" [the orchestra].

21. According to Riensch 1960, Italian operas, ballets, and dramatic works were performed in the two theaters, Teatro Principal and Teatro Alegría.

22. The work on the Teatro Rubio, located half a block from Plaza Machado, was initiated by the entrepreneur Manuel Rubio. The theater was renamed in 1936 in honor of the Mexican diva Angela Peralta, who died of yellow fever in Mazatlán in 1883.

23. According to Gómez Flores (1889: 26), the term *kermesse* was introduced in the 1880s to designate particular social gatherings among upper-class Mazatlecos. Some, however, disliked the term for being too exotic (German!); instead they preferred the Spanish term *tertulia*.

24. For further information on Mexico's orchestras, see Campos 1930: 184–186, and 1928: 207–214.

25. El *correo de la tarde*, 17 July 1899: The suppliers were on a drinking spree with an orchestra. El *correo de la tarde*, 22 July 1901: The Orquesta de Eligio Mora played at dance events organized by the factory workers of El Vapor and El Dios de Amor (cigar and cigarette factories).

26. Programs of open-air concerts given by orchestras were published in El *correo de la tarde*.

27. El *correo de la tarde*, 17 May 1899: The night before, the orchestra of Navarro

was paid by the young admirer of the daughter of a prominent family to serenade her. *El correo de la tarde*, 16 November 1900: Paid by young merchants, two orchestras serenaded in the city's streets, keeping the young ladies awake. *El correo de la tarde*, 24 January 1902: The orchestras of Cirilo Rivas and of Abundio García serenaded in the city.

28. *El Pacífico*, 18 November 1888. *El correo de la tarde*, 25 and 26 April 1898. *El correo de la tarde*, 15 May 1901: The police arrested a hurdy-gurdy player for entertaining drunkards with the national anthem.

29. Nineteenth-century local newspapers are rich in information concerning urban lifestyles. Unfortunately, Sinaloa's archives hold only a few annual sets of *El occidental* (Mazatlán, 1874), *El Pacífico* (Mazatlán weekly newspaper, founded in 1861), *El correo de la tarde* (Mazatlán daily newspaper, founded in 1885), and *Mefistófeles* (Culiacán, founded in 1901). Even the National Library in Mexico City (UNAM) has only four (incomplete) annual sets of *El correo de la tarde* from around the turn of the century. Missing issues make it difficult, if not impossible, to document nineteenth-century urban life in Sinaloa systematically. Nevertheless, some attempts have been made; see Alarcón 1996 and Padilla Beltrán 1996.

30. Redfield (1930) was one of the first anthropologists interested in the contemporary changes in the growing industrial world that in the 1930s began to affect Mexico's rural population. He did a comparative study of four different communities (the village of the tribal Indians, the peasant village, the town, and the city) and developed a model to study their cultures. He proposed distinguishing between the "great tradition" and the "little tradition" in order to deal with social and cultural change.

31. *El correo de la tarde*, 18 December 1899: General Antonio Rosales's victorious battle in San Pedro (1864) was commemorated by Mazatlán's "important personalities" in adequate manner, that is, with cannon salvos and a literary matinee adorned by the notes of the garrison band, which played works of Beethoven and Giraud, the "Marcha Patriótica" by L. Rosas, and the national anthem. In the afternoon, they enjoyed an "audición vespertina" performed by the Orquesta of Eligio Mora in the Hidalgo square.

32. In the capital, "Christmas and certain other periods became the occasions of such disorders that the government had to issue restrictions" (Bancroft 1888: 622). In Mazatlán, Lieutenant Henry Bulls Watson (1990) observed on Christmas day 1845 "high doings on shore. Every species of gaming going on in the plaza, the streets from this time to the 6th of Jan. crowded by villains of every cast and harlots of every degree. Two open murders committed, the criminals go unpunished. The only amusement on shore is rolling nine pins."

33. *El correo de la tarde*, 18 December 1899, announced the program of a fiesta in honor of General Porfirio Díaz, which was celebrated on Christmas Day. Organized by the suppliers for *las clases populares* [the "popular" classes], one had to be prepared for a noisy and tumultuous day.

34. *El correo de la tarde*, 15 September 1892: The official program for Mexican Independence Day in 1892 also indicated the localities of the working-class dance

events organized by the Sociedad de Artesanos Unidos. The union was founded in 1870 in Mazatlán to improve the poor working and housing conditions afflicting the growing labor force.

35. *Murga* was a colloquial term for a band of street musicians. Maybe it is no coincidence that the foul-smelling liquid which runs from piled-up olives is called *murga* as well. In a figurative sense, *murga* means annoyance, nuisance, or molestation.

36. *El correo de la tarde*, 1 April 1901. See the above description of the fiesta by Lieutenant Wise (1849: 307–308).

37. *El correo de la tarde*, 12 April 1901: "We are enemies of this source of prostitution and scandals that under the pretext of celebrating one of the most legitimate glories of the fatherland is being requested with arrogance, challenging the integrity of the authorities. . . . [W]e continue our campaign against this smudgy mark of Mazatlán's culture."

38. Commemorative festivities were most often noticed. See, for example, *El correo de la tarde*, 9 May 1900: "The population of the village Siqueros celebrated the anniversary of the triumph in Zaragoza in a boisterous way." Early in the morning, the national flag was run up and saluted, and the musicians strolled through the main street playing *dianas* [a musical genre]. The afternoon program included bullfights, a concert played by a band in the main square, official speeches, the national anthem sung by local students, and dancing.

39. Carnival has its origins in the saturnalia and Bacchanalia of ancient Greece and Rome, during which, in Dionysian rituals involving the use of masks and disguises, sexual orgies, and much drinking, eating, singing, and dancing, the established social values and hierarchies that governed everyday life were temporarily inverted. But the festival has more direct and immediate ties to Christianity and the Christian calendar of the late Middle Ages. There are two explanations of the origins of the word "carnival": either from *carrum navalis*, an allegorical float in the form of a ship with dancers on it, which paraded through the streets during the Roman festivals; or from *carne vale* (farewell to meat), which describes the day before the Lenten fast of forty days. After the Counter-Reformation in the seventeenth century, these merry-makings were incorporated into the church calendar, and Carnival Sunday was established to occur seven weeks before Easter. Carnival is a period of relaxed inhibitions and a time to celebrate life's carnal pleasures before the abstinence of Lent.

40. On carnival festivals in the Caribbean, Haiti, and New Orleans, see Nunley 1988.

41. Vázquez Santa Ana and Dávila Garibi (1931) claim that no sources refer to carnival in Mexico City until 1844. According to the authors, carnival reached a peak in the 1850s and 1860s, but they do no explain what kind of carnival they refer to. It is true that very few travelers and settlers wrote about carnival practices in the capital, although many of them described feasts, festivals, and social entertainment in detail.

42. Olea alludes to "various references," which he unfortunately does not disclose.

43. The rowdy carnival of Cologne was reformed in 1823 by an active urban citizens' group comprising young entrepreneurs and intellectuals. Committees of

"educated citizens" began to organize well-behaved and refined carnival celebrations with parades featuring the "Carnival Hero." This type of festivity became a model for other local carnivals. Riensch came from the northwestern part of Germany and was familiar with the carnival customs of Cologne.

44. The circumstances under which carnival was celebrated were certainly special, so the following impression of Lieutenant Wise may be somewhat misleading: "The carnival was not carried out with much spirit, nor was Lent regarded with the same pious severity as in other Catholic countries. The Mazatlanese are not a pious people; there were, to be sure, a few processions, and fire-works, accompanied by a wooden piece of artillery, discharging salvos of sugar-plums, with nightly fandangos, but this was all" (1849: 188).

45. A collection of early documents on carnival in Mazatlán was recently published by the personnel of the Municipal Archive, Mazatlán, under the guidance of Enrique Vega Ayala (1996). See also the essay by Rodríguez (1997) and Manuel Gómez Rubio, "Desde mediados del siglo pasado festejaban alemanes aquí el carnaval," *Noroeste*, 1 March 1998. On carnival celebrations in Culiacán, see Verdugo Fálquez ([1949] 1981: 228–229) and Padilla Beltrán (1996: 290–291).

46. *El Pacífico*, 9 March 1890: "Masked balls. When the corruption of the customs has come to such a scandalous point, it is delicate to allow events such as the masked balls that are tolerated nowadays. The families already worry much about the upcoming popular dance events in which their servants will participate during the nights and will not show up for work the next day. Moreover, some adolescents who ought to distance themselves from such reunions will go there with the excuse of enjoying music and entertainment; the mischance that will happen to them is indescribable. The public morals request a corrective to this excess of evil passions which cannot happen as long as these masked balls continue."

47. According to *El correo de la tarde*, 30 January 1898, the parade of 1898 was "monstrous": it consisted of "a float of decorated carriages; masks and fantastic dresses; music of harps, chirimías [a double-reed instrument], and tamboras."

48. For a historiosociological account of the carnival queens and an analysis of carnival's role in the institutionalization of the beauty cult in Sinaloa, see Santamaría Gómez 1997.

49. *El correo de la tarde*, 15 February 1899; *El correo de la tarde*, 20 Februrary 1901: "The musicians exhibited the most eccentric and grotesque disguises."

50. *El correo de la tarde*, 27 January 1893: During the early morning hours, several music bands strolled through the city. *El correo de la tarde*, 17 September 1901: In the morning, the band roamed the streets playing the merriest pieces of its repertory. *Mefistófeles*, 3 March 1905: During the days of carnival, popular bands roamed the streets of Culiacán.

51. *El correo de la tarde*, 3 February 1900: Part of the opening celebration of the Mercado Romeo Rubio was the military band parade. During the early morning hours, the band went through the streets playing cheerful dianas.

52. *El correo de la tarde*, 29 January and 21 February 1900: "The banda del Quelite under the direction of the well-known Mr. Francisco Terríquez will give a concert . . . in the Plaza Machado."

53. *El correo de la tarde*, 28 February 1900. According to the carnival program, Sunday afternoon concerts were given by Terríquez's band in the Plaza Machado, by Enrique Mora's orchestra in the Plaza Hidalgo, and by Pedro Lizardi's trio in the Plazuela del Rastro.

54. For a good overview on the brass band movement in England, see Herbert 1991; for the United States, see Hazen and Hazen 1987; for German-speaking Europe, see Suppan 1976 and Biber 1995.

55. Although foreign merchants had sold musical instruments earlier in the century, several houses advertised their supply in Mazatlán's newspaper in the 1890s: the Mercería Alemana (Heymann Sucs.) advertised their "gran surtido" of pianos, organs, hurdy-gurdies, and other musical instruments. Nicolas Gómez publicized the sale of pianos, hurdy-gurdies, bandurrias, mandolins, and guitars. La Voz del Pueblo (Wöhler, Bartning y Cia.) and the Mercería Francesa (J. C. Charpentier) advertised musical instruments as well. In 1902, the Mercería Alemana publicized their stock of instruments in *El correo de la tarde* with a print of a clarinet and a valve trombone and the following text: "Nuestro Departamento de Música es el más extenso y mejor surtido en la Costa del Pacífico."

CHAPTER 5

1. It was commonly believed, even among scholars, that "folk expressions" needed some refinement in order to please the eye and the ear. The renowned Mexican musicologist Rúben M. Campos justified his selection and representation of folk songs in the preliminary note to his book (1946: xi): "To the man of letters, the literary efflorescence of a people made available by the folklorist is a discovery of precious stones awaiting to be polished. Relying on his taste, he shows the people what is beautiful of its own creation, selected and ennobled by the perception of the artist and his just appreciation."

2. For those who could afford it, the menu of the Hotel Central in Mazatlán (which opened in October 1888) contained, according to *El Pacífico*, 28 October 1888: "Déjeuner. Potage Velouté / Quenelles sauce Tomates / Cervelles au beurre noir / Volaille braisée aux champignons / Pommes Maître d'Hôtel / Entrecôtes sauce Moëlle / Haricots. Dessert. Gateau à la crème / Café. Souper. Consommé / Petits patés à la Reine / Rognons sautés / Ragout Napolitaine / Légume / Files rotis / Haricots. Dessert. Café / Thé Lait."

3. Among the most prominent composers were Juventino Rosas, Tomas León, Julio Ituarte, Ernesto Elorduy, Felipe Villanueva, and Ricardo Castro.

4. Manuel M. Ponce, the author of the famous "Estrellita ("Canciones mexicanas," 1912–13), was the initiator of the new musical ideology of the Revolution. Ponce was also the first to collect folk music systematically and to use popular and folk music elements in his compositions. Carlos Chávez composed the first nationalistic work, the *Cantos mexicanos* (1921). Nationalist ideas are also evident in the works of Silvestre Revueltas and El Grupo de los Cuatro—for instance, in Blas Galindo's *Sones de mariachis* (1940).

5. Toor observed that in contrast to dance occasions in the villages, where "neither girls nor the men dress up especially," city women dressed in their *china*

poblana [costume from Puebla] and men in *charro* costumes. Yet, "the traditional, century old costumes of the China and the Charro have undergone changes together with the dance in being adapted for the stage and to suit the taste of urban wearers, thus losing much of their old character and elegance" (1930: 26).

6. Focusing on the social and political dimensions of Mexican *folklórico* dances, Nájera Ramírez (1989) shows how Mexican folk dance was used as a cultural symbol during Mexico's postrevolutionary period and during the Chicano movement in the late 1960s in the United States, pointing out important differences between the specific social and political circumstances of each period as well as their ideological connections.

7. This conception, however, is not confined to earlier studies of mariachi—it was recently expressed by Mexico's most renowned mariachi scholars, Jesús Jáuregui and Ramón Mata Torres (30 April 1996, *Conversación en el Museo*, Regional Museum of Guadalajara). Whereas some simply note that contemporary mariachi, a relic of a rural genre, is daily becoming more of a tourist attraction, others are more passionate. For example, Fermín Herrera, a professor of Chicano studies in Los Angeles, criticized the (professional) mariachis in Plaza Garibaldi, Mexico City, for not interpreting the traditional *sones* as they should—that is, with soul. According to Herrera, only a few of the mariachis he heard were able to play the *sones abajeños*, the traditional dance accompaniment developed in the rural towns of Jalisco. "'I think we are better off here,' Herrera concluded. Throughout the Southwest United States, mariachis are making greater efforts to preserve the music, including the *son's* spirit evolved from nineteenth-century hybrids of Spanish, Indian and African music" (quoted in Victor Valle, "The Changing Sounds of Mariachi Music," *Los Angeles Times*, 1 March 1988). Only rarely is change accepted as inherent in a living music tradition; see, for example, Urrutia de Vázquez and Saldaña 1982: 448–467. Instead of arguing about mariachi's authenticity, the authors suggest the various kinds of mariachi be considered different phases of one and the same process.

8. The word was used in Mexico before the French Intervention of the 1860s. Hence it cannot be a distortion of the French word *mariage* as generally believed. For a correction, see the linguistic study of Rafael (1982). At least four other reasonable explanations for the origin of the word are provided by the Study Group of the Regional Museum, Guadalajara (see Urrutia de Vázquez and Saldaña 1982). "Mariachi" (or its variant, "mariache") was often used to designate any kind of popular musical ensemble and was not confined to the regions of Jalisco.

9. The *vihuela* [small five-stringed guitar] and the *guitarrón* [five-stringed bass guitar] seem to have appeared during the latter half of the century (Sonnichsen 1993: 4).

10. The U.S. companies Edison, Columbia, and Victor made the first recordings of this quartet in 1908. Four of their pieces are included in *Mariachi Coculense de Cirilo Marmolejo, 1926–1936*, Arhoolie Folklyric CD-7011 (1993). Liner notes by Jonathan Clark, "Cuarteto Coculense" (1993): 8–12.

11. According to Sonnichsen (1993: 3), the Mariachi Coculense de Cirilo Marmolejo was the first mariachi to appear in a stage show in a legitimate city theater, the first to appear in a sound film (*Santa*, 1931), and the first to make "electric"

recordings, thus initiating the era of the dominance of the mariachi style in radio and film, and on records. In 1933 it became the first mariachi to perform outside of Mexico (at the World's Fair in Chicago), and the first mariachi to record in the United States.

12. According to Urrutia de Vázquez and Saldaña 1982: 458–459, Silvestre Vargas, leader of the famous Mariachi de Tecalitlán, remembered that they were granted a loan in order to outfit the ensemble for the first time in the 1930s with a simple denim suit, wide-brimmed sombrero, tie, and boots.

13. According to Toor 1947: 286, the *mestizo ranchero* arose as a new social class in the seventeenth century. These rancheros had made such fortunes that they would adorn their horses' harnesses with silver and wear suits of rich materials with much embroidery, imitating the Spanish *matadors* and noblemen, who "lavished their wealth on horses, carriages, dress, showing off at bullfights, in riding games, promenades, and processions." Some of these ranchers would overload themselves with decorations to the point that "people of good taste" began to calling them *charros*, which means loud or flashy.

14. From the late 1930s on, three classes of charros could be distinguished: the *gentleman charro* of the cities and country; the *professional charro* of the movies; and the *vaquero charro* or herdsman. Although most of the professionals descended from the third class, they dressed more like the gentleman charros. In all three classes, the charro style of dress symbolized the glorification of masculinity and the enhancement of self-esteem and social prerogatives.

15. For example, the movie *Nosotros los pobres—Ustedes los ricos* (1947–48), which became the greatest box-office hit in the history of Mexican cinema.

16. XEW was started by the Mexican Music Company, a subsidiary of the Radio Corporation of America (RCA). Soon after going on the air, XEW became affiliated with the National Broadcasting Corporation (NBC).

17. The roots of the overseas band movements are buried deep in the musical traditions of western Europe. Precursors of modern wind bands began to appear in Germany and France in the seventeenth century. By 1750, small ensembles of wind instruments were to be found in many European towns and cities where they were employed for concerts, street parades, and ceremonial displays by the local military organizations. These ensembles, called *Harmonien*, utilized a variety of instrumentations involving some combination of oboes, clarinets, bassoons, and horns. The reorganization of the Prussian army by Frederick the Great in 1763 brought about uniformity to band instrumentation. Other European countries adopted similar patterns. The "Turkish elements," such as drums, cymbals, and triangle, were first incorporated into the Austrian military band in 1806.

18. According to *El correo de la tarde*, 24 January 1902, there was a rumor that the young musicians would be incorporated into the 11th Battalion. *El correo de la tarde*, 29 January 1902: The young musicians, directed by Angel Viderique, gave open-air concerts in the Plaza Machado, Mazatlán. Their repertory included pieces by Viderique. The band accompanied the governor on his journey and stayed for the Carnival season.

19. Like Viderique, many other bandmasters were active as teachers, especially

after the Revolution: Sebastian Sánchez in Concordia, Pedro Alvarez in Elota and Culiacán, Refugio "Cuco" Codina and Manuel Páez in the municipality of Mazatlán, Juan Gómez in Villa Unión, "El Nango" Sánchez in Ixpalino and San Javier, Ramón Millán in San Ignacio, Ildefonso Soto in Mocorito, and so forth. For more information on these individuals, see Flores Gastélum 1980. On bandas in Mocorito, see Velázquez 1997: 43–50 and Rubio Gutiérrez 1995: 104–110, 241–251.

20. Guadalupe "El Sirola" Ibarra Castro, personal communication, Culiacán, 1996. El Sirola (his father and brothers had the same nickname), was born into a musical dynasty in 1924: his grandfather, Alberto Ibarra, played the clarinet in the banda Los Alamitos (five Ibarras belonged to this banda, which had been established before the revolution); his father, Aristeo Castro, was head of the banda Los Sirolas, one of Culiacán's well-established bandas. Guadalupe joined Los Sirolas at the age of twelve. After his father's death in 1943, he took over the leadership. The banda eventually disbanded in 1955. For the next ten years Guadalupe was a member of the renowned Orquesta Embajadores del Ritmo in Culiacán. Later he joined (the new) Los Guamuchileños, Los Muñoz, and other bandas. In 1996, he was a member of Banda de Música Ejidal in Culiacán.

21. By 1927, the Union Pacific System alone boasted of seventeen active bands along its lines. Railroad bands in the United States were usually initiated by the workers, who also supplied their own instruments. Usually they were generously supported by the company, which bought uniforms, gave employment preference to bandsmen, and paid the men their hourly wage for performances presented during working hours (Hazen and Hazen 1987: 50).

22. El día, 19 March 1937: Union members offered to give public presentations in order to be exempt from paying taxes. This request was accepted by the municipality.

23. Contrary to a persistent notion that the municipality provided the instruments, banda musicians had to buy their instruments themselves. Very often such assumptions are kept alive in reference works: see Stanford 1980: 236, which claims that the instruments of the tambora sinaloense were frequently municipal property.

24. Manuel Flores believed on the basis of this observation that it was the mining towns and the surrounding rural areas rather than the coastal cities that gave birth to the regional bandas, and that this environment played a crucial role in the development of the popular repertory. The titles of the traditional sones are particularly strong evidence for this assumption.

25. The SEP was founded in 1921. Its primary goal was to educate the masses and to develop a national identity, as well as to collect and recover folk traditions.

26. El correo de la tarde, 15 October 1926: "Popular dances. Each Sunday dances are held in the shed, but we don't know for what purpose the money is being raised; the only thing we are aware of is that each time dances are held bloody crimes and abductions are reported." Crimes made the front-page headlines such as the following in El democráta, 5 September 1925: A poor musician was assassinated near Navolato; and in El correo de la tarde, 12 October 1926: The leader of Banda del Recodo was fatally injured in San Marcos. (See chapter 6.)

27. Quoted in Bob Schwartz, "Mariachis in Search of U.S. Respect," Los Angeles Times, 1 March 1988.

28. Quoted in Henry Muñoz Villalta, "La música del mariachi," *La opinión*, 30 April 1993.

29. From the song "No soy monedita de oro" [I'm Not a Gold Coin] by Cuco Sánchez, a well-known ranchera composer and singer.

30. *Banda Degollado*, Fonovisa MPC-5204 (1992). Banda Degollado's trademark is "La Mariachibanda"; see *Furia musical* 2, no. 6 (1994): 68–69.

31. *José Alfredo Jiménez con la Banda Sinaloense El Recodo de Cruz Lizárraga*, RCA, Bertelsmann 7303-2-RL. The song "El abandonado" has also been performed by bandas sinaloenses: for example, Banda Sinaloense El Recodo de Cruz Lizárraga, *15 éxitos (versiones originales)*, RCA, BMG 3195-2-RL.

32. Even well-meant comments are not always unreservedly enthusiastic. Herrera y Cairo, for instance, remarked that "*despite* the thunder of the drums, flutes, cornets and trombones, through that music man communicated with nature, transmitting love to life and bravery to such a degree that one felt like giving yells of joy" (1983: 89; emphasis mine).

33. There are only a few movies in which banda music is featured: in one scene of *Sobre las olas* [Over the Waves], Pedro Infante returns home, utterly drunk and accompanied by a banda (the music plays for less than three seconds); a banda plays in the background of the movie *Las mujeres de mi general* [My General's Women], most of the time covered by the dancers and drowned out by the protagonists' dialogue. Banda El Recodo's first appearance on the screen was for the movie *Contra viento y marea* [Against Wind and Tide], made in 1960.

34. The sources on this subject are contradictory: I was told by several individuals that Banda Los Guamuchileños was the first to visit Los Angeles in 1957. According to one of the many anecdotes told about bandas and their travel experiences, the American customs officers did not allow Banda Los Guamuchileños to cross the border because they found drugs hidden in the banda's instruments. Teodoro Ramírez, the tuba player for Banda Los Guamuchileños from 1946 to 1958, denied these allegations when I asked him about the banda's travels abroad. He told me that the banda had visited the United States already in 1948 to play in Los Angeles on the Fourth of July, American Independence Day. Banda El Recodo traveled to California in 1962. According to some musicians, they had crossed the border a year before with the help of some *coyotes* [a colloquial term for people who negotiate illegal border crossings].

35. For more details about the first recordings and their impact on the development of banda music, see chapter 6.

36. *José Alfredo Jiménez con la Banda Sinaloense El Recodo de Cruz Lizárraga*, RCA, BMG 7303-2-RL. The reference to Banda El Recodo is not part of the original text (1953), which reads: "es necesario que suene la guitarra."

CHAPTER 6

1. Performed by Adán Sánchez and accompanied by Banda Flor del Campo, headed by José Felipe Hernández; Adán Sánchez (El Compita), *Soy el hijo de Chalino*, RR Records CD-001.

2. This account is based upon two long conversations about his beginnings as a banda musician we had in Mazatlán in 1994 and 1996.

3. One piece, the *son* "Las tecualeñas," is included in *Que me siga la tambora* (Serie 30 éxitos), Orfeón JCD-049 (2 CDs). The recording is certainly not as bad as Don Chilolo remembers: it is a piece that could have been played by any regional village banda.

4. Most of this information is based on a conversation I had with Don Ramón before Christmas 1996 at his home in Mazatlán and in the presence of some of his children. In this relaxed atmosphere, he shared some intimate memories that put some earlier-published information into another light. I will make use of both sources of information. Where there are obvious contradictions of dates, I will rely upon my firsthand information. The following recollection is taken from an interview by Juan Manuel García, "Homenaje: Tres ases de la música sinaloense," *El sol del Pacífico* (supplement), 7 May 1995.

5. Loaiza was allegedly killed by the well-known *pistolero* Rodolfo Valdés ("El Gitano") in the early-morning hours of 21 February 1944. For details, see Astorga 1996: 63–68).

6. In the 1995 interview, he told Juan Manuel García: "One day Los Escamillas asked me to become their leader, and I accepted. Later, I left . . . and I decided to form my own banda. We went for our first recording with CBS without having a name. It was Señor Peña, the artistic director, who baptized us with the name of 'La Costeña.' That was in 1957." When I asked Don Ramón, he confirmed 1964 as the correct date.

7. The following interview excerpt is taken from Apolo Escobedo and María Luisa Díaz, "Vida y arte de J. Cruz Lizárraga: El rey de la tambora" (1980). María de Jesús Lizárraga, Don Cruz's widow, kindly allowed me to use the material in this brochure for my own purpose.

8. Like RCA, Columbia also began with recording popular music in the Mexican provinces. In 1952 they recorded the *son* "El callejero," played by the Conjunto Mazatlán de Cruz Lizárraga (Columbia, Mex 2280-CO 2548-C). The other three pieces in this early 78 rpm recording were performed by Banda Típica Mazatlán: "La india bonita" (waltz), "Dos con el alma" (danza), and "Arriba San Marcos" (march by Carlos Lizárraga).

9. The order of these events is chronologically incorrect. Banda El Recodo was already in Mazatlán in the 1950s.

10. Interview by Apolo Escobedo, 1980, Mazatlán. The order of the events as told by Don Cruz is not chronological. According to Germán Lizárraga, it was in the late 1940s when his father talked the musicians of the village band into wearing a uniform. Don Cruz referred in this interview first to "la banda del lugar," that is, to the Banda de El Recodo under the direction of Carlos Lizárraga. When Don Carlos and his son Roberto ("El Güero Colorado") left Banda de El Recodo, Don Cruz became its representative. At that time, there was another band in the village: Banda Del Recodo, led by Manuel Rivera. Cruz Lizárraga formed his own Banda El Recodo ad hoc for the RCA recording in 1951 in Mazatlán. For that purpose, he brought several

musicians from his village to Mazatlán. Don Cruz was the first to add his own name to a band's name in order to distinguish bands of the same provenance.

11. The music of the 1960s can be found on the CD *Mis inicios*, by Banda El Recodo de Don Cruz Lizárraga (Banda Gold Series, vol. 2), Master Stereo CDBG-513.

12. Don Germán told me his story of how he became a banda musician on the way from Mazatlán to El Recodo in February 1998. We drove there with a reporter to shoot some videos of the village and the house where his father was born. Apart from Germán, four of Don Cruz's many other children became professional musicians: José Angel, leader of Lizárraga Musical; Alberto, leader of Míster Lobo; and Alfonso ("Poncho") and Joel, both members of Banda El Recodo.

13. Some of these recordings were reissued on CD by Bertelsmann: for example, Banda Sinaloense El Recodo de Cruz Lizárraga, *15 éxitos (versiones originales)*, RCA, BMG 3195-2-RL; *José Alfredo Jiménez con la Banda Sinaloense El Recodo de Cruz Lizárraga*, RCA, BMG 7303-2-RL (1994); Banda Sinaloense El Recodo de Cruz Lizárraga, *La chuchis y otros éxitos*, RCA, BMG CDV-1824; and *La Banda Sinaloense El Recodo de Cruz Lizárraga*, (serie 20 éxitos), RCA, BMG 3294-2-RL.

14. *Banda Pioneros*, Musical Vinny BCL-011 (cassette).

15. See also the memoirs of Galarza (1971: 157). Like Felipe Hernández, Galarza was intrigued by this particular piece: "On certain evenings the regimental band quartered in Mazatlán [in 1910] gave concerts in the plaza. . . . It was at these concerts that I heard 'El Niño Perdido' and decided to become a clarinet player."

16. This account is based upon a long conversation about his beginnings as a banda musician we had in 1997 in Compton, California.

17. In addition to jazz-band music, *orquestas* played Cuban popular music genres, in particular *danzones*. The *danzón* (or Cuban *guaracha*) had been introduced to Mexico's east coast around the turn of the century and became very popular in the capital in the 1920s. *Danzones* were again popular in the 1950s.

18. Traditional *sones* were not designed to showcase the virtuosity of skillful musicians. Thus, soloist improvisation was not germane to plebeian musical practice which had a rather egalitarian quality. The improvisatory element was probably introduced by jazz-band musicians.

19. Enrique Sánchez Alonso ("El Negrumo") acknowledged Peña Bátiz as "generoso protector de artistas cantantes y de las tamboras" [generous protector of the singers and of the tambora music]; see Figueroa Díaz 1987: 121. José Angel Espinoza ("Ferrusquilla") confirmed Peña Bátiz's generous support as well (personal communication, 1998, Mazatlán and Culiacán). Enrique Peña Batíz had a great affection for banda music as well as for baseball. He founded the Liga la Costa del Pacífico in 1945. The *liga's* fans always brought a banda to the stadium to support their team. This was the time when Ramón López Alvarado played in his father's banda for the "great encounters between Mazatlán and Culiacán" (see Don Ramón's memoirs, quoted in this chapter, after note 4). Peña Bátiz always supported Sinaloa's regional music. In later years, he set about promoting banda music. In October 1997 he organized the celebration of the first Día de la Tambora in Culiacán, and in March 1998 he launched the coronation of the first Tambora

Queen, the Sinaloan singer Patty Navidad. Shortly after, he died in Culiacán at the age of seventy-six.

20. Teodoro Ramírez left shortly before Los Guamuchileños disbanded. His narration reflects another point of view of the event described by Peña Batíz. At first sight, the account of Peña Batíz might look more accurate, yet Ramírez's lasting impression is as valuable. Indeed, it shows what was really important to one of the members of that banda. At the time of this interview, Teodoro Ramírez was a member of Banda Santa Cecilia in Guasave.

21. This is confirmed by an announcement published in one of Culiacán's local newspapers. El diario de Culiacán, 25 May 1952: "XECQ 16.00: Música popular sinaloense: con la Banda Guamuchileña [sic] (Abarrotes Nazario Frías, Vitalizadora y Renovadora México)." Banda Los Guamuchileños was also featured for the celebration of the radio station's five years of broadcasting: "Al dar las gracias al Comercio, a la Banca, a la Industria y al Público en General por el Favor de su Atención Durante 5 Años X.E.C.Q en compañía de su Madrina, la gentil señorita Rafaelita Montis, les invitan a escuchar su programación extraordinaria de Aniversario, hoy domingo, en transmisiones que se efectuarán desde los altos de la Biblioteca. . . . 7.00 Salutación a Sinaloa: Bandas Guamuchileña y lectura de cartas enviadas por C. Presidentes Municipales (Estudio Escamilla)" (emphasis mine). Other musical entertainment for that celebration included Conjunto Musical Galindo, Mariachi Culiacán, Conjunto Orquestal, Trío Rubí, and Orquesta Miguel Angel Valladares. The program of radio station XECQ in 1952 and 1953 regularly included: Miguel Aceves Mejía with mariachi, Pedro Infante with mariachi, Lola Beltrán, Luis Pérez Meza, las mejores orquestas [the best orchestras], Los Tres Diamantes, Las Hermanas Padilla, Los Hermanos Reyes, Andy Russell, Beny Moré, ritmos tropicales, boleros, mambos, and rancheras.

22. This recording was made by Columbia in mid-1953. It contains "El sinaloense" (son by Severiano Briseño, although several persons stated that this piece was originally authored by Enrique Sánchez Alonso ["El Negrumo"]), "El guanco" (polka), "El corrido de Agustín Jaime," "Culiacán" (danzón by Enrique Sánchez Alonso "El Negrumo"), "Ingrato dolor" (waltz), "Viva Gaxiola" (march), "Valentín Quintero" (corrido), and "Viva mi desgracia" (waltz by Francisco Cardenas); reissued on Bandas Sinaloenses: "Música Tambora," Las primeras grabaciones de la música de tambora (1952–1965) [The First Recordings of Tambora Music from the Mexican State of Sinaloa], Arhoolie/Folklyric CD-7048 (2001).

23. The first companies to record Sinaloan banda music were RCA Victor, Columbia, Peerless, Colony, and Azteca (issued in the United States). These early 78 rpm recordings feature Banda Los Guamuchileños de Culiacán (RCA, late 1952; Columbia, mid-1953), Banda Típica Mazatlán (Columbia, late 1952), Banda Sinaloense de El Recodo (Victor, c. 1953), Los Tamazulas de Culiacán (Azteca, c. 1953), Banda de Mocorito (Colony, c. 1954), Banda de El Limón (Peerless, early 1954), and Eduardo del Campo with Banda Regional Sinaloense (Peerless, late 1954). For detailed information on these early recordings, see Simonett 2001b.

24. The first telephone lines in Sinaloa were installed in the 1940s—but only in the cities. This account is largely based on a conversation I had with Luis "El

Gigante" Ramírez Vizcarra in 1996, El Bajío. Luis Ramírez, born in 1915, was an energetic music teacher in El Bajío as well as in the rest of the municipality of Mazatlán (hence his nickname of "El Gigante").

25. When I asked Chilolo Ramírez and Germán Lizárraga about those years of traveling, their stories corresponded largely with what El Serrucho had told me. But since each individual remembers the past somewhat differently, contradictory statements will always arise.

26. About the life of Luis Pérez Meza, see H. Hernández 1992. His early recordings were reissued on the CDs *Luis Pérez Meza con la Banda Los Sirolas de Culiacán*, Musart CDS-1822, and *Luis Pérez Meza* (with Banda Los Guamuchileños), Musart TTV-1005.

27. Anne Geyer, "Un espectáculo fantástico," *Los Angeles Times (Calendar)*, 25 November 1984.

28. Banda El Recodo was apparently not the first banda to travel to the United States. Information on this subject differs since various bandas claim to have been the first to perform in the United States. When I asked other musicians in Los Angeles about how and when the first banda crossed the border, I was told that the impresario Arnulfo Delgado ("El Gordo") had contracted Porfirio Amarillas and his Banda Los Mochis in 1957. Later, in 1962, Delgado arranged to bring Banda El Recodo over. Banda La Costeña followed in 1964. I intended to talk with Porfirio Amarillas. But unfortunately, when I returned to Sinaloa in the winter of 1996, Teodoro Ramírez informed me that Amarillas had passed away two months ago. I told him that I had wanted to ask Amarillas about Banda Los Mochis's first trip to the United States, when Don Teodoro revealed that Banda Los Guamuchileños had already crossed the border in 1948 to play at a Fourth of July celebration in Los Angeles. With the disintegration of the banda, this story sank into oblivion, and it would have been forgotten, had Don Teodoro not told it to me.

29. This song is covered by Luis Pérez Meza; *Luis Pérez Meza, 15 éxitos con banda*, Musivisa TUL 1562. An instrumental version of it can be found on *La Banda Sinaloense El Recodo de Cruz Lizárraga*, (Serie 20 éxitos), RCA 3294-2-RL, BMG International, U.S. Latin.

30. "El sinaloense" by Severiano Briseño; covered by Charro Avitia on *Que me siga la tambora* (Serie 30 éxitos), Orfeón JCD-049 (2 CDs). Its instrumental version is on many of Banda El Recodo's recordings: for example, *La Banda Sinaloense El Recodo de Cruz Lizárraga* (Serie 20 éxitos), RCA 3294-2-RL (BMG International, U.S. Latin); and *La Banda Sinaloense El Recodo de Cruz Lizárraga, 15 éxitos (versiones originales)*, RCA 3195-2-RL (BMG International, U.S. Latin).

31. "Andamos borrachos todos" by Julián Garza Arredondo; performed by Banda Clave Azul, *Los reyes de la banda*, Fonovisa TMCD-3036; Banda Clave Azul, *Un indio quiere llorar*, Fonovisa MPCD-5151.

32. See chapter 4.

33. Santamaría Gómez 1997 argues that the lack of female patron saints in Sinaloa encouraged an overstated worshiping of the beauty queen. Thus, "in the land of the beauty pageants," the cult of the virgin has turned into what locals call "reinitis."

34. Felipe Cobián, "Mazatlán: A los narcos les gusta imponer reinas de carnaval," *Proceso* 1112 (1998): 35–36.

35. The following groups played on the stages built up on the Paseo Olas Altas: Los Hermanos Romero, La de El Quelite, Pancho Barraza con su Mariachi y Banda Santa María, Mr. Charro, Banda San Marcos, Nueva Estrella, Colmillo Norteño, Junior Camino, San José de Mesillas, Jaguar, Gavilla, La Nueva Ilusión, Mr. Lobo, Alcatraz, Los Texanos de Tepuxta, Tormenta, Yesenica y sus Gitanos, Banda Azteca, and José Ledezma ("El Coyote") y la Banda Santa Elena.

36. Ana Bertha Trujillo Corza, "Gran reventón con El Recodo en el Carnaval de Mazatlán," *Furia musical* (U.S.A.) 6, no. 6 (1998).

37. Musicians are used to receiving direct payment after playing. One reason is that the banda personnel fluctuates, and it would be difficult for the bandleader to keep track of who had shown up for work and who had not.

38. Although carnival revelry provides felicitous conditions for bad-tempered encounters, it is not the excessive crowd density or the use of intoxicants, especially alcohol, that lead to conflicts. Rather, fights begin when the line between mock provocation and real provocation vanishes. This line, of course, is subjective. If an elbow, for instance, is thrown too aggressivly and maliciously, it might be interpreted as a real provocation and lead to a violent face-to-face encounter right on the spot. For a discussion of cultural conceptions of violence and of the subtle difference between playing to and playing over the limit, see Touro Linger 1992.

CHAPTER 7

1. DIFOCUR (Dirección de Investigación y Fomento de Cultura Regional) has published a number of academic studies in regional culture, and I was interested in purchasing any book related to my research topic.

2. Astorga's work has been helpful for my study. He affirms many of my own observations and ethnographical data. For an understanding of the significance of contemporary commercial corridos as a force for shaping social and cultural identity, see Paredes 1958, 1993, and (1976) 1995. Though on ballads of the border-conflict period, Paredes's work is still most seminal. My main references for historical, socioeconomic, and political information related to the drug trade are Toro 1995 and Mejía Prieto 1988. Valuable insight into the life of a Mexican drug lord is provided by Poppa 1990.

3. Hobsbawm defined social bandits as peasant outlaws who are regarded as criminals by the state and as heroes, champions, avengers, fighter for justice, or leaders of liberation by their people. As a phenomenon of social protest, social banditry has an affinity for revolution. "As men who have already won their freedom [bandits] may normally be contemptuous of the inert and passive mass, but in epochs of revolution this passivity disappears. Large numbers of peasants *become bandits*" (1969: 85). See also Hobsbawm 1959: 13–29.

4. "El bandido generoso" by Lino Valladares, quoted by Astorga (1995: 95).

5. "El bandido generoso" by Francisco Quintero, performed by Chalino Sánchez; Chalino Sánchez con Los Guamuchileños de Bernabé Martínez, *El bandido generoso*, Musart CDP-748.

6. "La muerte de Malverde" by Seferino Valladares, quoted in Astorga 1995: 96.

7. See note 6.

8. "Mañanitas a Malverde" by José Luis Jiménez; quoted in María Rivera, "En auge, el culto a Malverde, santo de narcos y poderosos," *La jornada*, 9 May 1998.

9. The price of such a shirt equals forty days' income for a peasant (the minimum daily wage in Mexico in 1996 equaled three U.S. dollars). The price for these silk shirts in Los Angeles ranges from fifty to two hundred dollars, and the golden chains and pendants start at ten thousand dollars.

10. On narco religion and double moral standards, see Trueba Lara 1995.

11. Odín Walkinshaw, "Narco-limosnas en Sinaloa: Evidente financiación del narcotráfico a obras sociales," *El sol del Pacífico*, 19 April 1996. According to the sociologist Luis Astorga, the scope of narco charity has been overstated; the belief in narcos' generosity is yet another element of narco mythology (personal communication, 1998, Mexico City).

12. Banda practice has always been male dominated. In general, banda music has been composed by men and hence reflects the world created and imagined by men. With the incorporation of a vocalist, new songs with text had to be composed. Of course, these new compositions center around masculine-oriented themes too. They give voice to regional notions of who "the Sinaloan" is. Although women cannot identify directly with the Sinaloan as portrayed in popular songs, they may well share the same notions of the Sinaloan, for he resembles their fathers, uncles, brothers, husbands, and sons. In the process of entertaining, popular songs have been instrumental in both reflecting and forming cultural attitudes and self-image. Thus, the Sinaloan is an imaginary image, but a living one.

13. Banda Sinaloense de El Recodo de Cruz Lizárraga, *50 años de tambora*, Karussell CDNPM 5136; Banda El Recodo en homenaje a Don Cruz Lizárraga, *Entiérrenme con la banda*, Sierra Records CD LRS-045.

14. This song as well as the next are performed by Carmina; Carmina con Banda El Pueblito, *Arriba mi Sinaloa*, Fonorama CD-50.

15. Performed by Carmina; see note 14. It is worth noting that when female singers interpret these songs, they almost never adjust masculine endings to their own gender. An adjustment would of course interfere with the correct rhyme (e.g., *colorado / enamorada*). This problem could be solved with a few modifications, but major changes would be required to alter all the chauvinistic macho utterances that often fill whole stanzas (e.g., verse 4 of "Que retumbe la tambora"). These songs are clearly written by men (and for men) and perpetuate the worst of patriarchal ideology.

16. Banda El Recodo, *Desde Paris, Francia: El orgullo de México* (Banda Gold Series), Master Stereo CDBGE-512.

17. Saúl Viera "El Gavilancillo" con Banda La Costeña, Discos Linda DL-230.

18. Jesús Palma (with Banda Sinaloense Los Huejoteños de Badiraguato), *Del mero Sinaloa*, "Mi oficio es matar" BM Record International BMC-050 (cassette).

19. Chalino Sánchez, *Mis mejores canciones, 17 súper éxitos*, vol. 2, EMI Latin Emid-27992.

20. For an excellent overview on the century-long history of narcotics in Sinaloa,

see Astorga 1996. A short overview is offered in Verdugo Quintero 1993 and the other essays collected in that volume.

21. One kilo of marijuana is as much worth as one ton of corn. Campesinos who grow opium poppies on their own land can earn between two thousand and four thousand U.S. dollars, compared to an income of four hundred dollars raising legitimate crops. Those who work in the field of others growing narcotics earn twice the minimum wage (numbers provided by the U.S. State Department's Bureau of International Narcotics Matters, 1987); see Barry, Browne, and Sims 1994: 59.

22. *Huaraches* are sandals commonly worn by peasants. According to Barry, Browne, and Sims 1994: 62, Culiacán's drug-related murder rate in 1986 was five per day.

23. Corrido performed by the norteño group Los Comodines de Durango, *Han vuelto los pistoleros*, Yael YR-0120 (cassette).

24. "Salvador López Beltrán" by Chalino Sánchez, *A pura banda*, vol. 2, EMI-Latin Emid-28547; and "Wence Carrillo" by Ignacio "Nacho" Hernández, *Eulogio Hernández "El Potro de Sinaloa" con La Banda Sinaloense Los Guamuchileños*, Maya Records MR-004 (cassette).

25. Sociological models developed to explain criminal behavior affirm this link. The so-called strain theory, for example, argues that crime is a substitute path to success for those who have been denied the opportunity to succeed by legitimate means; see Merton 1968.

26. The composer of this song, Julio C. Preciado, was Banda El Recodo's lead singer from 1992 to 1998. Banda El Recodo, *Los mejores corridos y rancheras de la gira Europa '95* (Banda Gold Series, vol. 2), Master Stereo CDBGE-510.

27. See chapter 8 on Chalino Sánchez.

28. Anne-Marie O'Connor, "Traditional Ballads in A New Key," *Los Angeles Times*, 3 January 1997.

29. Early scholars were mainly interested in compiling the vast repertory and in publishing corrido anthologies; see Mendoza 1954 and Menéndez Pidal 1939. Classifications of the vast repertory of *corridos del interior* [corridos of greater Mexico] were made according to thematic topics and/or literary forms; see Castañeda 1943. Early corrido scholars were principally interested in the evolution of the genre. According to Mendoza 1939, the Spanish *romance* and the *jácara* are the literary as well as musical predecessors of the Mexican narrative corrido; the lyrical corrido has its antecedents in the Spanish *coplas* and *cantares*. This view, however, is not shared by all scholars; see Serrano Martínez 1973. On the corrido's importance as a social and historical literary document, see Simmons 1957. Paredes 1958 and (1976) 1995 focus on *corridos norteños* [border corridos] and the border conflicts they describe. Herrera-Sobek (1979; 1990; 1993) took corridos as a source to write about immigrants' own migration experiences and about the representation of women in this male-dominated genre, respectively.

30. Some recent articles on the corrido tradition adhere to this somewhat romantic view of the corrido as a genre that is "rebellious and political in character" and that mirrors the social concerns of "the people"; see, for example, Lewis 1992 and Ruiz 1993.

31. Although one of the sources of ballads used in this book is the recording industry, the author does not address any questions that mass-media music poses for its analysis.

CHAPTER 8

1. Fidel Fausto, program director of KBUE-FM, personal communication, 1996, Los Angeles. "Lamberto Quintero," composed by Paulino Vargas, *Antonio Aguilar con tambora* (Disco de oro, vol. 2), Musart 1157. As is often the case, the "tambora" is not further identified on the CD cover, which here, however, is rather surprising: Aguilar recorded with one of the most outstanding Sinaloan bandas, Banda La Costeña from Mazatlán. Following in his father's footsteps, Pepe Aguilar recorded a corrido titled "El hijo de Lamberto Quintero" [Lamberto Quintero's Son]. It tells of a young man's torments, his hatred, and his dark thoughts of revenge, and cultivates the image of Lamberto as a noble man, beloved and remembered by the poor: *Pepe Aguilar con tambora* (with Banda Orquesta "Ahome"), Musart CMP 211 (cassette).

2. As of 1998, all six of the recent CDs of the norteño group Los Tucanes de Tijuana (signed by EMI Latin) had gone platinum. Their album *Catorce tucanazos bien pesados* [Fourteen Smash Hits] sold an estimated 1.2 million copies in Mexico and the United States. The Tucanes were the only artists other than Selena, the "Tex-Mex Queen" assassinated in 1995, to have six albums on the *Billboard* charts at once. Los Tigres del Norte's double album *Jefe de jefes* [Boss of Bosses] was nominated for a Grammy award in 1997.

3. The ban of narcocorridos from Sinaloa's radio program in 1987 and the appeal "Di no a la música violenta" [Say no to violent music] did not stop the commercialization of this type of music. The popularity of narco-music in the United States has provoked passionate discussions comparable to the gangsta rap debate. While critics are concerned about the negative influence of a music that excuses and glorifies drug trafficking and violence and, hence, want to ban narco-music from the airwaves in the United States, defenders view this music as a mirror of the contemporary Mexican political drama and, thus, a sensible artistic expression that reflects real life; see Anne-Marie O'Connor, "Traditional Ballads in a New Key," *Los Angeles Times*, 3 January 1997; and Elijah Wald, "The Ballad of a Mexican Musical Tradition," *Boston Globe*, 18 January 1998.

4. Banda El Recodo, the commercially most successful Sinaloan banda, sold an estimated 1.2 million copies of their compilation of corridos and rancheras; Banda El Recodo, *Los 20 mejores corridos y rancheras de la Gira Europa '95*, Master Stereo CD-BGE-510. According to *Billboard*, Mexico is Latin America's largest record market and the eighth-biggest record market in the world. Yet, a large proportion of Banda El Recodo's records is sold in the United States. Banda El Recodo has recently signed with Fonovisa, which is affiliated with Televisa Mexico, the world's largest Spanish-language media company. As of 1998, Fonovisa is the leading regional Mexican label in the United States.

5. Slobin (1993) has sketched a framework for thinking about and analyzing the complexity of "Western culture" by studying its micromusics. He proposes to distinguish between three culture terms—"superculture," "subculture," and

"interculture"—and to lay out the musical interplay between these cultures as well as between individual, community, small group, state, and industry. Hegemony authorizes the superculture to function as the overarching structure and dominating mainstream force, while subcultures are embedded units based on small-scale networks and affinity groups. Rather than proposing a single parameter that underlies all cultural expression, Slobin suggests analyzing music on different levels and acknowledging that paradigms shift, interact, and crosscut. Slobin's approach to micromusics is very intriguing not only for this chapter, which focuses on a specific subculture, but for any investigation into the cultural activities of people living in a multicultural environment.

6. During the last thirty years, Los Tigres del Norte have made numerous recordings and movies. In 1988 they were awarded a Grammy. But despite their most remarkable career, Los Tigres del Norte are virtually unknown to American society at large; see J. Martínez 1995. For a broader discussion of the immigration experience in the corrido, see Herrera-Sobek 1993.

7. "Jefe de jefes" (Teodoro Bello); Los Tigres del Norte, *Jefe de jefes*, Fonovisa FDCD-80711 (1997).

8. Quoted in Héctor Guardado, "Los Tigres del Norte," *Noroeste*, 9 November 1996.

9. Performed by Banda Los Pequeños, *Corridos con banda*, MCM CDER-8049; Banda El Recodo, *Los mejores corridos y rancheras de la gira Europa '95* (Banda Gold Series, vol. 2), Master Stereo CDBGE-510.

10. Banda El Cerrito, *Mira*, Fonorama CD-40.

11. Banda El Recodo, *Los mejores corridos y rancheras de la gira Europa '95* (Banda Gold Series, vol. 2), Master Stereo CDBGE-510.

12. Los Tucanes de Tijuana, *Tucanes de plata: 14 tucanazos censurados*, EMI Latin 56922. "Los tres animales," performed by banda on *Banda El Limón: Puro Sinaloa Compas*, Fonorama, Fonovisa FCCD-4021.

13. Banda Machos, *Los machos también lloran*, MCM CDER-8001.

14. "El destino cobra" by Manuel Eduardo Castro, *Banda El Chante de Jalisco*, Fonorama FCCD-4010 (1996); performed by Ezequiel Peña, former lead singer of Banda Vallarta Show, *Ezequiel Peña: Orgullo ranchero*, Fonovisa SDC-6046 (cassette).

15. On the character of the Sinaloans, see Nakayama Arce 1991.

16. The excerpts are taken from "Lucio Villarreal" by Chalino Sánchez on his album *Mis mejores canciones, 17 super éxitos*, vol. 2, EMI-Latin Emid-27992; and "Lalo Ríos" by El Güero Delgado, *La captura del Chapo Guzmán: Puros corridos con banda*, Kimo's CD-1003.

17. The following excerpts are from "Corrido de Jaimito" and "Agustín Nava," both by Chalino Sánchez, *Chalino Sánchez con Banda Sinaloense La Flor del Campo*, Musart MSC-741 (cassette); and from "Lalo Ríos" by El Güero Delgado, *La captura del Chapo Guzmán: Puros corridos con banda*, Kimo's CD-1003.

18. Since this direct relationship does not exist in commercial narcocorridos (rather than a particular client, the corrido author addresses an imagined mass audience), we observe a shift from the "I"-corridista and the "he"-narco to the fictive "I"-narco. This shift allows the author of commercial narcocorridos to speak directly to his audience.

19. Excerpts from "Joaquín Santana" and "Rigo Coria" by Chalino Sánchez, *Chalino Sánchez con Banda Sinaloense La Flor del Campo*, Musart MSC-741 (cassette).

20. The price for a master tape ranges from fifteen hundred to two thousand U.S. dollars. The composer sells a corrido for about seven hundred dollars, and a local banda charges seven hundred to one thousand dollars for the recording session. Norteño accompaniment is less expensive because the ensemble consists of only four to five men, compared to the twelve to sixteen members of a banda.

21. Excerpts from "Salvador López Beltrán" by Chalino Sánchez, *Chalino Sánchez con Banda Sinaloense La Flor del Campo*, Musart MSC-741 (cassette); and "Amador García" by the same author on his *Mis mejores canciones, 17 super éxitos*, vol. 2, EMI-Latin Emid-27992.

22. Excerpts from "Wence Carrillo" by Ignacio "Nacho" Hernández, *Eulogio Hernández "El Potro de Sinaloa" con La Banda Sinaloense Los Guamuchileños*, Maya Records MR-004 (cassette); and "Sinaloa y su gente" by Jésus Palma on his (with Banda Sinaloense Los Huejoteños de Badiraguato), *Del mero Sinaloa, "Mi oficio es matar,"* BM Record International BMC-050 (cassette).

23. "Amador García" by Chalino Sánchez; Chalino Sánchez, *Mis mejores canciones, 17 super éxitos*, vol. 2, EMI-Latin Emid-27992.

24. "Adiós, Hermanos Quintero" by Chalino Sánchez; *Chalino Sánchez con Los Guamuchileños de Bernabé Martínez: El bandido generoso*, Musart CDP-748.

25. "Corrido de Chalino Sánchez" by Jorge Romero Llamas, performed by Banda Super Galopes, *Corridos con banda*, MCM CDER-8049.

26. Luis Lim, "Chalino, el conocido cantante, su misma muerte, otro corrido," *Noroeste* (Mazatlán edition), 17 May 1992.

27. This as well as the following two corridos dedicated to Chalino can be found on *A pura banda*, vol. 2, EMI-Latin Emid-28547.

28. According to Valentín Velasco, director of Balboa Records (Musart), they have sold more than two million of Chalino's records during the four years since his death; quoted in *La llave musical* 2 (1996).

29. Quoted in Luis Lim, "Historia de un cantante sinaloense, parte II" *Noroeste* (Mazatlán edition), 24 May 1992.

30. "Chalino Sánchez" by José Felipe Hernández; *Banda Sinaloense Flor del Campo*, Ayana Musical AM-075 (1994).

31. "El gallo de los Sánchez" by Pedro Rivera; *Pedro Rivera, 17 éxitos con banda*, Cintas Acuario CAN-347 (1995).

32. Quoted in Luis Lim, "Historia de un cantante sinaloense," *Noroeste* (Mazatlán edition), 23 May 1992.

33. "Que me entierren cantando" by Oscar C. Hernández, performed by Chalino Sánchez, *Mis mejores canciones, 17 super éxitos*, vol. 2, EMI-Latin Emid-27992.

34. For example, "Entiérrenme con la banda" [Bury Me with the Banda] by Teodoro Bello; "Veinte mujeres" [Twenty Women], "Cruz de cemento" [Cross of Concrete] by Jesús Montoya; and "Cruz de madera" [Wooden Cross] by Chuy Luviano.

35. Chalino Sánchez also left behind a son Adán ("El Compita") (born in 1984), whose only idol is his late father (interview, 1996, Los Angeles). At the age of twelve,

he has already recorded four of his own compact disks—two with norteño, one with Banda Flor del Campo, and another with Banda Hermanos Rubio—and his biggest dream is to record one day with Banda El Recodo and Banda La Costeña. Adán, too, contributed to the body of corridos recorded in his father's memory: "Adiós padre querido" [Farewell My Beloved Father], "Un aplauso no sean gachos" [Applause, Don't Be Slack] and "Los pasos de mi padre" [My Father's Footsteps], both by Pedro Casanova, and the title song of his C D "Soy el hijo de Chalino" [I Am Chalino's Son], by Gabriel Benítez, Adán Sánchez (El Compita), (with Banda Sinaloense La Flor del Campo), *Soy el hijo de Chalino*, Rosalino Records R R CD-001 (1994).

36. Sam Quiñones, "Sing Now, Die Later: The Ballad of Chalino Sánchez," *LA Weekly*, 31 July–6 August 1998, 34.

CHAPTER 9

1. Quoted in José M. Vega, "La reina de las Bandas," *Tele guía de Chicago*, 6 August 1993.

2. Quoted in Juan Manuel García, "Homenaje: Tres ases de la música sinaloense," *El sol del Pacífico (Suplemento)*, 7 May 1995.

3. Quoted in Arturo Rivera Ruiz, "La mayoría ni bandas son," *Furia musical* 1, no. 5 (1993): 56.

4. Quoted in "Banda Machos se hace oír," *La opinión*, 24 March 1993.

5. Socorro Orozco, "Entérate," *El debate de Culiacán*, 18 September 1996.

6. Among the favorite bandas of *Furia musical* readers, Banda El Recodo was only number 7. The ranking list in July 1994 was the following: (1) Banda Machos, (2) Banda Vallarta Show, (3) El Mexicano, (4) Banda R-15, (5) Banda Cachorros, (6) Banda Móvil, (7) *Banda El Recodo*, (8) Banda Toro, (9) *Banda Pelillos*, (10) *Banda San Miguel*, (11) Vaquero's Musical, (12) *Banda Recoditos*, (13) Banda Brava, (14) Banda Súper Bandido, (15) Banda Maguey, and (16) Banda Pequeños Musical. (All bandas except the ones in italics are technobandas).

7. For more details on Julio Preciado and Banda El Recodo, see chapters 7 and 8.

8. Carlos Madrid, "La Costeña empieza a alternar con los grandes," *Furia musical* (USA) 4, no. 18 (1996): 61.

9. Banda La Costeña, *De puro arranque*, Musivisa T U L-1606 (1995).

10. *Banda La Costeña*, Musart C D P-1007 (1993).

11. Banda El Recodo, *Esta . . . ¡Sí es banda! Pegando con tubo* (Banda Gold Series), Master Stereo K B G E-514 (1993); Banda El Recodo, *De México y para el mundo* (Banda Gold Series), Master Stereo K B G E-519; Banda El Recodo de Cruz Lizárraga, *Desde el cielo y para siempre*, Musivisa TUT-1666 (1996).

12. Banda El Recodo even maintains a home page at http://www.bandaelrecodo.com.mx.

13. Banda El Recodo, *Tributo a Juan Gabriel*, Musivisa TUT-1919; Banda La Costeña, *Secreto de amor*, Fonovisa F P C D-9604.

14. "Música romántica" by Francisco Javier "Pancho" Barraza; performed by Banda La Tunera, *Las 30 bandas del siglo*, Fonovisa FTCD-80705; or Jorge Luis Cabrera (with Banda Tierra Blanca), *Música romántica*, Balboa Records BCDP-147 (1994).

15. See Gonzálo Escudero, "He impuesto un nuevo estilo de banda: Pancho

Barraza," *Furia musical* (U.S.A.) 4, no. 17 (1996), 12. Illustrative recordings are Pancho Barraza y su Banda Santa María, *Mis canciones de amor*, Balboa Records BPC-170 (1995); Banda Sinaloense Los Recoditos, *Canto para ti*, Musart CDP-1340 (1995); and Banda Sinaloense Los Recoditos, *Siempre te voy a recordar*, Musart CMP-1610 (1996).

16. *Banda Pelillos*, Fonorama FR-10-333 (1992); Banda El Chante de Jalisco, *Un amor como el mío*, Fonorama FRCD-2070 (1994); Banda Caña Verde, *Como poder olvidarte*, EMI-Latin Emid-54569 (1996).

17. For example, *Saúl Viera "El Gavilancillo" con la Banda Sinaloense*, Discos Linda DL-0204 (1992); *Saúl Viera "El Gavilancillo"con Banda La Costeña*, Discos Linda DL-230 (1993); El Puma de Sinaloa, *Después de mis errores*, EMI-Latin Emid-34951(1995); El Puma de Sinaloa con la Banda Nuevos Coyonquis, *A escondidas*, EMI-Latin Emid-34125 (1995); *El Monarca de Sinaloa con la Banda Santa Cruz*, BM Records BM-036 (1994); El Lobito de Sinaloa con Banda La Costeña de Ramón López Alvarado, *Se solicita novia*, BM Record BM-041 (1995). The recordings typically contain a mixture of romantic songs and corridos. One record producer in Los Angeles claimed that recordings without any narcocorrido and without a cover photograph suggesting "underworld" credibility would not sell in Los Angeles.

18. There is one exception: an all-female Sinaloan-style banda from Jalisco, Banda Las Tapatías. Apart from a notice in *El noroeste*, 1 February 1997, announcing the band's appearance in Mazatlán, I have never heard anything about this group.

19. Most prominent among the young female singers are Carmen Jara and Graciela Beltrán. Both have launched various hits with banda accompaniment: Carmen Jara, *La mujer . . . el nuevo folklore de México*, Fonovisa FPC-9109 (1993); Graciela Beltrán con Banda, *Tesoro*, EMI-Latin Emid-29343 (1994); and *Graciela Beltrán con la Banda Santa Cruz*, EMI-Latin Emid-42840.

20. For example, Aída Cuevas, Alicia Juárez, and Valentina Leyva on *Viva la banda sinaloense*, Quijote QUCD-7035 (1992); *Yolanda del Río con tambora*, Balboa Records BPC-911 (1993); and Lupe Mejía "La Yaqui," *La tamboreada* (with Banda de Música Sinaloense Los Recodeños), Peerless PCD-355-4 (1993).

21. Intense commercialization of tejano, as the various Texas-Mexican musical groups and their styles are labeled collectively, began in the mid-1980s. For tejano's increasing mainstream popularity in recent years, see Liera-Schwichtenberg 1998 and the various articles by Ramiro Burr and John Lannert, "Tejano: The Billboard Spotlight," *Billboard*, 2 September 1995: 39–48.

22. See Ramiro Burr, "Fresh Talent, Variety Key to Strong—but Changing—Regional and Tejano Markets," *Billboard*, 28 August 1999: LM–1.

23. The record industry has divided "Latin music" into three main categories: Latin pop (rock, dance, and reggae), tropical/salsa (merengue, son, bachata, etc.), and regional Mexican. The latter is divided into nine distinct subgenres: tejano, norteño, conjunto, grupo, mariachi, trio, tropical/cumbia, vallenato, and banda. See also chapter 1.

24. In 1994 Ezequiel Peña left the band to pursue his solo career as a ranchera singer. He exchanged his sequinned costumes for charro suits and began to sing accompanied by banda and by mariachi: Ezequiel Peña, *Orgullo ranchero*, Fonovisa SDCD-6046; Ezequiel Peña, *Me dicen el tirador*, Fonovisa SDCD-6061.

25. See chapter 6.

26. As of summer 1996, Banda Flor del Campo had played at the Farallón, Banda Los Guamuchileños at the Parral, and Banda Perla Azul at the Potrero. El Lido, the nightclub that first launched technobanda, used to hire local Sinaloan bandas such as Banda La Auténtica de Mazatlán, but after 1994 no *banda de planta* was contracted; instead the club began to diversify its music styles to cater to a more general Latino audience.

EPILOGUE

1. Among the contributions to Latino popular musics are, for example, Hill 1993, Pacini Hernández 1995, and Austerlitz 1997.

2. Zapatista leader and spokesman Subcomandante Marcos, quoted in *Zapatista*, A Big Noise Film (1998).

3. Alisa Valdes-Rodriguez, "More than a Single Voice: Diverse Sounds at Cinco de Mayo Festival Clearly Illustrate the Changing, Expanding Range of Latino Music in the L.A. Area," *Los Angeles Times*, 4 May 1999. Although Cinco de Mayo was originally a Mexican American celebration, other Latinos too enjoy the many festivals taking place during the first week of May. Paying tribute to these other Latino audiences, the festival organizers engaged the Colombian rock singer Shakira and Los Trio-O, the Puerto Rican pop singer Mayra, the Dominican bachata singer Juan Luis Guerra, and the Spanish ballad queen Rocío Durcal. Mexico was represented by the tejano group Cindy y Los Cholos, the norteño group Los Tiranos del Norte, and the ranchera singer Graciela Beltrán, accompanied by banda.

4. On transnational migration and new anthropological conceptualizations of space and community, see Rouse 1991.

Selected Bibliography

Acuña, Rodolfo F. 1996. *Anything but Mexican: Chicanos in Contemporary Los Angeles.* London: Verso.

Alarcón, R. Arturo Román. 1991. "La participación de comerciantes extranjeros de Mazatlán en la economía regional, 1877–1910." In *El porfiriato en Sinaloa,* edited by Gilberto López Alanís, pp. 153–163. Culiacán: Dirección de Investigación y Fomento de Cultura Regional.

———. 1996. "*El correo de la tarde,* espejo del Mazatlán porfirista." In *Historia y región,* edited by Jorge Verdugo Quintero and Víctor A. Miguel Vélez, pp. 185–201. Culiacán: Universidad Autónoma de Sinaloa.

Anderson, Benedict. 1983. *Imagined Communities: Reflections on the Origin and Spread of Nationalism.* London: Verso.

Aparicio, Frances R. 1998. *Listening to Salsa: Gender, Latin Popular Music, and Puerto Rican Cultures.* Hanover, N.H.: Wesleyan University Press.

Appadurai, Arjun. 1996. *Modernity at Large: Cultural Dimensions of Globalization.* Minneapolis: University of Minnesota Press.

Astorga, Luis. 1995. *Mitología del "narcotraficante" en México.* Mexico City: Universidad Nacional Autónoma de México.

———. 1996. *El siglo de las drogas: Usos, percepciones y personajes.* Mexico City: Espasa-Hoy.

Austerlitz, Paul. 1997. *Merengue: Dominican Music and Dominican Identity.* Philadelphia: Temple University Press.

Averill, Gage. 1997. *A Day for the Hunter, a Day for the Prey: Popular Music and Power in Haiti.* Chicago: University of Chicago Press.

Bancroft, Hubert H. 1888. *History of Mexico.* Vol. 6, 1861–1887. San Francisco: History Company.

Banerji, Sabita, and Gerd Baumann. 1990. "Bhangra 1984–8: Fusion and Professionalization in a Genre of South Asian Dance Music." In *Black Music in Britain: Essays on the Afro-Asian Contribution to Popular Music,* edited by Paul Oliver, pp. 137–152. Buckingham, United Kingdom: Open University Press.

Barnet, Richard, and John Cavanagh. 1996. "Homogenization of Global Culture." In *The Case against the Global Economy and for a Turn toward the Local,* edited by Jerry Mander and Edward Goldsmith, pp. 71–77. San Francisco: Sierra Club Books.

Barry, Tom, Harry Browne, and Beth Sims. 1994. *Crossing the Line: Immigrants, Economic Integration, and Drug Enforcement on the U.S.-Mexico Border.* Albuquerque: Resource Center Press.

Barth, Fredrik. 1969. Introduction to *Ethnic Groups and Boundaries: The Social*

Organization of Culture Difference, edited by Fredrik Barth, pp. 9–38. Boston: Little, Brown.

Bartky, Sandra L. 1990. *Femininity and Domination: Studies in the Phenomenology of Oppression*. New York: Routledge.

Bartra, Roger. 1992. *The Cage of Melancholy*. New Brunswick, N.J.: Rutgers University Press. Translation of *La jaula de la melancolía* (Mexico City: Grijalbo, 1987).

Bausinger, Hermann. [1961] 1986. *Volkskultur in der technischen Welt*. Frankfurt am Main: Campus Verlag.

Béhague, Gerard. 1979. *Music in Latin America: An Introduction*. Englewood Cliffs, N.J.: Prentice Hall.

———. 1985. "Popular Music." In *Handbook of Latin American Popular Culture*, edited by Harold E. Hinds, Jr., and Charles M. Tatum, pp. 3–38. Westport, Conn.: Greenwood Press.

Beraud, José Luis. 1996. *Actores históricos de la urbanización mazatleca*. Culiacán: Dirección de Investigación y Fomento de Cultura Regional.

Berger, Peter L., and Thomas Luckmann. 1967. *The Social Construction of Reality: A Treatise in the Sociology of Knowledge*. New York: Anchor Books.

Biber, Walter. 1995. *Von der Bläsermusik zum Blasorchester*. Lucerne: Maihof Verlag.

Boddy, Janice. 1989. *Wombs and Alien Spirits: Women, Men, and the Zar Cult in Northern Sudan*. Madison: University of Wisconsin Press.

Boehlert, Eric. 1993. "Banda Machos Takes Old Sound to New Heights." *Billboard* 105, no. 16 (17 April).

Bourdieu, Pierre. 1977. *Outline of a Theory of Practice*. Cambridge: University of Cambridge Press.

Buelna, Eustaquio. 1924. *Apuntes para la historia de Sinaloa, 1821–1882*. Mexico City: Secretaría de Educación.

Burke, Peter. 1978. *Popular Culture in Early Modern Europe*. New York: New York University Press.

Campos, Rubén M. 1928. *El folklore y la música mexicana: Investigación acerca de la cultura musical en México, 1525–1925*. Mexico City: Secretaría de Educación Pública.

———. 1930. *El folklore musical de las ciudades*. Mexico City: Secretaría de Educación Pública.

———. 1946. *El folklore literario y musical de México*. Mexico City: Secretaría de Educación Pública.

Castañeda, Daniel. 1941. "La música y la revolución mexicana." *Boletín Latino Americano de Música* 5, no. 5: 437–448.

———. 1943. *El corrido mexicano: Su técnica literaria y musical*. Mexico City: Editorial Surco.

Castillo, Ana. 1994. "The Ancient Roots of Machismo." In *Massacre of the Dreamers: Essays on Xicanisma*, pp. 63–84. Albuquerque: University of New Mexico Press.

Chambers, Iain. 1985. *Urban Rhythms*. New York: St. Martin's Press.

Clark, William A. V. 1996. "Residential Patterns: Avoidance, Assimilation, and

Succession." In *Ethnic Los Angeles*, edited by Roger Waldinger and Mehdi Bozorgmehr, pp. 109–138. New York: Russell Sage Foundation.

Clifford, James, and George E. Marcus, eds. 1986. *Writing Culture: The Poetics and Politics of Ethnography*. Berkeley: University of California Press.

Córdova, Nery. 1993. "Las mediaciones culturales y la communicación." In *Sinaloa: Historia, cultura y violencia*, pp. 37–47. Culiacán: Dirección de Investigación y Fomento Cultural Regional.

Cowan, Jane K. 1990. *Dance and the Body Politic in Northern Greece*. Princeton: Princeton University Press.

Dallal, Alberto. 1982. *El "dancing" mexicano*. Oaxaca: Editorial Oasis.

Daniel, Yvonne. 1995. *Rumba: Dance and Social Change in Contemporary Cuba*. Bloomington: Indiana University Press.

Danow, David K. 1995. *The Spirit of Carnival: Magical Realism and the Grotesque*. Lexington: University Press of Kentucky.

Duvall, Marius. 1957. *A Navy Surgeon in California, 1846–1847: The Journal of Marius Duvall*, edited by Fred B. Duvall. San Francisco: John Howell.

Eagleton, Terry. 1983. "Phenomenology, Hermeneutics, Reception Theory." In *Literary Theory: An Introduction*, pp. 54–90. Minneapolis: University of Minnesota Press.

Easley, Joan. 1993. "Strike Up the Banda." *Los Angeles Times Supplement*, 29 October.

Edwards, Henry. 1883. *A Mingled Yarn*. New York: G. P. Putnam's Sons.

Erlmann, Veit. 1996. *Nightsongs: Performance, Power, and Practice in South Africa*. Chicago: University of Chicago Press.

Estrada, Richard. 1995. "The Dynamics of Assimilation in the United States." In *Identity in North America: The Search for Community*, edited by Robert L. Earle and John D. Wirth, pp. 80–101. Stanford: Stanford University Press.

Featherstone, Mike. 1995. *Undoing Culture: Globalization, Postmodernism, and Identity*. London: Sage Publications.

Feld, Steven, and Keith H. Basso, eds. 1996. *Senses of Place*. Santa Fe, N.M.: School of American Research Press.

Figueroa Díaz, José María. 1987. *"El Negrumo": Partitura de un músico de peso completo*. Culiacán: Imprenta Minerva.

———. 1991. *La muerte de Lamberto Quintero*. Culiacán: Imprenta El Diario de Sinaloa.

Fischer, Michael M. J. 1986. "Ethnicity and the Post–Modern Arts of Memory." In *Writing Culture: The Poetics and Politics of Ethnography*, edited by James Clifford and George E. Marcus, pp. 194–233. Berkeley: University of California Press.

Fiske, John. 1989. *Understanding Popular Culture*. London: Routledge.

———. 1994. "Hybrid Vigor: Popular Culture in a Multicultural, Post-Fordist World." *Studies in Latin American Popular Culture* 15: 43–59.

Flippin, John R. 1889. *Sketches from the Mountains of Mexico*. Cincinnati: Standard Publishing Company.

Flores Gastélum, Manuel. 1980. *Historia de la música popular en Sinaloa*. Culiacán: Dirección de Investigación y Fomento de Cultura Regional.

Freund, Elizabeth. 1987. *The Return of the Reader: Reader-Response Criticism*. London: Methuen.

Frith, Simon. 1987. "Towards an Aesthetic of Popular Music." In *Music and Society: The Politics of Composition, Performance, and Reception*, edited by Richard Leppert and Susan McClary, pp. 133–149. Cambridge: Cambridge University Press.

———. 1992. "The Cultural Study of Popular Music." In *Cultural Studies*, edited by Lawrence Grossberg, Cary Nelson, and Paula A. Treichler, pp. 174–182. New York: Routledge.

Gadamer, Hans-Georg. 1994. *Truth and Method*. New York: Continuum. Translation of *Wahrheit und Methode* (Tübingen: J. C. B. Mohr, 1960).

Galarza, Ernesto. 1971. *Barrio Boy: The Story of a Boy's Acculturation*. Notre Dame: University of Notre Dame Press.

García Canclini, Néstor. 1990. *Culturas híbridas: Estrategias para entrar y salir de la modernidad*. Mexico City: Grijalbo.

García, Mario T. 1994. "Border Culture." In *From Different Shores: Perspectives on Race and Ethnicity in America*, edited by Ronald Takaki, pp. 72–81. Oxford: Oxford University Press.

Garofalo, Reebee. 1993. "Whose World, What Beat: The Transnational Music Industry, Identity, and Cultural Imperialism." *The World of Music* 35, no. 2: 16–31.

Garrido, Juan S. [1974] 1981. *Historia de la música popular en México, 1876–1973*. Mexico City: Editorial Extemporáneos.

Geertz, Clifford. 1973. *The Interpretation of Cultures*. New York: Basic Books.

———. 1996. Afterword to *Senses of Place*, edited by Steven Feld and Keith H. Basso, pp. 259–262. Santa Fe, N.M.: School of American Research Press.

Geijerstam, Claes af. 1976. *Popular Music in Mexico*. Albuquerque: University of New Mexico Press.

Gillpatrick, Owen W. 1911. *The Man Who Likes Mexico: The Spirited Chronicle of Adventurous Wandering in Mexican Highways and Byways*. New York: Century.

Gilmore, David. 1990. "Performance Excellence: Circum-Mediterranean." In *Manhood in the Making: Cultural Concept*, pp. 30–55. London: Yale University Press.

Gilroy, Paul. 1993. *The Black Atlantic: Double Consciousness and Modernity*. Cambridge, Mass.: Harvard University Press.

Glazer, Nathan, and Daniel P. Moynihan, eds. 1963. *Beyond the Melting Pot*. Cambridge: MIT Press and Harvard University Press.

Gómez Flores, Francisco. 1889. *Narraciones y caprichos: Apuntamientos de un viandante*, vol. 1. Culiacán: Ignacio M. Gastélum.

González Dávila, Amado. 1959. *Diccionario geográfico, histórico, biográfico y estadístico del estado de Sinaloa*. Culiacán: Gobierno del Estado de Sinaloa.

González, Ray, ed. 1996. *Muy Macho: Latino Men Confront Their Manhood*. New York: Anchor Books.

Gradante, William. 1982. "'El Hijo del Pueblo': José Alfredo Jiménez and the Mexican *Canción Ranchera*." *Latin American Music Review* 3, no. 1: 36–59.

Gregg, Josiah. 1944. *Diary and Letters of Josiah Gregg*. Excursions in Mexico and California: 1847–1850, edited by Maurice Garland Fulton. Norman: University of Oklahoma Press.

Greve, Martin. 1997. *Alla turca: Berliner Musik aus der Türkei*. Berlin: Ausländerbeauftragte des Senats.

Grossberg, Lawrence. 1984. "'I'd Rather Feel Bad than Not Feel Anything at All': Rock and Roll, Pleasure, and Power." *Enclictic* 8: 95–112.

———. 1996. "The Space of Culture, the Power of Space." In *The Post-Colonial Question: Common Skies, Divided Horizons*, edited by Iain Chambers and Lidia Curti, pp. 169–188. London: Routledge.

Gupta, Akhil, and James Ferguson. 1997. "Culture, Power, Place: Ethnography at the End of an Era." In *Culture, Power, Place: Explorations in Critical Anthropology*, edited by Akhil Gupta and James Ferguson, pp. 1–29. Durham, N.C.: Duke University Press.

Hall, Stuart. 1990. "Cultural Identity and Diaspora." In *Identity: Community, Culture, Difference*, edited by Jonathan Rutherford, pp. 222–237. London: Lawrence and Wishart.

Hamilton, Leonidas Le Cenci. 1883. *Hamilton's Mexican Handbook: A Complete Description of the Republic of Mexico*. Boston: D. Lothrop. Also published as *Border States of Mexico: Sonora, Sinaloa, Chihuahua, and Durango* (Chicago, 1882).

Hanna, Judith L. 1979. *To Dance Is Human: A Theory of Nonverbal Communication*. Austin: University of Texas Press.

Hardy, Robert W. H. [1829] 1871. *Travels in the Interior of Mexico, in 1825, 1826, 1827 and 1828*. Glorieta, N.M.: Rio Grande Press.

Haro, Carlos M., and Steven Loza. 1994. "The Evolution of Banda Music and the Current Banda Movement in Los Angeles." In *Musical Aesthetics and Multiculturalism in Los Angeles* (Selected Reports in Ethnomusicology, vol. 10), edited by Steven Loza, pp. 59–71. Los Angeles: UCLA Ethnomusicology Publications.

Hayes, Joy Elizabeth. 1993. "Early Mexican Radio Broadcasting: Media Imperialism, State Paternalism, or Mexican Nationalism?" *Studies in Latin American Popular Culture* 12: 31–55.

Hazen, Margaret H., and Robert M. Hazen. 1987. *The Music Men: An Illustrated History of Brass Band in America, 1800–1920*. Washington, D.C.: Smithsonian Institution Press.

Hebdige, Dick. 1979. *Subculture: The Meaning of Style*. London: Methuen.

Henestrosa, Andrés. 1977. *Espuma y flor de corridos mexicanos*. Mexico City: Editorial Porrúa.

Herbert, Trevor. 1991. "Nineteenth-Century Bands: The Making of a Movement." In *Bands: The Brass Band Movement in the Nineteenth and Twentieth Centuries*, edited by Trevor Herbert, pp. 7–56. Milton Keynes, Pa.: Open University Press.

Hernández, Guillermo D. 1995. "New Perspectives on the Corrido." In *Ballads and Boundaries: Narrative Singing in an Intercultural Context*, edited by James Porter, pp. 28–36. Los Angeles: Department of Ethnomusicology and Systematic Musicology, UCLA.

Hernández, Hernando. 1992. *Y sigue la yunta andando: Una semblanza de Luis Pérez Meza*. Mexico City: Universidad Pedagógica Nacional.

Herrera-Sobek, María. 1979a. "The Theme of Drug Smuggling in the Mexican Corrido." *Revista Chicano-Riqueña* 7, no. 4: 49–61.

———. 1979b. *The Bracero Experience: Elitelore versus Folklore.* Los Angeles: UCLA Latin American Center Publications.

———. 1990. *The Mexican Corrido: A Feminist Analysis.* Bloomington: Indiana University Press.

———. 1993. *Northward Bound: The Mexican Immigrant Experience in Ballad and Song.* Bloomington: Indiana University Press.

Herrera y Cairo, Sergio. 1983. *Tesoro en Mazatlán.* Mexico City: Ediciones Libros de México.

Hill, Donald R. 1993. *Calypso Calaloo: Early Carnival Music in Trinidad.* Gainesville: University Press of Florida.

Hobsbawm, Eric. 1959. *Primitive Rebels.* Manchester: Manchester University Press.

———. 1969. *Bandits.* New York: Delacorte Press.

———. 1983. *The Invention of Tradition.* Cambridge: Cambridge University Press.

Holub, Robert C. 1984. *Reception Theory: A Critical Introduction.* London: Methuen.

———. 1992. *Crossing Borders: Reception Theory, Poststructuralism, Deconstruction.* Madison: University of Wisconsin Press.

Ibarra, Alfredo, Jr. 1944. "El folklore musical de Sinaloa." In *Sinaloa en la cultura de México*, pp. 71–78. Mexico City: Editorial Hidalgo.

———. 1960. "El folklore en Sinaloa." In *Estudios históricos de Sinaloa*, edited by Antonio Pompa y Pompa, pp. 307–321. Mexico City: Congreso Mexicano de Historia.

———. 1987. "Cosalá: La música." *El Suplemento: Organo Cultural de Difocur* 22: 8.

Ihde, Don. 1993. *Postphenomenology: Essays in the Postmodern Context.* Evanston, Ill.: Northwestern University Press.

Iser, Wolfgang. 1978. *The Act of Reading: A Theory of Aesthetic Response.* Baltimore: John Hopkins University Press. Translation of *Der Akt des Lesens: Theorie ästhetischer Wirkung* (Munich: Wilhelm Fink Verlag, 1976).

Jaramillo, Carlos P. 1899. *Por México y California: Recuerdos de viaje.* Bogotá: Librería Nueva.

Jauss, Hans Robert. 1982. *Aesthetic Experience and Literary Hermeneutics.* Minneapolis: University of Minnesota Press. Translation of *Ästhetische Erfahrung und literarische Hermeneutik* (Munich: Wilhelm Fink Verlag, 1977).

Jones, Oakah L., Jr. 1979. *Los Paisanos: Spanish Settlers on the Northern Frontier of New Spain.* Norman: University of Oklahoma Press.

Kearney, Richard. 1991. "Between Tradition and Utopia: The Hermeneutical Problem of Myth." In *On Paul Ricoeur: Narrative and Interpretation*, edited by David Wood, pp. 55–73. London: Routledge.

Keefe, Susan E., and Amado M. Padilla. 1987. *Chicano Ethnicity.* Albuquerque: University of New Mexico.

Keil, Charles, and Angeliki V. Keil. 1992. *Polka Happiness.* Philadelphia: Temple University Press.

Lamb, Andrew. 1980. "Popular Music." In *The New Grove Dictionary of Music and Musicians*, 20 vols., edited by Stanley Sadie, 15: 87–97. London: Macmillan.

Lewis, George H. 1992. "La Pistola y El Corazón: Protest and Passion in Mexican-American Popular Music." *Journal of Popular Culture* 26, no. 1: 51–67.

Liera-Schwichtenberg, Ramona. 1998. "Crossing Over: Selena's Tejano Music and the Discourse of Borderlands." In *Mapping the Beat: Popular Music and Contemporary Theory*, edited by Thomas Swiss, John Sloop, and Andrew Herman, pp. 205–218. Malden, Mass.: Blackwell.

Limón, José. 1994. *Dancing With the Devil: Society and Cultural Poetics in Mexican-American South Texas*. Madison: University of Wisconsin Press.

Lipsitz, George. 1990. "Cruising around the Historical Bloc." In *Time Passages: Collective Memory and American Popular Culture*, pp. 133–160. Minneapolis: University of Minnesota Press. Originally published in *Culture Critique* 5 (1986–87): 157–177.

———. 1994. "The Bands of Tomorrow Are Here Today: The Proud, Progressive, and Postmodern Sounds of Las Tres and Goddess 13." In *Musical Aesthetics and Multiculturalism in Los Angeles* (Selected Reports in Ethnomusicology, vol. 10), edited by Steven Loza, pp. 139–147. Los Angeles: UCLA Ethnomusicology Publications.

———. 1999. "'Home Is Where the Hatred Is': Work, Music and the Transnational Economy." In *Home, Exile, Homeland: Film, Media, and the Politics of Place*, edited by Hamid Naficy, pp. 293–312. New York: Routledge.

López Alanís, Gilberto, ed. 1991. *El porfiriato en Sinaloa*. Culiacán: Dirección de Investigación y Fomento de Cultura Regional.

López, Sandra, and Yolanda Prat Meza. 1989. "La subcultura del narcotráfico." Master's thesis, Universidad Autónoma de Sinaloa, Mazatlán.

Lovewell, Bertha E. 1898. *The Life of St. Cecilia*. Boston: Lamson and Wolffe.

Loza, Steven. 1990. "Contemporary Ethnomusicology in Mexico." *Latin American Music Review* 11, no. 2: 201–250.

———. 1993. *Barrio Rhythm: Mexican American Music in Los Angeles*. Urbana: University of Illinois Press.

Lummis, Charles F. 1898. *The Awakening of a Nation: Mexico of Today*. New York: Harper and Brothers.

Manuel, Peter. 1988. *Popular Music of the Non-Western World*. New York: Oxford University Press.

———. 1995. "Music as Symbol, Music as Simulacrum: Postmodern, Pre-Modern, and Modern Aesthetics in Subcultural Popular Music." *Popular Music* 14, no. 2: 227–239.

———. 1997–98. "Music, Identity, and Images of India in the Indo-Caribbean Diaspora." *Asian Music* 29, no. 1: 17–35.

Martín Barbero, Jesús. 1998. "Experiencia audiovisual y desorden cultural." In *Cultura, medios y sociedad*, edited by Jesús Martín-Barbero and Fabio López de la Roche, pp. 27–64. Bogotá: Universidad Nacional de Colombia.

Martínez, Jesús. 1995. "Tigers in a Gold Cage: Binationalism and Politics in the Songs of Mexican Immigrants in Silicon Valley." In *Ballads and Boundaries: Narrative Singing in an Intercultural Context*, edited by James Porter, pp. 325–338. Los Angeles: Department of Ethnomusicology and Systematic Musicology, UCLA.

Martínez, Oscar J. 1994. *Border People: Life and Society in the U.S.-Mexico Borderlands*. Tucson: University of Arizona Press.

Mayer, Brantz. 1844. *Mexico as It Was and as It Is*. New York: J. Winchester, New World Press.

Mayer-Serra, Otto. 1946. *El estado presente de la música en México (The Present State of Music in Mexico)*. Washington, D.C.: Pan American Union.

McDonald, Barry. 1996. "The Idea of Tradition Examined in the Light of Two Australian Musical Studies." *Yearbook for Traditional Music* 28: 106–130.

McDowell, John. 1972. "The Mexican Corrido: Formula and Theme in a Ballad Tradition." *Journal of American Folklore* 85: 205–220.

———. 1981. "The Corrido of Greater Mexico as Discourse, Music, and Event." In *"And Other Neighborly Names": Social Processes and Cultural Image in Texas Folklore*, edited by Richard Baumann and Roger D. Abrahams, pp. 44–75. Austin: University of Texas Press.

McRobbie, Angela. 1984. "Dance and Social Fantasy." In *Gender and Generation*, edited by Angela McRobbie and Mica Nava, pp. 130–161. London: Macmillan.

Mejía Prieto, Jorge. 1988. *México y el narcotráfico*. Mexico City: Editorial Universo México.

Méndez Moreno, Rafael. 1961. *Apuntes sobre el pasado de mi tierra*. Mexico City: Costa-Amic.

Mendoza, Vicente T. 1939. *El romance español y el corrido mexicano*. Mexico City: Ediciones de la Universidad Nacional Autónoma de México.

———. 1954. *El corrido mexicano: Antología, introducción y notas*. Mexico City: Fondo de Cultura Económica.

Menéndez Pidal, Ramón. 1939. *Los romances de América, y otros estudios*. Buenos Aires: Espasa-Calpe Argentina.

Merton, Robert K. 1968. *Social Theory and Social Structure*. New York: Free Press.

Middleton, Richard. 1990. *Studying Popular Music*. Milton Keynes, Pa.: Open University Press.

Mintz, Jerome R. 1997. *Carnival Song and Society: Gossip, Sexuality, and Creativity in Andalusia*. Oxford: Berg.

Mora, Carl J. 1989. *Mexican Cinema: Reflections of a Society, 1896–1988*. Berkeley: University of California Press.

Moreno Rivas, Yolanda. [1979] 1989. *Historia de la música popular mexicana*. Mexico City: Consejo Nacional para la Cultura y las Artes and Alianza Editorial Mexicana.

Nájera Ramírez, Olga. 1989. "Social and Political Dimensions of Folklorico Dance: The Binational Dialectic of Residual and Emergent Culture." *Western Folklore* 48, no. 1: 15–32.

Nakayama Arce, Antonio. 1980. *Pioneros sinaloenses en California*. Culiacán: Universidad Autónoma de Sinaloa.

———. 1991. *Entre sonorenses y sinaloenses: Afinidades y diferencias*. Culiacán: Dirección de Investigación y Fomento Cultural Regional.

Ness, Sally A. 1992. *Body, Movement, and Culture: Kinesthetic and Visual Symbolism in a Philippine Community*. Philadelphia: University of Pennsylvania Press.

Nettl, Bruno. 1975. "The State of Research in Ethnomusicology, and Recent Developments." *Current Musicology* 20: 67–78.

Novak, Michael. 1972. *The Rise of the Unmeltable Ethnics: Politics and Culture in the Seventies*. New York: Macmillan.

Nunley, John W., ed. 1988. *Caribbean Festival Art*. Seattle and Washington: Saint Louis Art Museum and University of Washington Press.

Olea, Héctor R. 1985. *Los orígenes de la tambora*. Culiacán: Ediciones del Ayuntamiento de Culiacán.

O'Malley, Ilene V. 1986. *The Myth of the Revolution: Hero Cults and the Institutionalization of the Mexican State, 1920–1940*. New York: Greenwood Press.

Ortega, Sergio, and Edgardo López Mañón. 1987. *Sinaloa, una historia compartida*. Mexico City and Culiacán: Instituto de Investigaciones Dr. José María Luis Mora and Dirección de Investigación y Fomento Cultural Regional.

Ortiz, Vilma. 1996. "The Mexican-Origin Population: Permanent Working Class or Emerging Middle Class?" In *Ethnic Los Angeles*, edited by Roger Waldinger and Mehdi Bozorgmehr, pp. 247–277. New York: Russell Sage Foundation.

Pacini Hernández, Deborah. 1993. "A View from the South: Spanish Caribbean Perspectives on World Beat." *World of Music* 35, no. 2: 48–69.

———. 1995. *Bachata: A Social History of a Dominican Popular Music*. Philadelphia: Temple University Press.

Padilla Beltrán, Francisco. 1996. "Poririato y rida cotidiana en Culiacán." In *Historia y región*, edited by Jorge Verdugo Quintero and Víctor A. Miguel Vélez, pp. 283–295. Culiacán: Universidad Autónoma de Sinaloa.

Paredes, Américo. 1958. *"With His Pistol in His Hand": A Border Ballad and Its Hero*. Austin: University of Texas Press.

———. [1976] 1995. *A Texas-Mexican Cancionero: Folksongs of the Lower Border*. Austin: University of Texas Press.

———. 1993. *Folklore and Culture on the Texas-Mexican Border*. Austin: University of Texas Press.

Paredes, Américo, and Ellen J. Stekert, eds. 1971. *The Urban Experience and Folk Tradition*. Austin: University of Texas Press.

Paz, Octavio. 1959. *El laberinto de la soledad*. Mexico City: Fondo de Cultura Económica, Colección Popular.

Peña, Manuel. 1980. "Ritual Structure in a Chicano Dance." *Latin American Music Review* 1, no. 1: 47–73.

———. 1985. *The Texas-Mexican Conjunto: History of a Working-Class Music*. Austin: University of Texas Press.

———. 1999. *Música Tejana: The Cultural Economy of Artistic Transformation*. College Station: Texas A & M University Press.

Poppa, E. 1990. *Drug Lord: The Life and Death of a Mexican Kingpin*. New York: Pharos Books.

Preston, Peter W. 1997. *Political/Cultural Identity: Citizens and Nations in a Global Era*. London: Sage.

Quintanilla, Michael. 1993. "¡Que cool!" *Los Angeles Times*, 16 June.

Rafael, Hermes. 1982. *Origen e historia del mariachi*. Mexico City: Editorial Katún.

Ramos, Samuel. 1962. *Profile of Man and Culture in Mexico*. Austin: University of Texas Press. Translation of *El perfil del hombre y la cultura en México* (1934).

Redfield, Robert. 1930. *Tepoztlán, a Mexican Village: A Study of Folk Life*. Chicago: University of Chicago Press.

Reuter, Jas. 1980. *La música popular de México*. Mexico City: Panorama Editorial.

Riaño-Alcalá, Pilar. 1991. "Urban Space and Music in the Formation of Youth Culture: The Case of Bogotá, 1920–1980." *Studies in Latin American Popular Culture* 10: 87–106.

Rice, Timothy. 1987. "Toward the Remodeling of Ethnomusicology." *Ethnomusicology* 31, no. 3: 469–488.

———. 1994. *May It Fill Your Soul: Experiencing Bulgarian Music*. Chicago: University of Chicago Press.

Ricoeur, Paul. 1970. "Qu'est-ce qu'un texte?" In *Hermeneutik und Dialektik: Aufsätze II*, edited by Rüdiger Bubner, Konrad Cramer, and Reiner Wiehl, pp. 181–200. Tübingen: J. C. B. Mohr.

———. 1971. "The Model of the Text: Meaningful Action Considered as a Text." *Social Research* 38: 529–562.

———. 1981. *Hermeneutics and Human Sciences*. New York: Cambridge University Press.

———. 1984, 1985, 1988. *Time and Narrative*, vols. 1–3. Chicago: University of Chicago Press.

Rieff, David. 1991. *Los Angeles: Capital of the Third World*. New York: Simon and Schuster.

Riensch, Adolph. 1960. *Erinnerungen aus meinem Leben während der Jahre 1830–1855*. Hamburg: Verlag Hanseatischer Merkur.

Riesgo, Juan M., and Antonio J. Valdés. 1828. *Memoria estadística del Estado de Occidente*. Guadalajara: C. E. Alatorre.

Ríos-Bustamante, Antonio, and Pedro Castillo. 1986. *An Illustrated History of Mexican Los Angeles: 1781–1985*. Los Angeles: Chicano Studies Research Center Publications, UCLA.

Rodríguez, José. 1997. "Por aquí pasó la reina: El carnaval de Mazatlán." In *El carnaval de Mazatlán*, pp. 9–48. Culiacán: Colegio de Bachilleres del Estado de Sinaloa.

Romo, Ricardo. 1983. *East Los Angeles: The History of a Barrio*. Austin: University of Texas Press.

Roosens, Eugeen. 1989. *Creating Ethnicity: The Process of Ethnogenesis*. London: Sage Publications.

Rosaldo, Renato. 1993. *Culture and Truth: The Remaking of Social Analysis*. Boston: Beacon Press.

Rouse, Roger. 1991. "Mexican Migration and the Social Space of Postmodernism." *Diaspora* 1, no. 1: 8–23.

Rubio Gutiérrez, David. 1995. *Mocorito, un camino, un testimonio*. Culiacán: Academia Cultural "Roberto Hernández Rodríguez" and Dirección de Investigación y Fomento de Cultura Regional.

Ruiz, Reynaldo. 1993. "The *Corrido* as a Medium for Cultural Identification." In *Imagination, Emblems, and Expressions: Essays on Latin American, Caribbean, and*

Continental Culture and Identity, edited by Helen Ryan-Ranson, pp. 53–64. Bowling Green, Ky.: Bowling Green State University Popular Press.

Sagel, Jim. 1990. *Straight from the Heart: Portraits of Traditional Hispanic Musicians.* Albuquerque: University of New Mexico Press.

Sánchez, George J. 1993. *Becoming Mexican American: Ethnicity, Culture, and Identity in Chicano Los Angeles, 1900–1945.* Oxford: Oxford University Press.

Santamaría Gómez, Arturo. 1996. *México en los mass media hispanos de Estados Unidos: En sus orígenes y en la crisis de 1994–1995.* Culiacán: Universidad Autónoma de Sinaloa, and Los Angeles: California State University, Los Angeles.

———. 1997. *El culto de las reinas de Sinaloa y el poder de la belleza.* Culiacán: Universidad Autónoma de Sinaloa, Colegio de Bachilleres del Estado de Sinaloa, and CODETUR.

Sartorius, Carl Christian. 1961. *Mexico about 1850.* Stuttgart: F. A. Brockhaus. Originally published as *Mexico: Landscape and Popular Sketches* (1858).

Sarup, Madan. 1996. *Identity, Culture, and the Postmodern World.* Edinburgh: Edinburgh University Press.

Savage, Roger W. H. 1994. "Music and the Cultural Imagination." In *Musical Aesthetics and Multiculturalism in Los Angeles* (Selected Reports in Ethnomusicology, vol. 10), edited by Steven Loza, pp. 23–36. Los Angeles: UCLA Ethnomusicology Publications.

———. 1995. "The Cultural Work of Music: Revisiting the Question of 'Meaningful Action Considered as a Text'." Paper presented at the 40th Annual Meeting of the Society for Ethnomusicology, Los Angeles.

Schapp, Wilhelm. [1953] 1985. *In Geschichten verstrickt.* Frankfurt am Main: Vittorio Klostermann.

Schiller, Nina Glick, Linda Basch, and Cristina Blanc-Szanton. 1992. "Transnationalism: A New Analytic Framework for Understanding Migration." In *Transnational Perspective on Migration: Race, Class, Ethnicity, and Nationalism Reconsidered*, pp. 1–44. New York: New York Academy of Science.

Seemann, Berthold. 1853. *Narrative of the Voyage of H.M.S. Herald during the Years 1845–51*, vol. 1. London: Reeve.

Serrano Martínez, Celedonio. 1973. *El corrido mexicano no deriva del romance español.* Mexico City: Centro Cultural Guerrerense.

Shils, Edward. 1975. *Center and Periphery.* Chicago: University of Chicago Press.

———. 1981. *Tradition.* Chicago: University of Chicago Press.

Simmons, Merle E. 1957. *The Mexican Corrido as a Source for Interpretive Study of Modern Mexico (1870–1950).* Bloomington: Indiana University Press.

Simonett, Helena. 1996–97. "Waving Hats and Stomping Boots: A Transborder Music and Dance Phenomenon in Los Angeles' Mexican American Communities." *Pacific Review of Ethnomusicology* 8, no. 1: 41–50.

———. 1997. *Loud and Proud: The Social History and Cultural Power of Mexican Banda Music.* Ph.D. diss., University of California, Los Angeles.

———. 1999. "Strike Up the Tambora: A Social History of Sinaloan Band Music." *Latin American Music Review* 20, no. 1: 59–104.

————. 2001a. "Popular Musics and the Politics of Identity: The Empowering Sound of Technobanda." *Popular Music and Society*. Forthcoming.

————. 2001b. *Bandas sinaloenses: "Música Tambora."* Arhoolie/Folklyric CD-7048, insert annotations.

Slobin, Mark. 1993. *Subcultural Sounds: Micromusics of the West*. Hanover, N.H.: Wesleyan University Press.

Sollors, Werner. 1986. *Beyond Ethnicity: Consent and Descent in American Culture*. New York: Oxford University Press.

Sommers, Laurie K. 1991. "Inventing Latinismo: The Creation of 'Hispanic' Panethnicity in the United States." *Journal of American Folklore* 104: 32–53.

Sonnichsen, Philip. 1993. *Mariachi Coculense de Cirilo Marmolejo*. Arhoolie/Folklyric CD-7011, insert annotations.

Stanford, Thomas E. 1980. "Mexico: (II, 2) Mestizo Forms; (vi) Bands and Regional Orchestras." In *The New Grove Dictionary of Music and Musicians*, 20 vols., edited by Stanley Sadie, 12: 236. London: Macmillan.

Stokes, Martin, ed. 1994. *Ethnicity, Identity, and Music: The Musical Construction of Place*. Oxford: Berg.

Suárez-Orozco, Carola, and Marcelo Suárez-Orozco. 1995. "Migration: Generational Discontinuities and the Making of Latino Identities." In *Ethnic Identity: Creation, Conflict, and Accommodation*, edited by Lola Romanucci-Ross and George De Vos, pp. 321–347. Walnut Creek, Calif.: AltaMira Press.

Suleiman, Susan R. 1980. Introduction to *The Reader in the Text: Essays on Audience and Interpretation*, edited by Susan R. Suleiman and Inge Crosman, pp. 3–45. Princeton: Princeton University Press.

Suppan, Wolfgang. 1976. *Lexikon des Blasmusikwesens*. Freiburg im Breisgau: Blasmusikverlag Fritz Schulz.

Takaki, Ronald, ed. 1994. *From Different Shores: Perspectives on Race and Ethnicity in America*. Oxford: Oxford University Press.

Taylor, Bayard. 1850. *El Dorado, or Adventures in the Path of Empire*. New York: George P. Putnam.

Tempsky, Gustav F. 1858. *Mitla: A Narrative of Incidents and Personal Adventures on a Journey in Mexico, Guatemala, and Salvador in the Years 1853 to 1855*. London: Longman.

Toor, Frances. 1930. "El jarabe antiguo y moderno—The Old and New Jarabe." *Mexican Folk-Ways* 6: 26–37.

————. 1947. *A Treasury of Mexican Folkways: The Customs, Myths, Folklore, Traditions, Beliefs, Fiestas, Dances, Songs of the Mexican People*. New York: Crown.

Toro, María C. 1995. *Mexico's "War" on Drugs: Causes and Consequences*. Boulder, Colo.: L. Rienner Publishers.

Touro Linger, Daniel. 1992. *Dangerous Encounters: Meanings of Violence in a Brazilian City*. Stanford: Stanford University Press.

Trejo Delarbre, Raúl, ed. 1985. *Televisa, el quinto poder*. Mexico City: Editorial Claves Latinoamericanas.

Trueba Lara, José Luis. 1995. *Política y narcopoder en México*. Mexico City: Grupo Editorial Planeta de México.

Turino, Thomas. 1993. *Moving away from Silence: Music of the Peruvian Altiplano and the Experience of Urban Migration*. Chicago: University of Chicago Press.

Urrutia de Vázquez, Cristina A., and Martha C. Saldaña. 1982. "Origen y evolución del mariachi." In *Sabiduría popular*, pp. 448–467. Morelia: Fímax Publicistas.

Valdéz Aguilar, Rafael. 1993. *Sinaloa: Negritud y olvido*. Culiacán: El Diario de Sinaloa.

Vázquez Santa Ana, Higinio, and J. Ignacio Dávila Garibi. 1931. *El carnaval*. Mexico City: Talleres Gráficos de la Nación.

Vega Ayala, Enrique. 1991. *¡Ay mi Mazatlán!* Culiacán: Dirección de Investigación y Fomento Cultural Regional.

———. 1996. *Crónicas originales: Carnaval de Mazatlán, 1898–1905*. Mazatlán: CODETUR.

Velázquez, José Ramón. 1997. *Apuntes de Mocorito (segunda parte)*. Culiacán: Colegio de Bachilleres del Estado de Sinaloa.

Verdugo Quintero, Jorge. 1993. "Un esbozo de la violencia en Sinaloa." In *Sinaloa: Historia, cultura y violencia*, pp. 19–25. Culiacán: Dirección de Investigación y Fomento Cultural Regional.

Verdugo Fálquez, Francisco. [1949] 1981. *Las viejas calles de Culiacán*. Culiacán: Universidad Autónoma de Sinaloa.

Voss, Stuart F. 1982. *On the Periphery of Nineteenth-Century Mexico*. Tucson: University of Arizona Press.

Waldinger, Roger, and Mehdi Bozorgmehr, eds. 1996. *Ethnic Los Angeles*. New York: Russell Sage Foundation.

Walser, Robert. 1993. *Running with the Devil: Power, Gender, and Madness in Heavy Metal Music*. Hanover, N.H.: Wesleyan University Press.

Waterman, Christopher A. 1990. *Jùjú: A Social History and Ethnography of an African Popular Music*. Chicago: University of Chicago Press.

Watson, Henry Bulls. 1990. *The Journals of Marine Second Lieutenant Henry Bulls Watson, 1845–1848*, edited by Charles R. Smith. Washington, D.C.: History and Museums Division, Headquarters, U.S. Marine Corps.

Waters, Mary C. 1990. *Ethnic Options: Choosing Identities in America*. Berkeley: University of California Press.

Weidner, Frederick. 1882. *Sinaloa: The Topography, Ethnography, and the Natural and Mineral Resources of Sinaloa*. San Francisco: Spaulding.

Wheat, Marvin (pseudonym: Cincinnatus). 1857. *Travels on the Western Slope of the Mexican Cordillera in the Form of Fifty-One Letters*. San Francisco: Whitton, Towne.

Widenmann, E., and H. Hauff. 1837. *Mexicanische Zustände aus den Jahren 1830–1832*. Stuttgart: J. G. Cotta'sche Buchhandlung.

Wise, Henry A. 1849. *Los Gringos: Or, an Inside View of Mexico and California*. New York: Baker and Scribner.

Württemberg, Paul Wilhelm von. 1986. *Reisen und Streifzüge in Mexiko und Nordamerika, 1849–1856*. Stuttgart: Thienemann.

Selected Discography

BANDA SINALOENSE

Adán Sánchez (El Compita; with Banda Sinaloense La Flor del Campo). 1994. *Soy el hijo de Chalino*. RR Records CD-001.

Antonio Aguilar con tambora (Disco de oro, vol. 1). 1995. Musart CDE-1245.

Antonio Aguilar con tambora (Disco de oro, vol. 2). 1994. Musart CDN-1157.

A pura banda (vol. 2). 1994. EMI-Latin Emid-28547.

Banda Caña Verde. 1996. *Como poder olvidarte*. EMI-Latin Emid-54569.

Banda Chilolos de Isidoror Ramírez. 1999. *Tiene que haber un final*. Discos Elite CD-002.

Banda Clave Azul. *Un indio quiere llorar*. Fonovisa MPCD-5151.

Banda Degollado. 1992. Fonovisa MPC-5204 (cassette).

Banda El Cerrito. *Mira*. Fonorama CD-40.

Banda El Chante de Jalisco. 1996. Fonorama FCCD-4010.

Banda El Chante de Jalisco. 1994. *Un amor como el mío*. Fonorama FRCD-2070.

Banda El Limón. 1997. *Puro Sinaloa Compas*. Fonorama (Fonovisa) FCCD-4021.

Banda El Recodo. *De México y para el mundo* (Banda Gold Series). Master Stereo KBGE-519 (cassette).

Banda El Recodo. 1995. *Desde París, Francia: El orgullo de México* (Banda Gold Series). Master Stereo CDBGE-512.

Banda El Recodo. 1993. *Ésta . . . ¡Sí es banda! Pegando con tubo* (Banda Gold Series). Master Stereo KBGE-514 (cassette).

Banda El Recodo. 1995. *Los mejores corridos y rancheras de la gira Europa '95* (Banda Gold Series, vol. 2). Master Stereo CDBGE-510.

Banda El Recodo. 1996. *Tributo a Juan Gabriel*. Musivisa TUT-1919.

Banda El Recodo de Cruz Lizárraga. 1996. *Desde el cielo y para siempre*. Musivisa TUT-1666.

Banda El Recodo de Cruz Lizárraga. 1998. *Tengo una ilusión*. Fonovisa TFD2-2490 (2 CDs).

Banda El Recodo de Don Cruz Lizárraga. 1995. *Mis inicios* (Banda Gold Series, vol. 2). Master Stereo CDBG-513.

Banda El Recodo en homenaje a Don Cruz Lizárraga. 1995. *Entiérrenme con la banda*. Sierra Records CD LRS-045.

Banda Hermanos Rubio de Mocorito. 1998. *Sangre mexicana*. Discos MM CDMM-7759.

Banda Kora de Puerta de Mangos. 1983. Fonorama CA-FR-10-101 (cassette).

Banda Kora de Puerta de Mangos. 1984. Fonorama FR-1052 (cassette).

Banda La Costeña. 1993. Musart CDP-1007.

Banda La Costeña. *De puro arranque.* 1995. Musivisa TUL-1606.

Banda La Costeña de Don Ramón López Alvarado. 1997. *Secreto de amor.* Fonovisa FPCD-9604.

Banda La Costeña de Ramón López Alvarado. 1996. *Corazón de oro.* Musart CDP-1622.

Banda La Costeña de Ramón López Alvarado. 1995. *Tu me pagaste mal.* BM Record BM-010.

Banda Pelillos. 1992. Fonorama FR-10-333.

Banda Pioneros. 1995. Musical Vinny BCL-011 (cassette).

Banda Sinaloense Flor del Campo. 1994. Ayana Musical AM-075 (cassette).

Banda Sinaloense Los Recoditos. 1995. *Canto para ti.* Musart CDP-1340.

Banda Sinaloense Los Recoditos. 1996. *Siempre te voy a recordar.* Musart CMP-1610 (cassette).

Banda Sinaloense MM. 1999. *Viejtas pero bonitas* (vol. 2). Discos MM CDMM-7771.

Banda Sinaloense de El Recodo de Cruz Lizárraga. 1992. *50 años de tambora.* Karussell CDNPM-5136.

Banda Sinaloense El Recodo de Cruz Lizárraga (Serie 20 éxitos). 1991. RCA, BMG 3294-2-RL.

Banda Sinaloense El Recodo de Cruz Lizárraga. 1996 [1969]. *La chuchis y otros éxitos.* RCA, BMG CDV-1824.

Banda Sinaloense El Recodo de Cruz Lizárraga. 1984. *15 éxitos (Versiones originales).* RCA, BMG 3195-2-RL.

Carmen Jara. 1993. *La mujer . . . el nuevo folklore de México.* Fonovisa FPC-9109.

Carmina con Banda El Pueblito. *Arriba mi Sinaloa.* Fonorama CD-50.

Chalino Sánchez con Banda Sinaloense La Flor del Campo. Musart MSC-741 (cassette).

Chalino Sánchez con Los Guamuchileños de Bernabé Martínez. 1992. *El bandido generoso.* Musart CDP-748.

Chalino Sánchez. 1993. *Mis mejores canciones, 17 súper éxitos* (vol. 2). EMI Latin Emid-27992.

Corridos con banda. 1996. MCM CDER-8049.

El Lobito de Sinaloa con Banda La Costeña de Ramón López Alvarado. 1995. *Se solicita novia.* BM Record BM-041 (cassette).

El Monarca de Sinaloa con la Banda Santa Cruz. 1994. BM Records BM-036 (cassette).

El Puma de Sinaloa. 1995. *Después de mis errores.* EMI-Latin Emid-34951.

El Puma de Sinaloa con la Banda Nuevos Coyonquis. 1995. *A escondidas.* EMI-Latin Emid-34125.

Eulogio Hernández "El Potro de Sinaloa" con La Banda Sinaloense Los Guamuchileños. 1994. Maya Records MR-004 (cassette).

Ezequiel Peña. 1997. *Me dicen el tirador.* Fonovisa SDCD-6061.

Ezequiel Peña. 1996. *Orgullo ranchero.* Fonovisa SDC-6046 (cassette).

Graciela Beltrán con Banda. 1994. *Tesoro.* EMI-Latin Emid-29343.

Graciela Beltrán con la Banda Santa Cruz. EMI-Latin Emid-42840.

Jesús Palma (with Banda Sinaloense Los Huejoteños de Badiraguato). 1996. *Del mero Sinaloa, "Mi oficio es matar."* BM Record International BMC-050 (cassette).

Jorge Luis Cabrera (with Banda Tierra Blanca). 1994. *Música romántica.* Balboa Records BCDP-147.

José Alfredo Jiménez con la Banda Sinaloense El Recodo de Cruz Lizárraga. 1984.
RCA, Bertelsmann 7303-2-RL.
La captura del Chapo Guzmán: Puros corridos con banda. 1993. Kimo's CD-1003.
Luis Pérez Meza con la Banda Los Sirolas de Culiacán. 1998. Musart CDS-1822.
Luis Pérez Meza (with Banda Los Guamuchileños). Musart TTV-1005.
Lupe Mejía, "La Yaqui" (with Banda de Música Sinaloense Los Recodeños). 1993.
La tamboreada. Peerless PCD-355-4.
Pancho Barraza y su Banda Santa María. 1995. Mis canciones de amor.
Balboa Records BPC-170.
Pedro Rivera. 1995. 17 éxitos con banda. Cintas Acuario CAN-347.
Pepe Aguilar con tambora (with Banda Orquesta "Ahome"). 1991. Musart CMP 211
(cassette).
Que me siga la tambora (Serie 30 éxitos). Orfeón JCD-049 (2 CDs).
Saúl Viera "El Gavilancillo" con Banda La Costeña. 1993. Discos Linda DL-230.
Saúl Viera "El Gavilancillo" con la Banda Sinaloense. 1992. Discos Linda DL-0204.
Viva la banda sinaloense. 1992. Quijote QUCD-7035.
Yolanda del Río con tambora. 1993. Tocando puertas. Balboa Records BPC-911
(cassette).

TECHNOBANDA
Banda América. 1995. Muévanse todos. Sony Discos CD-81529.
Banda Arkángel R-15. 1996. Cumbiando con la mera, mera. Fonovisa (LMC)
LFCD-7006.
Banda Arkángel R-15. 1993. De dónde es la quebradita. Fonovisa (LMC) LXCD-4019.
Banda Arkángel R-15. 1992. La quebradita. LMC JUCD-9085.
Banda Machos. 1993. Los machos también lloran. MCM CDER-8001.
Banda Machos. 1992. Sangre de indio. Musical MCM CD-5104.
Banda Maguey. 1995. Fonovisa FPCD-9266.
Banda Móvil. 1995. Cuando los hombres lloran. Fonovisa (Disa) FPCD-9353.
Banda R-15. 1993. 15 grandes éxitos. Disa CD-484.
Banda Súper Zapo. 1994. Fonovisa (MCM) MPCD-5261.
Banda Toro. Toro mix. 1994. Musivisa Tune-1240.
Banda Zeta. Presumidas S.A. MCM RH-C-6005 (cassette).
Las 30 bandas del siglo. 1997. Fonovisa FTCD-80705.
Los reyes de la banda. 1993. Fonovisa TMCD-3036.
Mi Banda El Mexicano. 1995. Fuera de serie. Musart CMP-1318 (cassette).
Vaquero's Musical. Fonorama FR-10-200 (cassette).
Vaquero's Musical. 1994. A ritmo Vaquero's. Musart CDP-1142.

NORTEÑA
Los Comodines de Durango. 1996. Han vuelto los pistoleros. Yael YR-0120 (cassette).
Los Tigres del Norte. 1997. Jefe de jefes. Fonovisa FDCD-80711 (2 CDs).
Los Tucanes de Tijuana. 1997. Tucanes de plata: 14 tucanazos censurados. EMI Latin
Emid-56922.

Permissions

Every effort has been made to contact copyright holders for the materials appearing in this book. Permission to reprint song lyrics and photos is gratefully acknowledged.

"A bailar la quebradita" (VE7100, 1993), video cover photo. Used by permission of De Luna Publishing.

"Adiós, Hermanos Quintero" by Chalino Sánchez. Copyright © Vander Music, Inc. Used by permission.

"Agustín Nava" by Chalino Sánchez. Copyright © Cintas Acuario. Used by permission.

"Amador García" by Chalino Sánchez. Copyright © Cintas Acuario. Used by permission.

"A mover el guayín" by José de Jesús Meza. Copyright © ED. Musical del Centro, S.A., Mexico. Used by permission of Universal Música, Inc. c/o: EDIMCE (SACM).

"Andamos borrachos todos" by Julián Garza Arredondo. Copyright © Leo Musical, S.A., Mexico. Used by permission of Universal Música, Inc. c/o: Leo Musical, S.A. (SACM).

"Arriba mi Sinaloa" by Ignacio Jaime Peñuñuri. Copyright © 1953 by Promotora Hispano Americana de Música, S.A. Administered by Peer International Corporation. Copyright renewed. International copyright secured. Used by permission. All rights reserved.

"Báilame quebradito" by Lourdes Pérez. Copyright © De Luna Publishing. Used by permission.

Banda Arkángel, *La Quebradita* (1992), CD cover photo. Used by permission of De Luna Publishing.

Banda Machos, photo by Luis Sánchez. Copyright © 1997 Furia Musical/Editorial Televisa. Used by permission.

"Bigote mojado" by Joan Sebastian. Copyright © Vander Music, Inc. Used by permission.

"Chalino Sánchez" by José Felipe Hernández. Used by permission of the author.

Chalino Sánchez, CD cover photo. Used by permission of Pedro Rivera, Cintas Acuario.

"Clave privada" by Mario Quintero Lara. Copyright © Mas Flamingo Music. Courtesy of Flamingo, Inc.

"Corrido de Jaimito" by Chalino Sánchez. Copyright © Vander Music, Inc. Used by permission.

Index

MUSIC / CULTURE

A series from Wesleyan University Press

Edited by George Lipsitz, Susan McClary, and Robert Walser

My Music by Susan D. Crafts, Daniel Cavicchi, Charles Keil, and the Music in Daily Life Project

Running with the Devil: Power, Gender, and Madness in Heavy Metal Music by Robert Walser

Subcultural Sounds: Micromusics of the West by Mark Slobin

Upside Your Head! Rhythm and Blues on Central Avenue by Johnny Otis

Dissonant Identities: The Rock 'n' Roll Scene in Austin, Texas by Barry Shank

Black Noise: Rap Music and Black Culture in Contemporary America by Tricia Rose

Club Cultures: Music, Media and Subcultural Capital by Sarah Thornton

Music, Society, Education by Christopher Small

Listening to Salsa: Gender, Latin Popular Music, and Puerto Rican Cultures by Frances Aparicio

Any Sound You Can Imagine: Making Music/Consuming Technology by Paul Théberge

Voices in Bali: Energies and Perceptions in Vocal Music and Dance Theater by Edward Herbst

A Thousand Honey Creeks Later: My Life in Music from Basie to Motown—and Beyond by Preston Love

Musicking: The Meanings of Performing and Listening by Christopher Small

Music of the Common Tongue: Survival and Celebration in African American Music by Christopher Small

Singing Archaeology: Philip Glass's Akhnaten by John Richardson

Metal, Rock, and Jazz: Perception and the Phenomenology Musical Experience by Harris M. Berger

Music and Cinema edited by James Buhler, Caryl Flinn, and David Neumeyer

"You Better Work!": Underground Dance Music in New York City by Kai Fikentscher

Singing Our Way to Victory: French Cultural Politics and Music During the Great War by Regina M. Sweeney

Popular Music in Theory by Keith Negus

The Book of Music and Nature: An Anthology of Sounds, Words, Thoughts edited by David Rothenberg and Marta Ulvaeus

Global Noise: Rap and Hip-Hop outside the USA edited by Tony Mitchell

Recollecting from the Past: Musical Practice and Spirit Possession on the East Coast of Madagascar by Ron Emoff

Banda: Mexican Musical Life across Borders by Helena Simonett

Library of Congress Cataloging-in-Publication Data
Simonett, Helena.
Banda : Mexican musical life across borders / Helena Simonett.
   p. cm. — (Music/culture)
Includes bibliographical references (p.), discography (p.),
and index.
ISBN 0-8195-6429-X (cloth : alk. paper) —
ISBN 0-8195-6430-3 (paper : alk. paper)
1. Banda (Music)—History and criticism. 2. Popular music—
Mexico—Sinaloa (State)—History and criticism. 3. Popular
music—California—Los Angeles—History and criticism.
4. Sinaloa (Mexico : State)—Social conditions. 5. Los Angeles
(Calif.)—Social conditions. 6. Transnationalism. I. Title.
II. Series.
ML3485.7S56 S55 2001
784.4'164'089'6872—dc21   20010268987